Machine Learning in Action

Machine Learning in Action

PETER HARRINGTON

MANNING

Shelter Island

For online information and ordering of this and other Manning books, please visit
www.manning.com. The publisher offers discounts on this book when ordered in quantity.
For more information, please contact

> Special Sales Department
> Manning Publications Co.
> 20 Baldwin Road
> PO Box 261
> Shelter Island, NY 11964
> Email: orders@manning.com

Manning Publications Co.
20 Baldwin Road
PO Box 261
Shelter Island, NY 11964

Development editor: Jeff Bleiel
Technical proofreaders: Tricia Hoffman, Alex Ott
Copyeditor: Linda Recktenwald
Proofreader: Maureen Spencer
Typesetter: Gordan Salinovic
Cover designer: Marija Tudor

ISBN 9781617290183
Printed in the United States of America
2 3 4 5 6 7 8 9 10 – MAL – 17 16 15 14 13 12

To Joseph and Milo

brief contents

contents

PART 2   FORECASTING NUMERIC VALUES WITH REGRESSION 151

preface

After college I went to work for Intel in California and mainland China. Originally my plan was to go back to grad school after two years, but time flies when you are having fun, and two years turned into six. I realized I had to go back at that point, and I didn't want to do night school or online learning, I wanted to sit on campus and soak up everything a university has to offer. The best part of college is not the classes you take or research you do, but the peripheral things: meeting people, going to seminars, joining organizations, dropping in on classes, and learning what you don't know.

Sometime in 2008 I was helping set up for a career fair. I began to talk to someone from a large financial institution and they wanted me to interview for a position modeling credit risk (figuring out if someone is going to pay off their loans or not). They asked me how much stochastic calculus I knew. At the time, I wasn't sure I knew what the word *stochastic* meant. They were hiring for a geographic location my body couldn't tolerate, so I decided not to pursue it any further. But this stochastic stuff interested me, so I went to the course catalog and looked for any class being offered with the word "stochastic" in its title. The class I found was "Discrete-time Stochastic Systems." I started attending the class without registering, doing the homework and taking tests. Eventually I was noticed by the professor and she was kind enough to let me continue, for which I am very grateful. This class was the first time I saw probability applied to an algorithm. I had seen algorithms take an averaged value as input before, but this was different: the variance and mean were internal values in these algorithms. The course was about "time series" data where every piece of data is a regularly spaced sample. I found another course with Machine Learning in the title. In this class the data was not assumed to be uniformly spaced in time, and they covered more algorithms but with less rigor. I later realized that similar methods were also being taught in the economics, electrical engineering, and computer science departments.

In early 2009, I graduated and moved to Silicon Valley to start work as a software consultant. Over the next two years, I worked with eight companies on a very wide range of technologies and saw two trends emerge which make up the major thesis for this book: first, in order to develop a compelling application you need to do more than just connect data sources; and second, employers want people who understand theory and can also program.

A large portion of a programmer's job can be compared to the concept of connecting pipes—except that instead of pipes, programmers connect the flow of data—and monstrous fortunes have been made doing exactly that. Let me give you an example. You could make an application that sells things online—the big picture for this would be allowing people a way to post things and to view what others have posted. To do this you could create a web form that allows users to enter data about what they are selling and then this data would be shipped off to a data store. In order for other users to see what a user is selling, you would have to ship the data out of the data store and display it appropriately. I'm sure people will continue to make money this way; however to make the application really good you need to add a level of intelligence. This intelligence could do things like automatically remove inappropriate postings, detect fraudulent transactions, direct users to things they might like, and forecast site traffic. To accomplish these objectives, you would need to apply machine learning. The end user would not know that there is magic going on behind the scenes; to them your application "just works," which is the hallmark of a well-built product.

An organization may choose to hire a group of theoretical people, or "thinkers," and a set of practical people, "doers." The thinkers may have spent a lot of time in academia, and their day-to-day job may be pulling ideas from papers and modeling them with very high-level tools or mathematics. The doers interface with the real world by writing the code and dealing with the imperfections of a non-ideal world, such as machines that break down or noisy data. Separating thinkers from doers is a bad idea and successful organizations realize this. (One of the tenets of lean manufacturing is for the thinkers to get their hands dirty with actual doing.) When there is a limited amount of money to be spent on hiring, who will get hired more readily—the thinker or the doer? Probably the doer, but in reality employers want both. Things need to get built, but when applications call for more demanding algorithms it is useful to have someone who can read papers, pull out the idea, implement it in real code, and iterate.

I didn't see a book that addressed the problem of bridging the gap between thinkers and doers in the context of machine learning algorithms. The goal of this book is to fill that void, and, along the way, to introduce uses of machine learning algorithms so that the reader can build better applications.

acknowledgments

This is by far the easiest part of the book to write...

First, I would like to thank the folks at Manning. Above all, I would like to thank my editor Troy Mott; if not for his support and enthusiasm, this book never would have happened. I would also like to thank Maureen Spencer who helped polish my prose in the final manuscript; she was a pleasure to work with.

Next I would like to thank Jennie Si at Arizona State University for letting me sneak into her class on discrete-time stochastic systems without registering. Also Cynthia Rudin at MIT for pointing me to the paper "Top 10 Algorithms in Data Mining,"[1] which inspired the approach I took in this book. For indirect contributions I would like to thank Mark Bauer, Jerry Barkely, Jose Zero, Doug Chang, Wayne Carter, and Tyler Neylon.

Special thanks to the following peer reviewers who read the manuscript at different stages during its development and provided invaluable feedback: Keith Kim, Franco Lombardo, Patrick Toohey, Josef Lauri, Ryan Riley, Peter Venable, Patrick Goetz, Jeroen Benckhuijsen, Ian McAllister, Orhan Alkan, Joseph Ottinger, Fred Law, Karsten Strøbæk, Brian Lau, Stephen McKamey, Michael Brennan, Kevin Jackson, John Griffin, Sumit Pal, Alex Alves, Justin Tyler Wiley, and John Stevenson.

My technical proofreaders, Tricia Hoffman and Alex Ott, reviewed the technical content shortly before the manuscript went to press and I would like to thank them

---

[1] Xindong Wu, et al., "Top 10 Algorithms in Data Mining," *Journal of Knowledge and Information Systems* 14, no. 1 (December 2007).

both for their comments and feedback. Alex was a cold-blooded killer when it came to reviewing my code! Thank you for making this a better book.

Thanks also to all the people who bought and read early versions of the manuscript through the MEAP early access program and contributed to the Author Online forum (even the trolls); this book wouldn't be what it is without them.

I want to thank my family for their support during the writing of this book. I owe a huge debt of gratitude to my wife for her encouragement and for putting up with all the irregularities in my life during the time I spent working on the manuscript.

Finally, I would like to thank Silicon Valley for being such a great place for my wife and me to work and where we can share our ideas and passions.

about this book

This book sets out to introduce people to important machine learning algorithms. Tools and applications using these algorithms are introduced to give the reader an idea of how they are used in practice today. A wide selection of machine learning books is available, which discuss the mathematics, but discuss little of how to program the algorithms. This book aims to be a bridge from algorithms presented in matrix form to an actual functioning program. With that in mind, please note that this book is heavy on code and light on mathematics.

Audience

What is all this machine learning stuff and who needs it? In a nutshell, machine learning is making sense of data. So if you *have* data you want to understand, this book is for you. If you want to *get* data and make sense of it, then this book is for you too. It helps if you are familiar with a few basic programming concepts, such as recursion and a few data structures, such as trees. It will also help if you have had an introduction to linear algebra and probability, although expertise in these fields is not necessary to benefit from this book. Lastly, the book uses Python, which has been called "executable pseudo code" in the past. It is assumed that you have a basic working knowledge of Python, but do not worry if you are not an expert in Python—it is not difficult to learn.

Top 10 algorithms in data mining

Data and making data-based decisions are so important that even the content of this book was born out of data—from a paper which was presented at the IEEE International Conference on Data Mining titled, "Top 10 Algorithms in Data Mining" and appeared in the *Journal of Knowledge and Information Systems* in December, 2007. This paper was the result of the award winners from the KDD conference being asked to come up with the top 10 machine learning algorithms. The general outline of this book follows the algorithms identified in the paper. The astute reader will notice this book has 15 chapters, although there were 10 "important" algorithms. I will explain, but let's first look at the top 10 algorithms.

The algorithms listed in that paper are: C4.5 (trees), k-means, support vector machines, Apriori, Expectation Maximization, PageRank, AdaBoost, k-Nearest Neighbors, Naïve Bayes, and CART. Eight of these ten algorithms appear in this book, the notable exceptions being PageRank and Expectation Maximization. PageRank, the algorithm that launched the search engine giant Google, is not included because I felt that it has been explained and examined in many books. There are entire books dedicated to PageRank. Expectation Maximization (EM) was meant to be in the book but sadly it is not. The main problem with EM is that it's very heavy on the math, and when I reduced it to the simplified version, like the other algorithms in this book, I felt that there was not enough material to warrant a full chapter.

How the book is organized

The book has 15 chapters, organized into four parts, and four appendixes.

Part 1 Machine learning basics

The algorithms in this book do not appear in the same order as in the paper mentioned above. The book starts out with an introductory chapter. The next six chapters in part 1 examine the subject of classification, which is the process of labeling items. Chapter 2 introduces the basic machine learning algorithm: k-Nearest Neighbors. Chapter 3 is the first chapter where we look at decision trees. Chapter 4 discusses using probability distributions for classification and the Naïve Bayes algorithm. Chapter 5 introduces Logistic Regression, which is not in the Top 10 list, but introduces the subject of optimization algorithms, which are important. The end of chapter 5 also discusses how to deal with missing values in data. You won't want to miss chapter 6 as it discusses the powerful Support Vector Machines. Finally we conclude our discussion of classification with chapter 7 by looking at the AdaBoost ensemble method. Chapter 7 includes a section that looks at the classification imbalance problem that arises when the training examples are not evenly distributed.

Part 2 Forecasting numeric values with regression

This section consists of two chapters which discuss regression or predicting continuous values. Chapter 8 covers regression, shrinkage methods, and locally weighted linear regression. In addition, chapter 8 has a section that deals with the bias-variance tradeoff, which needs to be considered when turning a Machine Learning algorithm. This part of the book concludes with chapter 9, which discusses tree-based regression and the CART algorithm.

Part 3 Unsupervised learning

The first two parts focused on supervised learning which assumes you have target values, or you know what you are looking for. Part 3 begins a new section called "Unsupervised learning" where you do not know what you are looking for; instead we ask the machine to tell us, "what do these data have in common?" The first algorithm discussed is k-Means clustering. Next we look into association analysis with the Apriori algorithm. Chapter 12 concludes our discussion of unsupervised learning by looking at an improved algorithm for association analysis called FP-Growth.

Part 4 Additional tools

The book concludes with a look at some additional tools used in machine learning. The first two tools in chapters 13 and 14 are mathematical operations used to remove noise from data. These are principal components analysis and the singular value decomposition. Finally, we discuss a tool used to scale machine learning to massive datasets that cannot be adequately addressed on a single machine.

Examples

Many examples included in this book demonstrate how you can use the algorithms in the real world. We use the following steps to make sure we have not made any mistakes:

1 Get concept/algo working with very simple data
2 Get real-world data in a format usable by our algorithm
3 Put steps 1 and 2 together to see the results on a real-world dataset

The reason we can't just jump into step 3 is basic engineering of complex systems—you want to build things incrementally so you understand when things break, where they break, and why. If you just throw things together, you won't know if the implementation of the algorithm is incorrect or if the formatting of the data is incorrect. Along the way I include some historical notes which you may find of interest.

Code conventions and downloads

All source code in listings or in text is in a `fixed-width font like this` to separate it from ordinary text. Code annotations accompany many of the listings, highlighting important concepts. In some cases, numbered bullets link to explanations that follow the listing.

Source code for all working examples in this book is available for download from the publisher's website at www.manning.com/MachineLearninginAction.

Author Online

Purchase of *Machine Learning in Action* includes free access to a private web forum run by Manning Publications where you can make comments about the book, ask technical questions, and receive help from the author and from other users. To access the forum and subscribe to it, point your web browser to www.manning.com/ MachineLearninginAction. This page provides information on how to get on the forum once you're registered, what kind of help is available, and the rules of conduct on the forum.

Manning's commitment to our readers is to provide a venue where a meaningful dialog between individual readers and between readers and the author can take place. It's not a commitment to any specific amount of participation on the part of the author, whose contribution to the AO remains voluntary (and unpaid). We suggest you try asking the author some challenging questions lest his interest stray!

The Author Online forum and the archives of previous discussions will be accessible from the publisher's website as long as the book is in print.

about the author

Peter Harrington holds Bachelor's and Master's degrees in Electrical Engineering. He worked for Intel Corporation for seven years in California and China. Peter holds five U.S. patents and his work has been published in three academic journals. He is currently the chief scientist for Zillabyte Inc. Prior to joining Zillabyte, he was a machine learning software consultant for two years. Peter spends his free time competing in programming competitions and building 3D printers.

about the cover illustration

The figure on the cover of *Machine Learning in Action* is captioned a "Man from Istria," which is a large peninsula in the Adriatic Sea, off Croatia. This illustration is taken from a recent reprint of Balthasar Hacquet's *Images and Descriptions of Southwestern and Eastern Wenda, Illyrians, and Slavs* published by the Ethnographic Museum in Split, Croatia, in 2008. Hacquet (1739–1815) was an Austrian physician and scientist who spent many years studying the botany, geology, and ethnography of many parts of the Austrian Empire, as well as the Veneto, the Julian Alps, and the western Balkans, inhabited in the past by peoples of the Illyrian tribes. Hand drawn illustrations accompany the many scientific papers and books that Hacquet published.

The rich diversity of the drawings in Hacquet's publications speaks vividly of the uniqueness and individuality of the eastern Alpine and northwestern Balkan regions just 200 years ago. This was a time when the dress codes of two villages separated by a few miles identified people uniquely as belonging to one or the other, and when members of a social class or trade could be easily distinguished by what they were wearing. Dress codes have changed since then and the diversity by region, so rich at the time, has faded away. It is now often hard to tell the inhabitant of one continent from another and today the inhabitants of the picturesque towns and villages in the Slovenian Alps or Balkan coastal towns are not readily distinguishable from the residents of other parts of Europe or America.

We at Manning celebrate the inventiveness, the initiative, and the fun of the computer business with book covers based on costumes from two centuries ago brought back to life by illustrations such as this one.

Part 1

Classification

The first two parts of this book are on supervised learning. Supervised learning asks the machine to learn from our data when we specify a target variable. This reduces the machine's task to only divining some pattern from the input data to get the target variable.

We address two cases of the target variable. The first case occurs when the target variable can take only nominal values: true or false; reptile, fish, mammal, amphibian, plant, fungi. The second case of classification occurs when the target variable can take an infinite number of numeric values, such as 0.100, 42.001, 1000.743, ... This case is called regression. We'll study regression in part 2 of this book. The first part of this book focuses on classification.

Our study of classification algorithms covers the first seven chapters of this book. Chapter 2 introduces one of the simplest classification algorithms called k-Nearest Neighbors, which uses a distance metric to classify items. Chapter 3 introduces an intuitive yet slightly harder to implement algorithm: decision trees. In chapter 4 we address how we can use probability theory to build a classifier. Next, chapter 5 looks at logistic regression, where we find the best parameters to properly classify our data. In the process of finding these best parameters, we encounter some powerful optimization algorithms. Chapter 6 introduces the powerful support vector machines. Finally, in chapter 7 we see a meta-algorithm, AdaBoost, which is a classifier made up of a collection of classifiers. Chapter 7 concludes part 1 on classification with a section on classification imbalance, which is a real-world problem where you have more data from one class than other classes.

Machine learning basics

This chapter covers

- A brief overview of machine learning
- Key tasks in machine learning
- Why you need to learn about machine learning
- Why Python is so great for machine learning

I was eating dinner with a couple when they asked what I was working on recently. I replied, "Machine learning." The wife turned to the husband and said, "Honey, what's machine learning?" The husband replied, "Cyberdyne Systems T-800." If you aren't familiar with the Terminator movies, the T-800 is artificial intelligence gone very wrong. My friend was a little bit off. We're not going to attempt to have conversations with computer programs in this book, nor are we going to ask a computer the meaning of life. With machine learning we can gain insight from a dataset; we're going to ask the computer to make some sense from data. This is what we mean by learning, not cyborg rote memorization, and not the creation of sentient beings.

Machine learning is actively being used today, perhaps in many more places than you'd expect. Here's a hypothetical day and the many times you'll encounter machine learning: You realize it's your friend's birthday and want to send her a card via snail mail. You search for funny cards, and the search engine shows you the 10

3

most relevant links. You click the second link; the search engine learns from this. Next, you check some email, and without your noticing it, the spam filter catches unsolicited ads for pharmaceuticals and places them in the Spam folder. Next, you head to the store to buy the birthday card. When you're shopping for the card, you pick up some diapers for your friend's child. When you get to the checkout and purchase the items, the human operating the cash register hands you a coupon for $1 off a six-pack of beer. The cash register's software generated this coupon for you because people who buy diapers also tend to buy beer. You send the birthday card to your friend, and a machine at the post office recognizes your handwriting to direct the mail to the proper delivery truck. Next, you go to the loan agent and ask them if you are eligible for loan; they don't answer but plug some financial information about you into the computer and a decision is made. Finally, you head to the casino for some late-night entertainment, and as you walk in the door, the person walking in behind you gets approached by security seemingly out of nowhere. They tell him, "Sorry, Mr. Thorp, we're going to have to ask you to leave the casino. Card counters aren't welcome here." Figure 1.1 illustrates where some of these applications are being used.

Figure 1.1   Examples of machine learning in action today, clockwise from top left: face recognition, handwriting digit recognition, spam filtering in email, and product recommendations from Amazon.com

In all of the previously mentioned scenarios, machine learning was present. Companies are using it to improve business decisions, increase productivity, detect disease, forecast weather, and do many more things. With the exponential growth of technology, we not only need better tools to understand the data we currently have, but we also need to prepare ourselves for the data we will have.

Are you ready for machine learning? In this chapter you'll find out what machine learning is, where it's already being used around you, and how it might help you in the future. Next, we'll talk about some common approaches to solving problems with machine learning. Last, you'll find out why Python is so great and why it's a great language for machine learning. Then we'll go through a really quick example using a module for Python called NumPy, which allows you to abstract and matrix calculations.

1.1   *What is machine learning?*

In all but the most trivial cases, insight or knowledge you're trying to get out of the raw data won't be obvious from looking at the data. For example, in detecting spam email, looking for the occurrence of a single word may not be very helpful. But looking at the occurrence of certain words used together, combined with the length of the email and other factors, you could get a much clearer picture of whether the email is spam or not. Machine learning is turning data into information.

Machine learning lies at the intersection of computer science, engineering, and statistics and often appears in other disciplines. As you'll see later, it can be applied to many fields from politics to geosciences. It's a tool that can be applied to many problems. Any field that needs to interpret and act on data can benefit from machine learning techniques.

Machine learning uses statistics. To most people, statistics is an esoteric subject used for companies to lie about how great their products are. (There's a great manual on how to do this called *How to Lie with Statistics* by Darrell Huff. Ironically, this is the best-selling statistics book of all time.) So why do the rest of us need statistics? The practice of engineering is applying science to solve a problem. In engineering we're used to solving a deterministic problem where our solution solves the problem all the time. If we're asked to write software to control a vending machine, it had better work all the time, regardless of the money entered or the buttons pressed. There are many problems where the solution isn't deterministic. That is, we don't know enough about the problem or don't have enough computing power to properly model the problem. For these problems we need statistics. For example, the motivation of humans is a problem that is currently too difficult to model.

In the social sciences, being right 60% of the time is considered successful. If we can predict the way people will behave 60% of the time, we're doing well. How can this be? Shouldn't we be right all the time? If we're not right all the time, doesn't that mean we're doing something wrong?

Let me give you an example to illustrate the problem of not being able to model the problem fully. Do humans not act to maximize their own happiness? Can't we just predict the outcome of events involving humans based on this assumption? Perhaps, but it's difficult to define what makes everyone happy, because this may differ greatly from one person to the next. So even if our assumptions are correct about people maximizing their own happiness, the definition of happiness is too complex to model. There are many other examples outside human behavior that we can't currently model deterministically. For these problems we need to use some tools from statistics.

1.1.1 *Sensors and the data deluge*

We have a tremendous amount of human-created data from the World Wide Web, but recently more nonhuman sources of data have been coming online. The technology behind the sensors isn't new, but connecting them to the web is new. It's estimated that shortly after this book's publication physical sensors will create 20 percent of non-video internet traffic.[1]

The following is an example of an abundance of free data, a worthy cause, and the need to sort through the data. In 1989, the Loma Prieta earthquake struck northern California, killing 63 people, injuring 3,757, and leaving thousands homeless. A similarly sized earthquake struck Haiti in 2010, killing more than 230,000 people. Shortly after the Loma Prieta earthquake, a study was published using low-frequency magnetic field measurements claiming to foretell the earthquake.[2] A number of subsequent studies showed that the original study was flawed for various reasons.[3,4] Suppose we want to redo this study and keep searching for ways to predict earthquakes so we can avoid the horrific consequences and have a better understanding of our planet. What would be the best way to go about this study? We could buy magnetometers with our own money and buy pieces of land to place them on. We could ask the government to help us out and give us money and land on which to place these magnetometers. Who's going to make sure there's no tampering with the magnetometers, and how can we get readings from them? There exists another low-cost solution.

Mobile phones or smartphones today ship with three-axis magnetometers. The smartphones also come with operating systems where you can execute your own programs; with a few lines of code you can get readings from the magnetometers hundreds of times a second. Also, the phone already has its own communication system set up; if you can convince people to install and run your program, you could record a large amount of magnetometer data with very little investment. In addition to the magnetometers, smartphones carry a large number of other sensors including yaw-rate gyros, three-axis accelerometers, temperature sensors, and GPS receivers, all of which you could use to support your primary measurements.

---

[1] http://www.gartner.com/it/page.jsp?id=876512, retrieved 7/29/2010 4:36 a.m.

[2] Fraser-Smith et al., "Low-frequency magnetic field measurements near the epicenter of the Ms 7.1 Loma Prieta earthquake," *Geophysical Research Letters* 17, no. 9 (August 1990), 1465–68.

[3] W. H. Campbell, "Natural magnetic disturbance fields, not precursors, preceding the Loma Prieta earthquake," *Journal of Geophysical Research* 114, A05307, doi:10.1029/2008JA013932 (2009).

[4] J. N. Thomas, J. J. Love, and M. J. S. Johnston, "On the reported magnetic precursor of the 1989 Loma Prieta earthquake," *Physics of the Earth and Planetary Interiors* 173, no. 3–4 (2009), 207–15.

The two trends of mobile computing and sensor-generated data mean that we'll be getting more and more data in the future.

1.1.2   *Machine learning will be more important in the future*

In the last half of the twentieth century the majority of the workforce in the developed world has moved from manual labor to what is known as *knowledge work*. The clear definitions of "move this from here to there" and "put a hole in this" are gone. Things are much more ambiguous now; job assignments such as "maximize profits," "minimize risk," and "find the best marketing strategy" are all too common. The fire hose of information available to us from the World Wide Web makes the jobs of knowledge workers even harder. Making sense of all the data with our job in mind is becoming a more essential skill, as Hal Varian, chief economist at Google, said:

> *I keep saying the sexy job in the next ten years will be statisticians. People think I'm joking, but who would've guessed that computer engineers would've been the sexy job of the 1990s? The ability to take data—to be able to understand it, to process it, to extract value from it, to visualize it, to communicate it—that's going to be a hugely important skill in the next decades, not only at the professional level but even at the educational level for elementary school kids, for high school kids, for college kids. Because now we really do have essentially free and ubiquitous data. So the complementary scarce factor is the ability to understand that data and extract value from it. I think statisticians are part of it, but it's just a part. You also want to be able to visualize the data, communicate the data, and utilize it effectively. But I do think those skills—of being able to access, understand, and communicate the insights you get from data analysis— are going to be extremely important. Managers need to be able to access and understand the data themselves.*
>
> —*McKinsey Quarterly*, January 2009

With so much of the economic activity dependent on information, you can't afford to be lost in the data. Machine learning will help you get through all the data and extract some information. We need to go over some vocabulary that commonly appears in machine learning so it's clear what's being discussed in this book.

1.2   *Key terminology*

Before we jump into the machine learning algorithms, it would be best to explain some terminology. The best way to do so is through an example of a system someone may want to make. We'll go through an example of building a bird classification system. This sort of system is an interesting topic often associated with machine learning called *expert systems*. By creating a computer program to recognize birds, we've replaced an ornithologist with a computer. The ornithologist is a bird expert, so we've created an expert system.

In table 1.1 are some values for four parts of various birds that we decided to measure. We chose to measure weight, wingspan, whether it has webbed feet, and the color of its back. In reality, you'd want to measure more than this. It's common practice to measure just about anything you can measure and sort out the important parts later. The four things we've measured are called *features*; these are also called *attributes*, but we'll stick with the term *features* in this book. Each of the rows in table 1.1 is an *instance* made up of features.

Table 1.1 Bird species classification based on four features

	Weight (g)	Wingspan (cm)	Webbed feet?	Back color	Species
1	1000.1	125.0	No	Brown	Buteo jamaicensis
2	3000.7	200.0	No	Gray	Sagittarius serpentarius
3	3300.0	220.3	No	Gray	Sagittarius serpentarius
4	4100.0	136.0	Yes	Black	Gavia immer
5	3.0	11.0	No	Green	Calothorax lucifer
6	570.0	75.0	No	Black	Campephilus principalis

The first two features in table 1.1 are numeric and can take on decimal values. The third feature (webbed feet) is binary: it can only be 1 or 0. The fourth feature (back color) is an enumeration over the color palette we're using, and I just chose some very common colors. Say we ask the people doing the measurements to choose one of seven colors; then back color would be just an integer. (I know choosing one color for the back of a bird is a gross oversimplification; please excuse this for the purpose of illustration).

If you happen to see a Campephilus principalis (Ivory-billed Woodpecker), give me a call ASAP! Don't tell anyone else you saw it; just call me and keep an eye on the bird until I get there. (There's a $50,000 reward for anyone who can lead a biologist to a living Ivory-billed Woodpecker.)

One task in machine learning is *classification*; I'll illustrate this using table 1.1 and the fact that information about an Ivory-billed Woodpecker could get us $50,000. We want to identify this bird out of a bunch of other birds, and we want to profit from this. We could set up a bird feeder and then hire an ornithologist (bird expert) to watch it and when they see an Ivory-billed Woodpecker give us a call. This would be expensive, and the person could only be in one place at a time. We could also automate this process: set up many bird feeders with cameras and computers attached to them to identify the birds that come in. We could put a scale on the bird feeder to get the bird's weight and write some computer vision code to extract the bird's wingspan, feet type, and back color. For the moment, assume we have all that information. How do we then decide if a bird at our feeder is an Ivory-billed Woodpecker or something else? This task is called *classification*, and there are many machine learning algorithms that are good at classification. The class in this example is the bird species; more specifically, we can reduce our classes to Ivory-billed Woodpecker or everything else.

Say we've decided on a machine learning algorithm to use for classification. What we need to do next is train the algorithm, or allow it to learn. To train the algorithm we feed it quality data known as a *training set*. A training set is the set of training examples we'll use to train our machine learning algorithms. In table 1.1 our training set has six *training examples*. Each training example has four features and one *target variable*; this is depicted in figure 1.2. The target variable is what we'll be trying to predict with our machine learning algorithms. In classification the target variable takes on a nominal value, and in the task of regression its value could be continuous. In a training set the target variable is known. The machine learns by finding some relationship between the features and the target variable. The target variable is the species, and as I mentioned earlier, we can reduce this to take nominal values. In the classification problem the target variables are called *classes*, and there is assumed to be a finite number of classes.

> **NOTE** Features or attributes are the individual measurements that, when combined with other features, make up a training example. This is usually columns in a training or test set.

To test machine learning algorithms what's usually done is to have a training set of data and a separate dataset, called a *test set*. Initially the program is fed the training examples; this is when the machine learning takes place. Next, the test set is fed to the program. The target variable for each example from the test set isn't given to the program, and the program decides which class each example should belong to. The target variable or class that the training example belongs to is then compared to the predicted value, and we can get a sense for how accurate the algorithm is. There are better ways to use all the information in the test set and training set. We'll discuss them later.

In our bird classification example, assume we've tested the program and it meets our desired level of accuracy. Can we see what the machine has learned? This is called *knowledge representation*. The answer is it depends. Some algorithms have knowledge representation that's more readable by humans than others. The knowledge representation may be in the form of a set of rules; it may be a probability distribution or an example from the training set. In some cases we may not be interested in building an expert system but interested only in the knowledge representation that's acquired from training a machine learning algorithm.

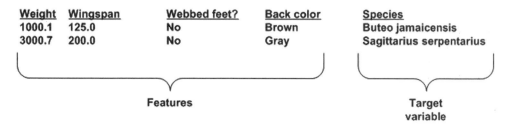

Figure 1.2 Features and target variable identified

We've covered a lot of key terms of machine learning, but we didn't cover them all. We'll introduce more key terms in later chapters as they're needed. We'll now address the big picture: what we can do with machine learning.

1.3   Key tasks of machine learning

In this section we'll outline the key jobs of machine learning and set a framework that allows us to easily turn a machine learning algorithm into a solid working application.

The example covered previously was for the task of classification. In classification, our job is to predict what class an instance of data should fall into. Another task in machine learning is *regression*. Regression is the prediction of a numeric value. Most people have probably seen an example of regression with a best-fit line drawn through some data points to generalize the data points. Classification and regression are examples of *supervised learning*. This set of problems is known as supervised because we're telling the algorithm what to predict.

The opposite of supervised learning is a set of tasks known as *unsupervised learning*. In unsupervised learning, there's no label or target value given for the data. A task where we group similar items together is known as *clustering*. In unsupervised learning, we may also want to find statistical values that describe the data. This is known as *density estimation*. Another task of unsupervised learning may be reducing the data from many features to a small number so that we can properly visualize it in two or three dimensions. Table 1.2 lists some common tasks in machine learning with algorithms used to solve these tasks.

Supervised learning tasks	
Classification	**Regression**
k-Nearest Neighbors	Linear
Naive Bayes	Locally weighted linear
Support vector machines	Ridge
Decision trees	Lasso
Unsupervised learning tasks	
Clustering	**Density estimation**
k-Means	Expectation maximization
DBSCAN	Parzen window

Table 1.2 Common algorithms used to perform classification, regression, clustering, and density estimation tasks

If you noticed in table 1.2 that multiple techniques are used for completing the same task, you may be asking yourself, "If these do the same thing, why are there four different methods? Why can't I just choose one method and master it?" I'll answer that question in the next section.

1.4   *How to choose the right algorithm*

With all the different algorithms in table 1.2, how can you choose which one to use? First, you need to consider your goal. What are you trying to get out of this? (Do you want a probability that it might rain tomorrow, or do you want to find groups of voters with similar interests?) What data do you have or can you collect? Those are the big questions. Let's talk about your goal.

If you're trying to predict or forecast a target value, then you need to look into supervised learning. If not, then unsupervised learning is the place you want to be. If you've chosen supervised learning, what's your target value? Is it a discrete value like Yes/No, 1/2/3, A/B/C, or Red/Yellow/Black? If so, then you want to look into classification. If the target value can take on a number of values, say any value from 0.00 to 100.00, or -999 to 999, or +∞ to -∞, then you need to look into regression.

If you're not trying to predict a target value, then you need to look into unsupervised learning. Are you trying to fit your data into some discrete groups? If so and that's all you need, you should look into clustering. Do you need to have some numerical estimate of how strong the fit is into each group? If you answer yes, then you probably should look into a density estimation algorithm.

The rules I've given here should point you in the right direction but are not unbreakable laws. In chapter 9 I'll show you how you can use classification techniques for regression, blurring the distinction I made within supervised learning. The second thing you need to consider is your data.

You should spend some time getting to know your data, and the more you know about it, the better you'll be able to build a successful application. Things to know about your data are these: Are the features nominal or continuous? Are there missing values in the features? If there are missing values, why are there missing values? Are there outliers in the data? Are you looking for a needle in a haystack, something that happens very infrequently? All of these features about your data can help you narrow the algorithm selection process.

With the algorithm narrowed, there's no single answer to what the best algorithm is or what will give you the best results. You're going to have to try different algorithms and see how they perform. There are other machine learning techniques that you can use to improve the performance of a machine learning algorithm. The relative performance of two algorithms may change after you process the input data. We'll discuss these in more detail later, but the point is that finding the best algorithm is an iterative process of trial and error.

Many of the algorithms are different, but there are some common steps you need to take with all of these algorithms when building a machine learning application. I'll explain these steps in the next section.

1.5   *Steps in developing a machine learning application*

Our approach to understanding and developing an application using machine learning in this book will follow a procedure similar to this:

1   *Collect data.* You could collect the samples by scraping a website and extracting data, or you could get information from an RSS feed or an API. You could have a device collect wind speed measurements and send them to you, or blood glucose levels, or anything you can measure. The number of options is endless. To save some time and effort, you could use publicly available data.

2   *Prepare the input data.* Once you have this data, you need to make sure it's in a useable format. The format we'll be using in this book is the Python list. We'll talk about Python more in a little bit, and lists are reviewed in appendix A. The benefit of having this standard format is that you can mix and match algorithms and data sources.

   You may need to do some algorithm-specific formatting here. Some algorithms need features in a special format, some algorithms can deal with target variables and features as strings, and some need them to be integers. We'll get to this later, but the algorithm-specific formatting is usually trivial compared to collecting data.

3   *Analyze the input data.* This is looking at the data from the previous task. This could be as simple as looking at the data you've parsed in a text editor to make sure steps 1 and 2 are actually working and you don't have a bunch of empty values. You can also look at the data to see if you can recognize any patterns or if there's anything obvious, such as a few data points that are vastly different from the rest of the set. Plotting data in one, two, or three dimensions can also help. But most of the time you'll have more than three features, and you can't easily plot the data across all features at one time. You could, however, use some advanced methods we'll talk about later to distill multiple dimensions down to two or three so you can visualize the data.

4   If you're working with a production system and you know what the data should look like, or you trust its source, you can skip this step. This step takes human involvement, and for an automated system you don't want human involvement. The value of this step is that it makes you understand you don't have garbage coming in.

5   *Train the algorithm.* This is where the machine learning takes place. This step and the next step are where the "core" algorithms lie, depending on the algorithm. You feed the algorithm good clean data from the first two steps and extract knowledge or information. This knowledge you often store in a format that's readily useable by a machine for the next two steps.

   In the case of unsupervised learning, there's no training step because you don't have a target value. Everything is used in the next step.

6   *Test the algorithm.* This is where the information learned in the previous step is put to use. When you're evaluating an algorithm, you'll test it to see how well it does. In the case of supervised learning, you have some known values you can use to evaluate the algorithm. In unsupervised learning, you may have to use some other metrics to evaluate the success. In either case, if you're not satisfied,

you can go back to step 4, change some things, and try testing again. Often the collection or preparation of the data may have been the problem, and you'll have to go back to step 1.

7 *Use it.* Here you make a real program to do some task, and once again you see if all the previous steps worked as you expected. You might encounter some new data and have to revisit steps 1–5.

Now we'll talk about a language to implement machine learning applications. We need a language that's understandable by a wide range of people. We also need a language that has libraries written for a number of tasks, especially matrix math operations. We also would like a language with an active developer community. Python is the best choice for these reasons.

1.6 *Why Python?*

Python is a great language for machine learning for a large number of reasons. First, Python has clear syntax. Second, it makes text manipulation extremely easy. A large number of people and organizations use Python, so there's ample development and documentation.

1.6.1 *Executable pseudo-code*

The clear syntax of Python has earned it the name *executable pseudo-code*. The default install of Python already carries high-level data types like lists, tuples, dictionaries, sets, queues, and so on, which you don't have to program in yourself. These high-level data types make abstract concepts easy to implement. (See appendix A for a full description of Python, the data types, and how to install it.) With Python, you can program in any style you're familiar with: object-oriented, procedural, functional, and so on.

With Python it's easy to process and manipulate text, which makes it ideal for processing non-numeric data. You can get by in Python with little to no regular expression usage. There are a number of libraries for using Python to access web pages, and the intuitive text manipulation makes it easy to extract data from HTML.

1.6.2 *Python is popular*

Python is popular, so lots of examples are available, which makes learning it fast. Second, the popularity means that there are lots of modules available for many applications.

Python is popular in the scientific and financial communities as well. A number of scientific libraries such as SciPy and NumPy allow you to do vector and matrix operations. This makes the code even more readable and allows you to write code that looks like linear algebra. In addition, the scientific libraries SciPy and NumPy are compiled using lower-level languages (C and Fortran); this makes doing computations with these tools much faster. We'll be using NumPy extensively in this book.

The scientific tools in Python work well with a plotting tool called Matplotlib. Matplotlib can plot 2D and 3D and can handle most types of plots commonly used in the scientific world. We'll be using Matplotlib extensively throughout this book.

Python also has an interactive shell, which allows you to view and inspect elements of the program as you're developing it.

A new module for Python, called Pylab, seeks to combine NumPy, SciPy, and Matplotlib into one environment and instillation. At the time of writing, this isn't yet done but shows great promise for the future.

1.6.3 *What Python has that other languages don't have*

There are high-level languages that allow you to do matrix math such as MATLAB and Mathematica. MATLAB has a number of built-in features that make machine learning easier. MATLAB is also very fast. The problem with MATLAB is that to legally use it will cost you a few thousand dollars. There are third-party add-ons to MATLAB but nothing on the scale of an open source project.

There are matrix math libraries for low-level languages such as Java and C. The problem with these languages is that it takes a lot of code to get simple things done. First, you have to typecast variables, and then with Java it seems that you have to write setters and getters every time you sneeze. Don't forget subclassing. You have to subclass methods even if you aren't going to use them. At the end of the day, you have written a lot of code—sometimes tedious code—to do simple things. This isn't the case with Python. Python is clean, concise, and easy to read. Python is easy for nonprogrammers to pick up. Java and C aren't so easy to pick up and much less concise than Python.

All of us learn to write in the second grade. Most of us go on to greater things.

—Bobby Knight

Perhaps one day I can replace "write" with "write code" in this quote. Some people are actually interested in programming languages. But for many people a programming language is simply a tool to accomplish some other task. Python is a higher-level language; this allows you to spend more time making sense of data and less time concerned with how a machine approximates the data. Python easily allows you to effortlessly express yourself.

1.6.4 *Drawbacks*

The only real drawback of Python is that it's not as fast as Java or C. You can, however, call C-compiled programs from Python. This gives you the best of both worlds and allows you to incrementally develop a program. If you experiment with an idea in Python and decide it's something you want to pursue in a production system, it will be easy to make that transition. If the program is built in a modular fashion, you could first get it up and running in Python and then to improve speed start building portions of the code in C. The Boost C++ library makes this easy to do. Other tools such as Cython and PyPy allow you write typed versions of Python with performance gains over regular Python.

If an idea for a program or application is flawed, then it will be flawed at low speed as well as high speed. If an idea is a bad idea, writing code to make it fast or scale to a large number of users doesn't change anything. This makes Python so beautiful that you can quickly see an idea in action and then optimize it if needed.

Now that you know the language we're going to be using, I'm sure you're ready to start using it. In the next section, we'll walk through use of the Python shell and NumPy.

1.7 Getting started with the NumPy library

We'll use NumPy heavily in this book because we'll be doing some linear algebra. Don't worry about linear algebra—we just want to do the same math operation on lots of different data points. If we represent our data as a matrix, we can do simple math without a bunch of messy loops. Before we get into any machine learning algorithms, you should make sure you have Python working and NumPy properly installed. NumPy is a separate module for Python that doesn't come with most distributions of Python, so you'll need to install it after you've installed Python. Start a Python shell by opening a command prompt in Windows or a terminal in Linux and Mac OS. At the command line, type `python` for Linux and Mac or `c:\Python27\python.exe` in Windows. From this point on, anytime you see these symbols

```
>>>
```

it will mean the Python shell. In the Python shell type the following command.

```
>>> from numpy import *
```

This imports all of the NumPy modules into the current namespace. This is shown in figure 1.3 on the Mac OS.

Next, type the following in the Python shell:

```
>>> random.rand(4,4)
array([[ 0.70328595,  0.40951383,  0.7475052 ,  0.07061094],
       [ 0.9571294 ,  0.97588446,  0.2728084 ,  0.5257719 ],
       [ 0.05431627,  0.01396732,  0.60304292,  0.19362288],
       [ 0.10648952,  0.27317698,  0.45582919,  0.04881605]])
```

This creates a random array of size 4x4; don't worry if the numbers you see are different from mine. These are random numbers, so your numbers should look different from mine.

```
Last login: Mon Nov 22 08:35:55 on ttys000
peter-harringtons-imac:~ pbharrin$ python
Python 2.6.1 (r261:67515, Feb 11 2010, 00:51:29)
[GCC 4.2.1 (Apple Inc. build 5646)] on darwin
Type "help", "copyright", "credits" or "license" for more information.
>>> from numpy import *
>>>
```

Figure 1.3 Starting Python from the command line and importing a module in the Python shell

> **NumPy matrix vs. array**
>
> In NumPy there are two different data types for dealing with rows and columns of numbers. Be careful of this because they look similar, but simple mathematical operations such as multiply on the two data types can have different meanings. The matrix data type behaves more like matrices in MATLAB.™

You can always convert an array to a matrix by calling the `mat()` function; type in the following:

```
>>> randMat = mat(random.rand(4,4))
```

You will probably have different values than I have here because we're getting random numbers:

```
>>> randMat.I
matrix([[ 0.24497106,  1.75854497, -1.77728665, -0.0834912 ],
        [ 1.49792202,  2.12925479,  1.32132491, -9.75890849],
        [ 2.76042144,  1.67271779, -0.29226613, -8.45413693],
        [-2.03011142, -3.07832136,  1.4420448 ,  9.62598044]])
```

The `.I` operator solves the inverse of a matrix. Very easy, huh? Try that in Python without NumPy. If you don't remember or never learned how to solve the inverse of a matrix, don't worry; it was just done for you:

```
>>> invRandMat = randMat.I
```

You can also do matrix multiplication. Let's see that in action:

```
>>> randMat*invRandMat
matrix([[  1.00000000e+00,   0.00000000e+00,   2.22044605e-16,
           1.77635684e-15],
        [  0.00000000e+00,   1.00000000e+00,   0.00000000e+00,
           0.00000000e+00],
        [  0.00000000e+00,   4.44089210e-16,   1.00000000e+00,
          -8.88178420e-16],
        [ -2.22044605e-16,   0.00000000e+00,   1.11022302e-16,
           1.00000000e+00]])
```

This gives you just the identity matrix, a 4x4 matrix where all elements are zero except the diagonals, which are one. This isn't exactly true. There are some very small elements left over in the array. Let's see the leftover results:

```
>>> myEye - eye(4)
matrix([[  0.00000000e+00,  -6.59194921e-17,  -4.85722573e-17,
          -4.99600361e-16],
        [  2.22044605e-16,   0.00000000e+00,  -6.03683770e-16,
          -7.77156117e-16],
        [ -5.55111512e-17,  -1.04083409e-17,  -3.33066907e-16,
          -2.22044605e-16],
        [  5.55111512e-17,   1.56125113e-17,  -5.55111512e-17,
```

The function `eye(4)` just creates an identity matrix of size 4.

If you got through this example, you have NumPy installed correctly. You're now ready to start making some powerful programs using machine learning. Don't worry if you haven't seen all these functions before. More NumPy functionality will be introduced as it's needed in further examples in this book.

1.8 Summary

Machine learning is already being used in your daily lives even though you may not be aware of it. The amount of data coming at you isn't going to decrease, and being able to make sense of all this data will be an essential skill for people working in a data-driven industry.

In machine learning, you look at instances of data. Each instance of data is composed of a number of features. Classification, one the popular and essential tasks of machine learning, is used to place an unknown piece of data into a known group. In order to build or train a classifier, you feed it data for which you know the class. This data is called your training set.

I don't claim that our expert system used to recognize birds will be perfect or as a good as a human. But building a machine with accuracy close to that of a human expert could greatly increase the quality of life. When we build software that can match the accuracy of a human doctor, people can more rapidly get treatment. Better prediction of weather could lead to fewer water shortages and a greater supply of food. The examples where machine learning could be useful are endless.

In the next chapter I'll introduce our first machine learning algorithm. This will be an example of classification, which is a type of supervised learning. The next six chapters will be on classification.

Classifying with k-Nearest Neighbors

2

This chapter covers

- The k-Nearest Neighbors classification algorithm
- Parsing and importing data from a text file
- Creating scatter plots with Matplotlib
- Normalizing numeric values

Have you ever seen movies categorized into genres? What defines these genres, and who says which movie goes into what genre? The movies in one genre are similar but based on what? I'm sure if you asked the people involved with making the movies, they wouldn't say that their movie is just like someone else's movie, but in some way you know they're similar. What makes an action movie similar to another action movie and dissimilar to a romance movie? Do people kiss in action movies, and do people kick in romance movies? Yes, but there's probably more kissing in romance movies and more kicking in action movies. Perhaps if you measured kisses, kicks, and other things per movie, you could automatically figure out what genre a movie belongs to. I'll use movies to explain some of the concepts of k-Nearest Neighbors; then we will move on to other applications.

In this chapter, we'll discuss our first machine-learning algorithm: k-Nearest Neighbors. k-Nearest Neighbors is easy to grasp and very effective. We'll first discuss the theory and how you can use the concept of a distance measurement to classify items. Next, you'll see how to easily import and parse data from text files using Python. We'll address some common pitfalls when working with distance calculations and data coming from numerous sources. We'll put all of this into action in examples for improving results from a dating website and recognizing handwritten digits.

2.1 *Classifying with distance measurements*

> ### k-Nearest Neighbors
>
> Pros: High accuracy, insensitive to outliers, no assumptions about data
>
> Cons: Computationally expensive, requires a lot of memory
>
> Works with: Numeric values, nominal values

The first machine-learning algorithm we'll look at is k-Nearest Neighbors (kNN). It works like this: we have an existing set of example data, our training set. We have labels for all of this data—we know what class each piece of the data should fall into. When we're given a new piece of data without a label, we compare that new piece of data to the existing data, every piece of existing data. We then take the most similar pieces of data (the nearest neighbors) and look at their labels. We look at the top k most similar pieces of data from our known dataset; this is where the *k* comes from. (*k* is an integer and it's usually less than 20.) Lastly, we take a majority vote from the k most similar pieces of data, and the majority is the new class we assign to the data we were asked to classify.

Let's run through a quick example classifying movies into romance or action movies. Someone watched a lot of movies and counted the number of kicks and kisses in each movie. I've plotted six movies by the number of kisses and kicks in each movie in figure 2.1. Now, you find a movie you haven't seen yet and want to know if it's a romance movie or an action movie. To determine this, we'll use the kNN algorithm.

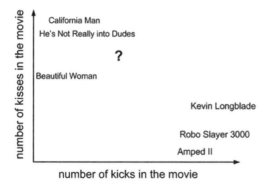

Figure 2.1　Classifying movies by plotting the number of kicks and kisses in each movie

We find the movie in question and see how many kicks and kisses it has. It's plotted as a large question mark along with a few other movies in figure 2.1. These values are listed in table 2.1.

Table 2.1   Movies with the number of kicks and number of kisses shown for each movie, along with our assessment of the movie type

Movie title	# of kicks	# of kisses	Type of movie
California Man	3	104	Romance
He's Not Really into Dudes	2	100	Romance
Beautiful Woman	1	81	Romance
Kevin Longblade	101	10	Action
Robo Slayer 3000	99	5	Action
Amped II	98	2	Action
?	18	90	Unknown

We don't know what type of movie the question mark movie is, but we have a way of figuring that out. First, we calculate the distance to all the other movies. I've calculated the distances and shown those in table 2.2. (Don't worry about how I did these calculations right now. We'll get into that in a few minutes.)

Movie title	Distance to movie "?"
California Man	20.5
He's Not Really into Dudes	18.7
Beautiful Woman	19.2
Kevin Longblade	115.3
Robo Slayer 3000	117.4
Amped II	118.9

Table 2.2   Distances between each movie and the unknown movie

Now that we have all the distances to our unknown movie, we need to find the k-nearest movies by sorting the distances in decreasing order. Let's assume k=3. Then, the three closest movies are *He's Not Really into Dudes*, *Beautiful Woman*, and *California Man*. The kNN algorithm says to take the majority vote from these three movies to determine the class of the mystery movie. Because all three movies are romances, we forecast that the mystery movie is a romance movie.

We'll work through a real machine learning algorithm in this chapter, and along the way I'll introduce the Python tools and machine learning terminology. First, however, we'll go over a simple example of the kNN algorithm to make sure we're using the algorithm correctly.

General approach to kNN

1. Collect: Any method.

2. Prepare: Numeric values are needed for a distance calculation. A structured data format is best.

3. Analyze: Any method.

4. Train: Does not apply to the kNN algorithm.

5. Test: Calculate the error rate.

6. Use: This application needs to get some input data and output structured numeric values. Next, the application runs the kNN algorithm on this input data and determines which class the input data should belong to. The application then takes some action on the calculated class.

2.1.1 *Prepare: importing data with Python*

First, we'll create a Python module called kNN.py, where we'll place all the code used in this chapter. You can create your own file and enter code as we progress, or you can copy the file kNN.py from the book's source code. The best way to learn is to start with a blank module and enter code as it's used.

First, let's create kNN.py or copy it from the source code repository. We'll create a few support functions before we create the full kNN algorithm. Add the following lines to kNN.py:

```
from numpy import *
import operator

def createDataSet():
    group = array([[1.0,1.1],[1.0,1.0],[0,0],[0,0.1]])
    labels = ['A','A','B','B']
    return group, labels
```

In this code, we import two modules. The first one is NumPy, which is our scientific computing package. The second module is the operator module, which is used later in the kNN algorithm for sorting; we'll get to that shortly.

The function `createDataSet()` is there for your convenience. This creates the dataset and labels, as shown in figure 2.1. Let's try this out: save kNN.py, change to the directory where you've stored kNN.py, and launch a Python interactive session. To get started you need to open a new terminal in Linux/Mac OS or in Windows, so open a command prompt. When you're using Linux or a Mac, you need to type `python` at the command line to get started, and in Windows you need to refer to the Python program directly, such as `c:\Python26\python.exe`, unless you have it aliased.

Once you've started Python to load your module, you need to type

```
>>> import kNN
```

This will load the kNN module. To make sure that we're looking at the same dataset, I created a function called `createDataSet`. Type the following at the Python command prompt:

```
>>> group,labels = kNN.createDataSet()
```

This creates two variables called `group` and `labels`. To inspect each variable, type its name at the Python command prompt:

```
>>> group
array([[ 1. ,  1.1],
       [ 1. ,  1. ],
       [ 0. ,  0. ],
       [ 0. ,  0.1]])
>>> labels
['A', 'A', 'B', 'B']
```

Here we have four pieces of data. Each piece of data has two attributes or features, things we know about it. In the group matrix each row is a different piece of data. Think of it as a different measurement or entry in some sort of log. As humans, we can visualize things in one, two, or sometimes three dimensions, but that's about the limit of our brains; to keep things easy to visualize, we'll use only two features for each data point.

The label's vector carries the labels we've given to each of the data points. There should be as many items in this vector as there are rows in the group matrix. We assigned the data point (1,1.1) to the class A, and similarly we assigned the data point (0,0.1) to the class B. The values in this example are arbitrarily chosen for the purpose of illustration, and the axes are unlabeled. The four data points with class labels are plotted in figure 2.2.

Now that you have an idea of how to parse and load data into Python, and you have an idea of how the kNN algorithm works, let's put it all together and do some classification.

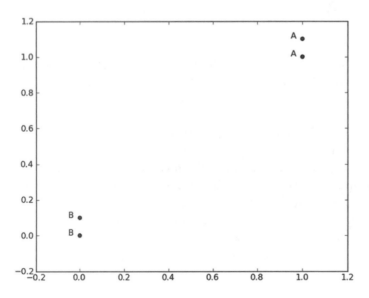

Figure 2.2 The four data points of our very simple kNN example

2.1.2 Putting the kNN classification algorithm into action

In this section we'll build a function, shown in listing 2.1, to run the kNN algorithm on one piece of data. I'll first show the function in pseudocode and then in actual Python, followed by a detailed explanation of what everything in the code does. Remember, the goal of this function is to use the kNN algorithm to classify one piece of data called inX. Pseudocode for this function would look like this:

For every point in our dataset:

    calculate the distance between inX and the current point

    sort the distances in increasing order

    take k items with lowest distances to inX

    find the majority class among these items

    return the majority class as our prediction for the class of inX

The Python code for the classify0() function is in the following listing.

Listing 2.1 k-Nearest Neighbors algorithm

```
def classify0(inX, dataSet, labels, k):
    dataSetSize = dataSet.shape[0]
    diffMat = tile(inX, (dataSetSize,1)) - dataSet
    sqDiffMat = diffMat**2
    sqDistances = sqDiffMat.sum(axis=1)
    distances = sqDistances**0.5
    sortedDistIndicies = distances.argsort()
    classCount={}
    for i in range(k):
        voteIlabel = labels[sortedDistIndicies[i]]
        classCount[voteIlabel] = classCount.get(voteIlabel,0) + 1
    sortedClassCount = sorted(classCount.iteritems(),
     key=operator.itemgetter(1), reverse=True)
    return sortedClassCount[0][0]
```

❶ Distance calculation

Voting with lowest k distances ❷

Sort ❸ dictionary

The function classify0() takes four inputs: the input vector to classify called inX, our full matrix of training examples called dataSet, a vector of labels called labels, and, finally, k, the number of nearest neighbors to use in the voting. The labels vector should have as many elements in it as there are rows in the dataSet matrix. You calculate the distances ❶ using the Euclidian distance where the distance between two vectors, xA and xB, with two elements, is given by

$$d = \sqrt{(xA_0 - xB_0)^2 + (xA_1 - xB_1)^2}$$

For example, the distance between points (0,0) and (1,2) is calculated by

$$\sqrt{(1-0)^2 + (2-0)^2}$$

If we are working with four features, the distance between points (1,0,0,1) and (7,6,9,4) would be calculated by

$$\sqrt{(7-1)^2 + (6-0)^2 + (9-0)^2 + (4-1)^2}$$

Following the distance calculation, the distances are sorted from least to greatest (this is the default). Next, ❷ the first k or lowest k distances are used to vote on the class of inX. The input k should always be a positive integer. Lastly, ❸ you take the classCount dictionary and decompose it into a list of tuples and then sort the tuples by the second item in the tuple using the `itemgetter` method from the operator module imported in the second line of the program. This sort is done in reverse so you have largest to smallest. Finally, you can return the label of the item occurring the most frequently.

To predict the class, type the following text at the Python prompt:

```
>>> kNN.classify0([0,0], group, labels, 3)
```

The result should be B. Try to change the [0,0] entry to see how the answer changes.

Congratulations, you just made your first classifier! You can do a lot with this simple classifier. Things will only get easier from here on out.

2.1.3   *How to test a classifier*

We built the kNN algorithm and saw that it was giving us answers we would expect. You may be asking yourself, "At what point does this break?" or "Is it always right?" No, it's not always right. There are different ways of exploring how often a classifier is right. Also, there are different things that impact the performance of a classifier, such as settings of the classifier and the dataset. Different algorithms perform differently on different datasets. That's why we have six chapters on classification.

To test out a classifier, you start with some known data so you can hide the answer from the classifier and ask the classifier for its best guess. You can add up the number of times the classifier was wrong and divide it by the total number of tests you gave it. This will give you the *error rate*, which is a common measure to gauge how good a classifier is doing on a dataset. An error rate of 0 means you have a perfect classifier, and an error rate of 1.0 means the classifier is always wrong. You'll see this in action with some solid data later.

The example in this section worked, but it wasn't useful. We're going to put kNN to use in real-world examples in the next two sections. First, we'll look at improving the results from a dating site with kNN, and then we'll look at an impressive handwriting recognition example. We'll employ testing in the handwriting recognition example to see if this algorithm is working.

2.2   *Example: improving matches from a dating site with kNN*

My friend Hellen has been using some online dating sites to find different people to go out with. She realized that despite the site's recommendations, she didn't like everyone she was matched with. After some introspection, she realized there were three types of people she went out with:

- People she didn't like
- People she liked in small doses
- People she liked in large doses

After discovering this, Hellen couldn't figure out what made a person fit into any of these categories. They all were recommended to her by the dating site. The people whom she liked in small doses were good to see Monday through Friday, but on the weekend she'd rather spend time with the people she liked in large doses. Hellen has asked us to help her filter future matches to categorize them. In addition, Hellen has collected some data that isn't recorded by the dating site, but she feels it's useful in selecting people to go out with.

Example: using kNN on results from a dating site

1. Collect: Text file provided.

2. Prepare: Parse a text file in Python.

3. Analyze: Use Matplotlib to make 2D plots of our data.

4. Train: Doesn't apply to the kNN algorithm.

5. Test: Write a function to use some portion of the data Hellen gave us as test examples. The test examples are classified against the non-test examples. If the predicted class doesn't match the real class, we'll count that as an error.

6. Use: Build a simple command-line program Hellen can use to predict whether she'll like someone based on a few inputs.

2.2.1   *Prepare: parsing data from a text file*

The data Hellen collected is in a text file called datingTestSet.txt. Hellen has been collecting this data for a while and has 1,000 entries. A new sample is on each line, and Hellen has recorded the following features:

- Number of frequent flyer miles earned per year
- Percentage of time spent playing video games
- Liters of ice cream consumed per week

Before we can use this data in our classifier, we need to change it to the format that our classifier accepts. In order to do this, we'll add a new function to kNN.py called `file2matrix`. This function takes a filename string and outputs two things: a matrix of training examples and a vector of class labels.

Add the following code to your kNN.py.

Listing 2.2   Text record to NumPy parsing code

```
def file2matrix(filename):
    fr = open(filename)
    numberOfLines = len(fr.readlines())
    returnMat = zeros((numberOfLines,3))
    classLabelVector = []
    fr = open(filename)
```

❶ Get number of lines in file

❷ Create NumPy matrix to return

```
        index = 0
        for line in fr.readlines():
            line = line.strip()
            listFromLine = line.split('\t')
            returnMat[index,:] = listFromLine[0:3]
            classLabelVector.append(int(listFromLine[-1]))
            index += 1
        return returnMat,classLabelVector
```

❸ Parse line
to a list

This code is a great place to demonstrate how easy it is to process text with Python. Initially, you'd like to know how many lines are in the file. ❶ It reads in the file and counts the number of lines. Next, ❷ you create a NumPy matrix (actually, it's a 2D array, but don't worry about that now) to populate and return. I've hard-coded in the size of this to be numberOfLines x 3, but you could add some code to make this adaptable to the various inputs. Finally, ❸ you loop over all the lines in the file and strip off the return line character with line.strip(). Next, you split the line into a list of elements delimited by the tab character: '\t'. You take the first three elements and shove them into a row of your matrix, and you use the Python feature of negative indexing to get the last item from the list to put into classLabelVector. You have to explicitly tell the interpreter that you'd like the integer version of the last item in the list, or it will give you the string version. Usually, you'd have to do this, but NumPy takes care of those details for you.

To use this, type the following at the Python prompt:

```
>>> reload(kNN)
>>> datingDataMat,datingLabels = kNN.file2matrix('datingTestSet.txt')
```

Make sure that the file datingTestSet.txt is in the same directory you're working from. Note that before executing the function, I reloaded the kNN.py module. When you change a module, you need to reload that module or you'll still be using the old version.

After successfully importing the datingTestSet.txt file, take a minute to explore the data in Python. You should get something similar to the following.

```
>>> datingDataMat
array([[  7.29170000e+04,   7.10627300e+00,   2.23600000e-01],
       [  1.42830000e+04,   2.44186700e+00,   1.90838000e-01],
       [  7.34750000e+04,   8.31018900e+00,   8.52795000e-01],
       ...,
       [  1.24290000e+04,   4.43233100e+00,   9.24649000e-01],
       [  2.52880000e+04,   1.31899030e+01,   1.05013800e+00],
       [  4.91800000e+03,   3.01112400e+00,   1.90663000e-01]])

>>> datingLabels[0:20]
['didntLike', 'smallDoses', 'didntLike', 'largeDoses', 'smallDoses',
 'smallDoses', 'didntLike', 'smallDoses', 'didntLike', 'didntLike',
'largeDoses', 'largeDose s', 'largeDoses', 'didntLike', 'didntLike',
'smallDoses', 'smallDoses', 'didntLike', 'smallDoses', 'didntLike']
```

Now that you have the data imported and properly formatted, let's take a look at it and see if we can make any sense of it. "Take a look" can mean many things. It can mean look at the values in a text file or look at a plot of the values. We'll next use some of Python's tools to make plots of the data. If we make a plot, we may be able to distinguish some patterns.

NumPy Array and Python's Array

We'll be using the NumPy array extensively in this book. In your Python shell you can import this using `from numpy import array`, or it will be imported when you import all of NumPy. There's another array type that comes with Python that we won't be using. Don't make the mistake of importing that array because the NumPy array methods won't work on it.

2.2.2 Analyze: creating scatter plots with Matplotlib

Let's look at the data in further detail by making some scatter plots of the data from Matplotlib. This isn't hard to do. From the Python console, type the following:

```
>>> import matplotlib
>>> import matplotlib.pyplot as plt
>>> fig = plt.figure()
>>> ax = fig.add_subplot(111)
>>> ax.scatter(datingDataMat[:,1], datingDataMat[:,2])
>>> plt.show()
```

You should see something like figure 2.3. We've plotted the second and third columns from the datingDataMat matrix. These are all of our values for the features "Percentage

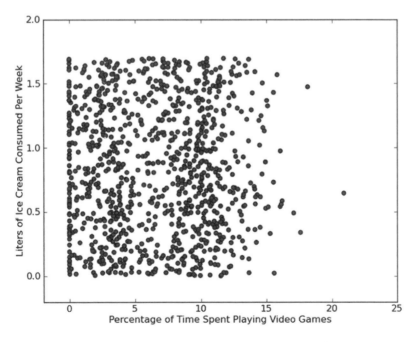

Figure 2.3 Dating data without class labels. From this plot it's difficult to discern which dot belongs to which group.

of time spent playing video games" and "Liters of ice cream consumed weekly" for all the classes put together.

It's hard to see any patterns in this data, but we have additional data we haven't used yet—the class values. If we can plot these in color or use some other markers, we can get a better understanding of the data. The Matplotlib scatter function has additional inputs we can use to customize the markers. Type the previous code again, but this time use the following for a scatter function:

```
>>> ax.scatter(datingDataMat[:,1], datingDataMat[:,2],
15.0*array(datingLabels), 15.0*array(datingLabels))
```

I provided a different marker size and color that depend on the class labels we have in datingLabels. You should see a plot similar to the one in figure 2.3. It doesn't look like you could make much sense of the data from figure 2.3; but if you plot columns 1 and 0 from our matrix, then you'll see a plot like the one in figure 2.4. From this image, you can make out three regions where the different classes lie.

Now that you can plot data using Matplotlib, you can get a better idea of exactly what's going on with our data. From figure 2.5, you can identify some regions where the different classes lie.

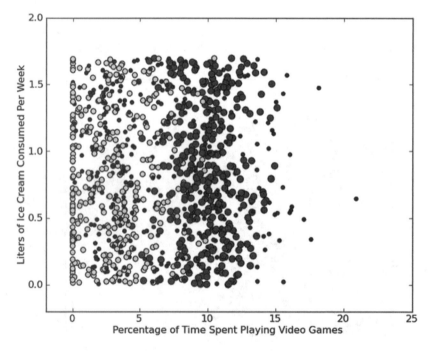

Figure 2.4   Dating data with markers changed by class label. It's easier to identify the different classes, but it's difficult to draw conclusions from looking at this data.

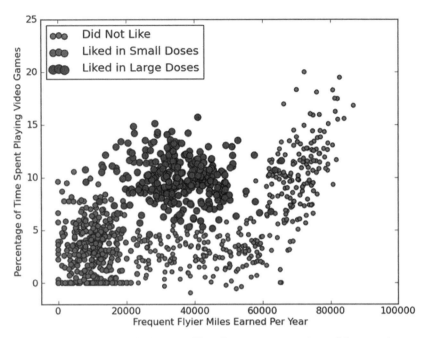

Figure 2.5 Dating data with frequent flier miles versus percentage of time spent playing video games plotted. The dating data has three features, and these two features show areas where the three different classes lie.

2.2.3 Prepare: normalizing numeric values

If you were to calculate the distance between person 3 and person 4 in table 2.3, you would have

$$\sqrt{(0-67)^2 + (20,000 - 32,000)^2 + (1.1 - 0.1)^2}$$

Which term in this equation do you think is going to make the most difference? The largest term, the number of frequent flyer miles earned per year, will have the most effect. The frequent flyer term will dominate even though the percentage of time spent playing video games and liters of ice cream consumed weekly have the largest differences of any two features in table 2.3. Why should frequent flyer miles be so important just because its values are large? It shouldn't have any extra importance, unless we want it to, but Hellen believes these terms are equally important.

Table 2.3 Sample of data from improved results on a dating site

	Percentage of time spent playing video games	Number of frequent flyer miles earned per year	Liters of ice cream consumed weekly	Category
1	0.8	400	0.5	1
2	12	134,000	0.9	3
3	0	20,000	1.1	2
4	67	32,000	0.1	2

When dealing with values that lie in different ranges, it's common to normalize them. Common ranges to normalize them to are 0 to 1 or -1 to 1. To scale everything from 0 to 1, you need to apply the following formula:

```
newValue = (oldValue-min)/(max-min)
```

In the normalization procedure, the variables `min` and `max` are the smallest and largest values in the dataset. This scaling adds some complexity to our classifier, but it's worth it to get good results. Let's create a new function in the file kNN.py called `autoNorm()` to automatically normalize the data to values between 0 and 1.

The `autoNorm()` function is given in the following listing.

Listing 2.3 Data-normalizing code

```
def autoNorm(dataSet):
    minVals = dataSet.min(0)
    maxVals = dataSet.max(0)
    ranges = maxVals - minVals
    normDataSet = zeros(shape(dataSet))
    m = dataSet.shape[0]
    normDataSet = dataSet - tile(minVals, (m,1))
    normDataSet = normDataSet/tile(ranges, (m,1))    ❶ Element-wise
    return normDataSet, ranges, minVals                  division
```

In the `autoNorm()` function, you get the minimum values of each column and place this in `minVals`; similarly, you get the maximum values. The 0 in `dataSet.min(0)` allows you to take the minimums from the columns, not the rows. Next, you calculate the range of possible values seen in our data and then create a new matrix to return. To get the normalized values, you subtract the minimum values and then divide by the range. The problem with this is that our matrix is 1000x3, while the `minVals` and `ranges` are 1x3. To overcome this, you use the NumPy `tile()` function to create a matrix the same size as our input matrix and then fill it up with many copies, or tiles. Note that it ❶ is element-wise division. In other numeric software packages, the / operator can be used for matrix division, but in NumPy you need to use `linalg.solve(matA,matB)` for matrix division.

To try out `autoNorm`, reload kNN.py, execute the function, and inspect the results at the Python prompt:

```
>>> reload(kNN)
>>> normMat, ranges, minVals = kNN.autoNorm(datingDataMat)
>>> normMat
array([[ 0.33060119,  0.58918886,  0.69043973],
       [ 0.49199139,  0.50262471,  0.13468257],
       [ 0.34858782,  0.68886842,  0.59540619],
       ...,
       [ 0.93077422,  0.52696233,  0.58885466],
       [ 0.76626481,  0.44109859,  0.88192528],
       [ 0.0975718 ,  0.02096883,  0.02443895]])
>>> ranges
array([ 8.78430000e+04,   2.02823930e+01,   1.69197100e+00])
>>> minVals
array([ 0.      ,  0.      ,   0.001818])
```

You could have returned just `normMat`, but you need the ranges and minimum values to normalize test data. You'll see this in action next.

2.2.4 *Test: testing the classifier as a whole program*

Now that you have the data in a format you can use, you're ready to test our classifier. After you test it, you can give it to our friend Hellen to use. One common task in machine learning is evaluating an algorithm's accuracy. One way you can use the existing data is to take some portion, say 90%, to train the classifier. Then you'll take the remaining 10% to test the classifier and see how accurate it is. There are more advanced ways of doing this, which we'll address later, but for now let's use this method. The 10% to be held back should be randomly selected. Our data isn't stored in a specific sequence, so you can take the first 10% or last 10% without upsetting any statistics professors.

Earlier, I mentioned that you can measure the performance of a classifier with the error rate. In classification, the error rate is the number of misclassified pieces of data divided by the total number of data points tested. An error rate of 0 means you have a perfect classifier, and an error rate of 1.0 means the classifier is always wrong. In our code, you'll measure the error rate with a counter that's incremented every time a piece of data is misclassified. The total number of errors divided by the total number of data points tested will give you the error rate.

To test the classifier, you'll create a new function in kNN.py called `datingClassTest`. This function is self-contained, so don't worry if you closed your Python shell earlier. You won't have to go back and type the code again. Enter the code in the following listing into kNN.py.

Listing 2.4 Classifier testing code for dating site

```
def datingClassTest():
    hoRatio = 0.10
    datingDataMat,datingLabels = file2matrix('datingTestSet.txt')
    normMat, ranges, minVals = autoNorm(datingDataMat)
    m = normMat.shape[0]
    numTestVecs = int(m*hoRatio)
    errorCount = 0.0
    for i in range(numTestVecs):
        classifierResult = classify0(normMat[i,:],normMat[numTestVecs:m,:],\
                    datingLabels[numTestVecs:m],3)
        print "the classifier came back with: %d, the real answer is: %d"\
                    % (classifierResult, datingLabels[i])
        if (classifierResult != datingLabels[i]): errorCount += 1.0
    print "the total error rate is: %f" % (errorCount/float(numTestVecs))
```

The `datingClassTest` function is shown in listing 2.4. This uses `file2matrix` and `autoNorm()` from earlier to get the data into a form you can use. Next, the number of test vectors is calculated, and this is used to decide which vectors from `normMat` will be used for testing and which for training. The two parts are then fed into our original kNN classifier, classify0. Finally, the error rate is calculated and displayed. Note that you're using the original classifier; you spent most of this section manipulating the data so that you could apply it to a simple classifier. Getting solid data is important and will be the subject of chapter 20.

To execute this, reload kNN and then type kNN.datingClassTest() at the Python prompt. You should get results similar to the following example:

```
>>> kNN.datingClassTest()
the classifier came back with: 1, the real answer is: 1
the classifier came back with: 2, the real answer is: 2
.
.
the classifier came back with: 1, the real answer is: 1
the classifier came back with: 2, the real answer is: 2
the classifier came back with: 3, the real answer is: 3
the classifier came back with: 3, the real answer is: 1
the classifier came back with: 2, the real answer is: 2
the total error rate is: 0.024000
```

The total error rate for this classifier on this dataset with these settings is 2.4%. Not bad. You can experiment with different hoRatios and different values of k inside the datingClassTest function. How does the error change as hoRatio is increased? Note that the results will vary by algorithm, dataset, and settings.

The example showed that we could predict the class with only a 2.4% error. To our friend Hellen, this means that she can enter a new person's information, and our system will predict whether she'll dislike or like the person in large or small doses.

2.2.5   *Use: putting together a useful system*

Now that you've tested the classifier on our data, it's time to use it to actually classify people for Hellen. We'll provide Hellen with a small program. Hellen will find someone on the dating site and enter his information. The program predicts how much she'll like this person.

Add the code from the following listing to kNN.py and reload kNN.

Listing 2.5   Dating site predictor function

```
def classifyPerson():
    resultList = ['not at all','in small doses', 'in large doses']
    percentTats = float(raw_input(\
                "percentage of time spent playing video games?"))
    ffMiles = float(raw_input("frequent flier miles earned per year?"))
    iceCream = float(raw_input("liters of ice cream consumed per year?"))
    datingDataMat,datingLabels = file2matrix('datingTestSet.txt')
    normMat, ranges, minVals = autoNorm(datingDataMat)
    inArr = array([ffMiles, percentTats, iceCream])
    classifierResult = classify0((inArr-\
                minVals)/ranges,normMat,datingLabels,3)
    print "You will probably like this person: ",\
                resultList[classifierResult - 1]
```

The code in listing 2.5 mostly uses things you saw earlier. The only new code is the function raw_input(). This gives the user a text prompt and returns whatever the user enters. To see the program in action, type in the following:

```
>>> kNN.classifyPerson()
percentage of time spent playing video games?10
frequent flier miles earned per year?10000
liters of ice cream consumed per year?0.5
You will probably like this person:  in small doses
```

You've seen how to create a classifier with some data. All of the data is easily read by a human, but how could you use a classifier on data that isn't easily read by a human? The next section contains another example, this time showing how you can apply kNN to things as diverse as images where the data is in binary form.

2.3 Example: a handwriting recognition system

We're going to work through an example of handwriting recognition with our kNN classifier. We'll be working only with the digits 0–9. Some examples are shown in figure 2.6. These digits were processed through image-processing software to make them all the same size and color.[1] They're all 32x32 black and white. The binary images were converted to text format to make this example easier, although it isn't the most efficient use of memory.

Example: using kNN on a handwriting recognition system

1. Collect: Text file provided.

2. Prepare: Write a function to convert from the image format to the list format used in our classifier, `classify0()`.

3. Analyze: We'll look at the prepared data in the Python shell to make sure it's correct.

4. Train: Doesn't apply to the kNN algorithm.

5. Test: Write a function to use some portion of the data as test examples. The test examples are classified against the non-test examples. If the predicted class doesn't match the real class, you'll count that as an error.

6. Use: Not performed in this example. You could build a complete program to extract digits from an image, such a system used to sort the mail in the United States.

2.3.1 Prepare: converting images into test vectors

The images are stored in two directories in the chapter 2 source code. The trainingDigits directory contains about 2,000 examples similar to those in figure 2.6. There are roughly 200 samples from each digit. The testDigits directory contains about 900 examples. We'll use the trainingDigits directory to train our classifier and testDigits to

---

[1] The dataset is a modified version of the "Optical Recognition of Handwritten Digits Data Set" by E. Alpaydin, C. Kaynak, Department of Computer Engineering at Bogazici University, 80815 Istanbul Turkey, retrieved from the UCI Machine Learning Repository (http://archive.ics.uci.edu/ml) on October 3, 2010.

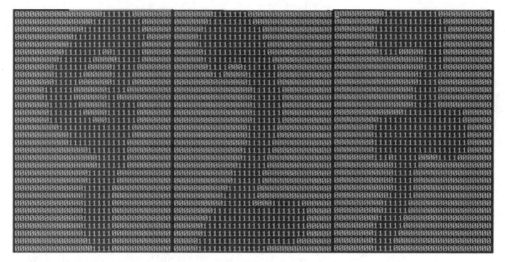

Figure 2.6   Examples of the handwritten digits dataset

test it. There'll be no overlap between the two groups. Feel free to take a look at the files in those folders.

We'd like to use the same classifier that we used in the previous two examples, so we're going to need to reformat the images to a single vector. We'll take the 32x32 matrix that is each binary image and make it a 1x1024 vector. After we do this, we can apply it to our existing classifier.

The following code is a small function called `img2vector`, which converts the image to a vector. The function creates a 1x1024 NumPy array, then opens the given file, loops over the first 32 lines in the file, and stores the integer value of the first 32 characters on each line in the NumPy array. This array is finally returned.

```
def img2vector(filename):
    returnVect = zeros((1,1024))
    fr = open(filename)
    for i in range(32):
        lineStr = fr.readline()
        for j in range(32):
            returnVect[0,32*i+j] = int(lineStr[j])
    return returnVect
```

Try out the `img2vector` code with the following commands in the Python shell, and compare the results to a file opened with a text editor:

```
>>> testVector = kNN.img2vector('testDigits/0_13.txt')
>>> testVector[0,0:31]
array([ 0.,  0.,  0.,  0.,  0.,  0.,  0.,  0.,  0.,  0.,  0.,  0.,  0.,
        0.,  1.,  1.,  1.,  1.,  0.,  0.,  0.,  0.,  0.,  0.,  0.,  0.,
        0.,  0.,  0.,  0.,  0.])
>>> testVector[0,32:63]
array([ 0.,  0.,  0.,  0.,  0.,  0.,  0.,  0.,  0.,  0.,  0.,  0.,  1.,
        1.,  1.,  1.,  1.,  1.,  0.,  0.,  0.,  0.,  0.,  0.,  0.,
        0.,  0.,  0.,  0.,  0.])
```

2.3.2 *Test: kNN on handwritten digits*

Now that you have the data in a format that you can plug into our classifier, you're ready to test out this idea and see how well it works. The function shown in listing 2.6, handwritingClassTest(), is a self-contained function that tests out our classifier. You can add it to kNN.py. Before you add it, make sure to add from os import listdir to the top of the file. This imports one function, listdir, from the os module, so that you can see the names of files in a given directory.

Listing 2.6 Handwritten digits testing code

```
def handwritingClassTest():
    hwLabels = []
    trainingFileList = listdir('trainingDigits')          ❶ Get contents of
    m = len(trainingFileList)                                 directory
    trainingMat = zeros((m,1024))
    for i in range(m):
        fileNameStr = trainingFileList[i]
        fileStr = fileNameStr.split('.')[0]               ❷ Process class num
        classNumStr = int(fileStr.split('_')[0])             from filename
        hwLabels.append(classNumStr)
        trainingMat[i,:] = img2vector('trainingDigits/%s' % fileNameStr)
    testFileList = listdir('testDigits')
    errorCount = 0.0
    mTest = len(testFileList)
    for i in range(mTest):
        fileNameStr = testFileList[i]
        fileStr = fileNameStr.split('.')[0]
        classNumStr = int(fileStr.split('_')[0])
        vectorUnderTest = img2vector('testDigits/%s' % fileNameStr)
        classifierResult = classify0(vectorUnderTest, \
                            trainingMat, hwLabels, 3)
        print "the classifier came back with: %d, the real answer is: %d"\
                            % (classifierResult, classNumStr)
        if (classifierResult != classNumStr): errorCount += 1.0
    print "\nthe total number of errors is: %d" % errorCount
    print "\nthe total error rate is: %f" % (errorCount/float(mTest))
```

In listing 2.6, you get the contents for the trainingDigits directory ❶ as a list. Then you see how many files are in that directory and call this m. Next, you create a training matrix with m rows and 1024 columns to hold each image as a single row. You parse out the class number from the filename. ❷ The filename is something like 9_45.txt, where 9 is the class number and it is the 45th instance of the digit 9. You then put this class number in the hwLabels vector and load the image with the function img2vector discussed previously. Next, you do something similar for all the files in the testDigits directory, but instead of loading them into a big matrix, you test each vector individually with our classify0 function. You didn't use the autoNorm() function from section 2.2 because all of the values were already between 0 and 1.

To execute this from the Python shell, type kNN.handwritingClassTest() at the Python prompt. It's quite interesting to watch. Depending on your machine's speed, it will take some time to load the dataset. Then, when the function begins testing, you can see the results as they come back. You should have output that's similar to the following example:

```
>>> kNN.handwritingClassTest()
the classifier came back with: 0, the real answer is: 0
the classifier came back with: 0, the real answer is: 0
.
.
.
the classifier came back with: 7, the real answer is: 7
the classifier came back with: 7, the real answer is: 7
the classifier came back with: 8, the real answer is: 8
the classifier came back with: 8, the real answer is: 8
the classifier came back with: 8, the real answer is: 8
the classifier came back with: 6, the real answer is: 8
.
.
.
the classifier came back with: 9, the real answer is: 9
the total number of errors is: 11
the total error rate is: 0.011628
```

Using the kNN algorithm on this dataset, you were able to achieve an error rate of 1.2%. You can vary k to see how this changes. You can also modify the `handwritingClassTest` function to randomly select training examples. That way, you can vary the number of training examples and see how that impacts the error rate.

Depending on your computer's speed, you may think this algorithm is slow, and you'd be right. For each of our 900 test cases, you had to do 2,000 distance calculations on a 1024-entry floating point vector. Additionally, our test dataset size was 2 MB. Is there a way to make this smaller and take fewer computations? One modification to kNN, called kD-trees, allows you to reduce the number of calculations.

2.4   *Summary*

The k-Nearest Neighbors algorithm is a simple and effective way to classify data. The examples in this chapter should be evidence of how powerful a classifier it is. kNN is an example of instance-based learning, where you need to have instances of data close at hand to perform the machine learning algorithm. The algorithm has to carry around the full dataset; for large datasets, this implies a large amount of storage. In addition, you need to calculate the distance measurement for every piece of data in the database, and this can be cumbersome.

An additional drawback is that kNN doesn't give you any idea of the underlying structure of the data; you have no idea what an "average" or "exemplar" instance from each class looks like. In the next chapter, we'll address this issue by exploring ways in which probability measurements can help you do classification.

3

Splitting datasets one feature at a time: decision trees

This chapter covers
- Introducing decision trees
- Measuring consistency in a dataset
- Using recursion to construct a decision tree
- Plotting trees in Matplotlib

Have you ever played a game called Twenty Questions? If not, the game works like this: One person thinks of some object and players try to guess the object. Players are allowed to ask 20 questions and receive only yes or no answers. In this game, the people asking the questions are successively splitting the set of objects they can deduce. A *decision tree* works just like the game Twenty Questions; you give it a bunch of data and it generates answers to the game.

The decision tree is one of the most commonly used classification techniques; recent surveys claim that it's *the* most commonly used technique.[1] You don't have to know much about machine learning to understand how it works.

If you're not already familiar with decisions trees, the concept is straightforward. Chances are good that you've already seen a decision tree without knowing it. Figure 3.1 shows a flowchart, which is a decision tree. It has *decision blocks* (rectangles) and *terminating blocks* (ovals) where some conclusion has been reached. The right and left arrows coming out of the decision blocks are known as *branches,* and they can lead to other decision blocks or to a terminating block. In this particular example, I made a hypothetical email classification system, which first checks the domain of the sending email address. If this is equal to myEmployer.com, it will classify the email as "Email to read when bored." If it isn't from that domain, it checks to see if the body of the email contains the word *hockey.* If the email contains the word *hockey,* then this email is classified as "Email from friends; read immediately"; if the body doesn't contain the word *hockey,* then it gets classified as "Spam; don't read."

The kNN algorithm in chapter 2 did a great job of classifying, but it didn't lead to any major insights about the data. One of the best things about decision trees is that humans can easily understand the data.

The algorithm you'll build in this chapter will be able to take a set of data, build a decision tree, and draw a tree like the one in figure 3.1. The decision tree does a great job of distilling data into knowledge. With this, you can take a set of unfamiliar data and extract a set of rules. The machine learning will take place as the machine creates these rules from the dataset. Decision trees are often used in expert systems, and the results obtained by using them are often comparable to those from a human expert with decades of experience in a given field.

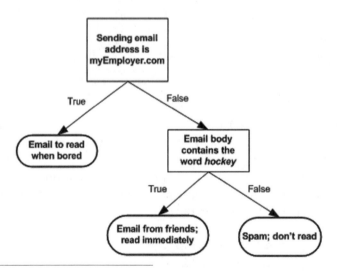

Figure 3.1   A decision tree in flowchart form

---

[1]   Giovanni Seni and John Elder, *Ensemble Methods in Data Mining: Improving Accuracy Through Combining Predictions,* Synthesis Lectures on Data Mining and Knowledge Discovery (Morgan and Claypool, 2010), 28.

Now that you know a little of what decision trees are good for, we're going to get into the process of building them from nothing but a pile of data. In the first section, we'll discuss methods used to construct trees and start writing code to construct a tree. Next, we'll address some metrics that we can use to measure the algorithm's success. Finally, we'll use recursion to build our classifier and plot it using Matplotlib. When we have the classifier working, we'll take some data of a contact lens prescription and use our classifier to try to predict what lenses people will need.

3.1 Tree construction

> **Decision trees**
>
> Pros: Computationally cheap to use, easy for humans to understand learned results, missing values OK, can deal with irrelevant features
>
> Cons: Prone to overfitting
>
> Works with: Numeric values, nominal values

In this section we're going to walk through the decision tree–building algorithm, with all its fine details. We'll first discuss the mathematics that decide how to split a dataset using something called *information theory*. We'll then write some code to apply this theory to our dataset, and finally we'll write some code to build a tree.

To build a decision tree, you need to make a first decision on the dataset to dictate which feature is used to split the data. To determine this, you try every feature and measure which split will give you the best results. After that, you'll split the dataset into subsets. The subsets will then traverse down the branches of the first decision node. If the data on the branches is the same class, then you've properly classified it and don't need to continue splitting it. If the data isn't the same, then you need to repeat the splitting process on this subset. The decision on how to split this subset is done the same way as the original dataset, and you repeat this process until you've classified all the data.

Pseudo-code for a function called `createBranch()` would look like this:

Check if every item in the dataset is in the same class:
> *If so return the class label*
> *Else*
>> *find the best feature to split the data*
>> *split the dataset*
>> *create a branch node*
>>> *for each split*
>>>> *call createBranch and add the result to the branch node*
>> *return branch node*

Please note the recursive nature of `createBranch`. It calls itself in the second-to-last line. We'll write this in Python later, but first, we need to address how to split the dataset.

General approach to decision trees

1. Collect: Any method.

2. Prepare: This tree-building algorithm works only on nominal values, so any continuous values will need to be quantized.

3. Analyze: Any method. You should visually inspect the tree after it is built.

4. Train: Construct a tree data structure.

5. Test: Calculate the error rate with the learned tree.

6. Use: This can be used in any supervised learning task. Often, trees are used to better understand the data.

Some decision trees make a binary split of the data, but we won't do this. If we split on an attribute and it has four possible values, then we'll split the data four ways and create four separate branches. We'll follow the ID3 algorithm, which tells us how to split the data and when to stop splitting it. (See http://en.wikipedia.org/wiki/ID3_algorithm for more information.) We're also going to split on one and only one feature at a time. If our training set has 20 features, how do we choose which one to use first?

See the data in table 3.1. It contains five animals pulled from the sea and asks if they can survive without coming to the surface and if they have flippers. We would like to classify these animals into two classes: fish and not fish. Now we want to decide whether we should split the data based on the first feature or the second feature. To answer this question, we need some quantitative way of determining how to split the data. We'll discuss that next.

	Can survive without coming to surface?	Has flippers?	Fish?
1	Yes	Yes	Yes
2	Yes	Yes	Yes
3	Yes	No	No
4	No	Yes	No
5	No	Yes	No

Table 3.1   Marine animal data

3.1.1   *Information gain*

We choose to split our dataset in a way that makes our unorganized data more organized. There are multiple ways to do this, and each has its own advantages and disadvantages. One way to organize this messiness is to measure the information. Using information theory, you can measure the information before and after the split. Information theory is a branch of science that's concerned with quantifying information.

The change in information before and after the split is known as the *information gain.* When you know how to calculate the information gain, you can split your data across every feature to see which split gives you the highest information gain. The split with the highest information gain is your best option.

Before you can measure the best split and start splitting our data, you need to know how to calculate the information gain. The measure of information of a set is known as the *Shannon entropy,* or just *entropy* for short. Its name comes from the father of information theory, Claude Shannon.

Claude Shannon

Claude Shannon is considered one of the smartest people of the twentieth century. In William Poundstone's 2005 book *Fortune's Formula,* he wrote this of Claude Shannon:

"There were many at Bell Labs and MIT who compared Shannon's insight to Einstein's. Others found that comparison unfair—unfair to Shannon."[†]

[†] William Poundstone, *Fortune's Formula: The Untold Story of the Scientific Betting System that Beat the Casinos and Wall Street"* (Hill and Wang, 2005), 15.

If the terms *information gain* and *entropy* sound confusing, don't worry. They're meant to be confusing! When Claude Shannon wrote about information theory, John von Neumann told him to use the term *entropy* because people wouldn't know what it meant.

Entropy is defined as the expected value of the information. First, we need to define information. If you're classifying something that can take on multiple values, the information for symbol x^i is defined as

$$l(x_i) = log_2 p(x_i)$$

where $p(x^i)$ is the probability of choosing this class.

To calculate entropy, you need the expected value of all the information of all possible values of our class. This is given by

$$H = -\sum_{i=1}^{n} p(x_i) log_2 p(x_i)$$

where *n* is the number of classes.

Let's see how to calculate this in Python. To start, you'll create a file called trees.py. Insert the code from the following listing into trees.py. This listing will do entropy calculations on a given dataset for you.

Listing 3.1   Function to calculate the Shannon entropy of a dataset

```
from math import log

def calcShannonEnt(dataSet):
    numEntries = len(dataSet)
    labelCounts = {}
    for featVec in dataSet:
        currentLabel = featVec[-1]                          ❶ Create dictionary
        if currentLabel not in labelCounts.keys():            of all possible
        labelCounts[currentLabel] = 0                         classes
        labelCounts[currentLabel] += 1
    shannonEnt = 0.0
    for key in labelCounts:                                 ❷ Logarithm
        prob = float(labelCounts[key])/numEntries             base 2
        shannonEnt -= prob * log(prob,2)
    return shannonEnt
```

The code in listing 3.1 is straightforward. First, you calculate a count of the number of instances in the dataset. This could have been calculated inline, but it's used multiple times in the code, so an explicit variable is created for it. Next, you create a dictionary whose keys are the values in the final column. ❶ If a key was not encountered previously, one is created. For each key, you keep track of how many times this label occurs. Finally, you use the frequency of all the different labels to calculate the probability of that label. This probability is used to calculate the Shannon entropy, ❷ and you sum this up for all the labels. Let's try out this entropy stuff.

The simple data about fish identification from table 3.1 is provided in the trees.py file by utilizing the createDataSet() function. You can enter it yourself:

```
def createDataSet():
    dataSet = [[1, 1, 'yes'],
               [1, 1, 'yes'],
               [1, 0, 'no'],
               [0, 1, 'no'],
               [0, 1, 'no']]
    labels = ['no surfacing','flippers']
    return dataSet, labels
```

Enter the following in your Python shell:

```
>>> reload(trees.py)
>>> myDat,labels=trees.createDataSet()
>>> myDat
[[1, 1, 'yes'], [1, 1, 'yes'], [1, 0, 'no'], [0, 1, 'no'], [0, 1, 'no']]
>>> trees.calcShannonEnt(myDat)
0.97095059445466858
```

The higher the entropy, the more mixed up the data is. Let's make the data a little messier and see how the entropy changes. We'll add a third class, which is called maybe, and see how the entropy changes:

```
>>> myDat[0][-1]='maybe'
>>> myDat
[[1, 1, 'maybe'], [1, 1, 'yes'], [1, 0, 'no'], [0, 1, 'no'], [0, 1, 'no']]
>>> trees.calcShannonEnt(myDat)
1.3709505944546687
```

Let's split the dataset in a way that will give us the largest information gain. We won't know how to do that unless we actually split the dataset and measure the information gain.

Another common measure of disorder in a set is the Gini impurity,[2] which is the probability of choosing an item from the set and the probability of that item being misclassified. We won't get into the Gini impurity. Instead, we'll move on to splitting the dataset and building the tree.

3.1.2 Splitting the dataset

You just saw how to measure the amount of disorder in a dataset. For our classifier algorithm to work, you need to measure the entropy, split the dataset, measure the entropy on the split sets, and see if splitting it was the right thing to do. You'll do this for all of our features to determine the best feature to split on. Think of it as a two-dimensional plot of some data. You want to draw a line to separate one class from another. Should you do this on the X-axis or the Y-axis? The answer is what you're trying to find out here.

To see this in action, open your editor and add the following code to trees.py.

> **Listing 3.2 Dataset splitting on a given feature**

```
def splitDataSet(dataSet, axis, value):
    retDataSet = []                                    ◁── ❶ Create
    for featVec in dataSet:                                    separate list
        if featVec[axis] == value:
            reducedFeatVec = featVec[:axis]                 ❷ Cut out the
            reducedFeatVec.extend(featVec[axis+1:])            feature split on
            retDataSet.append(reducedFeatVec)
    return retDataSet
```

The code in listing 3.2 takes three inputs: the dataset we'll split, the feature we'll split on, and the value of the feature to return. Most of the time in Python, you don't have to worry about memory or allocation. Python passes lists by reference, so if you modify a list in a function, the list will be modified everywhere. To account for this, you create a new list at the beginning. ❶ You create a new list each time because you'll be calling this function multiple times on the same dataset and you don't want the original dataset modified. Our dataset is a list of lists; you iterate over every item in the list and if it contains the value you're looking for, you'll add it to your newly created list. Inside the `if` statement, you cut out the feature that you split on. ❷ This will be more obvious in the next section, but think of it this way: once you've split on a feature, you're finished with that feature. You used the `extend()` and `append()` methods of the Python list type. There's an important difference between these two methods when dealing with multiple lists.

Assume you have two lists, a and b:

---

[2] For more information, you should check out *Introduction to Data Mining* by Pan-Ning Tan, Vipin Kumar, and Michael Steinbach; Pearson Education (Addison-Wesley, 2005), 158.

```
>>> a=[1,2,3]
>>> b=[4,5,6]
>>> a.append(b)
>>> a
[1, 2, 3, [4, 5, 6]]
```

If you do `a.append(b)`, you have a list with four elements, and the fourth element is a list. However, if you do

```
>>> a=[1,2,3]
>>> a.extend(b)
>>> a
[1, 2, 3, 4, 5, 6]
```

you now have one list with all the elements from a and b.

Let's try out the `splitDataSet()` function on our simple example. Add the code from listing 3.2 to trees.py, and type in the following at your Python shell:

```
>>> reload(trees)
<module 'trees' from 'trees.pyc'>
>>> myDat,labels=trees.createDataSet()
>>> myDat
[[1, 1, 'yes'], [1, 1, 'yes'], [1, 0, 'no'], [0, 1, 'no'], [0, 1, 'no']]
>>> trees.splitDataSet(myDat,0,1)
[[1, 'yes'], [1, 'yes'], [0, 'no']]
>>> trees.splitDataSet(myDat,0,0)
[[1, 'no'], [1, 'no']]
```

You're now going to combine the Shannon entropy calculation and the `splitDataSet()` function to cycle through the dataset and decide which feature is the best to split on. Using the entropy calculation tells you which split best organizes your data.

Open your text editor and add the code from the following listing to trees.py.

Listing 3.3   Choosing the best feature to split on

```
def chooseBestFeatureToSplit(dataSet):
    numFeatures = len(dataSet[0]) - 1
    baseEntropy = calcShannonEnt(dataSet)
    bestInfoGain = 0.0; bestFeature = -1
    for i in range(numFeatures):
        featList = [example[i] for example in dataSet]          ❶ Create unique list
        uniqueVals = set(featList)                                 of class labels
        newEntropy = 0.0
        for value in uniqueVals:
            subDataSet = splitDataSet(dataSet, i, value)         ❷ Calculate
            prob = len(subDataSet)/float(len(dataSet))              entropy for
            newEntropy += prob * calcShannonEnt(subDataSet)         each split
        infoGain = baseEntropy - newEntropy
        if (infoGain > bestInfoGain):
            bestInfoGain = infoGain                              ❸ Find the best
            bestFeature = I                                         information gain
    return bestFeature
```

The code in listing 3.3 is the function `chooseBestFeatureToSplit()`. As you can guess, it chooses the feature that, when split on, best organizes your data. The functions from listing 3.2 and listing 3.1 are used in this function. We've made a few assumptions about the data. The first assumption is that it comes in the form of a list of lists, and all these lists are of equal size. The next assumption is that the last column in the data or the last item in each instance is the class label of that instance. You use these assumptions in the first line of the function to find out how many features you have available in the given dataset. We didn't make any assumption on the type of data in the lists. It could be a number or a string; it doesn't matter.

The next part of the code in listing 3.3 calculates the Shannon entropy of the whole dataset before any splitting has occurred. This gives you the base disorder, which you'll later compare to the post split disorder measurements. The first `for` loop loops over all the features in our dataset. You use list comprehensions to create a list of all the ith entries in our dataset, or all the possible values present in the data. ❶ Next, you use the Python native set data type. Sets are like lists, but a value can occur only once. Creating a new set from a list is one of the fastest ways of getting the unique values out of list in Python.

Next, you go through all the unique values of this feature and split the data for each feature. ❷ The new entropy is calculated and summed up for all the unique values of that feature. The information gain is the reduction in entropy or the reduction in messiness. I hope entropy makes sense when put in terms of reduction of disorder. Finally, you compare the information gain among all the features and return the index of the best feature to split on. ❸

Now let's see this in action. After you enter the code from listing 3.3 into trees.py, type the following at your Python shell:

```
>>> reload(trees)
<module 'trees' from 'trees.py'>
>>> myDat,labels=trees.createDataSet()
>>> trees.chooseBestFeatureToSplit(myDat)
0
>>> myDat
[[1, 1, 'yes'], [1, 1, 'yes'], [1, 0, 'no'], [0, 1, 'no'], [0, 1, 'no']]
```

What just happened? The code told you that the 0th feature was the best feature to split on. Is that right? Does that make any sense? It's the same data from table 3.1, so let's look at table 3.1, or the data from the variable myDat. If you split on the first feature, that is, put everything where the first feature is 1 in one group and everything where the first feature is 0 in another group, how consistent is the data? If you do that, the group where the first feature is 1 will have two yeses and one no. The other group will have zero yeses and two nos. What if you split on the second feature? The first group will have two yeses and two nos. The second group will have zero yeses and one no. The first split does a better job of organizing the data. If you're not convinced, you can use the calcShannonEntropy() function from listing 3.1 to test it.

Now that you can measure how organized a dataset is and you can split the data, it's time to put all of this together and build the decision tree.

3.1.3 *Recursively building the tree*

You now have all the components you need to create an algorithm that makes decision trees from a dataset. It works like this: you start with our dataset and split it based on the best attribute to split. These aren't binary trees, so you can handle more than two-way splits. Once split, the data will traverse down the branches of the tree to another node. This node will then split the data again. You're going to use the principle of recursion to handle this.

You'll stop under the following conditions: you run out of attributes on which to split or all the instances in a branch are the same class. If all instances have the same class, then you'll create a leaf node, or terminating block. Any data that reaches this leaf node is deemed to belong to the class of that leaf node. This process can be seen in figure 3.2.

The first stopping condition makes this algorithm tractable, and you can even set a bound on the maximum number of splits you can have. You'll encounter other decision-tree algorithms later, such as C4.5 and CART. These do not "consume" the features at each split. This creates a problem for these algorithms because they split

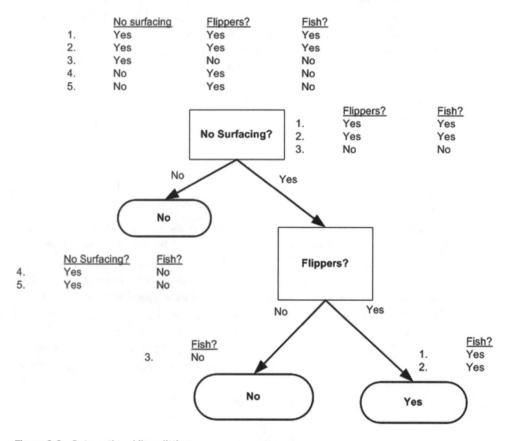

Figure 3.2   Data paths while splitting

the data, but the number of features doesn't decrease at each split. Don't worry about that for now. You can simply count the number of columns in our dataset to see if you've run out of attributes. If our dataset has run out of attributes but the class labels are not all the same, you must decide what to call that leaf node. In this situation, you'll take a majority vote.

Open your editor of choice. Before you add the next function, you need to add the following line to the top of trees.py: import operator. Now, add the following function to trees.py:

```
def majorityCnt(classList):
    classCount={}
    for vote in classList:
        if vote not in classCount.keys(): classCount[vote] = 0
        classCount[vote] += 1
    sortedClassCount = sorted(classCount.iteritems(),
     key=operator.itemgetter(1), reverse=True)
    return sortedClassCount[0][0]
```

This function may look familiar; it's similar to the voting portion of classify0 from chapter 2. This function takes a list of class names and then creates a dictionary whose keys are the unique values in classList, and the object of the dictionary is the frequency of occurrence of each class label from classList. Finally, you use the operator to sort the dictionary by the keys and return the class that occurs with the greatest frequency.

Open trees.py in your editor and add the code from the following listing.

Listing 3.4 Tree-building code

```
def createTree(dataSet,labels):
    classList = [example[-1] for example in dataSet]        ➊ Stop when all
    if classList.count(classList[0]) == len(classList):        classes are equal
        return classList[0]
    if len(dataSet[0]) == 1:                                  ➋ When no more features,
        return majorityCnt(classList)                           return majority
    bestFeat = chooseBestFeatureToSplit(dataSet)
    bestFeatLabel = labels[bestFeat]
    myTree = {bestFeatLabel:{}}
    del(labels[bestFeat])
    featValues = [example[bestFeat] for example in dataSet]   ➌ Get list of
    uniqueVals = set(featValues)                                 unique values
    for value in uniqueVals:
        subLabels = labels[:]
        myTree[bestFeatLabel][value] = createTree(splitDataSet\
                        (dataSet, bestFeat, value),subLabels)
    return myTree
```

The code in listing 3.4 takes two inputs: the dataset and a list of labels. The list of labels contains a label for each of the features in the dataset. The algorithm could function without this, but it would be difficult to make any sense of the data. All of the previous assumptions about the dataset still hold. You first create a list of all the class labels in our dataset and call this classList. The first stopping condition is that if all the class labels are the same, then you return this label. ❶ The second stopping condition is the case when there are no more features to split. ❷ If you don't meet the stopping conditions, then you use the function created in listing 3.3 to choose the best feature. Next, you create your tree.

You'll use the Python dictionary to store the tree. You could have created a special data type, but it's not necessary. The myTree dictionary will be used to store the tree, and you'll see how that works soon. You get all the unique values from the dataset for our chosen feature: bestFeat. ❸ The unique value code uses sets and is similar to a few lines in listing 3.3.

Finally, you iterate over all the unique values from our chosen feature and recursively call createTree() for each split of the dataset. This value is inserted into our myTree dictionary, so you end up with a lot of nested dictionaries representing our tree. Before we get into the nesting, note that the subLabels = labels[:] line makes a copy of labels and places it in a new list called subLabels. You do this because Python passes lists by reference and you'd like the original list to be the same every time you call createTree().

Let's try out this code. After you add the code from listing 3.4 to trees.py, enter the following in your Python shell:

```
>>> reload(trees)
<module 'trees' from 'trees.pyc'>
>>> myDat,labels=trees.createDataSet()
>>> myTree = trees.createTree(myDat,labels)
>>> myTree
{'no surfacing': {0: 'no', 1: {'flippers': {0: 'no', 1: 'yes'}}}}
```

The variable myTree contains the nested dictionaries, which you're using to represent our tree structure. Reading left to right, the first key, 'no surfacing', is the name of the first feature that was split by the create tree. The value of this key is another dictionary. This second dictionary's keys are the splits of the 'no surfacing' feature. The values of these keys are the children of the 'no surfacing' node. The values are either a class label or another dictionary. If the value is a class label, then that child is a leaf node. If the value is another dictionary, then that child node is a decision node and the format repeats itself. In our example, we have three leaf nodes and two decision nodes.

Now that you've properly constructed the tree, you need to display it so that humans can properly understand the information.

3.2   *Plotting trees in Python with Matplotlib annotations*

The tree you made in the previous section is great, but it's a little difficult to visualize. In this section, we'll use Matplotlib to create a tree you can look at. One of the greatest strengths of decision trees is that humans can easily understand them. The plotting library we used in the previous chapter is extremely powerful. Unfortunately, Python doesn't include a good tool for plotting trees, so we'll make our own. We'll write a program to draw a decision tree like the one in figure 3.3.

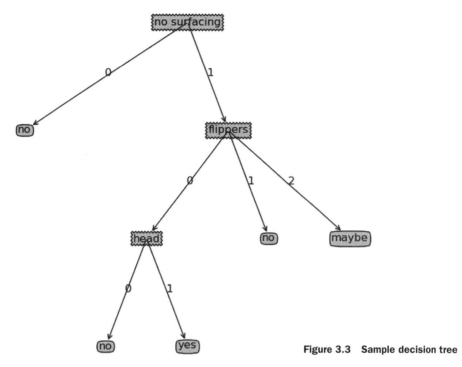

Figure 3.3   Sample decision tree

3.2.1   *Matplotlib annotations*

Matplotlib has a great tool, called *annotations*, that can add text near data in a plot. Annotations are usually used to explain some part of the data. But having the text on top of the data looks ugly, so the tool has a built-in arrow that allows you to draw the text a safe distance away from the data yet show what data you're talking about. Figure 3.4 shows this in action. We have a point at $(0.2, 0.1)$, and we placed some text at $(0.35, 0.3)$ and an arrow pointing to the point at $(0.2, 0.1)$.

> **Plot or graph?**
>
> Why use the word *plot*? Why not use the word *graph* for talking about showing data in an image? In some disciplines, the word *graph* has a different meaning. In applied mathematics, it's a representation of a set of objects (vertices) connected by edges. Any combination of the vertices can be connected by edges. In computer science, a graph is a data structure that's used to represent the concept from mathematics.

We're going to hijack the annotations and use them for our tree plotting. You can color in the box of the text and give it a shape you like. Next, you can flip the arrow and have it point from the data point to the text box. Open your text editor and create a new file called treePlotter.py. Add the code from the following listing.

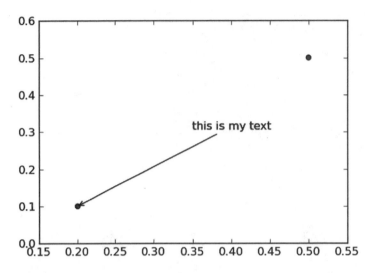

Figure 3.4
Matplotlib annotations
demonstration

Listing 3.5   Plotting tree nodes with text annotations

```
import matplotlib.pyplot as plt

decisionNode = dict(boxstyle="sawtooth", fc="0.8")
leafNode = dict(boxstyle="round4", fc="0.8")
arrow_args = dict(arrowstyle="<-")

def plotNode(nodeTxt, centerPt, parentPt, nodeType):
    createPlot.ax1.annotate(nodeTxt, xy=parentPt,
xycoords='axes fraction',
    xytext=centerPt, textcoords='axes fraction',
    va="center", ha="center", bbox=nodeType, arrowprops=arrow_args)

def createPlot():
    fig = plt.figure(1, facecolor='white')
    fig.clf()
    createPlot.ax1 = plt.subplot(111, frameon=False)
    plotNode('a decision node', (0.5, 0.1), (0.1, 0.5), decisionNode)
    plotNode('a leaf node', (0.8, 0.1), (0.3, 0.8), leafNode)
    plt.show()
```

❶ Define box and
   arrow formatting

❷ Draws annotations
   with arrows

If `createPlot()` doesn't look like `createPlot()` in the example text file, don't worry. You'll change it later. The code in the listing begins by defining some constants that you'll use for formatting the nodes. **❶** Next, you create the `plotNode()` function, which actually does the drawing. It needs a plot to draw these on, and the plot is the global variable `createPlot.ax1`. In Python, all variables are global by default, and if you know what you're doing, this won't get you into trouble. Lastly, you have the `createPlot()` function, which is the master. Here, you create a new figure, clear it, and then draw on two nodes to demonstrate the different types of nodes you'll use in plotting your tree.

To give this code a try, open your Python shell and import the treePlotter file.

```
>>> import treePlotter
>>> treePlotter.createPlot()
```

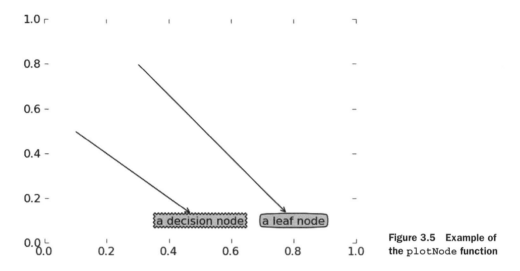

Figure 3.5 Example of the plotNode function

You should see something that looks like figure 3.5. You can alter the points in plotNode() ❷ to see how the X,Y position changes.

Now that you can plot the nodes, you're ready to combine more of these to plot a whole tree.

3.2.2 Constructing a tree of annotations

You need a strategy for plotting this tree. You have X and Y coordinates. Now, where do you place all the nodes? You need to know how many leaf nodes you have so that you can properly size things in the X direction, and you need to know how many levels you have so you can properly size the Y direction. You're going to create two new functions to get the two items you're looking for. The next listing has the functions getNumLeafs() and getTreeDepth(). Add these two functions to treePlotter.py.

Listing 3.6   Identifying the number of leaves in a tree and the depth

```
def getNumLeafs(myTree):
    numLeafs = 0
    firstStr = myTree.keys()[0]
    secondDict = myTree[firstStr]
    for key in secondDict.keys():
        if type(secondDict[key]).__name__=='dict':          ❶ Test if node is
            numLeafs += getNumLeafs(secondDict[key])              dictionary
        else:   numLeafs +=1
    return numLeafs

def getTreeDepth(myTree):
    maxDepth = 0
    firstStr = myTree.keys()[0]
    secondDict = myTree[firstStr]
    for key in secondDict.keys():
        if type(secondDict[key]).__name__=='dict':
```

```
            thisDepth = 1 + getTreeDepth(secondDict[key])
        else:   thisDepth = 1
        if thisDepth > maxDepth: maxDepth = thisDepth
    return maxDepth
```

The two functions in listing 3.6 have the same structure, which you'll use again later. The structure is built around how you store the tree in a Python dictionary. The first key is the label of the first split, and the values associated with that key are the children of the first node. You get out the first key and value, and then you iterate over all of the child nodes. You test to see if the child nodes are dictionaries by using the Python type() method. ❶ If the child node is of type dict, then it is another decision node and you must recursively call your function. The getNumLeafs() function traverses the entire tree and counts only the leaf nodes; then it returns this number. The second function, getTreeDepth(), counts the number of times you hit a decision node. The stopping condition is a leaf node, and once this is reached you back out of your recursive calls and increment the count. To save you some time, I added a simple function to output premade trees. This will save you the trouble of making a tree from data every time during testing.

Enter the following into treePlotter.py:

```
def retrieveTree(i):
    listOfTrees =[{'no surfacing': {0: 'no', 1: {'flippers': \
                    {0: 'no', 1: 'yes'}}}},
                  {'no surfacing': {0: 'no', 1: {'flippers': \
                    {0: {'head': {0: 'no', 1: 'yes'}}, 1: 'no'}}}}
                  ]
    return listOfTrees[i]
```

Save treePlotter.py and enter the following into your Python shell:

```
>>> reload(treePlotter)
<module 'treePlotter' from 'treePlotter.py'>
>>> treePlotter.retrieveTree (1)
{'no surfacing': {0: 'no', 1: {'surfacing': {0: {'head': {0: 'no', 1:
    'yes'}}, 1: 'no'}}}}
>>> myTree = treePlotter.retrieveTree (0)
>>> treePlotter.getNumLeafs(myTree)
3
>>> treePlotter.getTreeDepth(myTree)
2
```

The retrieveTree() function pulls out a predefined tree for testing. You can see that getNumLeafs() returns three leaves, which is what tree 0 has. The function getTreeDepth() also returns the proper number levels.

Now you can put all of these elements together and plot the whole tree. When you're finished, the tree will look something like the one in figure 3.6 but without the labels on the X and Y axes.

Open your text editor and enter the code from the following listing into treePlotter.py. Note that you probably already have a version of treePlotter(). Please change it to look like the following code.

Listing 3.7   The `plotTree` function

```
def plotMidText(cntrPt, parentPt, txtString):
    xMid = (parentPt[0]-cntrPt[0])/2.0 + cntrPt[0]
    yMid = (parentPt[1]-cntrPt[1])/2.0 + cntrPt[1]
    createPlot.ax1.text(xMid, yMid, txtString)

def plotTree(myTree, parentPt, nodeTxt):
    numLeafs = getNumLeafs(myTree)
    getTreeDepth(myTree)
    firstStr = myTree.keys()[0]
    cntrPt = (plotTree.xOff + (1.0 + float(numLeafs))/2.0/plotTree.totalW,\
                        plotTree.yOff)
    plotMidText(cntrPt, parentPt, nodeTxt)
    plotNode(firstStr, cntrPt, parentPt, decisionNode)
    secondDict = myTree[firstStr]
    plotTree.yOff = plotTree.yOff - 1.0/plotTree.totalD
    for key in secondDict.keys():
        if type(secondDict[key]).__name__=='dict':
            plotTree(secondDict[key],cntrPt,str(key))
        else:
            plotTree.xOff = plotTree.xOff + 1.0/plotTree.totalW
            plotNode(secondDict[key], (plotTree.xOff, plotTree.yOff),
                cntrPt, leafNode)
            plotMidText((plotTree.xOff, plotTree.yOff), cntrPt, str(key))
    plotTree.yOff = plotTree.yOff + 1.0/plotTree.totalD

def createPlot(inTree):
    fig = plt.figure(1, facecolor='white')
    fig.clf()
    axprops = dict(xticks=[], yticks=[])
    createPlot.ax1 = plt.subplot(111, frameon=False, **axprops)
    plotTree.totalW = float(getNumLeafs(inTree))
    plotTree.totalD = float(getTreeDepth(inTree))
    plotTree.xOff = -0.5/plotTree.totalW; plotTree.yOff = 1.0;
    plotTree(inTree, (0.5,1.0), '')
    plt.show()
```

① Plots text between child and parent

② Get the width and height

③ Plot child value

④ Decrement Y offset

The `createPlot()` function is the main function you'll use, and it calls `plotTree()`, which in turns calls many of the previous functions and `plotMidText()`. The function `plotTree()` does the majority of the work. The first thing that happens in `plotTree()` is the calculation of width and height of the tree. **②** Two global variables are set up to store the width (`plotTree.totalW`) and depth of the tree (`plotTree.totalD`). These variables are used in centering the tree nodes vertically and horizontally. The `plotTree()` function gets called recursively like `getNumLeafs()` and `getTreeDepth()` from listing 3.6. The width of the tree is used to calculate where to place the decision node. The idea is to place this in the middle of all the leaf nodes below it, not place it in the middle of its children. Also note that you use two global variables to keep track of what has already been plotted and the appropriate coordinate to place the next node. These values are stored in `plotTree.xOff` and `plotTree.yOff`. Another thing to point out is that you're plotting everything on the x-axis from 0.0 to 1.0 and on the y-axis from 0.0 to 1.0. Figure 3.6 has these values labeled for your convenience. The center point for the current node is plotted with its total width split by the total number of leafs in the global tree. This allows you to split the x-axis into as many segments as you have leaves. The beautiful thing about plotting everything in terms of the image width is that you can resize the image, and the node will be redrawn in its proper place. If this was drawn in terms of pixels, that wouldn't be the case. You couldn't resize the image as easily.

Next, you plot the child value or the value for the feature for the split going down that branch. ❸ The code in plotMidText() calculates the midpoint between the parent and child nodes and puts a simple text label in the middle. ❶

Next, you decrement the global variable plotTree.yOff to make a note that you're about to draw children nodes. ❹ These nodes could be leaf nodes or other decision nodes, but you need to keep track of this. You decrement rather than increment because you start drawing from the top of the image and draw downward. You next recursively go through the tree in a similar fashion as the getNumLeafs() and getTreeDepth() functions. If a node is a leaf node, you draw a leaf node. If not, you recursively call plotTree() again. Finally, after you finish plotting the child nodes, you increment the global Y offset.

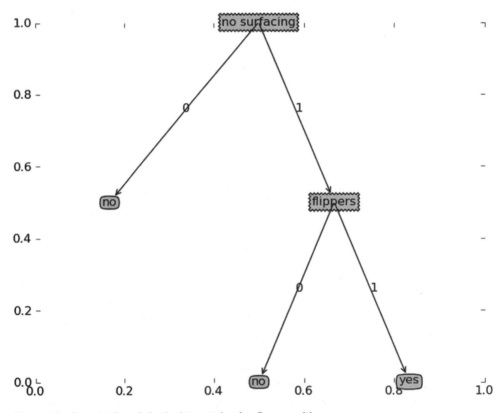

Figure 3.6   Tree plotting of simple dataset showing figure position axes

The last function in listing 3.7 is createPlot(), which handles setting up the image, calculating the global tree size, and kicking off the recursive plotTree() function.

Let's see this in action. After you add the function to treePlotter.py, type the following in your Python shell:

```
>>> reload(treePlotter)
<module 'treePlotter' from 'treePlotter.pyc'>
>>> myTree=treePlotter.retrieveTree (0)
>>> treePlotter.createPlot (myTree)
```

You should see something like figure 3.6 without the axis labels. Now let's alter the dictionary and plot it again.

```
>>> myTree['no surfacing'][3]='maybe'
>>> myTree
{'no surfacing ': {0: 'no', 1: {'flippers': {0: 'no', 1: 'yes'}}, 3:
    'maybe'}}
>>> treePlotter.createPlot (myTree)
```

You should see something that looks like figure 3.7 (and a lot like a headless stick figure.) Feel free to play around with the tree data structures and plot them out.

Now that you can build a decision tree and plot out the tree, you can to put it to use and see what you can learn from some data and this algorithm.

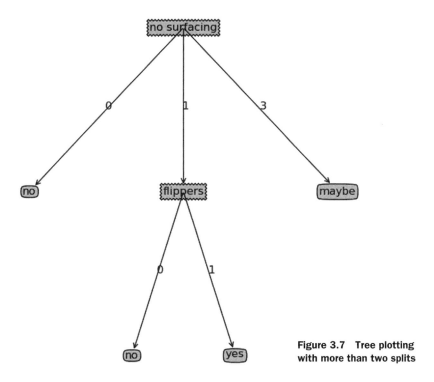

Figure 3.7 Tree plotting with more than two splits

3.3   *Testing and storing the classifier*

The main focus of the first section of this book is on classification. We've done a lot of work in this chapter so far building the tree from data and plotting the tree so a human can make some sense of the data, but we haven't yet done any classification.

In this section, you'll build a classifier that uses our tree, and then you'll see how to persist that classifier on disk for longer storage in a real application. Finally, you'll put our decision tree code to use on some real data to see if you can predict what type of contact lenses a person should use.

3.3.1   *Test: using the tree for classification*

You want to put our tree to use doing some classification after you've learned the tree from our training data, but how do you do that? You need our tree and the label vector that you used in creating the tree. The code will then take the data under test and compare it against the values in the decision tree. It will do this recursively until it hits a leaf node; then it will stop because it has arrived at a conclusion.

To see this in action, open your text editor and add the code in the following listing to trees.py.

> **Listing 3.8   Classification function for an existing decision tree**

```
def classify(inputTree,featLabels,testVec):
    firstStr = inputTree.keys()[0]
    secondDict = inputTree[firstStr]
    featIndex = featLabels.index(firstStr)            ❶ Translate label
    for key in secondDict.keys():                          string to index
        if testVec[featIndex] == key:
            if type(secondDict[key]).__name__=='dict':
                classLabel = classify(secondDict[key],featLabels,testVec)
            else:   classLabel = secondDict[key]
    return classLabel
```

The code in listing 3.8 follows the same format as the other recursive functions in this chapter. A problem with storing your data with the label as the feature's identifier is that you don't know where this feature is in the dataset. To clear this up, you first split on the "no surfacing" attribute, but where is that in the dataset? Is it first or second? The Labels list will tell you this. You use the index method to find out the first item in this list that matches firstStr. ❶ With that in mind, you can recursively travel the tree, comparing the values in testVec to the values in the tree. If you reach a leaf node, you've made your classification and it's time to exit.

After you've added the code in listing 3.8 to your trees.py file, enter the following in your Python shell:

```
>>> myDat,labels=trees.createDataSet()
>>> labels
['no surfacing', 'flippers']
>>> myTree=treePlotter.retrieveTree(0)
>>> myTree
{'no surfacing': {0: 'no', 1: {'flippers': {0: 'no', 1: 'yes'}}}}
```

```
>>> trees.classify(myTree,labels,[1,0])
'no'
>>> trees.classify(myTree,labels,[1,1])
'yes'
```

Compare these results to figure 3.6. You have a first node called "no surfacing" that has two children, one called 0, which has a label of "no", and one that's another decision node called "flippers". This checks out. The "flippers" node had two children. Is this the same as between the tree you plotted and the tree data structure? Yes.

Now that you've built a classifier, it would be nice to be able to store this so you don't have to rebuild the tree every time you want to do classification.

3.3.2   Use: persisting the decision tree

Building the tree is the majority of the work. It may take a few seconds with our small datasets, but, with large datasets, this can take a long time. When it's time to classify items with a tree, you can do it quickly. It would be a waste of time to build the tree every time you wanted to make a classification. To get around this, you're going to use a Python module, which is properly named *pickle*, to serialize objects, as shown in the following listing. Serializing objects allows you to store them for later use. Serializing can be done with any object, and dictionaries work as well.

> **Listing 3.9   Methods for persisting the decision tree with pickle**

```
def storeTree(in
putTree,filename):
    import pickle
    fw = open(filename,'w')
    pickle.dump(inputTree,fw)
    fw.close()

def grabTree(filename):
    import pickle
    fr = open(filename)
    return pickle.load(fr)
```

You can experiment with this in your Python shell by typing in the following:

```
>>> trees.storeTree(myTree,'classifierStorage.txt')
>>> trees.grabTree('classifierStorage.txt')
{'no surfacing': {0: 'no', 1: {'flippers': {0: 'no', 1: 'yes'}}}}
```

Now you have a way of persisting your classifier so that you don't have to relearn it every time you want to classify something. This is another advantage of decision trees over another machine learning algorithm like kNN from chapter 2; you can distill the dataset into some knowledge, and you use that knowledge only when you want to classify something. Let's use the tools you've learned thus far on the Lenses dataset.

3.4   Example: using decision trees to predict contact lens type

In this section, we'll go through an example that predicts the contacts lens type that should be prescribed. You'll take a small dataset and see if you can learn anything from it. You'll see if a decision tree can give you any insight as to how the eye doctor prescribes contact lenses. You can predict the type of lenses people will use and understand the underlying processes with a decision tree.

Example: using decision trees to predict contact lens type

1. Collect: Text file provided.

2. Prepare: Parse tab-delimited lines.

3. Analyze: Quickly review data visually to make sure it was parsed properly. The final tree will be plotted with `createPlot()`.

4. Train: Use `createTree()` from section 3.1.

5. Test: Write a function to descend the tree for a given instance.

6. Use: Persist the tree data structure so it can be recalled without building the tree; then use it in any application.

The Lenses dataset[3] is one of the more famous datasets. It's a number of observations based on patients' eye conditions and the type of contact lenses the doctor prescribed. The classes are hard, soft, and no contact lenses. The data is from the UCI database repository and is modified slightly so that it can be displayed easier. The data is stored in a text file with the source code download.

You can load the data by typing the following into your Python shell:

```
>>> fr=open('lenses.txt')
>>> lenses=[inst.strip().split('\t') for inst in fr.readlines()]
>>> lensesLabels=['age', 'prescript', 'astigmatic', 'tearRate']
>>> lensesTree = trees.createTree(lenses,lensesLabels)
>>> lensesTree
{'tearRate': {'reduced': 'no lenses', 'normal': {'astigmatic': {'yes':
{'prescript': {'hyper': {'age': {'pre': 'no lenses', 'presbyopic':
'no lenses', 'young':'hard'}}, 'myope': 'hard'}}, 'no': {'age': {'pre':
'soft', 'presbyopic': {'prescript': {'hyper': 'soft', 'myope':
'no lenses'}}, 'young': 'soft'}}}}}}
>>> treePlotter.createPlot(lensesTree)
```

That tree looks difficult to read as a line of text; it's a good thing you have a way to plot it. The tree plotted using our `createPlot()` function is shown in figure 3.8. If you follow the different branches of the tree, you can see what contact lenses should be prescribed to a given individual. One other conclusion you can draw from figure 3.8 is that a doctor has to ask at most four questions to determine what type of lenses a patient will need.

---

[3] The dataset is a modified version of the Lenses dataset retrieved from the UCI Machine Learning Repository November 3, 2010 [http://archive.ics.uci.edu/ml/machine-learning-databases/lenses/]. The source of the data is Jadzia Cendrowska and was originally published in "PRISM: An algorithm for inducing modular rules," in *International Journal of Man-Machine Studies* (1987), 27, 349–70.

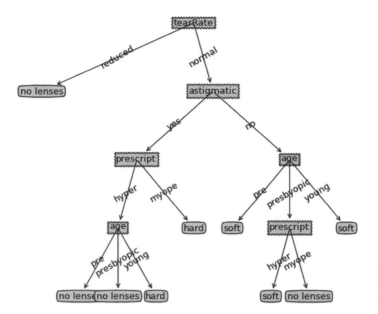

Figure 3.8　Decision tree generated by the ID3 algorithm

The tree in figure 3.8 matches our data well; however, it probably matches our data too well. This problem is known as *overfitting*. In order to reduce the problem of over-fitting, we can prune the tree. This will go through and remove some leaves. If a leaf node adds only a little information, it will be cut off and merged with another leaf. We'll investigate this further when we revisit decision trees in chapter 9.

In chapter 9 we'll also investigate another decision tree algorithm called CART. The algorithm we used in this chapter, ID3, is good but not the best. ID3 can't handle numeric values. We could use continuous values by quantizing them into discrete bins, but ID3 suffers from other problems if we have too many splits.

3.5　*Summary*

A decision tree classifier is just like a work-flow diagram with the terminating blocks representing classification decisions. Starting with a dataset, you can measure the inconsistency of a set or the entropy to find a way to split the set until all the data belongs to the same class. The ID3 algorithm can split nominal-valued datasets. Recursion is used in tree-building algorithms to turn a dataset into a decision tree. The tree is easily represented in a Python dictionary rather than a special data structure.

Cleverly applying Matplotlib's annotations, you can turn our tree data into an easily understood chart. The Python Pickle module can be used for persisting our tree. The contact lens data showed that decision trees can try too hard and overfit a dataset. This overfitting can be removed by pruning the decision tree, combining adjacent leaf nodes that don't provide a large amount of information gain.

There are other decision tree–generating algorithms. The most popular are C4.5 and CART. CART will be addressed in chapter 9 when we use it for regression.

The first two chapters in this book have drawn hard conclusions about data such as "This data instance is in this class!" What if we take a softer approach, such as "Well, I'm not quite sure where that data should go. Maybe here? Maybe there?" What if we assign a probability to a data instance belonging to a given class? This will be the focus of the next chapter.

Classifying with probability theory: naïve Bayes

This chapter covers

- Using probability distributions for classification
- Learning the naïve Bayes classifier
- Parsing data from RSS feeds
- Using naïve Bayes to reveal regional attitudes

In the first two chapters we asked our classifier to make hard decisions. We asked for a definite answer for the question "Which class does this data instance belong to?" Sometimes the classifier got the answer wrong. We could instead ask the classifier to give us a best guess about the class and assign a probability estimate to that best guess.

Probability theory forms the basis for many machine-learning algorithms, so it's important that you get a good grasp on this topic. We touched on probability a bit in chapter 3 when we were calculating the probability of a feature taking a given value. We calculated the probability by counting the number of times the feature equals that value divided by the total number of instances in the dataset. We're going to expand a little from there in this chapter.

We'll look at some ways probability theory can help us classify things. We start out with the simplest probabilistic classifier and then make a few assumptions and learn the naïve Bayes classifier. It's called naïve because the formulation makes some naïve assumptions. Don't worry; you'll see these in detail in a bit. We'll take full advantage of Python's text-processing abilities to split up a document into a word vector. This will be used to classify text. We'll build another classifier and see how it does on a real-world spam email dataset. We'll review conditional probability in case you need a refresher. Finally, we'll show how you can put what the classifier has learned into human-readable terms from a bunch of personal ad postings.

4.1   Classifying with Bayesian decision theory

> **Naïve Bayes**
>
> Pros: Works with a small amount of data, handles multiple classes
>
> Cons: Sensitive to how the input data is prepared
>
> Works with: Nominal values

Naïve Bayes is a subset of Bayesian decision theory, so we need to talk about Bayesian decision theory quickly before we get to naïve Bayes.

Assume for a moment that we have a dataset with two classes of data inside. A plot of this data is shown in figure 4.1.

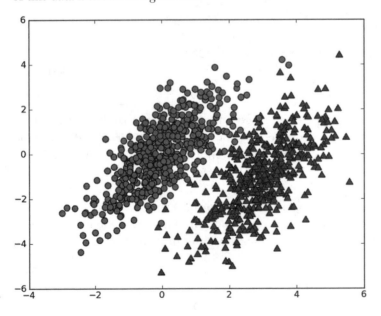

Figure 4.1 Two probability distributions with known parameters describing the distribution

We have the data shown in figure 4.1 and we have a friend who read this book; she found the statistical parameters of the two classes of data. (Don't worry about how to find the statistical parameters for this type of data now; we'll get to that in chapter 10.) We have an equation for the probability of a piece of data belonging to Class 1 (the circles): `p1(x, y)`, and we have an equation for the class belonging to Class 2 (the triangles): `p2(x, y)`. To classify a new measurement with features (x, y), we use the following rules:

If `p1(x, y) > p2(x, y)`, then the class is 1.
If `p2(x, y) > p1(x, y)`, then the class is 2.

Put simply, we choose the class with the higher probability. That's Bayesian decision theory in a nutshell: choosing the decision with the highest probability. Let's get back to the data in figure 4.1. If you can represent the data in six floating-point numbers, and the code to calculate the probability is two lines in Python, which would you rather do?

1 Use kNN from chapter 1, and do 1,000 distance calculations.
2 Use decision trees from chapter 2, and make a split of the data once along the x-axis and once along the y-axis.
3 Compute the probability of each class, and compare them

The decision tree wouldn't be very successful, and kNN would require a lot of calculations compared to the simple probability calculation. Given this problem, the best choice would be the probability comparison we just discussed.

We're going to have to expand on the p1 and p1 probability measures I provided here. In order to be able to calculate p1 and p2, we need to discuss conditional probability. If you feel that you have a good handle on conditional probability, you can skip the next section.

> ### Bayes?
> This interpretation of probability that we use belongs to the category called Bayesian probability; it's popular and it works well. Bayesian probability is named after Thomas Bayes, who was an eighteenth-century theologian. Bayesian probability allows prior knowledge and logic to be applied to uncertain statements. There's another interpretation called *frequency probability*, which only draws conclusions from data and doesn't allow for logic and prior knowledge.

4.2 Conditional probability

Let's spend a few minutes talking about probability and conditional probability. If you're comfortable with the $p(x, y | c_1)$ symbol, you may want to skip this section.

Let's assume for a moment that we have a jar containing seven stones. Three of these stones are gray and four are black, as shown in figure 4.2. If we stick a hand into this jar and randomly pull out a stone, what are the chances that the stone will be gray? There are seven possible stones and three are gray, so the probability is 3/7. What is the

probability of grabbing a black stone? It's 4/7. We
write the probability of gray as P(gray). We calculated the probability of drawing a gray stone
P(gray) by counting the number of gray stones
and dividing this by the total number of stones.

What if the seven stones were in two buckets?
This is shown in figure 4.3.

If you want to calculate the P(gray) or
P(black), would knowing the bucket change the
answer? If you wanted to calculate the probability of drawing a gray stone from bucket B, you

Figure 4.2   A collection has seven
stones that are gray or black. If we
randomly select a stone from this set,
the probability it will be a gray stone
is 3/7. Similarly, the probability of
selecting a black stone is 4/7.

could probably figure out how do to that. This is known as *conditional probability*. We're
calculating the probability of a gray stone, given that the unknown stone comes from
bucket B. We can write this as P(gray|bucketB), and this would be read as "the prob-
ability of gray given bucket B." It's not hard to see that P(gray|bucketA) is 2/4 and
P(gray|bucketB) is 1/3.

To formalize how to calculate the conditional probability, we can say

```
P(gray|bucketB) = P(gray and bucketB)/P(bucketB)
```

Let's see if that makes sense: P(gray and bucketB) = 1/7. This was calculated by taking
the number of gray stones in bucket B and dividing by the total number of stones. Now,
P(bucketB) is 3/7 because there are three stones in bucket B of the total seven stones.
Finally, P(gray|bucketB) = P(gray and bucketB)/P(bucketB) = (1/7) / (3/7) = 1/3.
This formal definition may seem like too much work for this simple example, but it will
be useful when we have more features. It's also useful to have this formal definition if
we ever need to algebraically manipulate the conditional probability.

Another useful way to manipulate conditional probabilities is known as Bayes' rule.
Bayes' rule tells us how to swap the symbols in a conditional probability statement. If
we have P(x|c) but want to have P(c|x), we can find it with the following:

$$p(c|x) = \frac{p(x|c)p(c)}{p(x)}$$

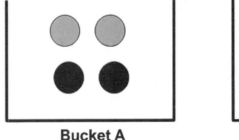

Bucket A   **Bucket B**

Figure 4.3   Seven stones sitting in two buckets

Now that we've discussed conditional probability, we need to see how to apply this to our classifier. The next section will discuss how to use conditional probabilities with Bayesian decision theory.

4.3 *Classifying with conditional probabilities*

In section 4.1, I said that Bayesian decision theory told us to find the two probabilities:

If `p1(x, y) > p2(x, y)`, then the class is 1.
If `p2(x, y) > p1(x, y)`, then the class is 2.

These two rules don't tell the whole story. I just left them as `p1()` and `p2()` to keep it as simple as possible. What we really need to compare are `p(c₁|x,y)` and `p(c₂|x,y)`. Let's read these out to emphasize what they mean. Given a point identified as x,y, what is the probability it came from class c_1? What is the probability it came from class c_2?. The problem is that the equation from our friend is `p(x,y|c₁)`, which is not the same. We can use Bayes' rule to switch things around. Bayes' rule is applied to these statements as follows:

$$p(c_i|x,y) = \frac{p(x,y|c_i)p(c_i)}{p(x,y)}$$

With these definitions, we can define the Bayesian classification rule:

If `P(c₁|x, y) > P(c₂|x, y)`, the class is c_1.
If `P(c₁|x, y) < P(c₂|x, y)`, the class is c_2.

Using Bayes' rule, we can calculate this unknown from three known quantities. We'll soon write some code to calculate these probabilities and classify items using Bayes' rule. Now that we've introduced a bit of probability theory, and you've seen how you can build a classifier with it, we're going to put this in action. The next section will introduce a simple yet powerful application of the Bayesian classifier.

4.4 *Document classification with naïve Bayes*

One important application of machine learning is automatic document classification. In document classification, the whole document such as an individual email is our instance and the features are things in that email. Email is an example that keeps coming up, but you could classify news stories, message board discussions, filings with the government, or any type of text. You can look at the documents by the words used in them and treat the presence or absence of each word as a feature. This would give you as many features as there are words in your vocabulary. Naïve Bayes—an extension of the Bayesian classifier introduced in the last section—is a popular algorithm for the document-classification problem.

Earlier I mentioned that we're going to use individual words as features and look for the presence or absence of each word. How many features is that? Which (human) language are we assuming? It may be more than one language. The estimated total

General approach to naïve Bayes

1. Collect: Any method. We'll use RSS feeds in this chapter.

2. Prepare: Numeric or Boolean values are needed.

3. Analyze: With many features, plotting features isn't helpful. Looking at histograms is a better idea.

4. Train: Calculate the conditional probabilities of the independent features.

5. Test: Calculate the error rate.

6. Use: One common application of naïve Bayes is document classification. You can use naïve Bayes in any classification setting. It doesn't have to be text.

number of words in the English language is over 500,000.[1]] To be able to read in English, it's estimated that you need to understand thousands of words.

Let's assume that our vocabulary is 1,000 words long. In order to generate good probability distributions, we need enough data samples. Let's call this N samples. In previous examples in this book, we had 1,000 examples for the dating site, 200 examples per digit in the handwriting recognition, and 24 examples for our decision tree. Having 24 examples was a little bit low, 200 samples was better, and 1,000 samples was great. In the dating example we had three features. Statistics tells us that if we need N samples for one feature, we need N^{10} for 10 features and N^{1000} for our 1,000-feature vocabulary. The number will get very large very quickly.

If we assume independence among the features, then our N^{1000} data points get reduced to 1000*N. By *independence* I mean statistical independence; one feature or word is just as likely by itself as it is next to other words. We're assuming that the word *bacon* is as likely to appear next to *unhealthy* as it is next to *delicious*. We know this assumption isn't true; *bacon* almost always appears near *delicious* but very seldom near *unhealthy*. This is what is meant by *naïve* in the naïve Bayes classifier. The other assumption we make is that every feature is equally important. We know that isn't true either. If we were trying to classify a message board posting as inappropriate, we probably don't need to look at 1,000 words; maybe 10 or 20 will do. Despite the minor flaws of these assumptions, naïve Bayes works well in practice.

At this point you know enough about this topic to get started with some code. If everything doesn't make sense right now, it might help to see this in action. In the next section, we'll start to implement the naïve Bayes classifier in Python. We'll go through everything that's needed to classify text with Python.

---

[1] http://hypertextbook.com/facts/2001/JohnnyLing.shtml retrieved October 20, 2010.

4.5 *Classifying text with Python*

In order to get features from our text, we need to split up the text. But how do we do that? Our features are going to be tokens we get from the text. A *token* is any combination of characters. You can think of tokens as words, but we may use things that aren't words such as URLs, IP addresses, or any string of characters. We'll reduce every piece of text to a vector of tokens where 1 represents the token existing in the document and 0 represents that it isn't present.

To see this in action, let's make a quick filter for an online message board that flags a message as inappropriate if the author uses negative or abusive language. Filtering out this sort of thing is common because abusive postings make people not come back and can hurt an online community. We'll have two categories: abusive and not. We'll use 1 to represent abusive and 0 to represent not abusive.

First, we're going to show how to transform lists of text into a vector of numbers. Next, we'll show how to calculate conditional probabilities from these vectors. Then, we'll create a classifier, and finally, we'll look at some practical considerations for implementing naïve Bayes in Python.

4.5.1 *Prepare: making word vectors from text*

We're going to start looking at text in the form of word vectors or token vectors, that is, transform a sentence into a vector. We consider all the words in all of our documents and decide what we'll use for a vocabulary or set of words we'll consider. Next, we need to transform each individual document into a vector from our vocabulary. To get started, open your text editor, create a new file called bayes.py, and add the code from the following listing.

> **Listing 4.1 Word list to vector function**

```
def loadDataSet():
    postingList=[['my', 'dog', 'has', 'flea', \
                  'problems', 'help', 'please'],
                 ['maybe', 'not', 'take', 'him', \
                  'to', 'dog', 'park', 'stupid'],
                 ['my', 'dalmation', 'is', 'so', 'cute', \
                  'I', 'love', 'him'],
                 ['stop', 'posting', 'stupid', 'worthless', 'garbage'],
                 ['mr', 'licks', 'ate', 'my', 'steak', 'how',\
                  'to', 'stop', 'him'],
                 ['quit', 'buying', 'worthless', 'dog', 'food', 'stupid']]
    classVec = [0,1,0,1,0,1]    #1 is abusive, 0 not
    return postingList,classVec

def createVocabList(dataSet):
    vocabSet = set([])                                    ❶ Create an empty set
    for document in dataSet:
        vocabSet = vocabSet | set(document)               ❷ Create the union of two sets
    return list(vocabSet)

def setOfWords2Vec(vocabList, inputSet):
```

❶ Create an empty set

❷ Create the union of two sets

```
        returnVec = [0]*len(vocabList)                              Create a vector
        for word in inputSet:                              ◀─┐  ❸  of all 0s
            if word in vocabList:
                returnVec[vocabList.index(word)] = 1
            else: print "the word: %s is not in my Vocabulary!" % word
        return returnVec
```

The first function creates some example data to experiment with. The first variable returned from `loadDatSet()` is a tokenized set of documents from a Dalmatian (spotted breed of dog) lovers message board. The text has been broken up into a set of tokens. Punctuation has been removed from this text as well. We'll return to text processing later. The second variable of `loadDatSet()` returns a set of class labels. Here you have two classes, `abusive` and `not` `abusive`. The text has been labeled by a human and will be used to train a program to automatically detect abusive posts.

Next, the function `createVocabList()` will create a list of all the unique words in all of our documents. To create this unique list you use the Python set data type. You can give a list of items to the set constructor, and it will only return a unique list. First, you create an empty set. ❶ Next, you append the set with a new set from each document. ❷ The | operator is used for union of two sets; recall that this is the bitwise `OR` operator from C. Bitwise `OR` and set union also use the same symbols in mathematical notation.

Finally, after you have our vocabulary list, you can use the function `setOfWords2Vec()`, which takes the vocabulary list and a document and outputs a vector of 1s and 0s to represent whether a word from our vocabulary is present or not in the given document. You then create a vector the same length as the vocabulary list and fill it up with 0s. ❸ Next, you go through the words in the document, and if the word is in the vocabulary list, you set its value to 1 in the output vector. If everything goes well, you shouldn't need to test if a word is in `vocabList`, but you may use this later.

Now let's look at these functions in action. Save bayes.py, and enter the following into your Python shell:

```
>>> import bayes
>>> listOPosts,listClasses = bayes.loadDataSet()
>>> myVocabList = bayes.createVocabList(listOPosts)
>>> myVocabList
['cute', 'love', 'help', 'garbage', 'quit', 'I', 'problems', 'is', 'park',
'stop', 'flea', 'dalmation', 'licks', 'food', 'not', 'him', 'buying',
'posting', 'has', 'worthless', 'ate', 'to', 'maybe', 'please', 'dog',
'how', 'stupid', 'so', 'take', 'mr', 'steak', 'my']
```

If you examine this list, you'll see that there are no repeated words. The list is unsorted, and if you want to sort it, you can do that later.

Let's look at the next function `setOfWords2Vec()`:

```
>>> bayes.setOfWords2Vec(myVocabList, listOPosts[0])
[0, 0, 1, 0, 0, 0, 1, 0, 0, 0, 1, 0, 0, 0, 0, 0, 0, 0, 1, 0, 0, 0, 0, 1, 1,
0, 0, 0, 0, 0, 0, 1]
>>> bayes.setOfWords2Vec(myVocabList, listOPosts[3])
[0, 0, 0, 1, 0, 0, 0, 0, 0, 1, 0, 0, 0, 0, 0, 0, 0, 1, 0, 1, 0, 0, 0, 0, 0,
0, 1, 0, 0, 0, 0, 0]
```

This has taken our vocabulary list or list of all the words you'd like to examine and created a feature for each of them. Now when you apply a given document (a posting to the Dalmatian site), it will be transformed into a word vector. Check to see if this makes sense. What's the word at index 2 in `myVocabList`? It should be *help*. This word should be in our first document. Now check to see that it isn't in our fourth document.

4.5.2 *Train: calculating probabilities from word vectors*

Now that you've seen how to convert from words to numbers, let's see how to calculate the probabilities with these numbers. You know whether a word occurs in a document, and you know what class the document belongs to. Do you remember Bayes' rule from section 3.2? It's rewritten here, but I've changed the x,y to **w**. The bold type means that it's a vector; that is, we have many values, in our case as many values as words in our vocabulary.

$$p(c_i|\mathbf{w}) = \frac{p(\mathbf{w}|c_i)p(c_i)}{p(\mathbf{w})}$$

We're going to use the right side of the formula to get the value on the left. We'll do this for each class and compare the two probabilities. How do we get the stuff on the right? We can calculate $p(c_i)$ by adding up how many times we see class i (abusive posts or non-abusive posts) and then dividing by the total number of posts. How can we get $p(\mathbf{w}|c_i)$? This is where our naïve assumption comes in. If we expand **w** into individual features, we could rewrite this as $p(w_0, w_1, w_2..w_N|c_i)$. Our assumption that all the words were independently likely, and something called conditional independence, says we can calculate this probability as $p(w_0|c_i)p(w_1|c_i)p(w_2|c_i)...p(w_N|c_i)$. This makes our calculations a lot easier.

Pseudocode for this function would look like this:

Count the number of documents in each class
for every training document:
    for each class:
        if a token appears in the document → increment the count for that token
        increment the count for tokens
    for each class:
      for each token:
        divide the token count by the total token count to get conditional probabilities
    return conditional probabilities for each class

The code in the following listing will do these calculations for us. Open your text editor and insert this code into bayes.py. This function uses some functions from NumPy, so make sure you add `from numpy import *` to the top of bayes.py.

Listing 4.2 Naïve Bayes classifier training function

```
def trainNB0(trainMatrix,trainCategory):
    numTrainDocs = len(trainMatrix)
    numWords = len(trainMatrix[0])
```

```
pAbusive = sum(trainCategory)/float(numTrainDocs)
p0Num = zeros(numWords); p1Num = zeros(numWords)
p0Denom = 0.0; p1Denom = 0.0
for i in range(numTrainDocs):
    if trainCategory[i] == 1:
        p1Num += trainMatrix[i]
        p1Denom += sum(trainMatrix[i])
    else:
        p0Num += trainMatrix[i]
        p0Denom += sum(trainMatrix[i])
p1Vect = p1Num/p1Denom          #change to log()
p0Vect = p0Num/p0Denom          #change to log()
return p0Vect,p1Vect,pAbusive
```

1 Initialize probabilities

2 Vector addition

3 Element-wise division

The function in listing 4.2 takes a matrix of documents, `trainMatrix`, and a vector with the class labels for each of the documents, `trainCategory`. The first thing you do is calculate the probability the document is an abusive document (class=1). This is `P(1)` from above; because this is a two-class problem, you can get `P(0)` by `1-P(1)`. For more than a two-class problem, you'd need to modify this a little.

You initialize the numerator and denominator for the $p(w_i|c_1)$ and $p(w_i|c_0)$ calculations. **1** Since you have so many ws, you're going to use NumPy arrays to calculate these values quickly. The numerator is a NumPy array with the same number of elements as you have words in your vocabulary. In the `for` loop you loop over all the documents in `trainMatrix`, or our training set. Every time a word appears in a document, the count for that word (`p1Num` or `p0Num`) gets incremented, and the total number of words for a document gets summed up over all the documents. **2** You do this for both classes.

Finally, you divide every element by the total number of words for that class. **3** This is done compactly in NumPy by dividing an array by a float. This can't be done with regular Python lists. Try it out to see for yourself. Finally, the two vectors and one probability are returned.

Let's try this out. After you've added the code from listing 4.2 to bayes.py, open your Python shell and enter the following:

```
>>> from numpy import *
>>> reload(bayes)
<module 'bayes' from 'bayes.py'>
>>> listOPosts,listClasses = bayes.loadDataSet()
This loads the data from preloaded values.
>>> myVocabList = bayes.createVocabList(listOPosts)
You've now created a list of all our words in myVocabList.
>>> trainMat=[]
>>> for postinDoc in listOPosts:
...     trainMat.append(bayes.setOfWords2Vec(myVocabList, postinDoc))
...
```

This `for` loop populates the `trainMat` list with word vectors. Now let's get the probabilities of being abusive and the two probability vectors:

```
>>> p0V,p1V,pAb=bayes.trainNB0(trainMat,listClasses)
```

Let's look inside each of these variables:

```
>>> pAb
0.5
This is just the probability of any document being abusive.
>>> p0V
array([ 0.04166667,  0.04166667,  0.04166667,  0.         ,  0.         ,
          .
          .
          .
        0.04166667,  0.         ,  0.04166667,  0.         ,  0.04166667,
        0.04166667,  0.125      ])
>>> p1V
array([ 0.         ,  0.         ,  0.         ,  0.05263158,  0.05263158,
          .
          .
          .
        0.         ,  0.15789474,  0.         ,  0.05263158,  0.         ,
        0.         ,  0.         ])
```

First, you found the probability that a document was abusive: pAb; this is 0.5, which is correct. Next, you found the probabilities of the words from our vocabulary given the document class. Let's see if this makes sense. The first word in our vocabulary is *cute*. This appears once in the 0 class and never in the 1 class. The probabilities are 0.04166667 and 0.0. This makes sense. Let's look for the largest probability. That's 0.15789474 in the P(1) array at index 21. If you look at the word in myVocabList at index 26, you'll see that it's the word *stupid*. This tells you that the word *stupid* is most indicative of a class 1 (abusive).

Before we can go on to classification with this, we need to address a few flaws in the previous function.

4.5.3 *Test: modifying the classifier for real-world conditions*

When we attempt to classify a document, we multiply a lot of probabilities together to get the probability that a document belongs to a given class. This will look something like $p(w_0|1)p(w_1|1)p(w_2|1)$. If any of these numbers are 0, then when we multiply them together we get 0. To lessen the impact of this, we'll initialize all of our occurrence counts to 1, and we'll initialize the denominators to 2.

Open bayes.py in your text editor, and change lines 4 and 5 of trainNB0() to

```
p0Num = ones(numWords); p1Num = ones(numWords)
p0Denom = 2.0; p1Denom = 2.0
```

Another problem is underflow: doing too many multiplications of small numbers. When we go to calculate the product $p(w_0|c_i)p(w_1|c_i)p(w_2|c_i)\ldots p(w_N|c_i)$ and many of these numbers are very small, we'll get underflow, or an incorrect answer. (Try to multiply many small numbers in Python. Eventually it rounds off to 0.) One solution to this is to take the natural logarithm of this product. If you recall from algebra, $ln(a*b) = ln(a)+ln(b)$. Doing this allows us to avoid the underflow or round-off error problem. Do we lose anything by using the natural log of a number rather than the number itself? The answer is no. Figure 4.4 plots two functions, f(x) and ln(f(x)). If you examine both of these plots, you'll see that they increase and

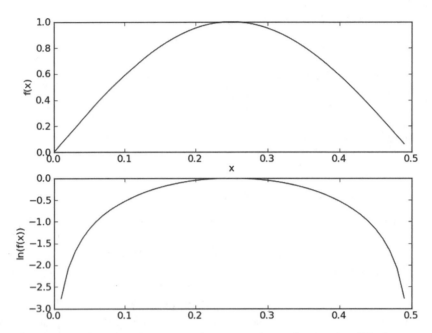

Figure 4.4 Arbitrary functions `f(x)` and `ln(f(x))` increasing together. This shows that the natural log of a function can be used in place of a function when you're interested in finding the maximum value of that function.

decrease in the same areas, and they have their peaks in the same areas. Their values are different, but that's fine. To modify our classifier to account for this, modify the last two lines before the return to look like this:

```
p1Vect = log(p1Num/p1Denom)
p0Vect = log(p0Num/p0Denom)
```

We're now ready to build the full classifier. It's quite simple when we're using vector math with NumPy. Open your text editor and add the code from the following listing to bayes.py.

Listing 4.3   Naïve Bayes classify function

```
def classifyNB(vec2Classify, p0Vec, p1Vec, pClass1):
    p1 = sum(vec2Classify * p1Vec) + log(pClass1)          Element-wise
    p0 = sum(vec2Classify * p0Vec) + log(1.0 - pClass1)  ❶ multiplication
    if p1 > p0:
        return 1
    else:
        return 0

def testingNB():
    listOPosts,listClasses = loadDataSet()
    myVocabList = createVocabList(listOPosts)
    trainMat=[]
    for postinDoc in listOPosts:
        trainMat.append(setOfWords2Vec(myVocabList, postinDoc))
```

```
pOV,p1V,pAb = trainNB0(array(trainMat),array(listClasses))
testEntry = ['love', 'my', 'dalmation']
thisDoc = array(setOfWords2Vec(myVocabList, testEntry))
print testEntry,'classified as: ',classifyNB(thisDoc,pOV,p1V,pAb)
testEntry = ['stupid', 'garbage']
thisDoc = array(setOfWords2Vec(myVocabList, testEntry))
print testEntry,'classified as: ',classifyNB(thisDoc,pOV,p1V,pAb)
```

The code in listing 4.3 takes four inputs: a vector to classify called vec2Classify and three probabilities calculated in the function `trainNB0()`. You use NumPy arrays to multiply two vectors. ❶ The multiplication is element–wise; that is, you multiply the first elements of both vectors, then the second elements, and so on. You next add up the values for all of the words in our vocabulary and add this to the log probability of the class. Finally, you see which probability is greater and return the class label. That isn't too hard, is it?

The second function in listing 4.3 is a convenience function to wrap up everything properly and save you some time from typing all the code from section 4.3.1.

Let's try it out. After you've added the code from listing 4.3, enter the following into your Python shell:

```
>>> reload(bayes)
<module 'bayes' from 'bayes.pyc'>
>>>bayes.testingNB()
['love', 'my', 'dalmation'] classified as:  0
['stupid', 'garbage'] classified as:  1
```

Change the text and see what the classifier spits out. This example is overly simplistic, but it demonstrates how the naïve Bayes classifier works. We'll next make a few changes to it so that it will work even better.

4.5.4 *Prepare: the bag-of-words document model*

Up until this point we've treated the presence or absence of a word as a feature. This could be described as a set-of-words model. If a word appears more than once in a document, that might convey some sort of information about the document over just the word occurring in the document or not. This approach is known as a bag-of-words model. A *bag* of words can have multiple occurrences of each word, whereas a *set* of words can have only one occurrence of each word. To accommodate for this we need to slightly change the function `setOfWords2Vec()` and call it `bagOfWords2VecMN()`.

The code to use the bag-of-words model is given in the following listing. It's nearly identical to the function `setOfWords2Vec()` listed earlier, except every time it encounters a word, it increments the word vector rather than setting the word vector to 1 for a given index.

> **Listing 4.4 Naïve Bayes bag-of-words model**

```
def bagOfWords2VecMN(vocabList, inputSet):
    returnVec = [0]*len(vocabList)
    for word in inputSet:
        if word in vocabList:
            returnVec[vocabList.index(word)] += 1
    return returnVec
```

Now that we have a classifier built, we should be able to put this into action classifying spam.

4.6 Example: classifying spam email with naïve Bayes

In the previous simple example we imported a list of strings. To use naïve Bayes on some real-life problems we'll need to be able to go from a body of text to a list of strings and then a word vector. In this example we're going to visit the famous use of naïve Bayes: email spam filtering. Let's first look at how we'd approach this problem with our general framework.

> **Example: using naïve Bayes to classify email**
>
> 1. Collect: Text files provided.
>
> 2. Prepare: Parse text into token vectors.
>
> 3. Analyze: Inspect the tokens to make sure parsing was done correctly.
>
> 4. Train: Use `trainNB0()` that we created earlier.
>
> 5. Test: Use `classifyNB()` and create a new testing function to calculate the error rate over a set of documents.
>
> 6. Use: Build a complete program that will classify a group of documents and print misclassified documents to the screen.

First, we'll create some code to parse text into tokens. Next, we'll write a function that ties together the parsing and the classification code from earlier in this chapter. This function will also test the classifier and give us an error rate.

4.6.1 Prepare: tokenizing text

The previous section showed how to create word vectors and use naïve Bayes to classify with these word vectors. The word vectors in the previous section came premade. Let's see how to create your own lists of words from text documents.

If you have a text string, you can split it using the Python string `.split()` method. Let's see this in action. Enter the following into your Python shell:

```
>>> mySent='This book is the best book on Python or M.L. I have ever laid
➥ eyes upon.'
>>> mySent.split()
['This', 'book', 'is', 'the', 'best', 'book', 'on', 'Python', 'or', 'M.L.',
 'I', 'have', 'ever', 'laid', 'eyes', 'upon.']
```

That works well, but the punctuation is considered part of the word. You can use regular expressions to split up the sentence on anything that isn't a word or number:

```
>>> import re
>>> regEx = re.compile('\\W*')
>>> listOfTokens = regEx.split(mySent)
```

```
>>> listOfTokens
['This', 'book', 'is', 'the', 'best', 'book', 'on', 'Python', 'or', 'M',
'L', '', 'I', 'have', 'ever', 'laid', 'eyes', 'upon', '']
```

Now you have a list of words. But you have some empty strings you need to get rid of. You can count the length of each string and return only the items greater than 0.

```
>>> [tok for tok in listOfTokens if len(tok) > 0]
```

Finally, the first word in the sentence is capitalized. If you were looking at sentences, this would be helpful. You're just looking at a bag of words, so you want all the words to look the same whether they're in the middle, end, or beginning of a sentence. Python has built-in methods for converting strings to all lowercase (`.lower()`) or all uppercase (`.upper()`). This will solve our problem. Let's change our list comprehension to the following:

```
>>> [tok.lower() for tok in listOfTokens if len(tok) > 0]
['this', 'book', 'is', 'the', 'best', 'book', 'on', 'python', 'or', 'm',
'l', 'i', 'have', 'ever', 'laid', 'eyes', 'upon']
```

Now let's see this in action with a full email from our email dataset. The email dataset is in a folder called email, with two subfolders called spam and ham.

```
>>> emailText = open('email/ham/6.txt').read()
>>> listOfTokens=regEx.split(emailText)
```

The file named 6.txt in the ham folder is quite long. It's from a company telling me that they no longer support something. One thing to notice is that we now have words like *en* and *py* because they were originally part of a URL: /answer.py?hl=en&answer=174623. When we split the URL we got a lot of words. We'd like to get rid of these words, so we'll filter out words with less than three characters. We used one blanket text-parsing rule for this example. In a real-world parsing program, you should have more advanced filters that look for things like HTML and URIs. Right now, a URI will wind up as one of our words; www.whitehouse.com will wind up as three words. Text parsing can be an involved process. We'll create a bare-bones function, and you can modify as you see fit.

4.6.2 *Test: cross validation with naïve Bayes*

Let's put this text parser to work with a whole classifier. Open your text editor and add the code from this listing to bayes.py.

> **Listing 4.5   File parsing and full spam test functions**

```
def textParse(bigString):
    import re
    listOfTokens = re.split(r'\W*', bigString)
    return [tok.lower() for tok in listOfTokens if len(tok) > 2]

def spamTest():
    docList=[]; classList = []; fullText =[]
    for i in range(1,26):
```

```
        wordList = textParse(open('email/spam/%d.txt' % i).read())
        docList.append(wordList)
        fullText.extend(wordList)
        classList.append(1)
        wordList = textParse(open('email/ham/%d.txt' % i).read())
        docList.append(wordList)                              Load and parse ❶
        fullText.extend(wordList)                                text files
        classList.append(0)
    vocabList = createVocabList(docList)
    trainingSet = range(50); testSet=[]
    for i in range(10):                                       ❷ Randomly
        randIndex = int(random.uniform(0,len(trainingSet)))      create the
        testSet.append(trainingSet[randIndex])                   training set
        del(trainingSet[randIndex])
    trainMat=[]; trainClasses = []
    for docIndex in trainingSet:
        trainMat.append(setOfWords2Vec(vocabList, docList[docIndex]))
        trainClasses.append(classList[docIndex])
    p0V,p1V,pSpam = trainNB0(array(trainMat),array(trainClasses))
    errorCount = 0
    for docIndex in testSet:
        wordVector = setOfWords2Vec(vocabList, docList[docIndex])
        if classifyNB(array(wordVector),p0V,p1V,pSpam) !=
    classList[docIndex]:                            Classify the ❸
            errorCount += 1                            test set
    print 'the error rate is: ',float(errorCount)/len(testSet)
```

The first function, textParse(), takes a big string and parses out the text into a list of strings. It eliminates anything under two characters long and converts everything to lowercase. There's a lot more parsing you could do in this function, but it's good enough for our purposes.

The second function, spamTest(), automates the naïve Bayes spam classifier. You load the spam and ham text files into word lists. ❶ Next, you create a test set and a training set. The emails that go into the test set and the training set will be randomly selected. In this example, we have 50 emails total (not very many). Ten of the emails are randomly selected to be used in the test set. The probabilities will be computed from only the documents in the training set. The Python variable trainingSet is a list of integers from 0 to 49. Next, you randomly select 10 of those files. ❷ As a number is selected, it's added to the test set and removed from the training set. This randomly selecting a portion of our data for the training set and a portion for the test set is called *hold-out cross validation*. You've done only one iteration, but to get a good estimate of our classifier's true error, you should do this multiple times and take the average error rate.

The next for loop iterates through all the items in the test set and creates word vectors from the words of each email and the vocabulary using setOfWords2Vec(). These words are used in traindNB0() to calculate the probabilities needed for classification. You then iterate through the test set and classify each email in the test set. ❸ If the email isn't classified correctly, the error count is incremented, and finally the total percentage error is reported.

Give this a try. After you've entered the code from listing 4.5, enter the following into your Python shell:

```
>>> bayes.spamTest()
the error rate is:  0.0
>>> bayes.spamTest()
classification error ['home', 'based', 'business', 'opportunity',
'knocking', 'your', 'door', 'don', 'rude', 'and', 'let', 'this', 'chance',
'you', 'can', 'earn', 'great', 'income', 'and', 'find', 'your',
'financial', 'life', 'transformed', 'learn', 'more', 'here', 'your',
'success', 'work', 'from', 'home', 'finder', 'experts']
the error rate is:  0.1
```

The function `spamTest()` displays the error rate from 10 randomly selected emails. Since these are randomly selected, the results may be different each time. If there's an error, it will display the word list for that document to give you an idea of what was misclassified. To get a good estimate of the error rate, you should repeat this procedure multiple times, say 10, and average the results. I did that and got an average error rate of 6%.

The error that keeps appearing is a piece of spam that was misclassified as ham. It's better that a piece of spam sneaks through the filter than a valid email getting shoved into the spam folder. There are ways to bias the classifier to not make these errors, and we'll talk about these in chapter 7.

Now that we've used naïve Bayes to classify documents, we're going to look at another use for it. The next example will show how to interpret the knowledge acquired from training the naïve Bayes classifier.

4.7 Example: using naïve Bayes to reveal local attitudes from personal ads

Our next and final example is a fun one. We looked at two practical applications of the naïve Bayes classifier. The first one was to filter out malicious posts on a website, and the second was to filter out spam in email. There are a number of other uses for classification. I've seen someone take the naïve Bayes classifier and train it with social network profiles of women he liked and women he didn't like and then use the classifier to test how he would like an unknown person. The range of possibilities is limited only by your imagination. It's been shown that the older someone is, the better their vocabulary becomes. Could we guess a person's age by the words they use? Could we guess other factors about the person? Advertisers would love to know specific demographics about a person to better target the products they promote. Where would you get such training material? The internet abounds with training material. Almost every imaginable niche has a dedicated community where people have identified themselves as belonging to that community. The Dalmatian owners' site used in section 4.3.1 is a great example.

In this last example, we'll take some data from personals ads from multiple people for two different cities in the United States. We're going to see if people in different cities use different words. If they do, what are the words they use? Can the words people use give us some idea what's important to people in different cities?

Example: using naïve Bayes to find locally used words

1. Collect: Collect from RSS feeds. We'll need to build an interface to the RSS feeds.

2. Prepare: Parse text into token vectors.

3. Analyze: Inspect the tokens to make sure parsing was done correctly.

4. Train: Use `trainNB0()` that we created earlier.

5. Test: We'll look at the error rate to make sure this is actually working. We can make modifications to the tokenizer to improve the error rate and results.

6. Use: We'll build a complete program to wrap everything together. It will display the most common words given in two RSS feeds.

We're going to use the city that each ad comes from to train a classifier and then see how well it does. Finally, we're not going to use this to classify anything. We're going to look at the words and conditional probability scores to see if we can learn anything specific to one city over another.

4.7.1   Collect: importing RSS feeds

The first thing we're going to need to do is use Python to download the text. Luckily, the text is readily available in RSS form. Now all we need is an RSS reader. Universal Feed Parser is the most common RSS library for Python.

You can view documentation here: http://code.google.com/p/feedparser/. You should be able to install it like other Python packages, by unzipping the downloaded package, changing your directory to the unzipped package, and then typing `>>python setup.py install` at the command prompt.

We're going to use the personal ads from Craigslist, and hopefully we'll stay Terms Of Service compliant. To open the RSS feed from Craigslist, enter the following at your Python shell:

```
>>> import feedparser
>>>ny=feedparser.parse('http://newyork.craigslist.org/stp/index.rss')
```

I've decided to use the step, or strictly platonic, section from Craigslist because other sections can get a little lewd. You can play around with the feed and check out the great documentation at feedparser.org. To access a list of all the entries type

```
>>> ny['entries']
>>> len(ny['entries'])
100
```

You can create a function similar to `spamTest()` to automate your testing. Open your text editor and enter the code from the following listing.

Listing 4.6 RSS feed classifier and frequent word removal functions

```
def calcMostFreq(vocabList,fullText):
    import operator
    freqDict = {}
    for token in vocabList:
        freqDict[token]=fullText.count(token)
    sortedFreq = sorted(freqDict.iteritems(), key=operator.itemgetter(1),\
                    reverse=True)
    return sortedFreq[:30]

def localWords(feed1,feed0):
    import feedparser
    docList=[]; classList = []; fullText =[]
    minLen = min(len(feed1['entries']),len(feed0['entries']))
    for i in range(minLen):
        wordList = textParse(feed1['entries'][i]['summary'])
        docList.append(wordList)
        fullText.extend(wordList)
        classList.append(1)
        wordList = textParse(feed0['entries'][i]['summary'])
        docList.append(wordList)
        fullText.extend(wordList)
        classList.append(0)
    vocabList = createVocabList(docList)
    top30Words = calcMostFreq(vocabList,fullText)
    for pairW in top30Words:
        if pairW[0] in vocabList: vocabList.remove(pairW[0])
    trainingSet = range(2*minLen); testSet=[]
    for i in range(20):
        randIndex = int(random.uniform(0,len(trainingSet)))
        testSet.append(trainingSet[randIndex])
        del(trainingSet[randIndex])
    trainMat=[]; trainClasses = []
    for docIndex in trainingSet:
        trainMat.append(bagOfWords2VecMN(vocabList, docList[docIndex]))
        trainClasses.append(classList[docIndex])
    p0V,p1V,pSpam = trainNB0(array(trainMat),array(trainClasses))
    errorCount = 0
    for docIndex in testSet:
        wordVector = bagOfWords2VecMN(vocabList, docList[docIndex])
        if classifyNB(array(wordVector),p0V,p1V,pSpam) != \
            classList[docIndex]:
            errorCount += 1
    print 'the error rate is: ',float(errorCount)/len(testSet)
    return vocabList,p0V,p1V
```

❶ Calculates frequency of occurrence

❷ Accesses one feed at a time

❸ Removes most frequently occurring words

The code in listing 4.6 is similar to the `spamTest()` function in listing 4.5 with some added features. One helper function is included in listing 4.6; the function is called `calcMostFreq()`. ❶ The helper function goes through every word in the vocabulary and counts how many times it appears in the text. The dictionary is then sorted by frequency from highest to lowest, and the top 100 words are returned. You'll see why this is important in a second.

The next function, `localWords()`, takes two feeds as arguments. The feeds should be loaded outside this function. The reason for doing this is that feeds can change over time, and if you want to make some changes to our code to see how it performs, you should have the same input data. Reloading the feeds will give you new data, and you won't be sure whether our code changed or new data changed our results. The function localWords() is mostly the same as spamTest() from listing 4.5. The differences are that you access feeds ❷ instead of files, and you call calcMostFreq() to get the top 100 words and then remove these words. ❸ The rest of the function is similar to spamTest(), except the last line returns values that you'll use later.

You can comment out the three lines that removed the most frequently used words and see the performance before and after. ❸ When I did this, I had an error rate of 54% without these lines and 70% with the lines included. An interesting observation is that the top 30 words in these posts make up close to 30% of all the words used. The size of the vocabList was ~3000 words when I was testing this. A small percentage of the total words makes up a large portion of the text. The reason for this is that a large percentage of language is redundancy and structural glue. Another common approach is to not just remove the most common words but to also remove this structural glue from a predefined list. This is known as a *stop word* list, and there are a number of sources of this available. (At the time of writing, http://www.ranks.nl/resources/stopwords.html has a good list of stop words in multiple languages.)

After you've entered the code from listing 4.6 into bayes.py, you can test it in Python by typing in the following:

```
>>> reload(bayes)
<module 'bayes' from 'bayes.py'>
>>>ny=feedparser.parse('http://newyork.craigslist.org/stp/index.rss')
>>>sf=feedparser.parse('http://sfbay.craigslist.org/stp/index.rss')
>>> vocabList,pSF,pNY=bayes.localWords(ny,sf)
the error rate is:  0.1
>>> vocabList,pSF,pNY=bayes.localWords(ny,sf)
the error rate is:  0.35
```

To get a good estimate of the error rate, you should do multiple trials of this and take the average. The error rate here is much higher than for the spam testing. That is not a huge problem because we're interested in the word probabilities, not actually classifying anything. You can play around the number of words removed by caclMostFreq() and see how the error rate changes.

4.7.2 Analyze: displaying locally used words

You can sort the vectors pSF and pNY and then print out the words from vocabList at the same index. There's one last piece of code that does this for you. Open bayes.py one more time and enter the code from the following listing.

Listing 4.7   Most descriptive word display function

```
def getTopWords(ny,sf):
    import operator
    vocabList,p0V,p1V=localWords(ny,sf)
    topNY=[]; topSF=[]
```

```
    for i in range(len(p0V)):
        if p0V[i] > -6.0 : topSF.append((vocabList[i],p0V[i]))
        if p1V[i] > -6.0 : topNY.append((vocabList[i],p1V[i]))
    sortedSF = sorted(topSF, key=lambda pair: pair[1], reverse=True)
    print "SF**SF**SF**SF**SF**SF**SF**SF**SF**SF**SF**SF**SF**"
    for item in sortedSF:
        print item[0]
    sortedNY = sorted(topNY, key=lambda pair: pair[1], reverse=True)
    print "NY**NY**NY**NY**NY**NY**NY**NY**NY**NY**NY**NY**NY **"
    for item in sortedNY:
        print item[0]
```

The function getTopWords() in listing 4.7 takes the two feeds and first trains and tests the naïve Bayes classifier. The probabilities used are returned. Next, you create two lists and store tuples inside the lists. Rather than just return the top *X* words, you return all words above a certain threshold. The tuples are then sorted by their conditional probabilities.

To see this in action, enter the following in your Python shell after you've saved bayes.py.

```
>>> reload(bayes)
<module 'bayes' from 'bayes.pyc'>
>>> bayes.getTopWords(ny,sf)
the error rate is:  0.2
SF**SF**SF**SF**SF**SF**SF**SF**SF**SF**SF**SF**SF**SF**SF**
love
time
will
there
hit
send
francisco
female
NY**NY**NY**NY**NY**NY**NY**NY**NY**NY**NY**NY**NY**NY**
friend
people
will
single
sex
female
night
420
relationship
play
hope
```

The words from this output are entertaining. One thing to note: a lot of stop words appear in the output. It would be interesting to see how things would change if you removed the fixed stop words. In my experience, the classification error will also go down.

4.8   *Summary*

Using probabilities can sometimes be more effective than using hard rules for classification. Bayesian probability and Bayes' rule gives us a way to estimate unknown probabilities from known values.

You can reduce the need for a lot of data by assuming conditional independence among the features in your data. The assumption we make is that the probability of one word doesn't depend on any other words in the document. We know this assumption is a little simple. That's why it's known as naïve Bayes. Despite its incorrect assumptions, naïve Bayes is effective at classification.

There are a number of practical considerations when implementing naïve Bayes in a modern programming language. Underflow is one problem that can be addressed by using the logarithm of probabilities in your calculations. The bag-of-words model is an improvement on the set-of-words model when approaching document classification. There are a number of other improvements, such as removing stop words, and you can spend a long time optimizing a tokenizer.

The probability theory you learned in this chapter will be used again later in the book, and this chapter was a great introduction to the full power of Bayesian probability theory. We're going to take a break from probability theory. You'll next see a classification method called logistic regression and some optimization algorithms.

Logistic regression

This is an exciting chapter because this is the first chapter where we encounter optimization algorithms. If you think about it, many of the things we do in life are optimization problems. Some examples of optimization from daily life are these: How do we get from point A to point B in the least amount of time? How do we make the most money doing the least amount of work? How do we design an engine to produce the most horsepower while using the least amount of fuel? The things we can do with optimization are powerful. I'll introduce a few optimization algorithms to train a nonlinear function for classification.

If you're not familiar with regression, don't worry. We're going to cover that in the next part of this book, which starts with chapter 8. Perhaps you've seen some data points and then someone fit a line called the *best-fit* line to these points; that's regression. What happens in logistic regression is we have a bunch of data, and with the data we try to build an equation to do classification for us. The exact math behind this you'll see in the next part of the book, but the regression aspects means that we try to find a best-fit set of parameters. Finding the best fit is similar to regression, and in this method it's how we train our classifier. We'll use optimization algorithms to find these best-fit parameters. This best-fit stuff is where the name *regression* comes from. We'll talk about the math behind making this a classifier that puts out one of two values.

General approach to logistic regression

1. Collect: Any method.

2. Prepare: Numeric values are needed for a distance calculation. A structured data format is best.

3. Analyze: Any method.

4. Train: We'll spend most of the time training, where we try to find optimal coefficients to classify our data.

5. Test: Classification is quick and easy once the training step is done.

6. Use: This application needs to get some input data and output structured numeric values. Next, the application applies the simple regression calculation on this input data and determines which class the input data should belong to. The application then takes some action on the calculated class.

In this chapter you'll first learn what logistic regression is, and then you'll learn some optimization algorithms. In our study of optimization algorithms, you'll learn gradient ascent, and then we'll look at a modified version called stochastic gradient ascent. These optimization algorithms will be used to train our classifier. Next, you'll see logistic regression in action predicting whether a horse with an illness will live or die.

5.1   *Classification with logistic regression and the sigmoid function: a tractable step function*

Logistic regression

Pros: Computationally inexpensive, easy to implement, knowledge representation easy to interpret

Cons: Prone to underfitting, may have low accuracy

Works with: Numeric values, nominal values

We'd like to have an equation we can give all of our features and it will predict the class. In the two-class case, the function will spit out a 0 or a 1. Perhaps you've seen this before; it's called the Heaviside step function, or sometimes just the step function. The problem with the Heaviside step function is that at the point where it steps from 0 to 1, it does so instantly. This instantaneous step is sometimes difficult to deal with. There's another function that behaves in a similar fashion, but it's much easier to deal with mathematically. This function is called the *sigmoid*. The sigmoid is given by the following equation:

$$\sigma(z) = \frac{1}{1 + e^{-z}}$$

Two plots of the sigmoid are given in figure 5.1. At 0 the value of the sigmoid is 0.5. For increasing values of x, the sigmoid will approach 1, and for decreasing values of x, the sigmoid will approach 0. On a large enough scale (the bottom frame of figure 5.1), the sigmoid looks like a step function.

For the logistic regression classifier we'll take our features and multiply each one by a weight and then add them up. This result will be put into the sigmoid, and we'll get a number between 0 and 1. Anything above 0.5 we'll classify as a 1, and anything below 0.5 we'll classify as a 0. You can also think of logistic regression as a probability estimate.

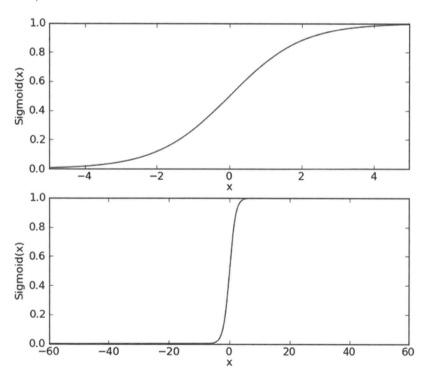

Figure 5.1   A plot of the sigmoid function on two scales; the top plot shows the sigmoid from -5 to 5, and it exhibits a smooth transition. The bottom plot shows a much larger scale where the sigmoid appears similar to a step function at x=0.

The question now becomes, what are the best weights, or regression coefficients to use, and how do we find them? The next section will address this question.

5.2   *Using optimization to find the best regression coefficients*

The input to the sigmoid function described will be z, where z is given by the following:

$$z = w_0 x_0 + w_1 x_1 + w_2 x_2 + \dots + w_n x_n$$

In vector notation we can write this as $z = w^T x$. All that means is that we have two vectors of numbers and we'll multiply each element and add them up to get one number. The vector **x** is our input data, and we want to find the best coefficients **w**, so that this classifier will be as successful as possible. In order to do that, we need to consider some ideas from optimization theory.

We'll first look at optimization with gradient ascent. We'll then see how we can use this method of optimization to find the best parameters to model our dataset. Next, we'll show how to plot the decision boundary generated with gradient ascent. This will help you visualize the successfulness of gradient ascent. Next, you'll learn about stochastic gradient ascent and how to make modifications to yield better results.

5.2.1   *Gradient ascent*

The first optimization algorithm we're going to look at is called gradient ascent. Gradient ascent is based on the idea that if we want to find the maximum point on a function, then the best way to move is in the direction of the gradient. We write the gradient with the symbol ∇ and the gradient of a function $f(x,y)$ is given by the equation

$$\nabla f(x,y) = \begin{pmatrix} \dfrac{\partial f(x,y)}{\partial x} \\ \dfrac{\partial f(x,y)}{\partial y} \end{pmatrix}$$

This is one of the aspects of machine learning that can be confusing. The math isn't difficult. You just need to keep track of what symbols mean. So this gradient means that we'll move in the x direction by amount $\frac{\partial f(x,y)}{\partial x}$ and in the y direction by amount $\frac{\partial f(x,y)}{\partial y}$. The function $f(x,y)$ needs to be defined and differentiable around the points where it's being evaluated. An example of this is shown in figure 5.2.

The gradient ascent algorithm shown in figure 5.2 takes a step in the direction given by the gradient. The gradient operator will always point in the direction of the greatest increase. We've talked about direction, but I didn't mention anything to do with magnitude of movement. The magnitude, or step size, we'll take is given by the parameter α. In vector notation we can write the gradient ascent algorithm as

$$w := w + \alpha \nabla_w f(w)$$

This step is repeated until we reach a stopping condition: either a specified number of steps or the algorithm is within a certain tolerance margin.

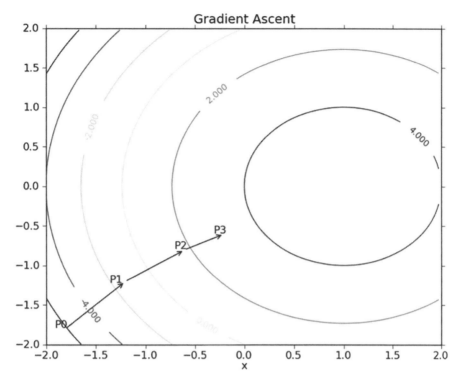

Figure 5.2 The gradient ascent algorithm moves in the direction of the gradient evaluated at each point. Starting with point P0, the gradient is evaluated and the function moves to the next point, P1. The gradient is then reevaluated at P1, and the function moves to P2. This cycle repeats until a stopping condition is met. The gradient operator always ensures that we're moving in the best possible direction.

Gradient descent

Perhaps you've also heard of gradient descent. It's the same thing as gradient ascent, except the plus sign is changed to a minus sign. We can write this as

$$w := w - \alpha \nabla_{\mathbf{w}} f(w)$$

With gradient descent we're trying to minimize some function rather than maximize it.

Let's put this into action on our logistic regression classifier and some Python. First, we need a dataset. Consider the dataset plotted in figure 5.3.

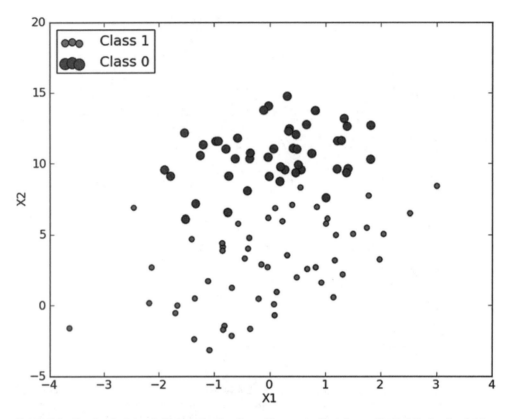

Figure 5.3   Our simple dataset. We're going to attempt to use gradient descent to find the best weights for a logistic regression classifier on this dataset.

5.2.2   *Train: using gradient ascent to find the best parameters*

There are 100 data points in figure 5.3. Each point has two numeric features: X1 and X2. We'll try to use gradient ascent to fit the best parameters for the logistic regression model to our data. We'll do this by finding the best weights for this given dataset.

Pseudocode for the gradient ascent would look like this:

Start with the weights all set to 1
Repeat R number of times:
   Calculate the gradient of the entire dataset
   Update the weights vector by alpha*gradient
   Return the weights vector

The code in the following listing implements gradient ascent. To see it in action, open your text editor and create a new file called `logRegres.py`. Then enter the following code.

Listing 5.1 Logistic regression gradient ascent optimization functions

```
def loadDataSet():
    dataMat = []; labelMat = []
    fr = open('testSet.txt')
    for line in fr.readlines():
        lineArr = line.strip().split()
        dataMat.append([1.0, float(lineArr[0]), float(lineArr[1])])
        labelMat.append(int(lineArr[2]))
    return dataMat,labelMat

def sigmoid(inX):
    return 1.0/(1+exp(-inX))

def gradAscent(dataMatIn, classLabels):
    dataMatrix = mat(dataMatIn)                              ❶ Convert to NumPy
    labelMat = mat(classLabels).transpose()                    matrix data type
    m,n = shape(dataMatrix)
    alpha = 0.001
    maxCycles = 500
    weights = ones((n,1))
    for k in range(maxCycles):
        h = sigmoid(dataMatrix*weights)                   Matrix ❷
        error = (labelMat - h)                       multiplication
        weights = weights + alpha * dataMatrix.transpose()* error
    return weights
```

The code in listing 5.1 starts out with a convenience function, loadDataSet(). This opens the text file testSet.txt and reads every line. The first two values on the line are X1 and X2, and the third value is the class label for our dataset. In addition, this sets the value of X0 to 1.0, which is a convention we use. The next function, sigmoid(), is our function from section 5.2.

The real work is done in the function gradAscent(), which takes two inputs. The first input, dataMatIn, is a 2D NumPy array, where the columns are the different features and the rows are the different training examples. Our example data has two features plus the 0th feature and 100 examples, so it will be a 100x3 matrix. In ❶ you take the input arrays and convert them to NumPy matrices. This is the first time in this book where you're using NumPy matrices, and if you're not familiar with matrix math, then some calculations can seem strange. NumPy can operate on both 2D arrays and matrices, and the results will be different if you assume the wrong data type. Please see appendix A for an introduction to NumPy matrices. The input classLabels is a 1x100 row vector, and for the matrix math to work, you need it to be a column vector, so you take the transpose of it and assign that to the variable labelMat. Next, you get the size of the matrix and set some parameters for our gradient ascent algorithm.

The variable alpha is the step size you'll take toward the target, and maxCycles is the number of times you're going to repeat the calculation before stopping. The for loop iterates over the dataset, and finally you return the weights. One thing I'd like to stress is that the calculations in ❷ are matrix operations. The variable h is not one number but a column vector with as many elements as you have data points, 100 in this example. The multiplication `dataMatrix * weights` is not one multiplication but actually 300.

Lastly, one thing I'd like to mention is that the first two lines in the formula in ❷ may not be familiar, and I haven't really derived them. A little math is needed to derive the equations used here, and I'll leave it to you to look into that further if desired. Qualitatively you can see we're calculating the error between the actual class and the predicted class and then moving in the direction of that error.

Let's see this in action. Open your text editor and add the code from listing 5.1.

Type the following at your Python shell:

```
>>> import logRegres
>>> dataArr,labelMat=logRegres.loadDataSet()
>>> logRegres.gradAscent(dataArr,labelMat)
matrix([[ 4.12414349],
        [ 0.48007329],
        [-0.6168482 ]])
```

5.2.3   *Analyze: plotting the decision boundary*

We're solving for a set of weights used to make a line that separates the different classes of data. How can we plot this line to understand this optimization procedure? In order to make a plot like this, you'll need the code in the next listing. Open logRegres.py and add in the following code.

> **Listing 5.2   Plotting the logistic regression best-fit line and dataset**

```
def plotBestFit(wei):
    import matplotlib.pyplot as plt
    weights = wei.getA()
    dataMat,labelMat=loadDataSet()
    dataArr = array(dataMat)
    n = shape(dataArr)[0]
    xcord1 = []; ycord1 = []
    xcord2 = []; ycord2 = []
    for i in range(n):
        if int(labelMat[i])== 1:
            xcord1.append(dataArr[i,1]); ycord1.append(dataArr[i,2])
        else:
            xcord2.append(dataArr[i,1]); ycord2.append(dataArr[i,2])
    fig = plt.figure()
    ax = fig.add_subplot(111)
    ax.scatter(xcord1, ycord1, s=30, c='red', marker='s')
    ax.scatter(xcord2, ycord2, s=30, c='green')
    x = arange(-3.0, 3.0, 0.1)
    y = (-weights[0]-weights[1]*x)/weights[2]        ◁──❶ Best-fit line
    ax.plot(x, y)
    plt.xlabel('X1'); plt.ylabel('X2');
    plt.show()
```

The code in listing 5.2 is a straightforward plot using Matplotlib. The only thing worth pointing out is ❶ where I set the sigmoid function to 0. If you remember

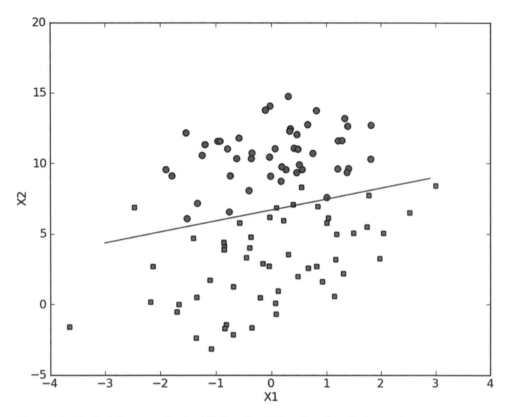

Figure 5.4 **The logistic regression best-fit line after 500 cycles of gradient ascent**

from section 5.2, an input of 0 was our center line to split things classified as a 1 and a 0. I set $0 = w_0x_0 + w_1x_1 + w_2x_2$ and solved for X2 in terms of X1 (remember, X0 was 0). To use the code in listing 5.2, type the following:

```
>>> reload(logRegres)
<module 'logRegres' from 'logRegres.py'>
>>> logRegres.plotBestFit(weights.getA())
```

You should get something similar to the plot in figure 5.4.

The classification is pretty good. From the image, it appears that we'll misclassify only two to four data points. One thing to stress is that this method took a lot of calculations; even our simple example used 300 multiplications on a tiny dataset. We'll need to alter the algorithm a little in order for it to work on real-world datasets, and we'll do that in the next section.

5.2.4 *Train: stochastic gradient ascent*

The previous optimization algorithm, gradient ascent, uses the whole dataset on each update. This was fine with 100 examples, but with billions of data points containing thousands of features, it's unnecessarily expensive in terms of computational resources. An alternative to this method is to update the weights using only one instance at a time. This is known as *stochastic gradient ascent*. Stochastic gradient ascent is an example of an online learning algorithm. This is known as *online* because we can incrementally update the classifier as new data comes in rather than all at once. The all-at-once method is known as *batch processing*.

Pseudo-code for the stochastic gradient ascent would look like this:

Start with the weights all set to 1
For each piece of data in the dataset:
  Calculate the gradient of one piece of data
  Update the weights vector by alpha*gradient
  Return the weights vector

The following listing contains the stochastic gradient ascent algorithm.

Listing 5.3   Stochastic gradient ascent

```
def stocGradAscent0(dataMatrix, classLabels):
    m,n = shape(dataMatrix)
    alpha = 0.01
    weights = ones(n)
    for i in range(m):
        h = sigmoid(sum(dataMatrix[i]*weights))
        error = classLabels[i] - h
        weights = weights + alpha * error * dataMatrix[i]
    return weights
```

You can see that stochastic gradient ascent is similar to gradient ascent except that the variables h and `error` are now single values rather than vectors. There also is no matrix conversion, so all of the variables are NumPy arrays.

To try this out, enter the code from listing 5.3 into logRegres.py and enter the following into your Python shell:

```
>>> reload(logRegres)
<module 'logRegres' from 'logRegres.py'>
>>> dataArr,labelMat=logRegres.loadDataSet()
>>> weights=logRegres.stocGradAscent0(array(dataArr),labelMat)
>>> logRegres.plotBestFit(weights)
```

After executing the code to plot the best-fit line, you should see something similar to figure 5.4; I've have plotted this in figure 5.5. The resulting best-fit line is OK but certainly not as great as the previous example from gradient ascent. If we were to use this as our classifier, we'd misclassify one-third of the results.

Directly comparing the stochastic gradient ascent algorithm in listing 5.3 to the code in listing 5.1 is unfair; the gradient ascent code had 500 iterations over the entire dataset. One way to look at how well the optimization algorithm is doing is to see if it's converging. That is, are the parameters reaching a steady value, or are they constantly changing? I took the stochastic gradient ascent algorithm in listing 5.3 and modified it to run through the dataset 200 times. I then plotted the weights, as shown in figure 5.6.

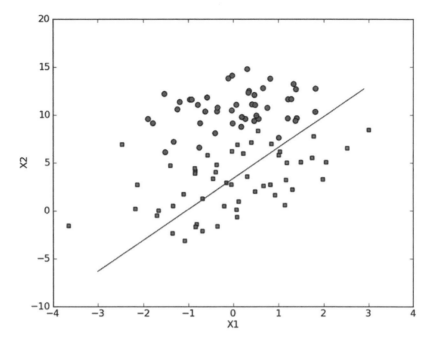

Figure 5.5   Our simple dataset with solution from stochastic gradient ascent after one pass through the dataset. The best-fit line isn't a good separator of the data.

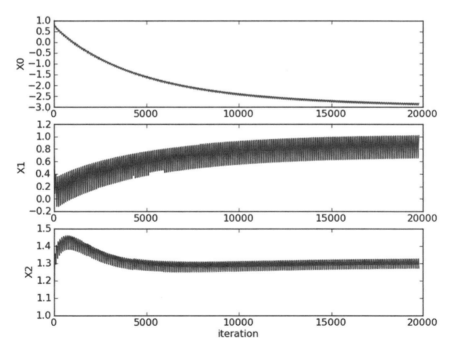

Figure 5.6   Weights versus iteration number for one pass through the dataset, with this method. It takes a large number of cycles for the weights to reach a steady-state value, and there are still local fluctuations.

Figure 5.6 shows how the weights change in our simple stochastic gradient ascent algorithm over 200 iterations of the algorithm. Weight 2, labeled X2 in figure 5.5, takes only 50 cycles to reach a steady value, but weights 1 and 0 take much longer. An additional item to notice from this plot is that there are small periodic variations, even though the large variation has stopped. If you think about what's happening, it should be obvious that there are pieces of data that don't classify correctly and cause a large change in the weights. We'd like to see the algorithm converge to a single value rather than oscillate, and we'd like to see the weights converge more quickly.

The stochastic gradient ascent algorithm of listing 5.3 has been modified to address the problems shown in figure 5.6, and this is given in the following listing.

Listing 5.4 Modified stochastic gradient ascent

```
def stocGradAscent1(dataMatrix, classLabels, numIter=150):
    m,n = shape(dataMatrix)
    weights = ones(n)
    for j in range(numIter):         dataIndex = range(m)
        for i in range(m):
            alpha = 4/(1.0+j+i)+0.01          ❶ Alpha changes with
            randIndex = int(random.uniform(0,len(dataIndex)))      each iteration
            h = sigmoid(sum(dataMatrix[randIndex]*weights))
            error = classLabels[randIndex] - h
            weights = weights + alpha * error * dataMatrix[randIndex]
            del(dataIndex[randIndex])
    return weights                    Update vectors are
                                      randomly selected  ❷
```

The code in listing 5.4 is similar to that of listing 5.3, but two things have been added to improve it.

The first thing to note is that in ❶ alpha changes on each iteration. This will improve the oscillations that occur in the dataset shown in figure 5.6 or high-frequency oscillations. Alpha decreases as the number of iterations increases, but it never reaches 0 because there's a constant term in ❶. You need to do this so that after a large number of cycles, new data still has some impact. Perhaps you're dealing with something that's changing with time. Then you may want to let the constant term be larger to give more weight to new values. The second thing about the decreasing alpha function is that it decreases by $1/(j+i)$; j is the index of the number of times you go through the dataset, and i is the index of the example in the training set. This gives an alpha that isn't strictly decreasing when $j<<max(i)$. The avoidance of a strictly decreasing weight is shown to work in other optimization algorithms, such as simulated annealing.

The second improvement in listing 5.4 appears in ❷. Here, you're randomly selecting each instance to use in updating the weights. This will reduce the periodic variations that you saw in figure 5.6. The way you randomly select a value from a list of integers and then delete it from the list is similar to what we did in chapter 3.

An optional argument to the function has also been added. If no third argument is given, then 150 iterations will be done. But if a third argument is given, that will override the default.

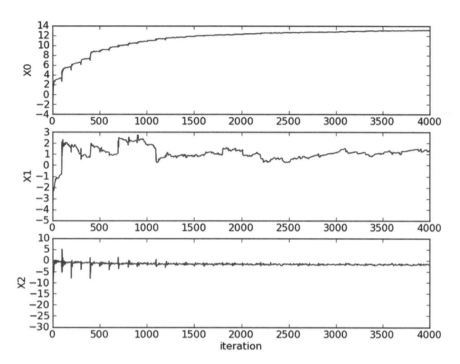

Figure 5.7 Coefficient convergence in `stocGradAscent1()` with random vector selection and decreasing alpha. This method is much faster to converge than using a fixed alpha.

Figure 5.7 shows how the weights change with each update similar to `stocGradAscent1()`.

If you compare figure 5.7 with figure 5.6, you'll notice two things. The first thing you may notice is that the coefficients in figure 5.7 don't show the regular motion like those in figure 5.6. This is due to the random vector selection of `stocGradAscent1()`. The second thing you'll notice is that the horizontal axis is much smaller in figure 5.7 than in figure 5.6. This is because with `stocGradAscent1()` we can converge on weights much more quickly. Here we use only 20 passes through the dataset, whereas we used 500 with the previous two methods.

Let's see this code in action on the same dataset as the previous examples. After you've entered the code from listing 5.4 into logRegres.py, enter the following in your Python shell:

```
>>> reload(logRegres)
<module 'logRegres' from 'logRegres.py'>
>>> dataArr,labelMat=logRegres.loadDataSet()
>>> weights=logRegres.stocGradAscent1(array(dataArr),labelMat)
>>> logRegres.plotBestFit(weights)
```

You should see a plot similar to that in figure 5.8. The results are similar to those of `GradientAscent()`, but far fewer calculations were involved.

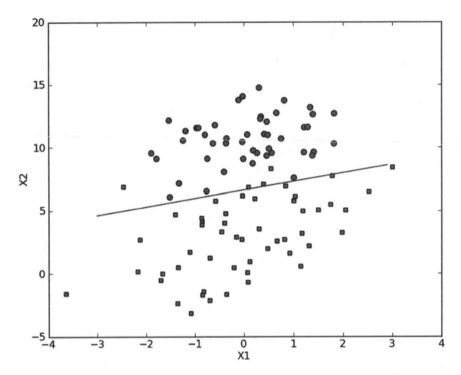

Figure 5.8 The coefficients with the improved stochastic gradient descent algorithm

The default number of iterations is 150, but you can change this by adding a third argument to `stocGradAscent1()` like

```
>>> weights=logRegres.stocGradAscent1(array(dataArr),labelMat, 500)
```

You've seen a few optimization algorithms so far. There are many more to explore. A number of books have been written on the subject. You can also adjust the parameters in our algorithm to give better results for a given dataset.

So far we've looked at how the weights change, but we haven't done a lot of classification, which is the purpose of this section and chapter. In the next section, we'll put stochastic gradient ascent to work on a problem of horse colic.

5.3   *Example: estimating horse fatalities from colic*

In this section, we'll use logistic regression to try to predict if a horse with colic will live or die. The data[1] has 368 instances with 28 features. I'm not a horse expert. From what I've read, horse colic is a general term used to describe gastrointestinal pain in horses. The pain may or may not be from gastrointestinal problems. The dataset contains

---

[1] Dataset retrieved from UCI Machine Learning Repository on 11/1/2010 (http://archive.ics.uci.edu/ml/datasets/Horse+Colic). Data originally created by Mary McLeish and Matt Cecile, Department of Computer Science, University of Guelph, Guelph, Ontario, Canada N1G 2W1.

measurements from horses seen by a hospital for colic. Some of the measurements are subjective, and some are difficult to measure, such as the pain level in the horse.

> **Example: using logistic regression to estimate horse fatalities from colic**
> 1. Collect: Data file provided.
>
> 2. Prepare: Parse a text file in Python, and fill in missing values.
>
> 3. Analyze: Visually inspect the data.
>
> 4. Train: Use an optimization algorithm to find the best coefficients.
>
> 5. Test: To measure the success, we'll look at error rate. Depending on the error rate, we may decide to go back to the training step to try to find better values for the regression coefficients by adjusting the number of iterations and step size.
>
> 6. Use: Building a simple command-line program to collect horse symptoms and output live/die diagnosis won't be difficult. I'll leave that up to you as an exercise.

In addition to the obvious problems with the data, there's another problem: 30% of the values are missing. We'll first handle the problem of how to deal with missing values in a dataset, and then we'll use logistic regression and stochastic gradient ascent to forecast whether a horse will live or die.

5.3.1 Prepare: dealing with missing values in the data

Missing values in your data is a big problem, and there have been many pages of text books dedicated to dealing with this problem. Well, why it is a problem? Say you have 100 instances with 20 features, and the data was collected by a machine. What if a sensor on this machine was broken and one feature was useless? Do you throw out all the data? What about the 19 other features; do they have anything useful to tell you? Yes, they do. Sometimes data is expensive, and you don't have the option to throw it out or collect it all over again, so you need a method for handling this problem.

Here are some options:

- Use the feature's mean value from all the available data.
- Fill in the unknown with a special value like -1.
- Ignore the instance.
- Use a mean value from similar items.
- Use another machine learning algorithm to predict the value.

The dataset we'll use in the next section will be preprocessed so that we can easily use it with our existing algorithm. During the preprocessing, I decided to do two things from the list. First, I had to replace all the unknown values with a real number because we're using NumPy, and in NumPy arrays can't contain a missing value. The number chosen was 0, which happens to work out well for logistic regression. The intuition is this: we want a value that won't impact the weight during the update. The weights are updated according to

```
weights = weights + alpha * error * dataMatrix[randIndex]
```

If `dataMatrix` is 0 for any feature, then the weight for that feature will simply be

```
weights = weights
```

Also, the error term will not be impacted by this because `sigmoid(0)=0.5`, which is totally neutral for predicting the class. For these reasons, replacing missing values with 0 allows us to keep our imperfect data without compromising the learning algorithm. Also, none of the features take on 0 in the data, so in some sense it's a special value.

Second, there was a missing class label in the test data. I simply threw it out. It's hard to replace a missing class label. This solution makes sense given that we're using logistic regression, but it may not make sense with something like kNN.

The data was preprocessed from its original form and the modified version was placed in two files, horseColicTest.txt and horseColicTraining.txt. You can see the data at http://archive.ics.uci.edu/ml/datasets/Horse+Colic if you want to compare the original data and the preprocessed data.

Now that we have a clean set of data and a good optimization algorithm, we're going to put all these parts together and build a classifier to see if we can predict whether a horse will die from colic.

5.3.2 *Test: classifying with logistic regression*

We spent a lot of time in the previous sections of this chapter talking about optimization algorithms. We didn't actually classify anything. With logistic regression you don't need to do much to classify an instance. All you have to do is calculate the sigmoid of the vector under test multiplied by the weights optimized earlier. If the sigmoid gives you a value greater than 0.5, the class is 1, and it's 0 otherwise.

To see this in action, open your favorite text editor and enter the following code in logRegres.py.

Listing 5.5 Logistic regression classification function

```
def classifyVector(inX, weights):
    prob = sigmoid(sum(inX*weights))
    if prob > 0.5: return 1.0
    else: return 0.0

def colicTest():
    frTrain = open('horseColicTraining.txt')
    frTest = open('horseColicTest.txt')
    trainingSet = []; trainingLabels = []
    for line in frTrain.readlines():
        currLine = line.strip().split('\t')
        lineArr =[]
        for i in range(21):
            lineArr.append(float(currLine[i]))
        trainingSet.append(lineArr)
```

```
            trainingLabels.append(float(currLine[21]))
        trainWeights = stocGradAscent1(array(trainingSet), trainingLabels, 500)
        errorCount = 0; numTestVec = 0.0
        for line in frTest.readlines():
            numTestVec += 1.0
            currLine = line.strip().split('\t')
            lineArr =[]
            for i in range(21):
                lineArr.append(float(currLine[i]))
            if int(classifyVector(array(lineArr), trainWeights))!=
                int(currLine[21]):
                errorCount += 1
        errorRate = (float(errorCount)/numTestVec)
        print "the error rate of this test is: %f" % errorRate
        return errorRate
def multiTest():
    numTests = 10; errorSum=0.0
    for k in range(numTests):
        errorSum += colicTest()
    print "after %d iterations the average error rate is:
        %f" % (numTests, errorSum/float(numTests))
```

The first function in listing 5.5 is classifyVector(). This takes the weights and an input vector and calculates the sigmoid. If the value of the sigmoid is more than 0.5, it's considered a 1; otherwise, it's a 0.

The next function in listing 5.5 is colicTest(). This is a standalone function that opens the test set and training set and properly formats the data. First, the training set is loaded. You use the convention that the last column contains the class value. Originally, the data had three class values representing what happened to the horse: lived, died, or was euthanized. For the purposes of this exercise, I bundled died and euthanized into one category called "did not live." After this data is loaded, the weights vector is calculated using stocGradAscent1(). I used 500 iterations in training the weights; this is shown to improve performance over the default 150 iterations. Feel free to change this value. After the weights are calculated, the test set is loaded and an error rate is calculated. colicTest() is totally a standalone function. If you run it multiple times, you'll get slightly different results because of the random components. If the weights totally converged in stocGradAscent1(), then there would be no random components.

The last function, multiTest(), runs the function colicTest() 10 times and takes the average. To see this in action, enter the following at your Python shell:

```
>>> reload(logRegres)
<module 'logRegres' from 'logRegres.py'>
>>> logRegres.multiTest()
the error rate of this test is: 0.358209
the error rate of this test is: 0.432836
the error rate of this test is: 0.373134
                        .

                        .
the error rate of this test is: 0.298507
the error rate of this test is: 0.313433
after 10 iterations the average error rate is: 0.353731
```

After 10 iterations, the data had a 35% error rate. This wasn't bad with over 30% of the values missing. You can alter the number of iterations in `colicTest()` and the alpha size in `stochGradAscent1()` to get results approaching a 20% error rate. We'll revisit this example in chapter 7.

5.4   Summary

Logistic regression is finding best-fit parameters to a nonlinear function called the sigmoid. Methods of optimization can be used to find the best-fit parameters. Among the optimization algorithms, one of the most common algorithms is gradient ascent. Gradient ascent can be simplified with stochastic gradient ascent.

Stochastic gradient ascent can do as well as gradient ascent using far fewer computing resources. In addition, stochastic gradient ascent is an online algorithm; it can update what it has learned as new data comes in rather than reloading all of the data as in batch processing.

One major problem in machine learning is how to deal with missing values in the data. There's no blanket answer to this question. It really depends on what you're doing with the data. There are a number of solutions, and each solution has its own advantages and disadvantages.

In the next chapter we're going to take a look at another classification algorithm similar to logistic regression. The algorithm is called support vector machines and is considered one of the best stock algorithms.

Support vector machines

This chapter covers

- Introducing support vector machines
- Using the SMO algorithm for optimization
- Using kernels to "transform" data
- Comparing support vector machines with other classifiers

I've seen more than one book follow this pattern when discussing support vector machines (SVMs): "Here's a little theory. Now SVMs are too hard for you. Just download libsvm and use that." I'm not going to follow that pattern. I think if you just read a little bit of the theory and then look at production C++ SVM code, you're going to have trouble understanding it. But if we strip out the production code and the speed improvements, the code becomes manageable, perhaps understandable.

Support vector machines are considered by some people to be the best stock classifier. By *stock*, I mean not modified. This means you can take the classifier in its basic form and run it on the data, and the results will have low error rates. Support vector machines make good decisions for data points that are outside the training set.

In this chapter you're going to learn what support vector machines are, and I'll introduce some key terminology. There are many implementations of support vector

101

machines, but we'll focus on one of the most popular implementations: the sequential minimal optimization (SMO) algorithm. After that, you'll see how to use something called *kernels* to extend SVMs to a larger number of datasets. Finally, we'll revisit the handwriting example from chapter 1 to see if we can do a better job with SVMs.

6.1 Separating data with the maximum margin

Support vector machines

Pros: Low generalization error, computationally inexpensive, easy to interpret results

Cons: Sensitive to tuning parameters and kernel choice; natively only handles binary classification

Works with: Numeric values, nominal values

To introduce the subject of support vector machines I need to explain a few concepts. Consider the data in frames A–D in figure 6.1; could you draw a straight line to put all of the circles on one side and all of the squares on another side? Now consider the data in figure 6.2, frame A. There are two groups of data, and the data points are separated enough that you could draw a straight line on the figure with all the points of one class on one side of the line and all the points of the other class on the other side of the line. If such a situation exists, we say the data is *linearly separable*. Don't worry if this assumption seems too perfect. We'll later make some changes where the data points can spill over the line.

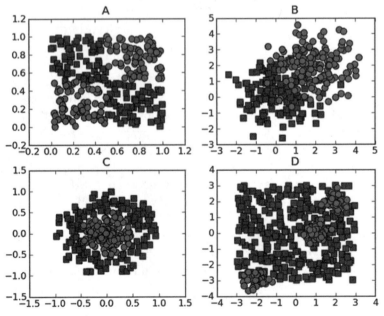

Figure 6.1   Four examples of datasets that aren't linearly separable

The line used to separate the dataset is called a *separating hyperplane*. In our simple 2D plots, it's just a line. But, if we have a dataset with three dimensions, we need a plane to separate the data; and if we have data with 1024 dimensions, we need something with 1023 dimensions to separate the data. What do you call something with 1023 dimensions? How about N-1 dimensions? It's called a *hyperplane*. The hyperplane is our decision boundary. Everything on one side belongs to one class, and everything on the other side belongs to a different class.

We'd like to make our classifier in such a way that the farther a data point is from the decision boundary, the more confident we are about the prediction we've made. Consider the plots in figure 6.2, frames B–D. They all separate the data, but which one does it best? Should we minimize the average distance to the separating hyperplane? In that case, are frames B and C any better than frame D in figure 6.2? Isn't something like that done with best-fit lines? Yes, but it's not the best idea here. We'd like to find the point closest to the separating hyperplane and make sure this is as far away from the separating line as possible. This is known as *margin*. We want to have the greatest possible margin, because if we made a mistake or trained our classifier on limited data, we'd want it to be as robust as possible.

The points closest to the separating hyperplane are known as *support vectors*. Now that we know that we're trying to maximize the distance from the separating line to the support vectors, we need to find a way to optimize this problem.

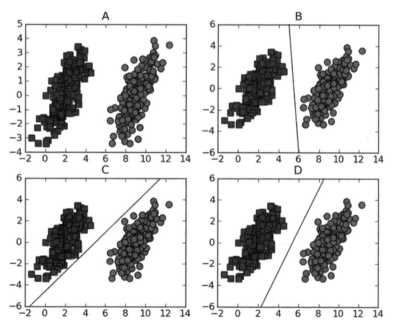

Figure 6.2   Linearly separable data is shown in frame A. Frames B, C, and D show possible valid lines separating the two classes of data.

6.2   *Finding the maximum margin*

How can we measure the line that best separates the data? To start with, look at figure 6.3. Our separating hyperplane has the form $\mathbf{w}^T\mathbf{x}+b$. If we want to find the distance from A to the separating plane, we must measure normal or perpendicular to the line. This is given by $|\mathbf{w}^T\mathbf{x}+b|/||\mathbf{w}||$. The constant b is just an offset like w_0 in logistic regression. All this w and b stuff describes the separating line, or hyperplane, for our data. Now, let's talk about the classifier.

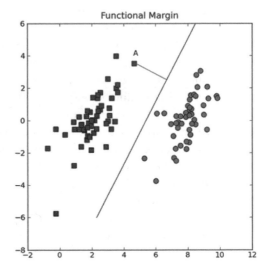

Figure 6.3   **The distance from point A to the separating plane is measured by a line normal to the separating plane.**

6.2.1   *Framing the optimization problem in terms of our classifier*

I've talked about the classifier but haven't mentioned how it works. Understanding how the classifier works will help you to understand the optimization problem. We'll have a simple equation like the sigmoid where we can enter our data values and get a class label out. We're going to use something like the Heaviside step function, $f(\mathbf{w}^T\mathbf{x}+b)$, where the function $f(u)$ gives us -1 if u<0, and 1 otherwise. This is different from logistic regression in the previous chapter where the class labels were 0 or 1.

Why did we switch from class labels of 0 and 1 to -1 and 1? This makes the math manageable, because -1 and 1 are only different by the sign. We can write a single equation to describe the margin or how close a data point is to our separating hyperplane and not have to worry if the data is in the -1 or +1 class.

When we're doing this and deciding where to place the separating line, this margin is calculated by $label*(\mathbf{w}^T\mathbf{x}+b)$. This is where the -1 and 1 class labels help out. If a point is far away from the separating plane on the positive side, then $\mathbf{w}^T\mathbf{x}+b$ will be a large positive number, and $label*(\mathbf{w}^T\mathbf{x}+b)$ will give us a large number. If it's far from the negative side and has a negative label, $label*(\mathbf{w}^T\mathbf{x}+b)$ will also give us a large positive number.

The goal now is to find the **w** and b values that will define our classifier. To do this, we must find the points with the smallest margin. These are the support vectors briefly mentioned earlier. Then, when we find the points with the smallest margin, we must maximize that margin. This can be written as

$$\arg\max_{w,b}\left\{\min_{n}\left(label\cdot(\boldsymbol{w}^T\boldsymbol{x}+b)\right)\cdot\frac{1}{\|\boldsymbol{w}\|}\right\}$$

Solving this problem directly is pretty difficult, so we can convert it into another form that we can solve more easily. Let's look at the inside of the previous equation, the part inside the curly braces. Optimizing multiplications can be nasty, so what we do is hold one part fixed and then maximize the other part. If we set label*(**w**ᵀ**x**+b) to be 1 for the support vectors, then we can maximize $||\mathbf{w}||^{-1}$ and we'll have a solution. Not all of the label*(**w**ᵀ**x**+b) will be equal to 1, only the closest values to the separating hyperplane. For values farther away from the hyperplane, this product will be larger.

The optimization problem we now have is a constrained optimization problem because we must find the best values, provided they meet some constraints. Here, our constraint is that label*(**w**ᵀ**x**+b) will be 1.0 or greater. There's a well-known method for solving these types of constrained optimization problems, using something called Lagrange multipliers. Using Lagrange multipliers, we can write the problem in terms of our constraints. Because our constraints are our data points, we can write the values of our hyperplane in terms of our data points. The optimization function turns out to be

$$\max_{\alpha} \left[\sum_{i=1}^{m} \alpha - \frac{1}{2} \sum_{i,j=1}^{m} label^{(i)} \cdot label^{(j)} \cdot a_i \cdot a_j \langle x^{(i)}, x^{(j)} \rangle \right]$$

subject to the following constraints:

$$\alpha \geq 0, and \sum_{i-1}^{m} \alpha_i \cdot label^{(i)} = 0$$

This is great, but it makes one assumption: the data is 100% linearly separable. We know by now that our data is hardly ever that clean. With the introduction of something called *slack variables*, we can allow examples to be on the wrong side of the decision boundary. Our optimization goal stays the same, but we now have a new set of constraints:

$$c \geq \alpha \geq 0, and \sum_{i-1}^{m} \alpha_i \cdot label^{(i)} = 0$$

The constant C controls weighting between our goal of making the margin large and ensuring that most of the examples have a functional margin of at least 1.0. The constant C is an argument to our optimization code that we can tune and get different results. Once we solve for our alphas, we can write the separating hyperplane in terms of these alphas. That part is straightforward. The majority of the work in SVMs is finding the alphas.

There have been some large steps taken in coming up with these equations here. I encourage you to seek a textbook to see a more detailed derivation if you're interested.[1,2]

---

[1] Christopher M. Bishop, *Pattern Recognition and Machine Learning* (Springer, 2006).

[2] Bernhard Schlkopf and Alexander J. Smola, *Learning with Kernels: Support Vector Machines, Regularization, Optimization, and Beyond* (MIT Press, 2001).

6.2.2 Approaching SVMs with our general framework

In chapter 1, we defined common steps for building machine learning–based applications. These steps may change from one machine learning task to another and from one algorithm to another. It's worth taking a few minutes to see how these will apply to the algorithm we're looking at in this chapter.

> **General approach to SVMs**
> 1. Collect: Any method.
> 2. Prepare: Numeric values are needed.
> 3. Analyze: It helps to visualize the separating hyperplane.
> 4. Train: The majority of the time will be spent here. Two parameters can be adjusted during this phase.
> 5. Test: Very simple calculation.
> 6. Use: You can use an SVM in almost any classification problem. One thing to note is that SVMs are binary classifiers. You'll need to write a little more code to use an SVM on a problem with more than two classes.

Now that we have a little bit of the theory behind us, we'd like to be able to program this problem so that we can use it on our data. The next section will introduce a simple yet powerful algorithm for doing so.

6.3 Efficient optimization with the SMO algorithm

The last two equations in section 6.2.1 are what we're going to minimize and some constraints that we have to follow while minimizing. A while back, people were using quadratic solvers to solve this optimization problem. (A *quadratic solver* is a piece of software that optimizes a quadratic function of several variables, subject to linear constraints on the variables.) These quadratic solvers take a lot of computing power and are complex. All of this messing around with optimization is to train our classifier. When we find the optimal values of α, we can get our separating hyperplane or line in 2D and then easily classify data.

We'll now discuss the SMO algorithm, and then we'll write a simplified version of it so that you can properly understand how it works. The simplified version works on small datasets. In the next section we'll move from the simplified to the full version, which works much faster than the simplified version.

6.3.1 Platt's SMO algorithm

In 1996 John Platt published a powerful algorithm he called SMO[3] for training the support vector machines. Platt's SMO stands for Sequential Minimal Optimization,

---

[3] John C. Platt, "Using Analytic QP and Sparseness to Speed Training of Support Vector Machines" in *Advances in Neural Information Processing Systems* 11, M. S. Kearns, S. A. Solla, D. A. Cohn, eds (MIT Press, 1999), 557–63.

and it takes the large optimization problem and breaks it into many small problems. The small problems can easily be solved, and solving them sequentially will give you the same answer as trying to solve everything together. In addition to getting the same answer, the amount of time is greatly reduced.

The SMO algorithm works to find a set of alphas and b. Once we have a set of alphas, we can easily compute our weights **w** and get the separating hyperplane.

Here's how the SMO algorithm works: it chooses two alphas to optimize on each cycle. Once a suitable pair of alphas is found, one is increased and one is decreased. To be suitable, a set of alphas must meet certain criteria. One criterion a pair must meet is that both of the alphas have to be outside their margin boundary. The second criterion is that the alphas aren't already clamped or bounded.

6.3.2 *Solving small datasets with the simplified SMO*

Implementing the full Platt SMO algorithm can take a lot of code. We'll simplify it in our first example to get an idea of how it works. After we get the simplified version working, we'll build on it to see the full version. The simplification uses less code but takes longer at runtime. The outer loops of the Platt SMO algorithm determine the best alphas to optimize. We'll skip that for this simplified version and select pairs of alphas by first going over every alpha in our dataset. Then, we'll choose the second alpha randomly from the remaining alphas. It's important to note here that we change two alphas at the same time. We need to do this because we have a constraint:

$$\sum a_i \cdot label^{(i)} = 0$$

Changing one alpha may cause this constraint to be violated, so we always change two at a time.

To do this we're going to create a helper function that randomly selects one integer from a range. We also need a helper function to clip values if they get too big. These two functions are given in the following listing. Open a text editor and add the code to svmMLiA.py.

> **Listing 6.1 Helper functions for the SMO algorithm**

```
def loadDataSet(fileName):
    dataMat = []; labelMat = []
    fr = open(fileName)
    for line in fr.readlines():
        lineArr = line.strip().split('\t')
        dataMat.append([float(lineArr[0]), float(lineArr[1])])
        labelMat.append(float(lineArr[2]))
    return dataMat,labelMat

def selectJrand(i,m):
    j=i
    while (j==i):
        j = int(random.uniform(0,m))
    return j

def clipAlpha(aj,H,L):
    if aj > H:
```

```
        aj = H
    if L > aj:
        aj = L
    return aj
```

The data that's plotted in figure 6.3 is available in the file testSet.txt. We'll use this dataset to develop the SMO algorithm. The first function in listing 6.1 is our familiar loadDatSet(), which opens up the file and parses each line into class labels, and our data matrix.

The next function, selectJrand(), takes two values. The first one, i, is the index of our first alpha, and m is the total number of alphas. A value is randomly chosen and returned as long as it's not equal to the input i.

The last helper function, clipAlpha(), clips alpha values that are greater than H or less than L. These three helper functions don't do much on their own, but they'll be useful in our classifier.

After you've entered the code from listing 6.1 and saved it, you can try these out using the following:

```
>>> import svmMLiA
>>> dataArr,labelArr = svmMLiA.loadDataSet('testSet.txt')
>>> labelArr
[-1.0, -1.0, 1.0, -1.0, 1.0, 1.0, 1.0, -1.0, -1.0, -1.0, -1.0, -1.0, -1.0,
1.0...
```

You can see that the class labels are -1 and 1 rather than 0 and 1.

Now that we have these working, we're ready for our first version of the SMO algorithm.

Pseudocode for this function would look like this:

Create an alphas vector filled with 0s
While the number of iterations is less than MaxIterations:
    For every data vector in the dataset:
        If the data vector can be optimized:
            Select another data vector at random
            Optimize the two vectors together
            If the vectors can't be optimized → break
    If no vectors were optimized → increment the iteration count

The code in listing 6.2 is a working version of the SMO algorithm. In Python, if we end a line with \, the interpreter will assume the statement is continued on the next line. There are a number of long lines in the following code that need to be broken up, so I've used the \ symbol for this. Open the file svmMLiA.py and enter the code from the following listing.

Listing 6.2   The simplified SMO algorithm

```
def smoSimple(dataMatIn, classLabels, C, toler, maxIter):
    dataMatrix = mat(dataMatIn); labelMat = mat(classLabels).transpose()
    b = 0; m,n = shape(dataMatrix)
```

```
        alphas = mat(zeros((m,1)))
        iter = 0
        while (iter < maxIter):
            alphaPairsChanged = 0
            for i in range(m):                                          Enter optimization  ❶
                fXi = float(multiply(alphas,labelMat).T*\               if alphas can be
                            (dataMatrix*dataMatrix[i,:].T)) + b              changed
                Ei = fXi - float(labelMat[i])
                if ((labelMat[i]*Ei < -toler) and (alphas[i] < C)) or \
                    ((labelMat[i]*Ei > toler) and \
                    (alphas[i] > 0)):
                    j = selectJrand(i,m)                                Randomly
                    fXj = float(multiply(alphas,labelMat).T*\           select
                                (dataMatrix*dataMatrix[j,:].T)) + b     second
                    Ej = fXj - float(labelMat[j])                    ❷ alpha
                    alphaIold = alphas[i].copy();
    alphaJold = alphas[j].copy();
                    if (labelMat[i] != labelMat[j]):
                        L = max(0, alphas[j] - alphas[i])          ❸ Guarantee
                        H = min(C, C + alphas[j] - alphas[i])          alphas stay
                    else:                                                between 0
                        L = max(0, alphas[j] + alphas[i] - C)          and C
                        H = min(C, alphas[j] + alphas[i])
                    if L==H: print "L==H"; continue
                    eta = 2.0 * dataMatrix[i,:]*dataMatrix[j,:].T - \
                        dataMatrix[i,:]*dataMatrix[i,:].T - \
                        dataMatrix[j,:]*dataMatrix[j,:].T
                    if eta >= 0: print "eta>=0"; continue          Update i by same  ❹
                    alphas[j] -= labelMat[j]*(Ei - Ej)/eta          amount as j in
                    alphas[j] = clipAlpha(alphas[j],H,L)          opposite direction
                    if (abs(alphas[j] - alphaJold) < 0.00001): print \
                            "j not moving enough"; continue
                    alphas[i] += labelMat[j]*labelMat[i]*\
                            (alphaJold - alphas[j])
                    b1 = b - Ei- labelMat[i]*(alphas[i]-alphaIold)*\
                        dataMatrix[i,:]*dataMatrix[i,:].T - \
                        labelMat[j]*(alphas[j]-alphaJold)*\
                        dataMatrix[i,:]*dataMatrix[j,:].T
                    b2 = b - Ej- labelMat[i]*(alphas[i]-alphaIold)*\
                        dataMatrix[i,:]*dataMatrix[j,:].T - \
                        labelMat[j]*(alphas[j]-alphaJold)*\          Set the       ❺
                        dataMatrix[j,:]*dataMatrix[j,:].T          constant term
                    if (0 < alphas[i]) and (C > alphas[i]): b = b1
                    elif (0 < alphas[j]) and (C > alphas[j]): b = b2
                    else: b = (b1 + b2)/2.0
                    alphaPairsChanged += 1
                    print "iter: %d i:%d, pairs changed %d" % \
                                    (iter,i,alphaPairsChanged)
            if (alphaPairsChanged == 0): iter += 1
            else: iter = 0
            print "iteration number: %d" % iter
        return b,alphas
```

This is one big function, I know. It's probably the biggest one you'll see in this book.
This function takes five inputs: the dataset, the class labels, a constant C, the tolerance,

and the maximum number of iterations before quitting. We've been building functions in this book with a common interface so you can mix and match algorithms and data sources. This function takes lists and inputs and transforms them into NumPy matrices so that you can simplify many of the math operations. The class labels are transposed so that you have a column vector instead of a list. This makes the row of the class labels correspond to the row of the data matrix. You also get the constants m and n from the shape of the dataMatIn. Finally, you create a column matrix for the alphas, initialize this to zero, and create a variable called iter. This variable will hold a count of the number of times you've gone through the dataset without any alphas changing. When this number reaches the value of the input maxIter, you exit.

In each iteration, you set alphaPairsChanged to 0 and then go through the entire set sequentially. The variable alphaPairsChanged is used to record if the attempt to optimize any alphas worked. You'll see this at the end of the loop. First, fXi is calculated; this is our prediction of the class. The error Ei is next calculated based on the prediction and the real class of this instance. If this error is large, then the alpha corresponding to this data instance can be optimized. This condition is tested ❶. In the if statement, both the positive and negative margins are tested. In this if statement, you also check to see that the alpha isn't equal to 0 or C. Alphas will be clipped at 0 or C, so if they're equal to these, they're "bound" and can't be increased or decreased, so it's not worth trying to optimize these alphas.

Next, you randomly select a second alpha, alpha[j], using the helper function described in listing 6.1 ❷. You calculate the "error" for this alpha similar to what you did for the first alpha, alpha[i]. The next thing you do is make a copy of alpha[i] and alpha[j]. You do this with the copy() method, so that later you can compare the new alphas and the old ones. Python passes all lists by reference, so you have to explicitly tell Python to give you a new memory location for alphaIold and alphaJold. Otherwise, when you later compare the new and old values, we won't see the change. You then calculate L and H ❸, which are used for clamping alpha[j] between 0 and C. If L and H are equal, you can't change anything, so you issue the continue statement, which in Python means "quit this loop now, and proceed to the next item in the for loop."

Eta is the optimal amount to change alpha[j]. This is calculated in the long line of algebra. If eta is 0, you also quit the current iteration of the for loop. This step is a simplification of the real SMO algorithm. If eta is 0, there's a messy way to calculate the new alpha[j], but we won't get into that here. You can read Platt's original paper if you really want to know how that works. It turns out this seldom occurs, so it's OK if you skip it. You calculate a new alpha[j] and clip it using the helper function from listing 6.1 and our L and H values.

Next, you check to see if alpha[j] has changed by a small amount. If so, you quit the for loop. Next, alpha[i] is changed by the same amount as alpha[j] but in the opposite direction ❹. After you optimize alpha[i] and alpha[j], you set the constant term b for these two alphas ❺.

Finally, you've finished the optimization, and you need to take care to make sure you exit the loops properly. If you've reached the bottom of the `for` loop without hitting a `continue` statement, then you've successfully changed a pair of alphas and you can increment `alphaPairsChanged`. Outside the `for` loop, you check to see if any alphas have been updated; if so you set `iter` to 0 and continue. You'll only stop and exit the `while` loop when you've gone through the entire dataset `maxIter` number of times without anything changing.

To see this in action, type in the following:

```
>>> b,alphas = svmMLiA.smoSimple(dataArr, labelArr, 0.6, 0.001, 40)
```

The output should look something like this:

```
iteration number: 29
j not moving enough
iteration number: 30
iter: 30 i:17, pairs changed 1
j not moving enough
iteration number: 0
j not moving enough
iteration number: 1
```

This will take a few minutes to converge. Once it's done, you can inspect the results:

```
>>> b
matrix([[-3.84064413]])
```

You can look at the alphas matrix by itself, but there'll be a lot of 0 elements inside. To see the number of elements greater than 0, type in the following:

```
>>> alphas[alphas>0]
matrix([[ 0.12735413,  0.24154794,  0.36890208]])
```

Your results may differ from these because of the random nature of the SMO algorithm. The command `alphas[alphas>0]` is an example of *array filtering*, which is specific to NumPy and won't work with a regular list in Python. If you type in `alphas>0`, you'll get a Boolean array with a true in every case where the inequality holds. Then, applying this Boolean array back to the original matrix will give you a NumPy matrix with only the values that are greater than 0.

To get the number of support vectors, type

```
>>> shape(alphas[alphas>0])
```

To see which points of our dataset are support vectors, type

```
>>> for i in range(100):
...     if alphas[i]>0.0: print dataArr[i],labelArr[i]
```

You should see something like the following:

```
...
[4.6581910000000004, 3.507396] -1.0
[3.4570959999999999, -0.082215999999999997] -1.0
[6.0805730000000002, 0.41888599999999998] 1.0
```

The original dataset with these points circled is shown in figure 6.4.

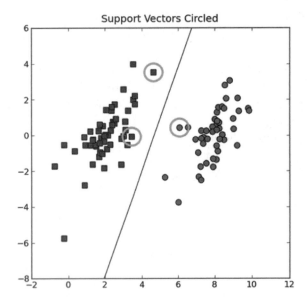

Figure 6.4   SMO sample dataset showing the support vectors circled and the separating hyperplane after the simplified SMO is run on the data

Using the previous settings, I ran this 10 times and took the average time. On my humble laptop this was 14.5 seconds. This wasn't bad, but this is a small dataset with only 100 points. On larger datasets, this would take a long time to converge. In the next section we're going speed this up by building the full SMO algorithm.

6.4   *Speeding up optimization with the full Platt SMO*

The simplified SMO works OK on small datasets with a few hundred points but slows down on larger datasets. Now that we've covered the simplified version, we can move on to the full Platt version of the SMO algorithm. The optimization portion where we change alphas and do all the algebra stays the same. The only difference is how we select which alpha to use in the optimization. The full Platt uses some heuristics that increase the speed. Perhaps in the previous section when executing the example you saw some room for improvement.

The Platt SMO algorithm has an outer loop for choosing the first alpha. This alternates between single passes over the entire dataset and single passes over non-bound alphas. The non-bound alphas are alphas that aren't bound at the limits 0 or C. The pass over the entire dataset is easy, and to loop over the non-bound alphas we'll first create a list of these alphas and then loop over the list. This step skips alphas that we know can't change.

The second alpha is chosen using an inner loop after we've selected the first alpha. This alpha is chosen in a way that will maximize the step size during optimization. In the simplified SMO, we calculated the error Ej after choosing j. This time, we're going to create a global cache of error values and choose from the alphas that maximize step size, or Ei-Ej.

Before we get into the improvements, we're going to need to clean up the code from the previous section. The following listing has a data structure we'll use to clean up the code and three helper functions for caching the E values. Open your text editor and enter the following code.

> **Listing 6.3 Support functions for full Platt SMO**

```
class optStruct:
    def __init__(self,dataMatIn, classLabels, C, toler):
        self.X = dataMatIn
        self.labelMat = classLabels
        self.C = C
        self.tol = toler
        self.m = shape(dataMatIn)[0]
        self.alphas = mat(zeros((self.m,1)))
        self.b = 0
        self.eCache = mat(zeros((self.m,2)))           ❶ Error
                                                          cache
def calcEk(oS, k):
    fXk = float(multiply(oS.alphas,oS.labelMat).T*\
        (oS.X*oS.X[k,:].T)) + oS.b
    Ek = fXk - float(oS.labelMat[k])
    return Ek
                                                       ❷ Inner-loop
def selectJ(i, oS, Ei):                                   heuristic
    maxK = -1; maxDeltaE = 0; Ej = 0
    oS.eCache[i] = [1,Ei]
    validEcacheList = nonzero(oS.eCache[:,0].A)[0]
    if (len(validEcacheList)) > 1:
        for k in validEcacheList:
            if k == i: continue
            Ek = calcEk(oS, k)
            deltaE = abs(Ei - Ek)
            if (deltaE > maxDeltaE):                   ❸ Choose j for
                maxK = k; maxDeltaE = deltaE; Ej = Ek     maximum step size
        return maxK, Ej
    else:
        j = selectJrand(i, oS.m)
        Ej = calcEk(oS, j)
    return j, Ej

def updateEk(oS, k):
    Ek = calcEk(oS, k)
    oS.eCache[k] = [1,Ek]
```

The first thing you do is create a data structure to hold all of the important values. This is done with an object. You don't use it for object-oriented programming; it's used as a data structure in this example. I moved all the data into a structure to save typing when you pass values into functions. You can now pass in one object. I could have done this just as easily with a Python dictionary, but that takes more work trying to access member variables; compare myObject.X to myObject['X']. To accomplish this, you create the class optStruct, which only has the init method. In this method, you populate the member variables. All of these are the same as in the simplified SMO code, but you've added the member variable eCache, which is an mx2 matrix **❶**. The first column is a flag bit stating whether the eCache is valid, and the second column is the actual E value.

The first helper function, calcEk(), calculates an E value for a given alpha and returns the E value. This was previously done inline, but you must take it out because it occurs more frequently in this version of the SMO algorithm.

The next function, selectJ(), selects the second alpha, or the inner loop alpha **❷**. Recall that the goal is to choose the second alpha so that we'll take the maximum step during each optimization. This function takes the error value associated with the first choice alpha (Ei) and the index i. You first set the input Ei to valid in the cache. *Valid* means that it has been calculated. The code nonzero(oS.eCache[:,0].A)[0] creates a list of nonzero values in the eCache. The NumPy function nonzero() returns a list containing indices of the input list that are—you guessed it—not zero. The nonzero() statement returns the alphas corresponding to non-zero E values, not the E values. You loop through all of these values and choose the value that gives you a maximum change **❸**. If this is your first time through the loop, you randomly select an alpha. There are more sophisticated ways of handling the first-time case, but this works for our purposes.

The last helper function in listing 6.3 is updateEk(). This calculates the error and puts it in the cache. You'll use this after you optimize alpha values.

The code in listing 6.3 doesn't do much on its own. But when combined with the optimization and the outer loop, it forms the powerful SMO algorithm.

Next, I'll briefly present the optimization routine, to find our decision boundary. Open your text editor and add the code from the next listing. You've already seen this code in a different format.

Listing 6.4 Full Platt SMO optimization routine

```
def innerL(i, oS):                                    Second-choice heuristic  ❶
    Ei = calcEk(oS, i)
    if ((oS.labelMat[i]*Ei < -oS.tol) and (oS.alphas[i] < oS.C)) or\
        ((oS.labelMat[i]*Ei > oS.tol) and (oS.alphas[i] > 0)):
        j,Ej = selectJ(i, oS, Ei)                           ◄───┘
        alphaIold = oS.alphas[i].copy(); alphaJold = oS.alphas[j].copy();
        if (oS.labelMat[i] != oS.labelMat[j]):
            L = max(0, oS.alphas[j] - oS.alphas[i])
            H = min(oS.C, oS.C + oS.alphas[j] - oS.alphas[i])
        else:
            L = max(0, oS.alphas[j] + oS.alphas[i] - oS.C)
            H = min(oS.C, oS.alphas[j] + oS.alphas[i])
        if L==H: print "L==H"; return 0
        eta = 2.0 * oS.X[i,:]*oS.X[j,:].T - oS.X[i,:]*oS.X[i,:].T - \
            oS.X[j,:]*oS.X[j,:].T
        if eta >= 0: print "eta>=0"; return 0
        oS.alphas[j] -= oS.labelMat[j]*(Ei - Ej)/eta
        oS.alphas[j] = clipAlpha(oS.alphas[j],H,L)        ❷  Updates
        updateEk(oS, j)                                ◄───┘   Ecache
```

```
        if (abs(oS.alphas[j] - alphaJold) < 0.00001):
            print "j not moving enough"; return 0
        oS.alphas[i] += oS.labelMat[j]*oS.labelMat[i]*\
                    (alphaJold - oS.alphas[j])
        updateEk(oS, i)
        b1 = oS.b - Ei- oS.labelMat[i]*(oS.alphas[i]-alphaIold)*\
            oS.X[i,:]*oS.X[i,:].T - oS.labelMat[j]*\
            (oS.alphas[j]-alphaJold)*oS.X[i,:]*oS.X[j,:].T
        b2 = oS.b - Ej- oS.labelMat[i]*(oS.alphas[i]-alphaIold)*\
            oS.X[i,:]*oS.X[j,:].T - oS.labelMat[j]*\
            (oS.alphas[j]-alphaJold)*oS.X[j,:]*oS.X[j,:].T
        if (0 < oS.alphas[i]) and (oS.C > oS.alphas[i]): oS.b = b1
        elif (0 < oS.alphas[j]) and (oS.C > oS.alphas[j]): oS.b = b2
        else: oS.b = (b1 + b2)/2.0
        return 1
    else: return 0
```

❷ **Updates Ecache**

The code in listing 6.4 is almost the same as the smoSimple() function given in listing 6.2. But it has been written to use our data structure. The structure is passed in as the parameter oS. The second important change is that selectJ() from listing 6.3 is used to select the second alpha rather than selectJrand() ❶. Lastly ❷, you update the Ecache after alpha values change. The final piece of code that wraps all of this up is shown in the following listing. This is the outer loop where you select the first alpha. Open your text editor and add the code from this listing to svmMLiA.py.

Listing 6.5 Full Platt SMO outer loop

```
def smoP(dataMatIn, classLabels, C, toler, maxIter, kTup=('lin', 0)):
    oS = optStruct(mat(dataMatIn),mat(classLabels).transpose(),C,toler)
    iter = 0
    entireSet = True; alphaPairsChanged = 0
    while (iter < maxIter) and ((alphaPairsChanged > 0) or (entireSet)):
        alphaPairsChanged = 0
        if entireSet:
            for i in range(oS.m):
                alphaPairsChanged += innerL(i,oS)
            print "fullSet, iter: %d i:%d, pairs changed %d" %\
    (iter,i,alphaPairsChanged)
            iter += 1
        else:
            nonBoundIs = nonzero((oS.alphas.A > 0) * (oS.alphas.A < C))[0]
            for i in nonBoundIs:
                alphaPairsChanged += innerL(i,oS)
                print "non-bound, iter: %d i:%d, pairs changed %d" % \
                    (iter,i,alphaPairsChanged)
            iter += 1
        if entireSet: entireSet = False
        elif (alphaPairsChanged == 0): entireSet = True
        print "iteration number: %d" % iter
    return oS.b,oS.alphas
```

❶ **Go over all values**

❷ **Go over non-bound values**

The code in listing 6.5 is the full Platt SMO algorithm. The inputs are the same as the function smoSimple(). Initially you create the data structure that will be used to hold all of your data. Next, you initialize some variables you'll use to control when you exit the function. The majority of the code is in the while loop, similar to smoSimple() but with a few more exit conditions. You'll exit from the loop whenever the number of iterations exceeds your specified maximum or you pass through the entire set without changing any alpha pairs. The maxIter variable has a different use from smoSimple() because in that function you counted an iteration as a pass through the entire set when no alphas were changed. In this function an iteration is defined as one pass through the loop regardless of what was done. This method is superior to the counting used in smoSimple() because it will stop if there are any oscillations in the optimization.

Inside the while loop is different from smoSimple(). The first for loop goes over any alphas in the dataset ❶. We call innerL() to choose a second alpha and do optimization if possible. A 1 will be returned if any pairs get changed. The second for loop goes over all the non-bound alphas, the values that aren't bound at 0 or C. ❷

You next toggle the for loop to switch between the non-bound loop and the full pass, and print out the iteration number. Finally, the constant b and the alphas are returned.

To see this in action, type the following in your Python shell:

```
>>> dataArr,labelArr = svmMLiA.loadDataSet('testSet.txt')
>>> b,alphas = svmMLiA.smoP(dataArr, labelArr, 0.6, 0.001, 40)
non-bound, iter: 2 i:54, pairs changed 0
non-bound, iter: 2 i:55, pairs changed 0
iteration number: 3
fullSet, iter: 3 i:0, pairs changed 0
fullSet, iter: 3 i:1, pairs changed 0
fullSet, iter: 3 i:2, pairs changed 0
```

You can inspect b and alphas similarly to what you did here. Was this method faster? On my humble laptop I did this algorithm with the settings listed previously 10 times and took the average. The average time on my machine was 0.78 seconds. Compare this to smoSimple() on the same dataset, which took an average of 14.5 seconds. The results will be even better on larger datasets, and there are many ways to make this even faster.

What happens if you change the tolerance value? How about if you change the value of C? I mentioned briefly at the end of section 6.2 that the constant C gives weight to different parts of the optimization problem. C controls the balance between making sure all of the examples have a margin of at least 1.0 and making the margin as wide as possible. If C is large, the classifier will try to make all of the examples properly classified by the separating hyperplane. The results from this optimization run are shown in figure 6.5. Comparing figure 6.5 to 6.4 you see that there are more support vectors in figure 6.5. If you recall, figure 6.4 was generated by our simplified algorithm, which randomly picked pairs of alphas. This method worked, but it wasn't as good as the full version of the algorithm, which covered the entire dataset. You may also think that the support vectors chosen should always be closest to the separating hyperplane. Given the settings we have for C, the support vectors circled give us a

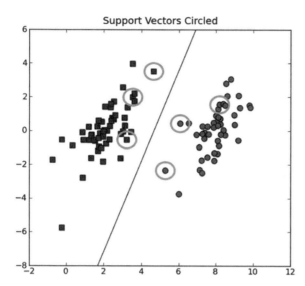

Figure 6.5 Support vectors shown after the full SMO algorithm is run on the dataset. The results are slightly different from those in figure 6.4.

solution that satisfies the algorithm. When you have a dataset that isn't linearly separable, you'll see the support vectors bunch up closer to the hyperplane.

You might be thinking, "We just spent a lot of time figuring out the alphas, but how do we use this to classify things?" That's not a problem. You first need to get the hyperplane from the alphas. This involves calculating ws. The small function listed here will do that for you:

```
def calcWs(alphas,dataArr,classLabels):
    X = mat(dataArr); labelMat = mat(classLabels).transpose()
    m,n = shape(X)
    w = zeros((n,1))
    for i in range(m):
        w += multiply(alphas[i]*labelMat[i],X[i,:].T)
    return w
```

The most important part of the code is the `for` loop, which just multiplies some things together. If you looked at any of the alphas we calculated earlier, remember that most of the alphas are 0s. The non-zero alphas are our support vectors. This `for` loop goes over all the pieces of data in our dataset, but only the support vectors matter. You could just as easily throw out those other data points because they don't contribute to the w calculations.

To use the function listed previously, type in the following:

```
>>> ws=svmMLiA.calcWs(alphas,dataArr,labelArr)
>>> ws
array([[ 0.65307162],
    [-0.17196128]])
```

Now to classify something, say the first data point, type in this:

```
>>> datMat=mat(dataArr)
>>> datMat[0]*mat(ws)+b
matrix([[-0.92555695]])
```

If this value is greater than 0, then its class is a 1, and the class is -1 if it's less than 0. For point 0 you should then have a label of -1. Check to make sure this is true:

```
>>> labelArr[0]
-1.0
```

Now check to make sure other pieces of data are properly classified:

```
>>> datMat[2]*mat(ws)+b
matrix([[ 2.30436336]])
>>> labelArr[2]
1.0
>>> datMat[1]*mat(ws)+b
matrix([[-1.36706674]])
>>> labelArr[1]
-1.0
```

Compare these results to figure 6.5 to make sure it makes sense.

Now that we can successfully train our classifier, I'd like to point out that the two classes fit on either side of a straight line. If you look at figure 6.1, you can probably find shapes that would separate the two classes. What if you want your classes to be inside a circle or outside a circle? We'll next talk about a way you can change the classifier to account for different shapes of regions separating your data.

6.5 Using kernels for more complex data

Consider the data in figure 6.6. This is similar to the data in figure 6.1, frame C. Earlier, this was used to describe data that isn't linearly separable. Clearly there's some pattern in this data that we can recognize. Is there a way we can use our powerful tools to capture this pattern in the same way we did for the linear data? Yes, there is. We're going to use something called a *kernel* to transform our data into a form that's easily understood by our classifier. This section will explain kernels and how we can use them to support vector machines. Next, you'll see one popular type of kernel called the *radial bias function*, and finally we'll apply this to our existing classifier.

6.5.1 Mapping data to higher dimensions with kernels

The points in figure 6.1 are in a circle. The human brain can recognize that. Our classifier, on the other hand, can only recognize greater than or less than 0. If we just plugged in our X and Y coordinates, we wouldn't get good results. You can probably think of some ways to change the circle data so that instead of X and Y, you'd have some new variables that would be better on the greater-than- or less-than-0 test. This is an example of transforming the data from one feature space to another so that you can deal with it easily with your existing tools. Mathematicians like to call this *mapping from one feature space to another feature space*. Usually, this mapping goes from a lower-dimensional feature space to a higher-dimensional space.

This mapping from one feature space to another is done by a *kernel*. You can think of the kernel as a wrapper or interface for the data to translate it from a difficult formatting to an easier formatting. If this mapping from a feature space to another feature

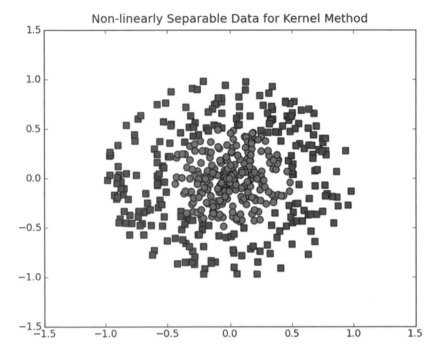

Figure 6.6 **This data can't be easily separated with a straight line in two dimensions, but it's obvious that some pattern exists separating the squares and the circles.**

space sounds confusing, you can think of it as another distance metric. Earlier we encountered distance metrics. There were many different ways to measure the distance, and the same is true with kernels, as you'll see soon. After making the substitution, we can go about solving this linear problem in high-dimensional space, which is equivalent to solving a nonlinear problem in low-dimensional space.

One great thing about the SVM optimization is that all operations can be written in terms of *inner products*. Inner products are two vectors multiplied together to yield a scalar or single number. We can replace the inner products with our kernel functions without making simplifications. Replacing the inner product with a kernel is known as the *kernel trick* or *kernel substation*.

Kernels aren't unique to support vector machines. A number of other machine-learning algorithms can use kernels. A popular kernel is the radial bias function, which we'll introduce next.

6.5.2 *The radial bias function as a kernel*

The *radial bias function* is a kernel that's often used with support vector machines. A radial bias function is a function that takes a vector and outputs a scalar based on the vector's distance. This distance can be either from 0,0 or from another vector. We'll use the Gaussian version, which can be written as

$$k(x,y) = exp\left(\frac{-\|x - y\|^2}{2\sigma^2}\right)$$

where σ is a user-defined parameter that determines the "reach," or how quickly this falls off to 0.

This Gaussian version maps the data from its feature space to a higher feature space, infinite dimensional to be specific, but don't worry about that for now. This is a common kernel to use because you don't have to figure out exactly how your data behaves, and you'll get good results with this kernel. In our example we have data that's basically in a circle; we could have looked over the data and realized we only needed to measure the distance to the origin; however, if we encounter a new dataset that isn't in that format, then we're in big trouble. We'll get great results with this Gaussian kernel, and we can use it on many other datasets and get low error rates there too.

If you add one function to our svmMLiA.py file and make a few modifications, you'll be able to use kernels with our existing code. Open your svmMLiA.py code and enter the function kernelTrans(). Also, modify our class, optStruct, so that it looks like the code given in the following listing.

Listing 6.6   Kernel transformation function

```
def kernelTrans(X, A, kTup):
    m,n = shape(X)
    K = mat(zeros((m,1)))
    if kTup[0]=='lin': K = X * A.T
    elif kTup[0]=='rbf':
        for j in range(m):
            deltaRow = X[j,:] - A
            K[j] = deltaRow*deltaRow.T          ❶ Element-wise
        K = exp(K /(-1*kTup[1]**2))                 division
    else: raise NameError('Houston We Have a Problem -- \
    That Kernel is not recognized')
    return K

class optStruct:
    def __init__(self,dataMatIn, classLabels, C, toler, kTup):
        self.X = dataMatIn
        self.labelMat = classLabels
        self.C = C
        self.tol = toler
        self.m = shape(dataMatIn)[0]
        self.alphas = mat(zeros((self.m,1)))
        self.b = 0
        self.eCache = mat(zeros((self.m,2)))
        self.K = mat(zeros((self.m,self.m)))
        for i in range(self.m):
            self.K[:,i] = kernelTrans(self.X, self.X[i,:], kTup)
```

I think it's best to look at our new version of optStruct. This has everything the same as the previous optStruct with one new input: kTup. This kTup is a generic tuple that contains the information about the kernel. You'll see this in action in a little bit. At the end of the initialization method a matrix K gets created and then populated by calling a function kernelTrans(). This global K gets calculated once. Then, when you want to use the kernel, you call it. This saves some redundant computations as well.

When the matrix K is being computed, the function kernelTrans() is called multiple times. This takes three inputs: two numeric types and a tuple. The tuple kTup holds information about the kernel. The first argument in the tuple is a string describing what type of kernel should be used. The other arguments are optional arguments that may be needed for a kernel. The function first creates a column vector and then checks the tuple to see which type of kernel is being evaluated. Here, only two choices are given, but you can expand this to many more by adding in other elif statements.

In the case of the linear kernel, a dot product is taken between the two inputs, which are the full dataset and a row of the dataset. In the case of the radial bias function, the Gaussian function is evaluated for every element in the matrix in the for loop. After the for loop is finished, you apply the calculations over the entire vector. It's worth mentioning that in NumPy matrices the division symbol means element-wise rather than taking the inverse of a matrix, as would happen in MATLAB. ❶

Lastly, you raise an exception if you encounter a tuple you don't recognize. This is important because you don't want the program to continue in this case.

Code was changed to use the kernel functions in two preexisting functions: innerL() and calcEk(). The changes are shown in listing 6.7. I hate to list them out like this. But relisting the entire functions would take over 90 lines, and I don't think anyone would be happy with that. You can copy the code from the source code download to get these changes without manually adding them. Here are the changes:

Listing 6.7 Changes to innerL() and calcEk() needed to user kernels

```
innerL():
                      .
                      .
                      .

eta = 2.0 * oS.K[i,j] - oS.K[i,i] - oS.K[j,j]
                      .
                      .
                      .

b1 = oS.b - Ei- oS.labelMat[i]*(oS.alphas[i]-alphaIold)*oS.K[i,i] -\
                oS.labelMat[j]*(oS.alphas[j]-alphaJold)*oS.K[i,j]
b2 = oS.b - Ej- oS.labelMat[i]*(oS.alphas[i]-alphaIold)*oS.K[i,j]-\
                oS.labelMat[j]*(oS.alphas[j]-alphaJold)*oS.K[j,j]
                      .
                      .
                      .

def calcEk(oS, k):
    fXk = float(multiply(oS.alphas,oS.labelMat).T*oS.K[:,k] + oS.b)
    Ek = fXk - float(oS.labelMat[k])
    return Ek
```

Now that you see how to apply a kernel during training, let's see how you'd use it during testing.

6.5.3 *Using a kernel for testing*

We're going to create a classifier that can properly classify the data points in figure 6.6. We'll create a classifier that uses the radial bias kernel. The function earlier had one user-defined input: σ. We need to figure out how big to make this. We'll create a function to train and test the classifier using the kernel. The function is shown in the following listing. Open your text editor and add in the function testRbf().

Listing 6.8 Radial bias test function for classifying with a kernel

```
def testRbf(k1=1.3):
    dataArr,labelArr = loadDataSet('testSetRBF.txt')
    b,alphas = smoP(dataArr, labelArr, 200, 0.0001, 10000, ('rbf', k1))
    datMat=mat(dataArr); labelMat = mat(labelArr).transpose()
    svInd=nonzero(alphas.A>0)[0]
    sVs=datMat[svInd]                                          Create matrix of
    labelSV = labelMat[svInd];                                 support vectors
    print "there are %d Support Vectors" % shape(sVs)[0]
    m,n = shape(datMat)
    errorCount = 0
    for i in range(m):
        kernelEval = kernelTrans(sVs,datMat[i,:],('rbf', k1))
        predict=kernelEval.T * multiply(labelSV,alphas[svInd]) + b
        if sign(predict)!=sign(labelArr[i]): errorCount += 1
    print "the training error rate is: %f" % (float(errorCount)/m)
    dataArr,labelArr = loadDataSet('testSetRBF2.txt')
    errorCount = 0
    datMat=mat(dataArr); labelMat = mat(labelArr).transpose()
    m,n = shape(datMat)
    for i in range(m):
        kernelEval = kernelTrans(sVs,datMat[i,:],('rbf', k1))
        predict=kernelEval.T * multiply(labelSV,alphas[svInd]) + b
        if sign(predict)!=sign(labelArr[i]): errorCount += 1
    print "the test error rate is: %f" % (float(errorCount)/m)
```

This code only has one input, and that's optional. The input is the user-defined variable for the Gaussian radial bias function. The code is mostly a collection of stuff you've done before. The dataset is loaded from a file. Then, you run the Platt SMO algorithm on this, with the option 'rbf' for a kernel.

After the optimization finishes, you make matrix copies of the data to use in matrix math later, and you find the non-zero alphas, which are our support vectors. You also take the labels corresponding to the support vectors and the alphas. Those are the only values you'll need to do classification.

The most important lines in this whole listing are the first two lines in the for loops. These show how to classify with a kernel. You first use the kernelTrans() function you used in the structure initialization method. After you get the transformed data, you do a multiplication with the alphas and the labels. The other important thing to note in these lines is how you use only the data for the support vectors. The rest of the data can be tossed out.

The second for loop is a repeat of the first one but with a different dataset—the test dataset. You now can compare how different settings perform on the test set and the training set.

To test out the code from listing 6.8, enter the following at the Python shell:

```
>>> reload(svmMLiA)
<module 'svmMLiA' from 'svmMLiA.pyc'>
>>> svmMLiA.testRbf()
                   .
                 .
               .
fullSet, iter: 11 i:497, pairs changed 0
fullSet, iter: 11 i:498, pairs changed 0
fullSet, iter: 11 i:499, pairs changed 0
iteration number: 12
there are 27 Support Vectors
the training error rate is: 0.030000
the test error rate is: 0.040000
```

You can play around with the k1 parameter to see how the test error, training error, and number of support vectors change with k1. The first example with sigma very small (0.1) is shown in figure 6.7.

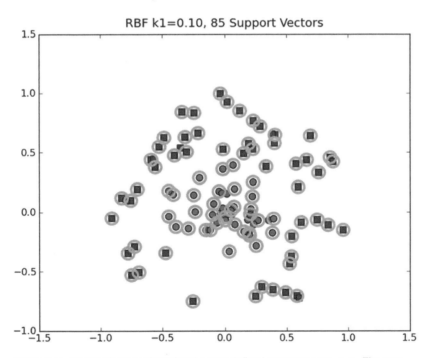

Figure 6.7 Radial bias function with the user-defined parameter k1=0.1. The user-defined parameter reduces the influence of each support vector, so you need more support vectors.

In figure 6.7 we have 100 data points, and 85 of them are support vectors. The optimization algorithm found it needed these points in order to properly classify the data. This should give you the intuition that the reach of the radial bias is too small. You can increase sigma and see how the error rate changes. I increased sigma and made another plot, shown in figure 6.8.

Compare figure 6.8 with figure 6.7. Now we have only 27 support vectors. This is much smaller. If you watch the output of the function `testRbf()`, you'll see that the test error has gone down too. This dataset has an optimum somewhere around this setting. If you make the sigma smaller, you'll get a lower training error but a higher testing error.

There is an optimum number of support vectors. The beauty of SVMs is that they classify things efficiently. If you have too few support vectors, you may have a poor decision boundary (this will be demonstrated in the next example). If you have too many support vectors, you're using the whole dataset every time you classify something—that's called k-Nearest Neighbors.

Feel free to play around with other settings in the SMO algorithm or to create new kernels. We're now going to put our support vector machines to use with some larger data and compare it with a classifier you saw earlier.

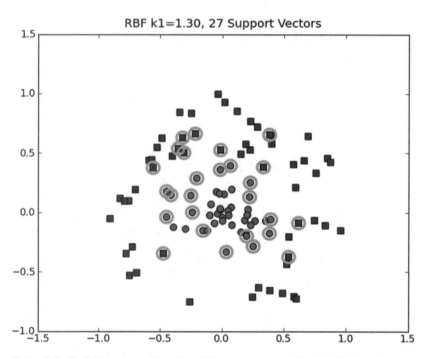

Figure 6.8   Radial bias kernel function with user parameter `k1=1.3`. Here we have fewer support vectors than in figure 6.7. The support vectors are bunching up around the decision boundary.

6.6　*Example: revisiting handwriting classification*

Consider the following hypothetical situation. Your manager comes to you and says, "That handwriting recognition program you made is great, but it takes up too much memory and customers can't download our application over the air. (At the time of writing there's a 10 MB limit on certain applications downloaded over the air. I'm sure this will be laughable at some point in the future.) We need you to keep the same performance with less memory used. I told the CEO you'd have this ready in a week. How long will it take?" I'm not sure how you'd respond, but if you wanted to comply with their request, you could consider using support vector machines. The k-Nearest Neighbors algorithm used in chapter 2 works well, but you have to carry around all the training examples. With support vector machines, you can carry around far fewer examples (only your support vectors) and achieve comparable performance.

Example: digit recognition with SVMs

1. Collect: Text file provided.

2. Prepare: Create vectors from the binary images.

3. Analyze: Visually inspect the image vectors.

4. Train: Run the SMO algorithm with two different kernels and different settings for the radial bias kernel.

5. Test: Write a function to test the different kernels and calculate the error rate.

6. Use: A full application of image recognition requires some image processing, which we won't get into.

Using some of the code from chapter 2 and the SMO algorithm, let's build a system to test a classifier on the handwritten digits. Open svmMLiA.py and copy over the function `img2vector()` from knn.py in chapter 2. Then, add the code in the following listing.

Listing 6.9　Support vector machine handwriting recognition

```
def loadImages(dirName):
    from os import listdir
    hwLabels = []
    trainingFileList = listdir(dirName)
    m = len(trainingFileList)
    trainingMat = zeros((m,1024))
    for i in range(m):
        fileNameStr = trainingFileList[i]
        fileStr = fileNameStr.split('.')[0]
        classNumStr = int(fileStr.split('_')[0])
        if classNumStr == 9: hwLabels.append(-1)
        else: hwLabels.append(1)
        trainingMat[i,:] = img2vector('%s/%s' % (dirName, fileNameStr))
    return trainingMat, hwLabels
```

```
def testDigits(kTup=('rbf', 10)):
    dataArr,labelArr = loadImages('trainingDigits')
    b,alphas = smoP(dataArr, labelArr, 200, 0.0001, 10000, kTup)
    datMat=mat(dataArr); labelMat = mat(labelArr).transpose()
    svInd=nonzero(alphas.A>0)[0]
    sVs=datMat[svInd]
    labelSV = labelMat[svInd];
    print "there are %d Support Vectors" % shape(sVs)[0]
    m,n = shape(datMat)
    errorCount = 0
    for i in range(m):
        kernelEval = kernelTrans(sVs,datMat[i,:],kTup)
        predict=kernelEval.T * multiply(labelSV,alphas[svInd]) + b
        if sign(predict)!=sign(labelArr[i]): errorCount += 1
    print "the training error rate is: %f" % (float(errorCount)/m)
    dataArr,labelArr = loadImages('testDigits')
    errorCount = 0
    datMat=mat(dataArr); labelMat = mat(labelArr).transpose()
    m,n = shape(datMat)
    for i in range(m):
        kernelEval = kernelTrans(sVs,datMat[i,:],kTup)
        predict=kernelEval.T * multiply(labelSV,alphas[svInd]) + b
        if sign(predict)!=sign(labelArr[i]): errorCount += 1
    print "the test error rate is: %f" % (float(errorCount)/m)
```

The function loadImages() appeared as part of handwritingClassTest() earlier in kNN.py. It has been refactored into its own function. The only big difference is that in kNN.py this code directly applied the class label. But with support vector machines, you need a class label of -1 or +1, so if you encounter a 9 it becomes -1; otherwise, the label is +1. Actually, support vector machines are only a binary classifier. They can only choose between +1 and -1. Creating a multiclass classifier with SVMs has been studied and compared. If you're interested, I suggest you read a paper called "A Comparison of Methods for Multiclass Support Vector Machines" by C. W. Hus et al.[4] Because we're doing binary classification, I've taken out all of the data except the 1 and 9 digits.

The next function, testDigits(), isn't super new. It's almost the exact same code as testRbf(), except it calls loadImages() to get the class labels and data. The other small difference is that the kernel tuple kTup is now an input, whereas it was assumed that you were using the rbf kernel in testRbf(). If you don't add any input arguments to testDigits(), it will use the default of ('rbf', 10) for kTup.

After you've entered the code from listing 6.9, save svmMLiA.py and type in the following:

```
>>> svmMLiA.testDigits(('rbf', 20))
            .
            .
            .
L==H
fullSet, iter: 3 i:401, pairs changed 0
iteration number: 4
```

---

[4] C. W. Hus, and C. J. Lin, "A Comparison of Methods for Multiclass Support Vector Machines," *IEEE Transactions on Neural Networks* 13, no. 2 (March 2002), 415–25.

```
there are 43 Support Vectors
the training error rate is: 0.017413
the test error rate is: 0.032258
```

I tried different values for sigma as well as trying the linear kernel and summarized them in table 6.1.

Table 6.1 Handwritten digit performance for different kernel settings

Kernel, settings	Training error (%)	Test error (%)	# Support vectors
RBF, 0.1	0	52	402
RBF, 5	0	3.2	402
RBF, 10	0	0.5	99
RBF, 50	0.2	2.2	41
RBF, 100	4.5	4.3	26
Linear	2.7	2.2	38

The results in table 6.1 show that we achieve a minimum test error with the radial bias function kernel somewhere around 10. This is much larger than our previous example, where our minimum test error was roughly 1.3. Why is there such a huge difference? The data is different. In the handwriting data, we have 1,024 features that could be as high as 1.0. In the example in section 6.5, our data varied from -1 to 1, but we had only two features. How can you tell what settings to use? To be honest, I didn't know when I was writing this example. I just tried some different settings. The answer is also sensitive to the settings of C. There are other formulations of the SVM that bring C into the optimization procedure, such as v-SVM. A good discussion about v-SVM can be found in chapter 3 of *Pattern Recognition*, by Sergios Theodoridis and Konstantinos Koutroumbas.[5]

It's interesting to note that the minimum training error doesn't correspond to a minimum number of support vectors. Also note that the linear kernel doesn't have terrible performance. It may be acceptable to trade the linear kernel's error rate for increased speed of classification, but that depends on your application.

6.7   *Summary*

Support vector machines are a type of classifier. They're called machines because they generate a binary decision; they're decision machines. Support vectors have good generalization error: they do a good job of learning and generalizing on what they've learned. These benefits have made support vector machines popular, and they're considered by some to be the best stock algorithm in unsupervised learning.

---

[5] Sergios Theodoridis and Konstantinos Koutroumbas, *Pattern Recognition*, 4th ed. (Academic Press, 2009), 133.

Support vector machines try to maximize margin by solving a quadratic optimization problem. In the past, complex, slow quadratic solvers were used to train support vector machines. John Platt introduced the SMO algorithm, which allowed fast training of SVMs by optimizing only two alphas at one time. We discussed the SMO optimization procedure first in a simplified version. We sped up the SMO algorithm a lot by using the full Platt version over the simplified version. There are many further improvements that you could make to speed it up even further. A commonly cited reference for further speed-up is the paper titled "Improvements to Platt's SMO Algorithm for SVM Classifier Design."[6]

Kernel methods, or the kernel trick, map data (sometimes nonlinear data) from a low-dimensional space to a high-dimensional space. In a higher dimension, you can solve a linear problem that's nonlinear in lower-dimensional space. Kernel methods can be used in other algorithms than just SVM. The radial-bias function is a popular kernel that measures the distance between two vectors.

Support vector machines are a binary classifier and additional methods can be extended to classification of classes greater than two. The performance of an SVM is also sensitive to optimization parameters and parameters of the kernel used.

Our next chapter will wrap up our coverage of classification by focusing on something called *boosting*. A number of similarities can be drawn between boosting and support vector machines, as you'll soon see.

---

[6] S. S. Keerthi, S. K. Shevade, C. Bhattacharyya, and K. R. K. Murthy, "Improvements to Platt's SMO Algorithm for SVM Classifier Design," *Neural Computation* 13, no. 3,(2001), 637–49.

Improving classification with the AdaBoost meta-algorithm

This chapter covers
- Combining similar classifiers to improve performance
- Applying the AdaBoost algorithm
- Dealing with classification imbalance

If you were going to make an important decision, you'd probably get the advice of multiple experts instead of trusting one person. Why should the problems you solve with machine learning be any different? This is the idea behind a meta-algorithm. Meta-algorithms are a way of combining other algorithms. We'll focus on one of the most popular meta-algorithms called AdaBoost. This is a powerful tool to have in your toolbox because AdaBoost is considered by some to be the best-supervised learning algorithm.

In this chapter we're first going to discuss different ensemble methods of classification. We'll next focus on boosting and AdaBoost, an algorithm for boosting.

We'll then build a decision stump classifier, which is a single-node decision tree. The AdaBoost algorithm will be applied to our decision stump classifier. We'll put our classifier to work on a difficult dataset and see how it quickly outperforms other classification methods.

Finally, before we leave the subject of classification, we're going to talk about a general problem for all classifiers: classification imbalance. This occurs when we're trying to classify items but don't have an equal number of examples. Detecting fraudulent credit card use is a good example of this: we may have 1,000 negative examples for every positive example. How do classifiers work in such a situation? You'll see that you may need to use alternate metrics to evaluate a classifier's performance. This subject isn't unique to AdaBoost, but because this is the last classification chapter, it's a good time to discuss it.

7.1   *Classifiers using multiple samples of the dataset*

AdaBoost

Pros: Low generalization error, easy to code, works with most classifiers, no parameters to adjust

Cons: Sensitive to outliers

Works with: Numeric values, nominal values

You've seen five different algorithms for classification. These algorithms have individual strengths and weaknesses. One idea that naturally arises is combining multiple classifiers. Methods that do this are known as *ensemble methods or meta-algorithms*. Ensemble methods can take the form of using different algorithms, using the same algorithm with different settings, or assigning different parts of the dataset to different classifiers. We'll next talk about two methods that use multiple instances of the same classifier and alter the dataset applied to these classifiers. Finally, we'll discuss how to approach AdaBoost with our general framework for approaching machine-learning problems.

7.1.1   *Building classifiers from randomly resampled data: bagging*

Bootstrap aggregating, which is known as bagging, is a technique where the data is taken from the original dataset S times to make S new datasets. The datasets are the same size as the original. Each dataset is built by randomly selecting an example from the original with replacement. By "with replacement" I mean that you can select the same example more than once. This property allows you to have values in the new dataset that are repeated, and some values from the original won't be present in the new set.

After the S datasets are built, a learning algorithm is applied to each one individually. When you'd like to classify a new piece of data, you'd apply our S classifiers to the new piece of data and take a majority vote.

There are more advanced methods of bagging, such as random forests. A good discussion of these methods can be found at http://www.stat.berkeley.edu/~breiman/ RandomForests/cc_home.htm. We'll now turn our attention to *boosting*: an ensemble method similar to bagging.

7.1.2 Boosting

Boosting is a technique similar to bagging. In boosting and bagging, you always use the same type of classifier. But in boosting, the different classifiers are trained sequentially. Each new classifier is trained based on the performance of those already trained. Boosting makes new classifiers focus on data that was previously misclassified by previous classifiers.

Boosting is different from bagging because the output is calculated from a weighted sum of all classifiers. The weights aren't equal as in bagging but are based on how successful the classifier was in the previous iteration.

There are many versions of boosting, but this chapter will focus on the most popular version, called AdaBoost.

General approach to AdaBoost

1. Collect: Any method.

2. Prepare: It depends on which type of weak learner you're going to use. In this chapter, we'll use decision stumps, which can take any type of data. You could use any classifier, so any of the classifiers from chapters 2–6 would work. Simple classifiers work better for a weak learner.

3. Analyze: Any method.

4. Train: The majority of the time will be spent here. The classifier will train the weak learner multiple times over the same dataset.

5. Test: Calculate the error rate.

6. Use: Like support vector machines, AdaBoost predicts one of two classes. If you want to use it for classification involving more than two classes, then you'll need to apply some of the same methods as for support vector machines.

We're now going to discuss some of the theory behind AdaBoost and why it works so well.

7.2   Train: improving the classifier by focusing on errors

An interesting theoretical question is can we take a weak classifier and use multiple instances of it to create a strong classifier? By "weak" I mean the classifier does a better job than randomly guessing but not by much. That is to say, its error rate is greater than 50% in the two-class case. The "strong" classifier will have a much lower error rate. The AdaBoost algorithm was born out of this question.

AdaBoost is short for *adaptive boosting*. AdaBoost works this way: A weight is applied to every example in the training data. We'll call the weight vector D. Initially, these weights are all equal. A weak classifier is first trained on the training data. The errors from the weak classifier are calculated, and the weak classifier is trained a second time with the same dataset. This second time the weak classifier is trained, the weights of the training set are adjusted so the examples properly classified the first time are weighted less and the examples incorrectly classified in the first iteration are weighted more. To get one answer from all of these weak classifiers, AdaBoost assigns α values to each of the classifiers. The α values are based on the error of each weak classifier. The error ε is given by

$$\varepsilon = \frac{number\ of\ incorrectly\ classified\ examples}{total\ number\ of\ examples}$$

and α is given by

$$\alpha = \frac{1}{2} \ln \left(\frac{1-\varepsilon}{\varepsilon} \right)$$

The AdaBoost algorithm can be seen schematically in figure 7.1.

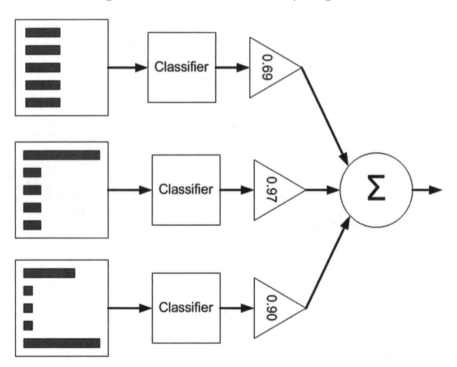

Figure 7.1   Schematic representation of AdaBoost; with the dataset on the left side, the different widths of the bars represent weights applied to each instance. The weighted predictions pass through a classifier, which is then weighted by the triangles (α values). The weighted output of each triangle is summed up in the circle, which produces the final output.

After you calculate α, you can update the weight vector D so that the examples that are correctly classified will decrease in weight and the misclassified examples will increase in weight. D is given by

$$D_i^{(t+1)} = \frac{D_i^{(t)} e^{-\alpha}}{Sum(D)}$$

if correctly predicted and

$$D_i^{(t+1)} = \frac{D_i^{(t)} e^{\alpha}}{Sum(D)}$$

if incorrectly predicted.

After D is calculated, AdaBoost starts on the next iteration. The AdaBoost algorithm repeats the training and weight-adjusting iterations until the training error is 0 or until the number of weak classifiers reaches a user-defined value.

We're going to build up to the full AdaBoost algorithm. But, before we can do that, we need to first write some code to create a weak classifier and to accept weights for the dataset.

7.3 Creating a weak learner with a decision stump

A *decision stump* is a simple decision tree. You saw how decision trees work earlier. Now, we're going to make a decision stump that makes a decision on one feature only. It's a tree with only one split, so it's a stump.

While we're building the AdaBoost code, we're going to first work with a simple dataset to make sure we have everything straight. You can create a new file called adaboost.py and add the following code:

```
def loadSimpData():
    datMat = matrix([[ 1. ,   2.1],
        [ 2. ,   1.1],
        [ 1.3,   1. ],
        [ 1. ,   1. ],
        [ 2. ,   1. ]])
    classLabels = [1.0, 1.0, -1.0, -1.0, 1.0]
    return datMat,classLabels
```

You can see this data in figure 7.2. Try choosing one value on one axis that totally separates the circles from the squares. It's not possible. This is the famous 45 problem that decision trees are notorious for having difficulty with. AdaBoost will need to use multiple decision stumps to properly classify this dataset. By using multiple decision stumps, we'll be able to build a classifier to completely classify the data.

You can load the dataset and class labels by typing in

```
>>> import adaboost
>>> datMat,classLabels=adaboost.loadSimpData()
```

Now that you have the dataset loaded, we can create a few functions to build our decision stump.

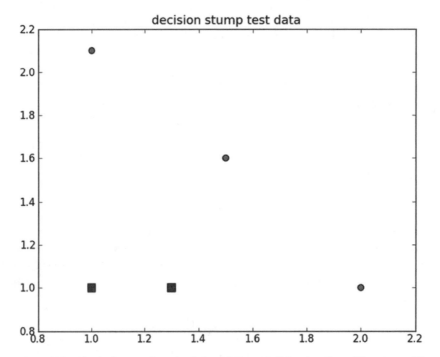

Figure 7.2   Simple data used to check the AdaBoost building functions. It's not possible to choose one threshold on one axis that separates the squares from the circles. AdaBoost will need to combine multiple decision stumps to classify this set without error.

The first one will be used to test if any of values are less than or greater than the threshold value we're testing. The second, more involved function will loop over a weighted version of the dataset and find the stump that yields the lowest error. The pseudo-code will look like this:

Set the minError to +∞
For every feature in the dataset:
     For every step:
      For each inequality:
       Build a decision stump and test it with the weighted dataset
       If the error is less than minError: set this stump as the best stump
Return the best stump

Let's now build this function. Enter the code from the following listing into adaboost.py and save the file.

Listing 7.1   Decision stump–generating functions

```
def stumpClassify(dataMatrix,dimen,threshVal,threshIneq):
    retArray = ones((shape(dataMatrix)[0],1))
    if threshIneq == 'lt':
```

```
            retArray[dataMatrix[:,dimen] <= threshVal] = -1.0
        else:
            retArray[dataMatrix[:,dimen] > threshVal] = -1.0
        return retArray

def buildStump(dataArr,classLabels,D):
    dataMatrix = mat(dataArr); labelMat = mat(classLabels).T
    m,n = shape(dataMatrix)
    numSteps = 10.0; bestStump = {}; bestClasEst = mat(zeros((m,1)))
    minError = inf
    for i in range(n):
        rangeMin = dataMatrix[:,i].min(); rangeMax = dataMatrix[:,i].max();
        stepSize = (rangeMax-rangeMin)/numSteps
        for j in range(-1,int(numSteps)+1):
            for inequal in ['lt', 'gt']:
                threshVal = (rangeMin + float(j) * stepSize)
                predictedVals = \
                        stumpClassify(dataMatrix,i,threshVal,inequal)
                errArr = mat(ones((m,1)))
                errArr[predictedVals == labelMat] = 0
                weightedError = D.T*errArr
                #print "split: dim %d, thresh %.2f, thresh ineqal: \
                        %s, the weighted error is %.3f" %\
                        (i, threshVal, inequal, weightedError)
                if weightedError < minError:
                    minError = weightedError
                    bestClasEst = predictedVals.copy()
                    bestStump['dim'] = i
                    bestStump['thresh'] = threshVal
                    bestStump['ineq'] = inequal
    return bestStump,minError,bestClasEst
```

Calculate
weighted
error ❶

The code in listing 7.1 contains two functions. The first function, `stumpClassify()`, performs a threshold comparison to classify data. Everything on one side of the threshold is thrown into class -1, and everything on the other side is thrown into class +1. This is done using array filtering, by first setting the return array to all 1s and then setting values that don't meet the inequality to -1. You can make this comparison on any feature in the dataset, and you can also switch the inequality from greater than to less than.

The next function, `buildStump()`, will iterate over all of the possible inputs to `stumpClassify()` and find the best decision stump for our dataset. Best here will be with respect to the data weight vector D. You'll see how this is done in a bit. The function starts out by making sure the input data is in the proper format for matrix math. Then, it creates an empty dictionary called `bestStump`, which you'll use to store the classifier information corresponding to the best choice of a decision stump given this weight vector D. The variable `numSteps` will be used to iterate over the possible values of the features. You also initialize the variable `minError` to positive infinity; this variable is used in finding the minimum possible error later.

The main portion of the code is three nested `for` loops. The first one goes over all the features in our dataset. You're considering numeric values, and you calculate the minimum and maximum to see how large your step size should be. Then, the next `for` loop loops over these values. It might make sense to set the threshold outside the extremes of your range, so there are two extra steps outside the range. The last `for` loop toggles your inequality between greater than and less than.

Inside the nested three `for` loops, you call `stumpClassify()` with the dataset and your three loop variables. `stumpClassify()` returns its class prediction based on these loop variables. You next create the column vector `errArr`, which contains a 1 for any value in `predictedVals` that isn't equal to the actual class in `labelMat`. You multiply these errors by the weights in `D` and sum the results to give you a single number: `weightedError`. ❶ This is the line where AdaBoost interacts with the classifier. You're evaluating your classifier based on the weights `D`, not on another error measure. If you want to use another classifier, you'd need to include this calculation to define the best classifier for `D`.

You next print out all the values. This line can be commented out later, but it's helpful in understanding how this function works. Last, you compare the error to your known minimum error, and if it's below it, you save this decision stump in your dictionary `bestStump`. The dictionary, the error, and the class estimates are all returned to the AdaBoost algorithm.

To see this in action, enter the following in the Python shell:

```
>>> D = mat(ones((5,1))/5)
>>> adaboost.buildStump(datMat,classLabels,D)
split: dim 0, thresh 0.90, thresh ineqal: lt, the weighted error is 0.400
split: dim 0, thresh 0.90, thresh ineqal: gt, the weighted error is 0.600
split: dim 0, thresh 1.00, thresh ineqal: lt, the weighted error is 0.400
split: dim 0, thresh 1.00, thresh ineqal: gt, the weighted error is 0.600
                                 .
                                 .
split: dim 1, thresh 2.10, thresh ineqal: lt, the weighted error is 0.600
split: dim 1, thresh 2.10, thresh ineqal: gt, the weighted error is 0.400
({'dim': 0, 'ineq': 'lt', 'thresh': 1.3}, matrix([[ 0.2]]), array([[-1.],
        [ 1.],
        [-1.],
        [-1.],
        [ 1.]]))
```

As `buildStump` iterates over all of the possible values, you can see the output, and finally you can see the dictionary returned. Does this dictionary correspond to the lowest possible weighted error? Are there other settings that have this same error?

The decision stump generator that you made is a simplified version of a decision tree. It's what you'd call the weak learner, which means a weak classification algorithm. Now that you've built the decision stump–generating code, we're ready to move on to the full AdaBoost algorithm. In the next section, we'll create the AdaBoost code to use multiple weak learners.

7.4   *Implementing the full AdaBoost algorithm*

In the last section, we built a classifier that could make decisions based on weighted input values. We now have all we need to implement the full AdaBoost algorithm.

We'll implement the algorithm outlined in section 7.2 with the decision stump built in section 7.3.

Pseudo-code for this will look like this:

For each iteration:
  Find the best stump using buildStump()
  Add the best stump to the stump array
  Calculate alpha
  Calculate the new weight vector – D
  Update the aggregate class estimate
  If the error rate ==0.0 : break out of the for loop

To put this function into Python, open adaboost.py and add the code from the following listing.

Listing 7.2   AdaBoost training with decision stumps

```
def adaBoostTrainDS(dataArr,classLabels,numIt=40):
    weakClassArr = []
    m = shape(dataArr)[0]
    D = mat(ones((m,1))/m)
    aggClassEst = mat(zeros((m,1)))
    for i in range(numIt):
        bestStump,error,classEst = buildStump(dataArr,classLabels,D)
        print "D:",D.T
        alpha = float(0.5*log((1.0-error)/max(error,1e-16)))
        bestStump['alpha'] = alpha
        weakClassArr.append(bestStump)
        print "classEst: ",classEst.T
        expon = multiply(-1*alpha*mat(classLabels).T,classEst)    ❶ Calculate D for next iteration
        D = multiply(D,exp(expon))
        D = D/D.sum()
        aggClassEst += alpha*classEst
        print "aggClassEst: ",aggClassEst.T
        aggErrors = multiply(sign(aggClassEst) !=                 ❷ Aggregate error calculation
                    mat(classLabels).T,ones((m,1)))
        errorRate = aggErrors.sum()/m
        print "total error: ",errorRate,"\n"
        if errorRate == 0.0: break
    return weakClassArr
>>> classifierArray = adaboost.adaBoostTrainDS(datMat,classLabels,9)
D: [[ 0.2   0.2   0.2   0.2   0.2]]
classEst:  [[-1.   1. -1. -1.   1.]]
aggClassEst:   [[-0.69314718  0.69314718 -0.69314718 -0.69314718
               0.69314718]]
total error:  0.2

D: [[ 0.5    0.125   0.125   0.125   0.125]]
classEst:  [[ 1.   1. -1. -1. -1.]]
aggClassEst:  [[ 0.27980789  1.66610226 -1.66610226 -1.66610226
               -0.27980789]]
total error:  0.2
```

```
D: [[ 0.28571429   0.07142857   0.07142857   0.07142857   0.5          ]]
classEst:  [[ 1.   1.   1.   1.   1.]]
aggClassEst:  [[ 1.17568763   2.56198199  -0.77022252  -0.77022252
             0.61607184]]
total error:  0.0
```

The AdaBoost algorithm takes the input dataset, the class labels, and one parameter, numIt, which is the number of iterations. This is the only parameter you specify for the whole AdaBoost algorithm.

You set the number of iterations to 9. But the algorithm reached a total error of 0 after the third iteration and quit, so you didn't get to see all nine iterations. Intermediate output from each of the iterations comes from the print statements. You'll comment these out later, but for now let's look at the output to see what's going on under the hood of the AdaBoost algorithm.

The DS at the end of the function names stands for decision stump. Decision stumps are the most popular weak learner in AdaBoost. They aren't the only one you can use. This function is built for decision stumps, but you could easily modify it for other base classifiers. Any classifier will work. You could use any of the algorithms we explored in the first part of this book. The algorithm will output an array of decision stumps, so you first create a new Python list to store these. You next get m, the number of data points in your dataset, and create a column vector, D.

The vector D is important. It holds the weight of each piece of data. Initially, you'll set all of these values equal. On subsequent iterations, the AdaBoost algorithm will increase the weight of the misclassified pieces of data and decrease the weight of the properly classified data. D is a probability distribution, so the sum of all the elements in D must be 1.0. To meet this requirement, you initialize every element to 1/m. You also create another column vector, aggClassEst, which gives you the aggregate estimate of the class for every data point.

The heart of the AdaBoost algorithm takes place in the for loop, which is executed numIt times or until the training error becomes 0. The first thing that is done in this loop is to build a decision stump with the buildStump() function described earlier. This function takes D, the weights vector, and returns the stump with the lowest error using D. The lowest error value is also returned as well as a vector with the estimated classes for this iteration D.

Next, alpha is calculated. This will tell the total classifier how much to weight the output from this stump. The statement max(error,1e-16) is there to make sure you don't have a divide-by-zero error in the case where there's no error. The alpha value is added to the bestStump dictionary, and the dictionary is appended to the list. This dictionary will contain all you need for classification.

The next three lines ❶ are used to calculate new weights D for the next iteration. In the case that you have 0 training error, you want to exit the for loop early. This is calculated ❷ by keeping a running sum of the estimated class in aggClassEst. This value is a floating point number, and to get the binary class you use the sign() function. If the total error is 0, you quit the for loop with the break statement.

Let's look at the intermediate output. Remember, our class labels were [1.0, 1.0, -1.0, -1.0, 1.0]. In the first iteration, all the D values were equal; then only one value, the first data point, was misclassified. So, in the next iteration, the D vector puts 0.5 weight on the first data point because it was misclassified previously. You can see the total class by looking at the sign of aggClassEst. After the second iteration, you can see that the first data point is correctly classified, but the last data point is now wrong. The D value now becomes 0.5 for the last element, and the other values in the D vector are much smaller. Finally, in the third iteration the sign of all the values in aggClassEst matches your class labels and the training error becomes 0, so you can quit.

To see classifierArray type in

```
>>> classifierArray
[{'dim': 0, 'ineq': 'lt', 'thresh': 1.3, 'alpha': 0.69314718055994529},
    {'dim': 1, 'ineq': 'lt', 'thresh': 1.0, 'alpha': 0.9729550745276565},
    {'dim': 0,'ineq': 'lt', 'thresh': 0.90000000000000002, 'alpha':
      0.89587973461402726}]
```

This array contains three dictionaries, which contain all of the information you'll need for classification. You've now built a classifier, and the classifier will reduce the training error to 0 if you wish. How does the test error look? In order to see the test error, you need to write some code for classification. The next section will discuss classification.

7.5 *Test: classifying with AdaBoost*

Once you have your array of weak classifiers and alphas for each classifier, testing is easy. You've already written most of the code in adaBoostTrainDS() in listing 7.2. All you need to do is take the train of weak classifiers from your training function and apply these to an instance. The result of each weak classifier is weighted by its alpha. The weighted results from all of these weak classifiers are added together, and you take the sign of the final weighted sum to get your final answer. The code to do this is given in the next listing. Add the following code to adaboost.py, and then you can use it to classify data with the classifier array from adaboostTrainDS().

Listing 7.3 AdaBoost classification function

```
def adaClassify(datToClass,classifierArr):
    dataMatrix = mat(datToClass)
    m = shape(dataMatrix)[0]
    aggClassEst = mat(zeros((m,1)))
    for i in range(len(classifierArr)):
        classEst = stumpClassify(dataMatrix,classifierArr[i]['dim'],\
                            classifierArr[i]['thresh'],\
                            classifierArr[i]['ineq'])
        aggClassEst += classifierArr[i]['alpha']*classEst
        print aggClassEst
    return sign(aggClassEst)
```

The function in listing 7.3 is adaClassify(), which, as you may have guessed, classifies with a train of weak classifiers. The inputs are datToClass, which can be multiple data instances or just one to be classified, and `classifierArr`, which is an array of weak classifiers. The function `adaClassify()` first converts `datToClass` to a NumPy matrix and gets m, the number of instances in `datToClass`. Then it creates `aggClassEst`, which is a column vector of all 0s. This is the same as `adaBoostTrainDS()`.

Next, you look over all of the weak classifiers in `classifierArr`, and for each of them you get a class estimate from `stumpClassify()`. You saw `stumpClassify()` earlier when you were building stumps. At that time you iterated over all of the possible stump values and chose the stump with the lowest weighted error. Here you're simply applying the stump. This class estimate is multiplied by the alpha value for each stump and added to the total: `aggClassEst`. I've added a `print` statement so you can see how `aggClassEst` evolves with each iteration. Finally, you return the sign of `aggClassEst`, which gives you a +1 if its argument is greater than 0 and a -1 if the argument is less than 0.

Let's see this in action. After you've added the code from listing 7.3, type the following at the Python shell:

```
>>> reload(adaboost)
<module 'adaboost' from 'adaboost.py'>
```

If you don't have the classifier array, you can enter the following:

```
>>> datArr,labelArr=adaboost.loadSimpData()
>>> classifierArr = adaboost.adaBoostTrainDS(datArr,labelArr,30)
```

Now you can classify by typing this:

```
>>> adaboost.adaClassify([0, 0],classifierArr)
[[-0.69314718]]
[[-1.66610226]]
[[-2.56198199]]
matrix([[-1.]])
```

You can see that the answer for point [0,0] gets stronger with each iteration. You can also do this with multiple points:

```
>>> adaboost.adaClassify([[5, 5],[0,0]],classifierArr)
[[ 0.69314718]
         .
         .
[-2.56198199]]
matrix([[ 1.],
        [-1.]])
```

The answer for both points gets stronger with each iteration. In the next section we're going to apply this to a much bigger and harder dataset from the real world.

7.6   *Example: AdaBoost on a difficult dataset*

In this section we're going to try AdaBoost on the dataset from chapter 4. It's the horse colic dataset. In chapter 4 we tried to predict whether a horse with colic would live or die by using logistic regression. Let's see if we can do better with AdaBoost and the decision stumps.

Example: using AdaBoost on a difficult dataset

1. Collect: Text file provided.

2. Prepare: We need to make sure the class labels are +1 and -1, not 1 and 0.

3. Analyze: Manually inspect the data.

4. Train: We'll train a series of classifiers on the data using the `adaBoost-TrainDS()` function.

5. Test: We have two datasets. With no randomization, we can have an apples-to-apples comparison of the AdaBoost results versus the logistic regression results.

6. Use: We'll look at the error rates in this example. But you could create a website that asks a trainer for the horse's symptoms and then predicts whether the horse will live or die.

Before you use the functions from the previous code listings in this chapter, you need to have a way to load data from a file. The familiar `loadDataSet()` is given in the following listing.

Listing 7.4 Adaptive load data function

```
def loadDataSet(fileName):
    numFeat = len(open(fileName).readline().split('\t'))
    dataMat = []; labelMat = []
    fr = open(fileName)
    for line in fr.readlines():
        lineArr =[]
        curLine = line.strip().split('\t')
        for i in range(numFeat-1):
            lineArr.append(float(curLine[i]))
        dataMat.append(lineArr)
        labelMat.append(float(curLine[-1]))
    return dataMat,labelMat
```

The function in listing 7.4 is `loadDataSet()`, which you've seen many times before. It's slightly improved this time because you don't have to specify the number of features in each file. It automatically detects this. The function also assumes that the last feature is the class label.

To use it, enter the following in your Python shell after you've saved adaboost.py:

```
>>> datArr,labelArr = adaboost.loadDataSet('horseColicTraining2.txt')
>>> classifierArray = adaboost.adaBoostTrainDS(datArr,labelArr,10)
total error: 0.284280936455
total error: 0.284280936455
            .
            .
total error: 0.230769230769
>>> testArr,testLabelArr = adaboost.loadDataSet('horseColicTest2.txt')
>>> prediction10 = adaboost.adaClassify(testArr,classifierArray)
To get the number of misclassified examples type in:
```

```
>>> errArr=mat(ones((67,1)))
>>> errArr[prediction10!=mat(testLabelArr).T].sum()
16.0
```

To get the error rate, divide this number by 67.

I've repeated the process for a number of weak classifiers between 1 and 10,000. The results are listed in table 7.1. The test error is excellent for this dataset. If you remember, in chapter 5 we looked at this dataset with logistic regression. At that time, the average error rate was 0.35. With AdaBoost we never have an error rate that high, and with only 50 weak learners we achieved high performance.

If you look at the Test Error column in table 7.1, you'll see that the test error reaches a minimum and then starts to increase. This sort of behavior is known as *overfitting*. It has been claimed in literature that for well-behaved datasets the test error for AdaBoost reaches a plateau and won't increase with more classifiers. Perhaps this dataset isn't "well behaved." It did start off with 30% missing values, and the assumptions made for the missing values were valid for logistic regression but they may not work for a decision tree. If you went back to our dataset and replaced all the 0s with other values—perhaps averages for a given class—would you have better performance?

Number of Classifiers	Training Error	Test Error
1	0.28	0.27
10	0.23	0.24
50	0.19	0.21
100	0.19	0.22
500	0.16	0.25
1000	0.14	0.31
10000	0.11	0.33

Table 7.1   AdaBoost test and training errors for a range of weak classifiers. This dataset is particularly difficult. Usually AdaBoost reaches a test error plateau, and the error doesn't increase with more classifiers.

AdaBoost and support vector machines are considered by many to be the most powerful algorithms in supervised learning. You can draw a number of similarities between the two. You can think of the weak learner in AdaBoost as a kernel in support vector machines. You can also write the AdaBoost algorithm in terms of maximizing a minimum margin. The way these margins are calculated is different and can lead to different results, especially with higher dimensions.

In the next section we're going to leave AdaBoost and talk about a problem common to all classifiers.

7.7   *Classification imbalance*

Before we leave the subject of classification, there's a topic that needs to be addressed. In all six chapters on classification, we assumed that the cost of classifying things is equal. In chapter 5, for example, we built a system to detect whether a horse with stomach pain would end up living or dying. We built the classifier but didn't talk about what happens after classification. Let's say someone brings a horse to us and asks us to predict whether the horse will live or die. We say die, and rather than delay the inevitable, making the animal suffer and incurring veterinary bills, they have it euthanized. Perhaps our prediction was wrong, and the horse would have lived. Our classifier is only 80% accurate, after all. If we predicted this incorrectly, then an expensive animal would have been destroyed, not to mention that a human was emotionally attached to the animal.

How about spam detection? Is it OK to let a few spam messages arrive in your inbox as long as real email never gets put into the spam folder? What about cancer detection? Is it better to tell someone to go for a second opinion as long as you never let someone with a disease go untreated?

The examples for this abound, and it's safe to say that in most cases the costs aren't equal. In this section, we'll examine a different method for measuring performance of our classifiers and some graphical techniques for visualizing the performance of different classifiers with respect to this problem. Then we'll look at two methods of altering our classification algorithms to take into account the costs of making different decisions.

7.7.1 Alternative performance metrics: precision, recall, and ROC

So far in this book we've measured the success of the classification tasks by the error rate. The error rate was the number of misclassified instances divided by the total number of instances tested. Measuring errors this way hides how instances were misclassified. There's a tool commonly used in machine learning that gives you a better view of classification errors called a *confusion matrix*. A confusion matrix for a three-class problem involving predicting animals found around the house is shown in table 7.2.

		Predicted		
		Dog	Cat	Rat
	Dog	24	2	5
Actual	Cat	2	27	0
	Rat	4	2	30

Table 7.2 Confusion matrix for a three-class problem

With a confusion matrix you get a better understanding of the classification errors. If the off-diagonal elements are all zero, then you have a perfect classifier.

Let's consider another confusion matrix, this time for the simple two-class problem. The confusion matrix is given in table 7.3. In the two-class problem, if you correctly classify something as positive, it's called a True Positive, and it's called a True Negative when you properly classify the negative class. The other two possible cases (False Negative and False Positive) are labeled in table 7.3.

		Predicted	
		+1	-1
Actual	+1	True Positive (TP)	False Negative (FN)
	-1	False Positive (FP)	True Negative (TN)

Table 7.3   Confusion matrix for a two-class problem, with different outcomes labeled

With these definitions we can define some new metrics that are more useful than error rate when detection of one class is more important than another class. The first term is *Precision = TP/(TP+FP)*. Precision tells us the fraction of records that were positive from the group that the classifier predicted to be positive. The second term we care about is *Recall = TP/(TP+FN)*. Recall measures the fraction of positive examples the classifier got right. Classifiers with a large recall don't have many positive examples classified incorrectly.

You can easily construct a classifier that achieves a high measure of recall or precision but not both. If you predicted everything to be in the positive class, you'd have perfect recall but poor precision. Creating a classifier that maximizes both precision and recall is a challenge.

Another tool used for measuring classification imbalance is the *ROC curve*. ROC stands for receiver operating characteristic, and it was first used by electrical engineers building radar systems during World War II. An example ROC curve is shown in figure 7.3.

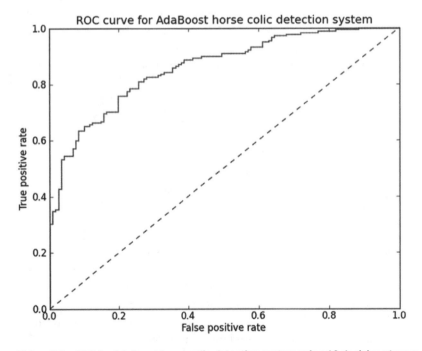

Figure 7.3   ROC for AdaBoost horse colic detection system using 10 decision stumps

The ROC curve in figure 7.3 has two lines, a solid one and a dashed one. The x-axis in figure 7.3 is the number of false positives, and the y-axis is the number of true positives. The ROC curve shows how the two rates change as the threshold changes. The leftmost point corresponds to classifying everything as the negative class, and the rightmost point corresponds to classifying everything in the positive class. The dashed line is the curve you'd get by randomly guessing.

ROC curves can be used to compare classifiers and make cost-versus-benefit decisions. Different classifiers may perform better for different threshold values, and it may make sense to combine them in some way. You wouldn't get this type of insight from simply looking at the error rate of a classifier.

Ideally, the best classifier would be in upper left as much as possible. This would mean that you had a high true positive rate for a low false positive rate. For example, in spam classification this would mean you catch all the spam and don't allow any legitimate emails to get put in the spam folder.

One metric to compare different ROC curves is the area under the curve (AUC). The AUC gives an average value of the classifier's performance and doesn't substitute for looking at the curve. A perfect classifier would have an AUC of 1.0, and random guessing will give you a 0.5.

In order to plot the ROC you need the classifier to give you a numeric score of how positive or negative each instance is. Most classifiers give this to you, but it's usually cleaned up before the final discrete class is delivered. Naïve Bayes gives you a probability. The input to the sigmoid in logistic regression is a numeric value. AdaBoost and SVMs both compute a numeric value that's input to the `sign()` function. All of these values can be used to rank how strong the prediction of a given classifier is. To build the ROC curve, you first sort the instances by their prediction strength. You start with the lowest ranked instance and predict everything below this to be in the negative class and everything above this to be the positive class. This corresponds to the point 1.0,1.0. You move to the next item in the list, and if that is the positive class, you move the true positive rate, but if that instance is in the negative class, you change the true negative rate.

This procedure probably sounds confusing but it will become clear when you look at the code in the following listing. Open adaboost.py and add the following code.

Listing 7.5   ROC plotting and AUC calculating function

```
def plotROC(predStrengths, classLabels):
    import matplotlib.pyplot as plt
    cur = (1.0,1.0)
    ySum = 0.0
    numPosClas = sum(array(classLabels)==1.0)
    yStep = 1/float(numPosClas)
    xStep = 1/float(len(classLabels)-numPosClas)
    sortedIndicies = predStrengths.argsort()          ❶ Get sorted
    fig = plt.figure()                                    index
    fig.clf()
    ax = plt.subplot(111)
    for index in sortedIndicies.tolist()[0]:
```

```
    if classLabels[index] == 1.0:
        delX = 0; delY = yStep;
    else:
        delX = xStep; delY = 0;
        ySum += cur[1]
    ax.plot([cur[0],cur[0]-delX],[cur[1],cur[1]-delY], c='b')
    cur = (cur[0]-delX,cur[1]-delY)
ax.plot([0,1],[0,1],'b--')
plt.xlabel('False Positive Rate'); plt.ylabel('True Positive Rate')
plt.title('ROC curve for AdaBoost Horse Colic Detection System')
ax.axis([0,1,0,1])
plt.show()
print "the Area Under the Curve is: ",ySum*xStep
```

The code in listing 7.5 takes two inputs; the first is a NumPy array or matrix in a row vector form. This is the strength of the classifier's predictions. Our classifier and our training functions generate this before they apply it to the `sign()` function. You'll see this function in action in a bit, but let's discuss the code first. The second input is the `classLabels` you used earlier. You first input `pyplot` and then create a tuple of floats and initialize it to 1.0,1.0. This holds your cursor for plotting. The variable `ySum` is used for calculating the AUC. You next calculate the number of positive instances you have, by using array filtering, and set this value to `numPosClas`. This will give you the number of steps you're going to take in the y direction. You're going to plot in the range of 0.0 to 1.0 on both the x- and y-axes, so to get the y step size you take 1.0/numPosClas. You can similarly get the x step size.

You next get the sorted index ❶, but it's from smallest to largest, so you start at the point 1.0,1.0 and draw to 0,0. The next three lines set up the plot, and then you loop over all the sorted values. The values were sorted in a NumPy array or matrix, but Python needs a list to iterate over, so you call the `tolist()` method. As you're going through the list, you take a step down in the y direction every time you get a class of 1.0, which decreases the true positive rate. Similarly, you take a step backward in the x direction (false positive rate) for every other class. This code is set up to focus only on the 1s so you can use either the 1,0 or +1,-1 class labels.

To compute the AUC, you need to add up a bunch of small rectangles. The width of each of these rectangles will be `xStep`, so you can add the heights of all the rectangles and multiply the sum of the heights by `xStep` once to get the total area. The height sum (`ySum`) increases every time you move in the x direction. Once you've decided whether you're going to move in the x or y direction, you draw a small, straight-line segment from the current point to the new point. The current point, `cur`, is then updated. Finally, you make the plot look nice and display it by printing the AUC to the terminal.

To see this in action, you'll need to alter the last line of `adaboostTrainDS()` to

```
return weakClassArr,aggClassEst
```

in order to get the `aggClassEst` out. Next, type in the following at your Python shell:

```
>>> reload(adaboost)
<module 'adaboost' from 'adaboost.pyc'>
>>> datArr,labelArr = adaboost.loadDataSet('horseColicTraining2.txt')
>>> classifierArray,aggClassEst =
    adaboost.adaBoostTrainDS(datArr,labelArr,10)
>>> adaboost.plotROC(aggClassEst.T,labelArr)
the Area Under the Curve is: 0.858296963506
```

You should also see an ROC plot identical to figure 7.3. This is the performance of our AdaBoost classifier with 10 weak learners. Remember, we had the best performance with 40 weak learners? How does the ROC curve compare? Is the AUC better?

7.7.2 *Manipulating the classifier's decision with a cost function*

Besides tuning the thresholds of our classifier, there are other approaches you can take to aid with uneven classification costs. One such method is known as *cost-sensitive learning*. Consider the cost matrix in table 7.4. The top table encodes the costs of classification as we've been using it up to this point. You calculate the total cost with this cost matrix by TP*0+FN*1+FP*1+TN*0. Now consider the cost matrix in the bottom frame of table 7.4. The total cost using this cost matrix will be TP*-5+FN*1+FP*50+TN*0. Using the second cost matrix, the two types of incorrect classification will have different costs. Similarly, the two types of correct classification will have different benefits. If you know these costs when you're building the classifier, you can select a classifier with the minimum cost.

		Predicted	
		+1	-1
Actual	+1	0	1
	-1	1	0

		Predicted	
		+1	-1
Actual	+1	-5	1
	-1	50	0

Table 7.4   Cost matrix for a two-class problem

There are many ways to include the cost information in classification algorithms. In AdaBoost, you can adjust the error weight vector D based on the cost function. In naïve Bayes, you could predict the class with the lowest expected cost instead of the class with the highest probability. In SVMs, you can use different C parameters in the cost function for the different classes. This gives more weight to the smaller class, which when training the classifier will allow fewer errors in the smaller class.

7.7.3   *Data sampling for dealing with classification imbalance*

Another way to tune classifiers is to alter the data used to train the classifier to deal with imbalanced classification tasks. This is done by either undersampling or oversampling the data. *Oversample* means to duplicate examples, whereas *undersample* means to delete examples. Either way, you're altering the data from its original form. The sampling can be done either randomly or in a predetermined fashion.

Usually there's a rare case that you're trying to identify, such as credit card fraud. As mentioned previously, the rare case is the positive class. You want to preserve as much information as possible about the rare case, so you should keep all of the examples from the positive class and undersample or discard examples from the negative class. One drawback of this approach is deciding which negative examples to toss out. The examples you choose to toss out could carry valuable information that isn't contained in the remaining examples.

One solution for this is to pick samples to discard that aren't near the decision boundary. For example, say you had a dataset with 50 fraudulent credit card transactions and 5,000 legitimate transactions. If you wanted to undersample the legitimate transactions to make the dataset equally balanced, you'd need to throw out 4,950 examples, which may also contain valuable information. This may seem extreme, so an alternative is to use a hybrid approach of undersampling the negative class and oversampling the positive class.

To oversample the positive class, you could replicate the existing examples or add new points similar to the existing points. One approach is to add a data point interpolated between existing data points. This process can lead to overfitting.

7.8   *Summary*

Ensemble methods are a way of combining the predictions of multiple classifiers to get a better answer than simply using one classifier. There are ensemble methods that use different types of classifiers, but we chose to look at methods using only one type of classifier.

Combining multiple classifiers exploits the shortcomings of single classifiers, such as overfitting. Combining multiple classifiers can help, as long as the classifiers are significantly different from each other. This difference can be in the algorithm or in the data applied to that algorithm.

The two types of ensemble methods we discussed are bagging and boosting. In bagging, datasets the same size as the original dataset are built by randomly sampling examples for the dataset with replacement. Boosting takes the idea of bagging a step further by applying a different classifier sequentially to a dataset. An additional ensemble method that has shown to be successful is random forests. Random forests aren't as popular as AdaBoost, so they aren't discussed in this book.

We discussed the most popular variant of boosting, called AdaBoost. AdaBoost uses a weak learner as the base classifier with the input data weighted by a weight vector. In the first iteration the data is equally weighted. But in subsequent iterations the data is weighted more strongly if it was incorrectly classified previously. This adapting to the errors is the strength of AdaBoost.

We built functions to create a classifier using AdaBoost and the weak learner, decision stumps. The AdaBoost functions can be applied to any classifier, as long as the classifier can deal with weighted data. The AdaBoost algorithm is powerful, and it quickly handled datasets that were difficult using other classifiers.

The classification imbalance problem is training a classifier with data that doesn't have an equal number of positive and negative examples. The problem also exists when the costs for misclassification are different from positive and negative examples. We looked at ROC curves as a way to evaluate different classifiers. We introduced precision and recall as metrics to measure the performance classifiers when classification of one class is more important than classification of the other class.

We introduced oversampling and undersampling as ways to adjust the positive and negative examples in a dataset. Another, perhaps better, technique was introduced for dealing with classifiers with unbalanced objectives. This method takes the costs of misclassification into account when training a classifier.

We've introduced a number of powerful classification techniques so far in this book. This is the last chapter on classification, and we'll move on to regression next to complete our study of supervised learning algorithms. Regression is much like classification, but instead of predicting a nominal class, we'll be predicting a continuous value.

Part 2

Forecasting numeric values with regression

This part of the book, chapters 8 and 9, covers regression. Regression is a continuation of supervised learning from chapters 1 through 7. Recall that supervised learning is machine learning when we have a target variable, or something we want to predict. The difference between regression and classification is that in regression our target variable is numeric and continuous.

Chapter 8 covers an introduction to linear regression, locally weighted linear regression, and shrinkage methods. Chapter 9 takes some ideas from tree building in chapter 3 and applies these to regression to create tree-based regression.

Predicting numeric
values: regression

This chapter covers

- Linear regression
- Locally weighted linear regression
- Ridge regression and stagewise linear regression
- Predicting the age of an abalone and an antique selling price

The previous chapters focused on classification that predicts only nominal values for the target variable. With the tools in this chapter you'll be able to start predicting target values that are continuous. You may be asking yourself, "What can I do with these tools?" "Just about anything" would be my answer. Companies may use this for boring things such as sales forecasts or forecasting manufacturing defects. One creative example I've seen recently is predicting the probability of celebrity divorce.

In this chapter, we'll first discuss linear regression, where it comes from, and how to do it in Python. We'll next look at a technique for locally smoothing our estimates to better fit the data. We'll explore *shrinkage* and a technique for getting a regression estimate in "poorly formulated" problems. We'll explore the theoretical notions of *bias* and *variance*. Finally, we'll put all of these techniques to use in forecasting the age of abalone and the future selling price of antique toys. To get the data on the antique toys, we'll first use Python to do some screen scraping. It's an action-packed chapter.

8.1   *Finding best-fit lines with linear regression*

Linear regression

Pros: Easy to interpret results, computationally inexpensive

Cons: Poorly models nonlinear data

Works with: Numeric values, nominal values

Our goal when using regression is to predict a numeric target value. One way to do this is to write out an equation for the target value with respect to the inputs. For example, assume you're trying to forecast the horsepower of your sister's boyfriend's automobile. One possible equation is

```
HorsePower = 0.0015*annualSalary - 0.99*hoursListeningToPublicRadio
```

This is known as a *regression equation*. The values 0.0015 and -0.99 are known as *regression weights*. The process of finding these regression weights is called *regression*. Once you've found the regression weights, forecasting new values given a set of inputs is easy. All you have to do is multiply the inputs by the regression weights and add them together to get a forecast.

When we talk about regression, we often mean linear regression, so the terms *regression* and *linear regression* are used interchangeably in this chapter. Linear regression means you can add up the inputs multiplied by some constants to get the output. There's another type of regression called *nonlinear regression* in which this isn't true; the output may be a function of the inputs multiplied together. For example, our horsepower equation written as

```
HorsePower = 0.0015*annualSalary/hoursListeningToPublicRadio
```

is an example of a nonlinear regression. We won't deal with nonlinear regression in this chapter.

General approach to regression

1. Collect: Any method.

2. Prepare: We'll need numeric values for regression. Nominal values should be mapped to binary values.

3. Analyze: It's helpful to visualized 2D plots. Also, we can visualize the regression weights if we apply shrinkage methods.

(continued)

4. Train: Find the regression weights.

5. Test: We can measure the R2, or correlation of the predicted value and data, to measure the success of our models.

6. Use: With regression, we can forecast a numeric value for a number of inputs. This is an improvement over classification because we're predicting a continuous value rather than a discrete category.

The origins of regression

What we know today as regression was invented by the cousin of Charles Darwin, Francis Galton. Galton did his first regression in 1877 to estimate the size of pea seeds based on the size of their parents' seeds. Galton performed regression on a number of things, including the heights of humans. He noticed that if parents were above average in height, their children also tended to be above average but not as much as their parents. The heights of children were regressing toward a mean value. Galton noticed this behavior in a number of things he studied, and so the technique is called regression, despite the English word having no relationship to predicting numeric values.[†]

[†] Ian Ayres, *Super Crunchers* (Bantam Books, 2008), 24.

How can we go from a bunch of data to our regression equation? Our input data is in the matrix **X**, and our regression weights in the vector w. For a given piece of data X_1 our predicted value is given by $y_1 = X^T_1 w$. We have the Xs and ys, but how can we find the ws? One way is to find the ws that minimize the error. We define error as the difference between predicted y and the actual y. Using just the error will allow positive and negative values to cancel out, so we use the squared error.

We can write this as

$$\sum_{i=1}^{m} (y_i - x_i^T w)^2$$

We can also write this in matrix notation as $(y-\mathbf{X}w)^T (y-\mathbf{X}w)$. If we take the derivative of this with respect to w, we'll get $\mathbf{X}^T (y-\mathbf{X}w)$. We can set this to zero and solve for w to get the following equation:

$$\hat{w} = (X^T X)^{-1} X^T y$$

The little symbol on top of the w tells us that this is the best solution we can come up with for w at the moment. The value we have for w is based on the data we have and may not perfectly describe the data, so we use a "hat" to describe our best estimate given the data.

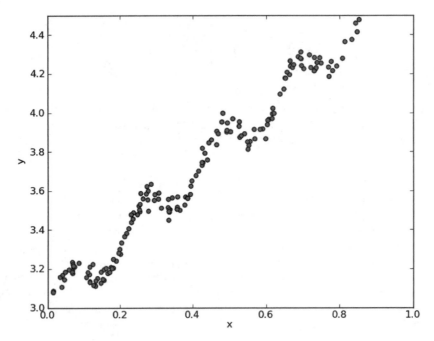

Figure 8.1 Example data from file ex0.txt

Something else to note about the equation is that it uses $\mathbf{X}^T\mathbf{X}^{-1}$, which is a matrix inverse. This equation will work provided the matrix inverse exists. The matrix inverse may not exist, and we'll need to check for this when putting this into code.

Solving this problem is one of the most common applications of statistics, and there are a number of ways to do it other than the matrix method. By using the matrix method with NumPy, we can write a few lines and get an answer. This method is also known as OLS, which stands for "ordinary least squares."

To see this in action, look at the plot in figure 8.1. We'd like to see how to create a best-fit line for this data.

The code in the following listing will allow you to create a best-fit line for the data in figure 8.1. Open a text editor and create a new file called regression.py, and then add the following code.

Listing 8.1 Standard regression function and data-importing functions

```
from numpy import *

def loadDataSet(fileName):
    numFeat = len(open(fileName).readline().split('\t')) - 1
    dataMat = []; labelMat = []
    fr = open(fileName)
    for line in fr.readlines():
        lineArr =[]
        curLine = line.strip().split('\t')
        for i in range(numFeat):
```

```
            lineArr.append(float(curLine[i]))
        dataMat.append(lineArr)
        labelMat.append(float(curLine[-1]))
    return dataMat,labelMat

def standRegres(xArr,yArr):
    xMat = mat(xArr); yMat = mat(yArr).T
    xTx = xMat.T*xMat
    if linalg.det(xTx) == 0.0:
        print "This matrix is singular, cannot do inverse"
        return
    ws = xTx.I * (xMat.T*yMat)
    return ws
```

The first function, `loadDataSet()`, is the same as `loadDataSet()` from chapter 7. This function opens a text file with tab-delimited values and assumes the last value is the target value. The second function, `standRegres()`, is the function that computes the best-fit line. You first load the x and y arrays and then convert them into matrices. Next you compute X^{T}X and then test if its determinate is zero. If the determinate is zero, then you'll get an error when you try to compute the inverse. NumPy has a linear algebra library called linalg, which has a number of useful functions; you can call `linalg.det()` to compute the determinate. If the determinate is nonzero, you compute the ws and return them. If you didn't check to see if the determinate was zero before attempting to compute the inverse, you'd get an error. NumPy's linear algebra library also has a function for solving for unknown matrices, with which you could have written `ws = xTx.I * (xMat.T*yMat)` as `ws = linalg.solve(xTx,xMat.T*yMatT)`.

Let's see this in action. Using `loadDataSet()`, you can import the data into two arrays, one for the X values and one for Y values. The Y values are our target values similar to our class labels in all of the classification algorithms.

```
>>> import regression
>>> from numpy import *
>>> xArr,yArr=regression.loadDataSet('ex0.txt')
```

Let's look at the first two pieces of data:

```
>>> xArr[0:2]
[[1.0, 0.067732000000000001], [1.0, 0.42781000000000002]]
```

The first value is always a 1.0. This is our X0 value, and we assume it's a 1.0 to account for a constant offset. The second value, X1, is our value in the plot.

Now let's see `standRegres()` in action:

```
>>> ws = regression.standRegres(xArr,yArr)
>>> ws
matrix([[ 3.00774324],
        [ 1.69532264]])
```

The variable ws is now our weights, which we multiply by our constant tern, and the second one we multiply by our input variable X1. Because we're assuming X0=1, we'll get y=ws[0]+ws[1]*X1. We also want to call this predicted y something other than the actual data, so this is called yHat. Let's compute yHat with our new ws:

```
>>> xMat=mat(xArr)
>>> yMat=mat(yArr)
>>> yHat = xMat*ws
```

Now we can plot this to see a plot of our data and our best-fit line:

```
>>> import matplotlib.pyplot as plt
>>> fig = plt.figure()
>>> ax = fig.add_subplot(111)
>>> ax.scatter(xMat[:,1].flatten().A[0], yMat.T[:,0].flatten().A[0])
    <matplotlib.collections.CircleCollection object at 0x04ED9D30>
```

These commands create the figure and plot the original data. To plot the best-fit line we've calculated, we need to plot yHat. Pyplot will have a problem if the points on our line are out of order, so we first sort the points in ascending order:

```
>>> xCopy=xMat.copy()
>>> xCopy.sort(0)
>>> yHat=xCopy*ws
>>> ax.plot(xCopy[:,1],yHat)
[<matplotlib.lines.Line2D object at 0x0343F570>]
>>> plt.show()
```

You should see a plot similar to the one in figure 8.2.

You can make a model of almost any dataset, but how good is the model? Consider for a moment the two plots in figure 8.3. If you do a linear regression on both of the plots, you'll get the exact same results. The plots are obviously not the same, but how can you measure the difference? One way you can calculate how well the predicted value, yHat, matches our actual data, y, is with the correlation between the two series.

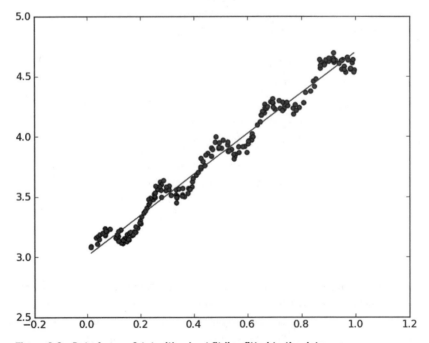

Figure 8.2   Data from ex0.txt with a best-fit line fitted to the data

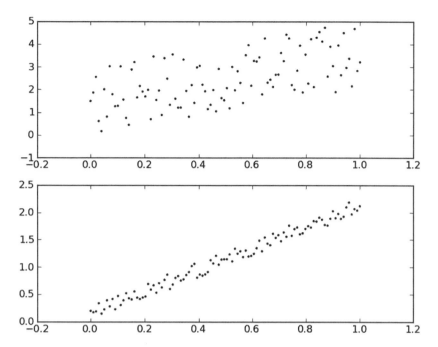

Figure 8.3 Two sets of data, which both give the same regression weights of 0,2.0. The top plot has a correlation coefficient of 0.58, whereas the bottom plot has a correlation coefficient of 0.99.

In Python the NumPy library comes with a command to generate the correlation coefficients. You can calculate the correlation between the estimate output and the actual outputs by the command corrcoef(yEstimate,yActual. Let's try this out on the data points from the previous example.

First, you need to get an estimate, as we did at the beginning of the example:

```
>>> yHat = xMat*ws
```

Now you can look at the correlation coefficients. You need to transpose yMat so that you have both of the vectors as row vectors:

```
>>> corrcoef(yHat.T, yMat)
array([[ 1.        ,  0.98647356],
       [ 0.98647356,  1.        ]])
```

This gives you the correlation between all possible pairs; elements on the diagonal are 1.0 because the correlation between yMat and yMat is perfect. The correlation between yHat and yMat is 0.98.

The best-fit line does a great job of modeling the data as if it were a straight line. But it looks like the data has some other patterns we may want to take advantage of. How can we take advantage of these patterns? One way is to locally adjust our forecast based on the data. We'll discuss such an approach next.

8.2   *Locally weighted linear regression*

One problem with linear regression is that it tends to underfit the data. It gives us the lowest mean-squared error for unbiased estimators. With the model underfit, we aren't getting the best predictions. There are a number of ways to reduce this mean-squared error by adding some bias into our estimator.

One way to reduce the mean-squared error is a technique known as locally weighted linear regression (LWLR). In LWLR we give a weight to data points near our data point of interest; then we compute a least-squares regression similar to section 8.1. This type of regression uses the dataset each time a calculation is needed, similar to kNN. The solution is now given by

$$\hat{w} = (X^T W X)^{-1} X^T W y$$

where W is a matrix that's used to weight the data points.

LWLR uses a kernel something like the kernels demonstrated in support vector machines to weight nearby points more heavily than other points. You can use any kernel you like. The most common kernel to use is a Gaussian. The kernel assigns a weight given by

$$w(i,i) = \exp\left(\frac{\left| x^{(i)} - x \right|}{-2k^2}\right)$$

This builds the weight matrix **W**, which has only diagonal elements. The closer the data point x is to the other points, the larger w(i,i) will be. There also is a user-defined constant k that will determine how much to weight nearby points. This is the only parameter that we have to worry about with LWLR. You can see how different values of k change the weights matrix in figure 8.4.

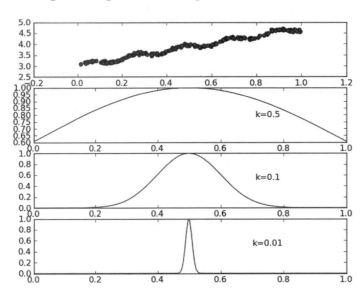

Figure 8.4   Plot showing the original data in the top frame and the weights applied to each piece of data (if we were forecasting the value of x=0.5.) The second frame shows that with k=0.5, most of the data is included, whereas the bottom frame shows that if k=0.01, only a few local points will be included in the regression.

To see this in action, open your text editor and add the code from the following listing to regression.py.

Listing 8.2 Locally weighted linear regression function

```
def lwlr(testPoint,xArr,yArr,k=1.0):
    xMat = mat(xArr); yMat = mat(yArr).T
    m = shape(xMat)[0]
    weights = mat(eye((m)))
    for j in range(m):
        diffMat = testPoint - xMat[j,:]
        weights[j,j] = exp(diffMat*diffMat.T/(-2.0*k**2))
    xTx = xMat.T * (weights * xMat)
    if linalg.det(xTx) == 0.0:
        print "This matrix is singular, cannot do inverse"
        return
    ws = xTx.I * (xMat.T * (weights * yMat))
    return testPoint * ws

def lwlrTest(testArr,xArr,yArr,k=1.0):
    m = shape(testArr)[0]
    yHat = zeros(m)
    for i in range(m):
        yHat[i] = lwlr(testArr[i],xArr,yArr,k)
    return yHat
```

❶ Create diagonal matrix
❷ Populate weights with exponentially decaying values

The code in listing 8.2 is used to generate a yHat estimate for any point in the x space. The function lwlr() creates matrices from the input data similar to the code in listing 8.1; then it creates a diagonal weights matrix called weights. ❶ The weights matrix is a square matrix with as many elements as data points. This assigns one weight to each data point. The function next iterates over all of the data points and computes a value, which decays exponentially as you move away from the testPoint. ❷ The input k controls how quickly the decay happens. After you've populated the weights matrix, you can find an estimate for testPoint similar to standRegres().

The other function in listing 8.2 is lwlrTest(), which will call lwlr() for every point in the dataset. This is helpful for evaluating the size of k.

Let's see this in action. After you've entered the code from listing 8.2 into regression.py, save it and type the following in the Python shell:

```
>>> reload(regression)
<module 'regression' from 'regression.py'>
```

If you need to reload the dataset, you can type in

```
>>> xArr,yArr=regression.loadDataSet('ex0.txt')
```

You can estimate a single point with the following:

```
>>> yArr[0]
3.1765129999999999
>>> regression.lwlr(xArr[0],xArr,yArr,1.0)
matrix([[ 3.12204471]])
>>> regression.lwlr(xArr[0],xArr,yArr,0.001)
matrix([[ 3.20175729]])
```

To get an estimate for all the points in our dataset, you can use `lwlrTest()`:

```
>>> yHat = regression.lwlrTest(xArr, xArr, yArr,0.003)
```

You can inspect yHat, so now let's plot these estimates with the original values. Plot needs the data to be sorted, so let's sort xArr:

```
xMat=mat(xArr)
>>> srtInd = xMat[:,1].argsort(0)
>>> xSort=xMat[srtInd][:,0,:]
```

Now you can plot this with Matplotlib:

```
>>> import matplotlib.pyplot as plt
>>> fig = plt.figure()
>>> ax = fig.add_subplot(111)
>>> ax.plot(xSort[:,1],yHat[srtInd])
[<matplotlib.lines.Line2D object at 0x03639550>]
>>> ax.scatter(xMat[:,1].flatten().A[0], mat(yArr).T.flatten().A[0] , s=2,
        c='red')
<matplotlib.collections.PathCollection object at 0x03859110>
>>> plt.show()
```

You should see something similar to the plot in the bottom frame of figure 8.5. Figure 8.5 has plots for three different values of k. With k=1.0, the weights are so large that they appear to weight all the data equally, and you have the same best-fit line as using standard regression. Using k=0.01 does a much better job of capturing the underlying pattern in the data. The bottom frame in figure 8.5 has k=0.003. This is too noisy and fits the line closely to the data. The bottom panel is an example of overfitting, whereas the top panel is an example of underfitting. You'll see how to quantitatively measure overfitting and underfitting in the next section.

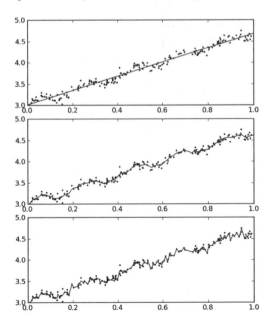

Figure 8.5 Plot showing locally weighted linear regression with three smoothing values. The top frame has a smoothing value of k=1.0, the middle frame has k=0.01, and the bottom frame has k=0.003. The top value of k is no better than least squares. The middle value captures some of the underlying data pattern. The bottom frame fits the best-fit line to noise in the data and results in overfitting.

One problem with locally weighted linear regression is that it involves numerous computations. You have to use the entire dataset to make one estimate. Figure 8.5 demonstrated that using k=0.01 gave you a good estimate of the data. If you look at the weights for k=0.01 in figure 8.4, you'll see that they're near 0 in for most of the data points. You could save a lot of computing time by avoiding these calculations.

Now that you've seen two methods of finding best-fit lines, let's put it to use predicting the age of an abalone.

8.3 Example: predicting the age of an abalone

Let's see our regression example in action on some real live data. In the data folder there is some data from the UCI data repository describing the age of a shellfish called abalone. The year is known by counting the number of layers in the shell of the abalone.

Add the following code to regression.py:

```
def rssError(yArr,yHatArr):
    return ((yArr-yHatArr)**2).sum()
```

```
>>> abX,abY=regression.loadDataSet('abalone.txt')
>>> yHat01=regression.lwlrTest(abX[0:99],abX[0:99],abY[0:99],0.1)
>>> yHat1=regression.lwlrTest(abX[0:99],abX[0:99],abY[0:99],1)
>>> yHat10=regression.lwlrTest(abX[0:99],abX[0:99],abY[0:99],10)
```

The function `rssError()` will give us a single number describing the error of our estimate:

```
>>> regression.rssError(abY[0:99],yHat01.T)
56.842594430533545
>>> regression.rssError(abY[0:99],yHat1.T)
429.89056187006685
>>> regression.rssError(abY[0:99],yHat10.T)
549.11817088257692
```

Using a smaller kernel will give us a lower error, so why don't we use the smallest kernel all the time? Using the smallest kernel will overfit our data. This may or may not give us the best results on new data. Let's see how well these predictions work on new data:

```
>>> yHat01=regression.lwlrTest(abX[100:199],abX[0:99],abY[0:99],0.1)
>>> regression.rssError(abY[100:199],yHat01.T)
25619.926899338669
>>> yHat1=regression.lwlrTest(abX[100:199],abX[0:99],abY[0:99],1)
>>> regression.rssError(abY[100:199],yHat1.T)
573.5261441895808
>>> yHat10=regression.lwlrTest(abX[100:199],abX[0:99],abY[0:99],10)
>>> regression.rssError(abY[100:199],yHat10.T)
517.57119053830979
```

Did you see that? This is our test error, and the smallest value of the test error occurred with a kernel size of 10. The kernel size of 10 gave us the largest training error. Let's see how these errors compare to our simple linear regression:

```
>>> ws = regression.standRegres(abX[0:99],abY[0:99])
>>> yHat=mat(abX[100:199])*ws
>>> regression.rssError(abY[100:199],yHat.T.A)
518.63631532450131
```

Simple linear regression did almost as well as the locally weighted linear regression. This demonstration illustrates one fact, and that is that in order to choose the best model you have to see how the model does on unknown data. Is 10 the best kernel size? Perhaps, but to get a better estimate you should do the previous test 10 times with 10 different samples of data and compare the results.

This example showed how one method—locally weighted linear regression—can be used to build a model that may be better at forecasting than regular regression. The problem with locally weighted linear regression is that you need to "carry around" the dataset. You need to have the training data available to make predictions. We'll now explore a second class of methods for improving forecasting accuracy. These methods have some added benefits, as you'll soon see.

8.4 Shrinking coefficients to understand our data

What if we have more features than data points? Can we still make a prediction using linear regression and the methods we've seen already? Then answer is no, not using the methods we've seen already. The reason for this is that when we try to compute $(\mathbf{X}^T\mathbf{X})^{-1}$ we'll get an error.

If we have more features than data points (n>m), we say that our data matrix $\mathbf{X}$ isn't full rank. When the data isn't full rank, we'll have a difficult time computing the inverse.

To solve this problem, statisticians introduced the concept of *ridge regression*, which is the first of two shrinkage methods we'll look at in this section. We'll then discuss the lasso, which is better but difficult to compute. We'll finally examine a second shrinkage method called forward stagewise regression, which is an easy way to approximate the lasso.

8.4.1 Ridge regression

Ridge regression adds an additional matrix $\lambda\mathbf{I}$ to the matrix $\mathbf{X}^T\mathbf{X}$ so that it's non-singular, and we can take the inverse of the whole thing: $\mathbf{X}^T\mathbf{X} + \lambda\mathbf{I}$. The matrix $\mathbf{I}$ is an mxm identity matrix where there are 1s in the diagonal elements and 0s elsewhere. The symbol λ is a user-defined scalar value, which we'll discuss shortly. The formula for estimating our coefficients is now

$$\hat{w} = (X^T X + \lambda I)^{-1} X^T y$$

Ridge regression was originally developed to deal with the problem of having more features than data points. But it can also be used to add bias into our estimations, giving us a better estimate. We can use the λ value to impose a maximum value on the sum of all our ws. By imposing this penalty, we can decrease unimportant parameters. This decreasing is known as *shrinkage* in statistics.

> ## What is the *ridge* in ridge regression?
>
> Ridge regression uses the identity matrix multiplied by some constant λ. If you look at **I** (the identity matrix), you'll see that there are 1s across the diagonal and 0s elsewhere. This ridge of 1s in a plane of 0s gives you the ridge in ridge regression.

Shrinkage methods allow us to throw out unimportant parameters so that we can get a better feel and human understanding of the data. Additionally, shrinkage can give us a better prediction value than linear regression.

We choose λ to minimize prediction error. This is similar to other parameter-selection methods we used in the chapters on classification. We take some of our data, set it aside for testing, and then use the remaining data to determine the ws. We then test this model against our test data and measure its performance. This is repeated with different λ values until we find a λ that minimizes prediction error.

Let's see this in action. First, open regression.py and add the code from the following listing.

Listing 8.3 Ridge regression

```
def ridgeRegres(xMat,yMat,lam=0.2):
    xTx = xMat.T*xMat
    denom = xTx + eye(shape(xMat)[1])*lam
    if linalg.det(denom) == 0.0:
        print "This matrix is singular, cannot do inverse"
        return
    ws = denom.I * (xMat.T*yMat)
    return ws

def ridgeTest(xArr,yArr):
    xMat = mat(xArr); yMat=mat(yArr).T
    yMean = mean(yMat,0)
    yMat = yMat - yMean
    xMeans = mean(xMat,0)                          ❶ Normalization
    xVar = var(xMat,0)                               code
    xMat = (xMat - xMeans)/xVar
    numTestPts = 30
    wMat = zeros((numTestPts,shape(xMat)[1]))
    for i in range(numTestPts):
        ws = ridgeRegres(xMat,yMat,exp(i-10))
        wMat[i,:]=ws.T
    return wMat
```

The code in listing 8.3 contains two functions: one to calculate weights, `ridgeRegres()`, and one to test this over a number of lambda values, `ridgeTest()`.

The first function, `ridgeRegres()`, implements ridge regression for any given value of lambda. If no value is given, lambda defaults to 0.2. Lambda is a reserved keyword in Python, so you use the variable `lam` instead. You first construct the matrix $\mathbf{x}^T\mathbf{x}$. Next, you add on the ridge term multiplied by our scalar `lam`. The identity matrix is created by the NumPy function `eye()`. Ridge regression should work on datasets that would give an error with regular regression, so you shouldn't need to check to see if the determinant is zero, right? Someone could enter 0 for lambda and you'd have a problem, so you put in a check. If the matrix isn't singular, the last thing the code does is calculate the weights and return them.

To use ridge regression and all shrinkage methods, you need to first normalize your features. If you read chapter 2, you'll remember that we normalized our data to give each feature equal importance regardless of the units it was measured in. The second function in listing 8.3, `ridgeTest()`, shows an example of how to normalize the data. This is done by subtracting off the mean from each feature and dividing by the variance. ❶

After the regularization is done, you call `ridgeRegres()` with 30 different lambda values. The values vary exponentially so that you can see how very small values of lambda and very large values impact your results. The weights are packed into a matrix and returned.

Let's see this in action on our abalone dataset.

```
>>> reload(regression)
>>> abX,abY=regression.loadDataSet('abalone.txt')
>>> ridgeWeights=regression.ridgeTest(abX,abY)
```

We now have the weights for 30 different values of lambda. Let's see what these look like. To plot them out, enter the following commands in your Python shell:

```
>>> import matplotlib.pyplot as plt
>>> fig = plt.figure()
>>> ax = fig.add_subplot(111)
>>> ax.plot(ridgeWeights)
>>> plt.show()
```

You should see a plot similar to figure 8.6. In figure 8.6 you can see the regression coefficients plotted versus $\log(\lambda)$. On the very left where λ is the smallest, you have

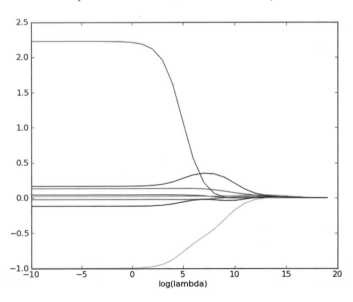

Figure 8.6 Regression coefficient values while using ridge regression. For very small values of λ the coefficients are the same as regular regression, whereas for very large values of λ the regression coefficients shrink to 0. Somewhere in between these two extremes, you can find values that allow you to make better predictions.

the full values of our coefficients, which are the same as linear regression. On the right side, the coefficients are all zero. Somewhere in the middle, you have some coefficient values that will give you better prediction results. To find satisfactory answers, you'd need to do cross-validation testing. A plot, shown in figure 8.6, also tells you which variables are most descriptive in predicting your output, by the magnitude of these coefficients.

There are other shrinkage methods such as the lasso, LAR, PCA regression,[1] and subset selection. These methods can be used to improve prediction accuracy and improve your ability to interpret regression coefficients similarly to ridge regression. We'll now talk about a method called the lasso.

8.4.2   The lasso

It can be shown that the equation for ridge regression is the same as our regular least-squares regression and imposing the following constraint:

$$\sum_{k=1}^{n} w_k^2 \leq \lambda$$

This means that the sum of the squares of all our weights has to be less than or equal to λ. When two or more of the features are correlated, we may have a very large positive weight and a very large negative weight using regular least-squares regression. By using ridge regression we're avoiding this problem because the weights are subject to the previous constraint.

Similar to ridge regression, there's another shrinkage technique called the *lasso*. The lasso imposes a different constraint on the weights:

$$\sum_{k=1}^{n} |w_k| \leq \lambda$$

The only difference is that we're taking the absolute value instead of the square of all the weights. Using a slightly different constraint will give us different results. If λ is small enough, some of the weights are forced to be exactly 0, which makes it easier to understand our data. The mathematical difference of the constraints may seem trivial, but it makes things a lot harder to solve. To solve this we now need a quadratic programming algorithm. Instead of using the quadratic solver, I'll introduce an easier method for getting results similar to the lasso. This is called *forward stagewise regression*.

8.4.3   Forward stagewise regression

There's an easier algorithm than the lasso that gives close results: stagewise linear regression. This algorithm is a greedy algorithm in that at each step it makes the decision that will reduce the error the most at that step. Initially, all the weights are

---

[1] Trevor Hastie, Robert Tibshirani, and Jerome Friedman, *The Elements of Statistical Learning: Data Mining, Inference, and Prediction*, 2nd ed. (Springer, 2009).

set to 0. The decision that's made at each step is increasing or decreasing a weight by some small amount.

Pseudo-code would look like this:

Regularize the data to have 0 mean and unit variance
For every iteration:
　Set lowestError to +∞
　For every feature:
　　For increasing and decreasing:
　　　Change one coefficient to get a new W
　　　Calculate the Error with new W
　　　If the Error is lower than lowestError: set Wbest to the current W
　　Update set W to Wbest

To see this in action, open regression.py and add the code from the following listing.

Listing 8.4   Forward stagewise linear regression

```
def stageWise(xArr,yArr,eps=0.01,numIt=100):
    xMat = mat(xArr); yMat=mat(yArr).T
    yMean = mean(yMat,0)
    yMat = yMat - yMean
    xMat = regularize(xMat)
    m,n=shape(xMat)
    ws = zeros((n,1)); wsTest = ws.copy(); wsMax = ws.copy()
    for i in range(numIt):
        print ws.T
        lowestError = inf;
        for j in range(n):
            for sign in [-1,1]:
                wsTest = ws.copy()
                wsTest[j] += eps*sign
                yTest = xMat*wsTest
                rssE = rssError(yMat.A,yTest.A)
                if rssE < lowestError:
                    lowestError = rssE
                    wsMax = wsTest
        ws = wsMax.copy()
        returnMat[i,:]=ws.T
    return returnMat
```

The function `stageWise()` in listing 8.4 is a demonstration of the stagewise linear regression algorithm, which approaches the lasso solution but is much easier to compute. The function takes the following inputs: our input data, `xArr`; and the variable we're forecasting, `yArr`. Additionally there are two parameters. One is `eps`, the step size to take at each iteration, and the second is `numIt`, which is the number of iterations.

You start off by converting the input data into matrices and normalizing the features to 0 mean and unit variance. You next make a vector, `ws`, to hold our w values, and you create two copies for use in the greedy optimization. Next, you loop over the optimization procedure `numIt` times. In each of these iterations you print out the `w` vector so you have some idea what's going on inside.

The greedy optimization is two `for` loops that loop over all the possible features and see how the error changes if you increase or decrease that feature. The error is measured by the squared error, which is calculated by the `rssError()` function given earlier. You initially set this error to $+\infty$ and then compare all the errors. The value giving the lowest error is chosen. You then repeat this procedure.

Let's see this in action. After you've entered the code from listing 8.4 into regression.py, save it and type the following in your Python shell:

```
>>> reload(regression)
<module 'regression' from 'regression.pyc'>
>>> xArr,yArr=regression.loadDataSet('abalone.txt')
>>> regression.stageWise(xArr,yArr,0.01,200)
[[ 0.    0.    0.    0.    0.    0.    0.    0.]]
[[ 0.    0.    0.    0.01  0.    0.    0.    0.  ]]
[[ 0.    0.    0.    0.02  0.    0.    0.    0.  ]]
                            .
                            .
[[ 0.04  0.    0.09  0.03  0.31 -0.64  0.    0.36]]
[[ 0.05  0.    0.09  0.03  0.31 -0.64  0.    0.36]]
[[ 0.04  0.    0.09  0.03  0.31 -0.64  0.    0.36]]
```

One thing to notice is that w_1 and w_6 are exactly 0. This means they don't contribute anything to the result. These variables are probably not needed. With the `eps` variable set to 0.01, after some time the coefficients will all saturate and oscillate between certain values because the step size is too large. Here you can see that the first weight is oscillating between 0.04 and 0.005.

Let's try again with a smaller step size and many more steps:

```
>>> regression.stageWise(xArr,yArr,0.001,5000)
[[ 0.    0.    0.    0.    0.    0.    0.    0.]]
[[ 0.    0.    0.    0.001 0.    0.    0.    0.  ]]
[[ 0.    0.    0.    0.002 0.    0.    0.    0.  ]]
                            .
                            .
[[ 0.044 -0.011 0.12  0.022 2.023 -0.963 -0.105 0.187]]
[[ 0.043 -0.011 0.12  0.022 2.023 -0.963 -0.105 0.187]]
[[ 0.044 -0.011 0.12  0.022 2.023 -0.963 -0.105 0.187]]
```

Let's compare these answers to the least-squares weights. You can get the least-squares weights by typing in the following:

```
>>> xMat=mat(xArr)
>>> yMat=mat(yArr).T
>>> xMat=regression.regularize(xMat)
>>> yM = mean(yMat,0)
>>> yMat = yMat - yM
>>> weights=regression.standRegres(xMat,yMat.T)
>>> weights.T
matrix([[ 0.0430442 , -0.02274163,  0.13214087,  0.02075182,  2.22403814,
         -0.99895312, -0.11725427,  0.16622915]])
```

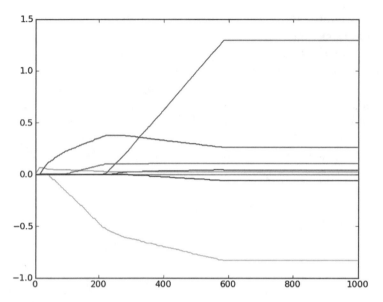

Figure 8.7   Coefficient values from the abalone dataset versus iteration of the stagewise linear regression algorithm. Stagewise linear regression gives values close to the lasso values with a much simpler algorithm.

You can see after 5,000 iterations that the results from the stagewise linear regression algorithm are close to the results using regular least squares. Results from 1,000 iterations with an epsilon value of 0.005 are shown in figure 8.7.

The practical benefit of the stagewise linear regression algorithm isn't that you can make these cool plots like the one in figure 8.7. The benefit is this algorithm allows you to better understand your models and build better models. When building a model, you'd want to run this algorithm and find out which features are important. You may choose to stop collecting data for unimportant features. Ultimately, you'd want to build many models with w values from the algorithm and after every 100 iterations test these. To test these models, you'd do something like tenfold cross validation and choose the model that minimizes error.

When we apply a shrinkage method such as stagewise linear regression or ridge regression, we say we're adding *bias* to our model. At the same time, we're reducing the model variance. The next section will explain the relationship and how these affect our results.

8.5   *The bias/variance tradeoff*

Anytime you have a difference between your model and your measurements, you have an error. When thinking about "noise" or error in our model, you have to consider the sources. You could be trying to simplify a complex process. This will create so-called noise or errors between your model and your measurements so that you won't be able to understand the true process that's generating your data. This will also cause differences. There could also be noise or problems with your measurement process. Let me show you an example. In sections 8.1 and 8.2, we played around with some two-dimensional data. This data was loaded from a file. To tell you the truth, I generated the data. The equation I used to generate the data was

```
y = 3.0 + 1.7x + 0.1sin(30x)+0.06N(0,1),
```

where `N(0,1)` is a normal distribution with 0 mean and unit variance. We were trying to model this with a straight line. The best we could do with this type of model was to get the `3.0 + 1.7x` part, and we'd still have an error of `0.1sin(30x)+0.06N(0,1)`. We came close to this in section 8.1. In sections 8.2 and 8.3, we used locally weighted linear regression to capture the underlying structure. That structure was hard to understand, so we used different amounts of local weights to find a solution that gave us the smallest test error.

A plot of training and test error is shown in figure 8.8. The top curve is the test error, and the bottom curve is training error. If you remember from section 8.3, as we decreased the size of the kernel, our training error got smaller. This corresponds to starting on the left side of figure 8.8 and then moving to the right as the kernel becomes smaller.

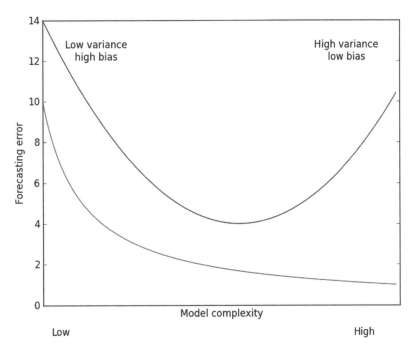

Figure 8.8 **The bias variance tradeoff illustrated with test error and training error. The training error is the top curve, which has a minimum in the middle of the plot. In order to create the best forecasts, we should adjust our model complexity where the test error is at a minimum.**

It's popular to think of our errors as a sum of three components: bias, error, and random noise. In sections 8.2 and 8.3, we were adding variance to our model by adding an increasingly smaller kernel.

In section 8.4, when we applied our shrinkage methods, some of the coefficients became small and some became zero. This is an example of adding bias to our model. By shrinking some of our components to exactly zero, we were reducing the complexity of our model. We had eight features. When we eliminated two of them, our model was easier for a human to understand, but it could give us smaller prediction error also. The left side of figure 8.8 shows our coefficients taking on very small values. The right side of the figure shows our coefficients totally unconstrained.

Variance is something we can measure. If we took a random sample of our abalone data, say, 100 points, and generated a linear model, we'd have a set of weights. Say we took another set of random points and generated another linear model. Comparing the amount that the weights change will tell us the variance in our model. This concept of a bias and variance tradeoff is popular in machine learning and will come up again and again.

Now let's see if we can put some of these ideas to use. We'll next examine some data from a real-world auction site and experiment with some regression methods. You'll see the bias/variance trade-off in action as we find the best ridge regression model for our data.

8.6   *Example: forecasting the price of LEGO sets*

Are you familiar with the LEGO brand of toys? If not, LEGO makes construction toys that are composed of many small plastic blocks of varying size. Because of the high quality of the parts, the blocks hold together without any adhesives. Beyond being a simple toy, LEGO sets are popular with many adults. Usually the blocks are sold as sets, which include all the pieces to make something specific such as a boat, castle, or famous building. LEGO makes a number of amazing sets varying from 10s of pieces to 5,000 pieces.

A LEGO set will typically be available for a few years and then will be discontinued. After the sets are discontinued, they continue to be traded by collectors. My friend Dangler would like to predict how much LEGO sets will sell for. We'll help him by building a model using the regression techniques in this chapter.

Example: using regression to predict the price of a LEGO set

1. Collect: Collect from Google Shopping API.
2. Prepare: Extract price data from the returned JSON.
3. Analyze: Visually inspect the data.
4. Train: We'll build different models with stagewise linear regression and straightforward linear regression.
5. Test: We'll use cross validation to test the different models to see which one performs the best.
6. Use: The resulting model will be the object of this exercise.

In this example we'll get some data on the prices for different datasets. Then, we'll build a regression model with that data. The first thing we need to figure out is how we can get the data.

8.6.1 Collect: using the Google shopping API

The wonderful people at Google have provided us with an API for retrieving prices via the Search API for Shopping. Before you can use the API, you'll need to sign up for a Google account and then visit the Google API console to enable this Shopping API. Now you can make HTTP requests and get back information about available products in JSON form. Python comes with a module for parsing JSON, so all you have to do is sort through the returned JSON for the information you want. You can read more about the API and what is returned with the Shopping API at http://code.google.com/apis/shopping/search/v1/getting_started.html.

Open regression.py and add the code from the following listing to implement code to retrieve this information.

Listing 8.5 Shopping information retrieval function

```
from time import sleep
import json
import urllib2
def searchForSet(retX, retY, setNum, yr, numPce, origPrc):
    sleep(10)
    myAPIstr = 'get from code.google.com'
    searchURL = 'https://www.googleapis.com/shopping/search/v1/public/
     products?\
      key=%s&country=US&q=lego+%d&alt=json' % (myAPIstr, setNum)
    pg = urllib2.urlopen(searchURL)
    retDict = json.loads(pg.read())
    for i in range(len(retDict['items'])):
        try:
            currItem = retDict['items'][i]
            if currItem['product']['condition'] == 'new':
                newFlag = 1
            else: newFlag = 0
            listOfInv = currItem['product']['inventories']
            for item in listOfInv:
                sellingPrice = item['price']
                if  sellingPrice > origPrc * 0.5:         ◁--❶ Filter out
                    print "%d\t%d\t%d\t%f\t%f" %\             fractional sets
                        (yr,numPce,newFlag,origPrc, sellingPrice)
                    retX.append([yr, numPce, newFlag, origPrc])
                    retY.append(sellingPrice)
        except: print 'problem with item %d' % i

def setDataCollect(retX, retY):
    searchForSet(retX, retY, 8288, 2006, 800, 49.99)
    searchForSet(retX, retY, 10030, 2002, 3096, 269.99)
    searchForSet(retX, retY, 10179, 2007, 5195, 499.99)
    searchForSet(retX, retY, 10181, 2007, 3428, 199.99)
    searchForSet(retX, retY, 10189, 2008, 5922, 299.99)
    searchForSet(retX, retY, 10196, 2009, 3263, 249.99)
```

The first function in listing 8.5 is searchForSet(), which will call the Google Shopping API and extract the correct data. You need to import a few modules: time.sleep(), json, and urllib2. But first you sleep for 10 seconds, which is just a precaution to prevent making too many API calls too quickly. Next, you format the search URL with your API key and the set you're looking for. This is opened and parsed with the json.loads() method. Now you have a dictionary. All you have to do is find the price and the condition.

Part of the returned results is an array of items. You'll iterate over these items, extracting whether the item is new or not and the listed price. The LEGO sets are composed of many small pieces, and sometimes a used set will be missing some pieces. Sellers will offer fragments of a set. These fragments are sometimes returned with the search results, so you need a way to filter these out. You could look for common terms in the description or employ naïve Bayes. I've instead chosen a simple heuristic: if a set is selling for less than half of its original price, it's probably a fractional set. ❶ These sets are ignored. Successfully parsed sets are printed to the screen and appended to the lists retX and retY.

The final function in listing 8.5 is setDataCollect(), which calls searchForSet() multiple times. The additional arguments to searchForSet() are relevant data collected from www.brickset.com that pass through to the output file.

Let's see this in action. After you've added the code from listing 8.5, save regression.py and enter the following commands in your Python shell:

```
>>> lgX = []; lgY = []
>>> regression.setDataCollect(lgX, lgY)
2006      800      1       49.990000       549.990000
2006      800      1       49.990000       759.050000
2006      800      1       49.990000       316.990000
2002      3096     1       269.990000      499.990000
2002      3096     1       269.990000      289.990000
                           .
                           .
2009      3263     0       249.990000      524.990000
2009      3263     1       249.990000      672.000000
2009      3263     1       249.990000      580.000000
```

Inspect lgX and lgY to make sure they're not empty. We're next going to use the data to build a regression equation that will forecast the selling price of antique LEGO sets.

8.6.2 *Train: building a model*

Now that we've collected some real data from the internet, we'd like to use it to build a model. The model can be used to make predictions. It can also be used to give us a better understanding of the forces driving the data. Let's see how to do this with Python.

First, you should add in a 1 for X0. To do this, you create a matrix of all 1s:

```
>>> shape(lgX)
(58, 4)
>>> lgX1=mat(ones((58,5)))
```

Next, copy over our data to the first through fifth columns:

```
>>> lgX1[:,1:5]=mat(lgX)
```

Check to make sure that data was copied over correctly:

```
>>> lgX[0]
[2006.0, 800.0, 0.0, 49.990000000000002]
>>> lgX1[0]
matrix([[  1.00000000e+00,   2.00600000e+03,   8.00000000e+02,
           0.00000000e+00,   4.99900000e+01]])
```

The data is the same, but now it has a 1 in the 0th feature. Finally, let's compute a regression for this dataset:

```
>>> ws=regression.standRegres(lgX1,lgY)
>>> ws
matrix([[  5.53199701e+04],
        [ -2.75928219e+01],
        [ -2.68392234e-02],
        [ -1.12208481e+01],
        [  2.57604055e+00]])
```

Check out the results, to see if this works:

```
>>> lgX1[0]*ws
matrix([[ 76.07418853]])
>>> lgX1[-1]*ws
matrix([[ 431.17797672]])
>>> lgX1[43]*ws
matrix([[ 516.20733105]])
```

The regression works. Now let's look at the model it constructed. The model says the price of a set will be

```
$55319.97-27.59*Year-0.00268*NumPieces-11.22*NewOrUsed+2.57*original price
```

The predictions were pretty good, but the model isn't satisfactory. It may fit the data, but it doesn't seem to make sense. It seems that sets with more pieces will sell for less, and there's a penalty for a set being new.

Let's try this again but with one of our shrinkage methods, say ridge regression. Earlier you saw how to shrink coefficients, but now you'll see how to determine the best coefficients. Open regression.py and insert the following code:

Listing 8.6 Cross-validation testing with ridge regression

```
def crossValidation(xArr,yArr,numVal=10):
    m = len(yArr)
    indexList = range(m)
    errorMat = zeros((numVal,30))
    for i in range(numVal):
        trainX=[]; trainY=[]          ❶ Create training and
        testX = []; testY = []           test containers
        random.shuffle(indexList)
        for j in range(m):
```

```
          if j < m*0.9:
              trainX.append(xArr[indexList[j]])
              trainY.append(yArr[indexList[j]])                    ❷  Split data
          else:                                                       into test and
              testX.append(xArr[indexList[j]])                       training sets
              testY.append(yArr[indexList[j]])
      wMat = ridgeTest(trainX,trainY)
      for k in range(30):
          matTestX = mat(testX); matTrainX=mat(trainX)            ❸  Regularize test
          meanTrain = mean(matTrainX,0)                              with training
          varTrain = var(matTrainX,0)                                params
          matTestX = (matTestX-meanTrain)/varTrain
          yEst = matTestX * mat(wMat[k,:]).T + mean(trainY)
          errorMat[i,k]=rssError(yEst.T.A,array(testY))
  meanErrors = mean(errorMat,0)
  minMean = float(min(meanErrors))
  bestWeights = wMat[nonzero(meanErrors==minMean)]
  xMat = mat(xArr); yMat=mat(yArr).T
  meanX = mean(xMat,0); varX = var(xMat,0)
  unReg = bestWeights/varX
  print "the best model from Ridge Regression is:\n",unReg     ❹  Undo
  print "with constant term: ",\                                   regularization
      -1*sum(multiply(meanX,unReg)) + mean(yMat)
```

The function crossValidation() in listing 8.6 takes three arguments; the first two, lgX and lgY, are assumed to be lists of the X and Y values of a dataset in question. The third argument, crossValidation(), takes the number of cross validations to run. If no value is entered, it will default to 10. Both lgX and lgY are assumed to have the same length. The crossValidation() function starts by measuring the number of data points, m. This will be used to split the data into two sets: one test set and one training set. ❶ The split between training and test sets will be done with 90% going to the training set and 10% going to the test set. You first create containers for the training and test sets. ❷ Next, you create a list and randomly shuffle the elements of that list using the NumPy random.shuffle() function. You'll use this to randomly select a set of data points for the training or test set.

Once you've randomly shuffled the data points, you create a new matrix, wMat, to store all of the coefficients from ridge regression. If you recall from section 8.4.1, ridgeTest() uses 30 different values of λ to create 30 different weights. You next loop over all 30 sets of weights and test them using the test set created earlier. Ridge regression assumes that the data has been normalized, so you have to normalize your test data with the same parameters used to normalize the training data. ❸ The error for each of these is calculated using the rssError() function and stored in wMat.

After all of the cross validations have been done, errorMat has a number of error estimates for the different λ values used in ridgeTest(). The average of all these error estimates is calculated. You next want to display the weights and compare them to the least-squares solution obtained by standRegres(). The problem with comparing the weights is that ridge regression uses regularized values whereas standRegres() doesn't. To have a direct comparison you need to undo the regularization. The regularization is undone and the values are displayed. ❹

To see all of this in action, enter the code from listing 8.6, save regression.py, and type in the following:

```
>>> regression.crossValidation(lgX,lgY,10)
The best model from Ridge Regression is:
[[ -2.96472902e+01 -1.34476433e-03 -3.38454756e+01  2.44420117e+00]]
with constant term: 59389.2069537
```

Let's compare this to the regular least-squares solution. The price is given by

```
$59389.21-29.64*Year-0.00134*NumPieces-33.85*NewOrUsed+2.44*original price.
```

This isn't wildly different from the least-squares solution. What you were looking for was a model that was easier to interpret. You didn't get that. In order to get that, you need to look at how the regularized coefficients change as you apply the shrinkage. To do that, type in the following:

```
>>> regression.ridgeTest(lgX,lgY)
array([[ -1.45288906e+02,  -8.39360442e+03,  -3.28682450e+00,
    4.42362406e+04],
[ -1.46649725e+02,  -1.89952152e+03,  -2.80638599e+00,
        4.27891633e+04],
                                        .
                                        .
[ -4.91045279e-06,   5.01149871e-08,   2.40728171e-05,
    8.14042912e-07]])
```

These are the regularized coefficients for different levels of shrinkage. Looking at the first line, you can see that the magnitude of the fourth term is 5 times larger than the second term, which is 57 times larger than the first term. You get the idea. These results tell you that if you had to choose one feature to predict the future, you should choose the fourth feature, which is the original price. If you had to choose two features, you should choose the fourth and the second terms.

This sort of analysis allows you to digest a large amount of data. It may not seem critical when you have only 4 features, but if you have 100 or more features, it will be more important to understand which features are critical and which aren't.

8.7 Summary

Regression is the process of predicting a target value similar to classification. The difference between regression and classification is that the variable forecasted in regression is continuous, whereas it's discrete in classification. Regression is one of the most useful tools in statistics. Minimizing the sum-of-squares error is used to find the best weights for the input features in a regression equation. Regression can be done on any set of data provided that for an input matrix X, you can compute the inverse of $\mathbf{X}^T\mathbf{X}$. Just because you can compute a regression equation for a set of data doesn't mean that the results are very good. One test of how "good" or significant the results are is the correlation between the predicted values yHat and the original data y.

When you have more features than data points, you can't compute the inverse of $\mathbf{X}^T\mathbf{X}$. If you have more data points than features, you still may not be able to compute

$\mathbf{x}^T\mathbf{x}$ if the features are highly correlated. Ridge regression is a regression method that allows you to compute regression coefficients despite being unable to compute the inverse of $\mathbf{x}^T\mathbf{x}$.

Ridge regression is an example of a shrinkage method. Shrinkage methods impose a constraint on the size of the regression coefficients. Another shrinkage method that's powerful is the lasso. The lasso is difficult to compute, but stagewise linear regression is easy to compute and gives results close to those of the lasso.

Shrinkage methods can also be viewed as adding bias to a model and reducing the variance. The bias/variance tradeoff is a powerful concept in understanding how altering a model impacts the success of a model.

The methods explored in this chapter are powerful. Sometimes our data will have complex interactions, perhaps nonlinear interactions that will be difficult to model with linear models. The next chapter explores a few techniques that use trees to create forecasts for our data.

Tree-based regression

9

This chapter covers
- The CART algorithm
- Regression and model trees
- Tree-pruning algorithms
- Building a GUI in Python

The linear regression methods we looked at in chapter 8 contain some powerful methods. These methods create a model that needs to work for all of the data points (locally weighted linear regression is the exception). When the data has many features that interact in complicated ways, building a global model can be difficult if not foolish. We know there are many nonlinearities in real life. How can we expect to model everything with a global linear model?

One way to build a model for our data is to subdivide the data into sections that can be modeled easily. These partitions can then be modeled with linear regression techniques from chapter 8. If we first partition the data and the results don't fit a linear model, then we can partition the partitions. Trees and recursion are useful tools for this sort of portioning.

We'll first examine a new algorithm for building trees, called CART. CART is an acronym for Classification And Regression Trees. It can be applied to regression or classification, so this is a valuable tool to learn. Next, we'll build and plot the trees in Python. We'll make the code flexible enough that it can be used for multiple problems. We'll next apply the CART algorithm to create regression trees. We'll explore a technique called tree pruning, which helps to prevent overfitting our trees to our data. Next, we'll explore a more advanced algorithm called model trees. In a model tree, we build a linear model at each leaf node instead of using mean values as in regression trees. The algorithms to build these trees have a few adjustable parameters, so we'll next see how to create a GUI in Python with the Tkinter module. Finally, we'll use this GUI to explore the impact of various tree-building parameters.

9.1   *Locally modeling complex data*

Tree-based regression

Pros: Fits complex, nonlinear data

Cons: Difficult to interpret results

Works with: Numeric values, nominal values

In chapter 3, we used decision trees for classification. Decision trees work by successively splitting the data into smaller segments until all of the target variables are the same or until the dataset can no longer be split. Decision trees are a type of greedy algorithm that makes the best choice at a given time without concern for global optimality.

The algorithm we used to construct trees in chapter 3 was ID3. ID3 chooses the best feature on which to split the data and then splits the data into all possible values that the feature can take. If a feature can take on four possible values, then there will be a four-way split. After the data is split on a given feature, that feature is consumed or removed from future splitting opportunities. There is some argument that this type of splitting separates the data too quickly. Another way to split the data is to do binary splits. If a piece of data has a feature equal to the desired split value, then it will go down the left side of the tree; otherwise, it will go down the right.

The ID3 algorithm had another limitation: it couldn't directly handle continuous features. Continuous features can be handled in ID3 if they're first made into discrete features. This quantization destroys some of the inherent information in a continuous variable. Using binary splits allows us to easily adapt our tree-building algorithm to handle continuous features. To handle continuous variables, we choose a feature; values greater than the desired value go on the left side of the tree and all the other values go on the right side. Binary splits also save time during the tree construction, but this is a moot point because we usually build the tree offline and time isn't a huge concern.

CART is a well-known and well-documented tree-building algorithm that makes binary splits and handles continuous variables. CART can handle regression with a simple modification. In chapter 3, we used the Shannon entropy as our measure of how unorganized the sets were. If we replace the Shannon entropy with some other measure, we can use a tree-building algorithm for regression.

We'll first build the CART algorithm with regression trees in mind. Regression trees are similar to trees used for classification but with the leaves representing a numeric value rather than a discrete one.

> **General approach to tree-based regression**
> 1. Collect: Any method.
> 2. Prepare: Numeric values are needed. If you have nominal values, it's a good idea to map them into binary values.
> 3. Analyze: We'll visualize the data in two-dimensional plots and generate trees as dictionaries.
> 4. Train: The majority of the time will be spent building trees with models at the leaf nodes.
> 5. Test: We'll use the R^2 value with test data to determine the quality of our models.
> 6. Use: We'll use our trees to make forecasts. We can do almost anything with these results.

With an idea of how to approach the problem, we can start writing some code. In the next section we'll discuss the best way to build a tree with the CART algorithm in Python.

9.2 Building trees with continuous and discrete features

As we build a tree, we'll need to have a way of storing the different types of data making up the tree. We're going to use a dictionary for our tree data structure, similar to chapter 3. The dictionary will have the following four items:

- *Feature*—A symbol representing the feature split on for this tree.
- *Value*—The value of the feature used to split.
- *Right*—The right subtree; this could also be a single value if the algorithm decides we don't need another split.
- *Left*—The left subtree similar to the right subtree.

This is a little different from the structure we used in chapter 3. In chapter 3, we had a dictionary to store every split. The dictionary could contain two or more values. In the CART algorithm, only binary splits are allowed, so we can fix our tree data structure. The tree will have a right key and a left key that will store either another branch or a value. The dictionary will also have two more keys: feature and value. These will tell us what feature of our data to split on and the value of that feature to make the split. You could also create this data structure using object-oriented programming patterns. You'd create the tree node in Python using the following code:

```
class treeNode():
    def __init__(self, feat, val, right, left):
        featureToSplitOn = feat
        valueOfSplit = val
        rightBranch = right
        leftBranch = left
```

When working with a less-flexible language like C++, you'd probably want to implement your trees using object-oriented patterns. Python is flexible enough that you can use dictionaries as your tree data structure and write less code than if you used a specific class. Python isn't strongly typed, so our branches can contain other trees, numeric values, or vectors, as you'll see later.

We're going to create two types of trees. The first type is called a *regression tree*, and it contains a single value for each leaf of the tree. We'll create this type in section 9.4. The second type of tree we'll create is called a *model tree*, and it has a linear equation at each leaf node. We'll create that in section 9.5. We'll try to reuse as much code as possible when creating the two types of trees. Let's start by making some tree-building code that can be used for either type of tree.

Pseudo-code for `createTree()` would look like this:

Find the best feature to split on:
    If we can't split the data, this node becomes a leaf node
    Make a binary split of the data
    Call createTree() on the right split of the data
    Call createTree() on the left split of the data

Open your favorite text editor and create a file called regTrees.py; then add the following code.

Listing 9.1 CART tree-building code

```
from numpy import *

def loadDataSet(fileName):
    dataMat = []
    fr = open(fileName)
    for line in fr.readlines():
        curLine = line.strip().split('\t')
        fltLine = map(float,curLine)          ❶ Map everything
        dataMat.append(fltLine)                  to float()
    return dataMat

def binSplitDataSet(dataSet, feature, value):
    mat0 = dataSet[nonzero(dataSet[:,feature] > value)[0],:][0]
    mat1 = dataSet[nonzero(dataSet[:,feature] <= value)[0],:][0]
    return mat0,mat1

def createTree(dataSet, leafType=regLeaf, errType=regErr, ops=(1,4)):
    feat, val = chooseBestSplit(dataSet, leafType, errType, ops)
    if feat == None: return val          ❷ Return leaf value if
    retTree = {}                            stopping condition met
    retTree['spInd'] = feat
```

```
retTree['spVal'] = val
lSet, rSet = binSplitDataSet(dataSet, feat, val)
retTree['left'] = createTree(lSet, leafType, errType, ops)
retTree['right'] = createTree(rSet, leafType, errType, ops)
return retTree
```

Listing 9.1 contains three functions. The first one, loadDataSet(), is similar to the previous versions of this function from other chapters. In previous chapters you broke the target variable off into its own list, but here you'll keep the data together. This function takes a file with tab-delimited values and breaks each line into a list of floats. ❶

The second function in listing 9.1 is binSplitDataSet(). This takes three arguments: a dataset, a feature on which to split, and a value for that feature. The function returns two sets. The two sets are created using array filtering for the given feature and value.

The last function in listing 9.1 is createTree(), which builds a tree. There are four arguments to createTree(): a dataset on which to build the tree and three optional arguments. The three optional arguments tell the function which type of tree to create. The argument leafType is the function used to create a leaf. The argument errType is a function used for measuring the error on the dataset. The last argument, ops, is a tuple of parameters for creating a tree.

The function createTree() is a recursive function that first attempts to split the dataset into two parts. The split is determined by the function chooseBestSplit(), which we haven't written yet. If chooseBestSplit() hits a stopping condition, it will return None and the value for a model type ❷. In the case of regression trees, this model is a constant value; in the case of model trees, this model is a linear equation. You'll see how these stopping conditions work later. If a stopping condition isn't hit, then you create a new dictionary and split the dataset into two portions. The function createTree() gets recursively called on the two splits.

The code in listing 9.1 is straightforward enough. You can't see createTree() in action until we write chooseBestSplit(), but you can test out the other two functions. After you've entered the code from listing 9.1 into regTrees.py, save it and type in the following:

```
>>> import regTrees
>>> testMat=mat(eye(4))
>>> testMat
matrix([[ 1.,   0.,   0.,   0.],
        [ 0.,   1.,   0.,   0.],
        [ 0.,   0.,   1.,   0.],
        [ 0.,   0.,   0.,   1.]])
```

You've created a simple matrix. Now let's split it by the value in a given column.

```
>>> mat0,mat1=regTrees.binSplitDataSet(testMat,1,0.5)
>>> mat0
matrix([[ 0.,   1.,   0.,   0.]])
>>> mat1
matrix([[ 1.,   0.,   0.,   0.],
        [ 0.,   0.,   1.,   0.],
        [ 0.,   0.,   0.,   1.]])
```

Entertaining isn't it? To see this do some more exciting stuff, let's fill out the `chooseBestSplit()` function for the case of regression trees. By filling out `chooseBestSplit()` with code specific to regression, we'll be able to use the CART code from listing 9.1 to build regression trees. In the next section, we'll finish this function and build regression trees.

9.3   *Using CART for regression*

In order to model the complex interactions of our data, we've decided to use trees to partition the data. How should we split up the partitions? How will we know when we've split up the data enough? The answer depends on how we're modeling the final values. The regression tree method breaks up data using a tree with constant values on the leaf nodes. This strategy assumes that the complex interactions of the data can be summarized by the tree.

In order to construct a tree of piecewise constant values, we need to be able to measure the consistency of data. In chapter 3, when we used trees for classification, we measured the disorder of the values at a given node. How can we measure the disorder of continuous values? Measuring this disorder for a set of data is quite easy. We first calculate the mean value of a set and then find how much each piece of data deviates from this mean value. In order to treat positive and negative deviations equally, we need to get the magnitude of the deviation from the mean. We can get this magnitude with the absolute value or the squared value. I've described something commonly done in statistics, and that's calculating the variance. The only difference is the variance is the mean squared error and we want the total error. We can get this total squared error by multiplying the variance of a dataset by the number of elements in a dataset.

With this error rule and the tree-building algorithm from the previous section, we can now write code to construct a regression tree from a dataset.

9.3.1   *Building the tree*

In order to build a regression tree, we need to create a few pieces of code to get `createTree()` from listing 9.1 to work. The first thing we need is a function, `chooseBestSplit()`, that given an error metric will find the best binary split for our data. The function `chooseBestSplit()` also needs to know when to stop splitting given our error metric and a dataset. When `chooseBestSplit()` does decide to stop splitting, we need to generate a leaf node. So `chooseBestSplit()` does only two things: split a dataset by the best possible split and generate a leaf node for a dataset.

If you noticed in listing 9.1, `chooseBestSplit()` has three arguments in addition to the data set. They're the `leafType`, `errType`, and `ops`. The `leafType` argument is a reference to a function that we use to create the leaf node. The `errType` argument is a reference to a function that will be used to calculate the squared deviation from the mean described earlier. Finally, `ops` is a tuple of user-defined parameters to help with tree building.

The function `chooseBestSplit()` is the most involved; this function finds the best place to split the dataset. It looks over every feature and every value to find the threshold that minimizes error. Pseudo-code would look like this:

For every feature:
  For every unique value:
    Split the dataset it two
    Measure the error of the two splits
    If the error is less than bestError → set bestSplit to this split and update bestError
Return bestSplit feature and threshold

To create the code for these three functions, open regTrees.py and enter the code from the following listing.

Listing 9.2 Regression tree split function

```
def regLeaf(dataSet):
    return mean(dataSet[:,-1])

def regErr(dataSet):
    return var(dataSet[:,-1]) * shape(dataSet)[0]

def chooseBestSplit(dataSet, leafType=regLeaf, errType=regErr, ops=(1,4)):
    tolS = ops[0]; tolN = ops[1]
    if len(set(dataSet[:,-1].T.tolist()[0])) == 1:          ❶ Exit if all values
        return None, leafType(dataSet)                         are equal
    m,n = shape(dataSet)
    S = errType(dataSet)
    bestS = inf; bestIndex = 0; bestValue = 0
    for featIndex in range(n-1):
        for splitVal in set(dataSet[:,featIndex]):
            mat0, mat1 = binSplitDataSet(dataSet, featIndex, splitVal)
            if (shape(mat0)[0] < tolN) or (shape(mat1)[0] < tolN): continue
            newS = errType(mat0) + errType(mat1)
            if newS < bestS:
                bestIndex = featIndex
                bestValue = splitVal
                bestS = newS                                ❷ Exit if low error
    if (S - bestS) < tolS:                                     reduction
        return None, leafType(dataSet)
    mat0, mat1 = binSplitDataSet(dataSet, bestIndex, bestValue)  ❸ Exit if split
    if (shape(mat0)[0] < tolN) or (shape(mat1)[0] < tolN):         creates small
        return None, leafType(dataSet)                             dataset
    return bestIndex,bestValue
```

The first function in listing 9.2 is `regLeaf()`, which generates the model for a leaf node. When `chooseBestSplit()` decides that you no longer should split the data, it will call `regLeaf()` to get a model for the leaf. The model in a regression tree is the mean value of the target variables.

The second function in listing 9.2 is our error estimate, `regErr()`. This function returns the squared error of the target variables in a given dataset. You could have first calculated the mean, then calculated the deviation, and then squared it, but it's easier to call var(), which calculates the mean squared error. You want the total squared error, not the mean, so you can get it by multiplying by the number of instances in a dataset.

The last function in listing 9.2 is chooseBestSplit(), which is the real workhorse of the classification tree. The job of this function is to find the best way to do a binary split on the data. If a "good" binary split can't be found, then this function returns None and tells createTree() to generate a leaf node. The value of the leaf node is also returned with None. There are three conditions that will generate a leaf node instead of split in chooseBestSplit(); you'll see them shortly. If a "good" split is found, the feature number and value of the split are returned.

The function chooseBestSplit() starts out by assigning the values of ops to tolS and tolN. These two values are user-defined settings that tell the function when to quit creating new splits. The variable tolS is a tolerance on the error reduction, and tolN is the minimum data instances to include in a split. The next thing chooseBestSplit() does is check the number of unique values by creating a set from all the target variables. If this set is length 1, then you don't need to try to split the set and you can return. ❶ Next, chooseBestSplit() measures the size of the dataset and measures the error on the existing dataset. This error S will be checked against new values of the error to see if splitting reduces the error. You'll see this shortly.

A few variables that will be used to find the best split are created and initialized. You next iterate over all the possible features and all the possible values of those features to find the best split. The best split is determined by the lowest error of the sets after the split. If splitting the dataset improves the error by only a small amount, you choose not to split and create a leaf node. ❷ Another test you perform is to check the size of the two splits. If this is less than our user-defined parameter tolN, you choose not to split and return a leaf node. Finally, if none of these early exit conditions have been met, you return the feature on which to split and the value to perform the split. ❸

9.3.2 *Executing the code*

Let's see this in action on some data. Consider the data plotted in figure 9.1. We'll generate a regression tree from this data.

After you've entered the code from listing 9.2 into regTrees.py, save it and enter the following commands in your Python shell:

```
>>>reload(regTrees)
<module 'regTrees' from 'regTrees.pyc'>
>>> from numpy import *
The data from figure 9.1 is stored in a file called ex00.txt.
>>> myDat=regTrees.loadDataSet('ex00.txt')
>>> myMat = mat(myDat)
>>> regTrees.createTree(myMat)
{'spInd': 0, 'spVal': matrix([[ 0.48813]]),
'right': -0.044650285714285733,
'left': 1.018096767241379}
```

Now let's try this out on some data with more splits. Consider the data in figure 9.2.

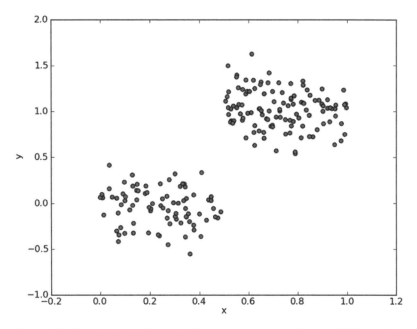

Figure 9.1   Simple dataset for evaluating regression trees with the CART algorithm

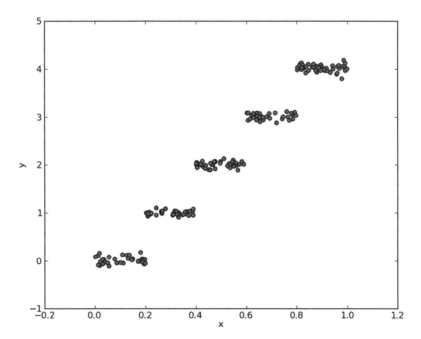

Figure 9.2   Piecewise constant data for testing regression trees

The data used to construct figure 9.2 is stored in a tab-delimited text file called ex0.txt. To build a tree from this data, enter the following commands in your Python shell:

```
>>> myDat1=regTrees.loadDataSet('ex0.txt')
>>> myMat1=mat(myDat1)
>>> regTrees.createTree(myMat1)
{'spInd': 1, 'spVal': matrix([[ 0.39435]]), 'right': {'spInd': 1, 'spVal':
matrix([[ 0.197834]]), 'right': -0.023838155555555553, 'left':
1.0289583666666664}, 'left': {'spInd': 1, 'spVal': matrix([[ 0.582002]]),
'right': 1.9800350714285717, 'left': {'spInd': 1, 'spVal': matrix([[
0.797583]]), 'right': 2.9836209534883724, 'left': 3.9871632000000004}}}
```

Check the tree data structure to make sure that there are five leaf nodes. Try out the regression trees on some more complex data and see what happens.

Now that we're able to build regression trees, we need to find a way to check if we've been doing something wrong. We'll next examine *tree pruning*, which modifies our decision trees so that we can make better predictions.

9.4   Tree pruning

Trees with too many nodes are an example of a model overfit to the data. How do we know when we're overfitting? In the previous chapters we used some form of cross-validation with a test set to find out when we're overfitting. Decision trees are no different. This section will talk about ways around this and ways to combat overfitting our data.

The procedure of reducing the complexity of a decision tree to avoid overfitting is known as *pruning*. You've done pruning already. By using the early stopping conditions in chooseBestSplit(), you were employing *prepruning*. Another form of pruning involves a test set and a training set. This is known as *postpruning*, and we'll investigate its effectiveness in this section, but first let's discuss some of the drawbacks of prepruning.

9.4.1   Prepruning

The results for these two simple experiments in the previous section were satisfactory, but there was something going on behind the scenes. The trees built are sensitive to the settings we used for tolS and tolN. For other values of our data we may not get such a nice answer as we did in the last section. To see what I mean, enter the following command in your Python shell:

```
>>> regTrees.createTree(myMat,ops=(0,1))
```

This creates a much bigger tree than the two-leaf tree in the previous section. It creates a leaf node for every instance in the dataset.

Consider for a second the plot in figure 9.3. This plot looks similar to the one in figure 9.1. If you look more closely at the y-axis, you'll see that figure 9.3 has 100x the magnitude as figure 9.1. That shouldn't be a problem, right? Well, let's try to build a

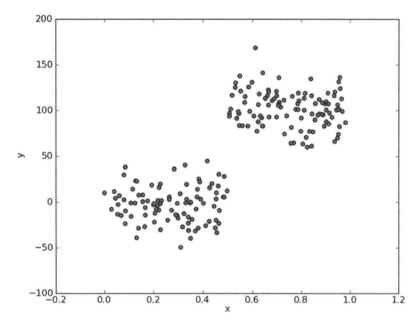

Figure 9.3 Simple piecewise constant data from figure 9.1 with magnitude enhanced 100x

tree using this data. The data is stored in a text file called ex2.txt. To create a tree, enter the following commands in your Python shell.

```
>>> myDat2=regTrees.loadDataSet('ex2.txt')
>>> myMat2=mat(myDat2)
>>> regTrees.createTree(myMat2)
{'spInd': 0, 'spVal': matrix([[ 0.499171]]), 'right': {'spInd': 0,
'spVal': matrix([[ 0.457563]]), 'right': -3.6244789069767438,
'left': 7.9699461249999999}, 'l
.
.
0, 'spVal': matrix([[ 0.958512]]), 'right': 112.42895575000001,
'left': 105.248
2350000001}}}}
```

What do you notice? The tree we built from figure 9.1 had only two leaf nodes. This tree has a lot more. The problem is that one of our stopping conditions, tolS, is sensitive to the magnitude of the errors. If we mess around with the options and square the error tolerance, perhaps we can get a tree with two leaves:

```
>>> regTrees.createTree(myMat2,ops=(10000,4))
{'spInd': 0, 'spVal': matrix([[ 0.499171]]), 'right': -2.6377193297872341,
 'left': 101.35815937735855}
```

We shouldn't have to mess around with the stopping conditions to give us the tree we're looking for. In fact, we're often not sure what we're looking for. That's what machine learning is all about. The machine is supposed to tell us the big picture.

The next section will discuss postpruning, which uses a test set to prune the tree. This is a more idealistic method of pruning because it doesn't use any user-defined parameters.

9.4.2 Postpruning

The method we'll use will first split our data into a test set and a training set. First, you'll build the tree with the setting that will give you the largest, most complex tree you can handle. You'll next descend the tree until you reach a node with only leaves. You'll test the leaves against data from a test set and measure if merging the leaves would give you less error on the test set. If merging the nodes will reduce the error on the test set, you'll merge the nodes.

Pseudo-code for prune() would look like this:

Split the test data for the given tree:
> *If the either split is a tree: call prune on that split*
> *Calculate the error associated with merging two leaf nodes*
> *Calculate the error without merging*
> *If merging results in lower error then merge the leaf nodes*

To see this in action, open regTrees.py and enter the code from the following listing.

Listing 9.3   Regression tree-pruning functions

```
def isTree(obj):
    return (type(obj).__name__=='dict')

def getMean(tree):
    if isTree(tree['right']): tree['right'] = getMean(tree['right'])
    if isTree(tree['left']): tree['left'] = getMean(tree['left'])
    return (tree['left']+tree['right'])/2.0

def prune(tree, testData):
    if shape(testData)[0] == 0: return getMean(tree)            ① Collapse tree if
    if (isTree(tree['right']) or isTree(tree['left'])):              no test data
        lSet, rSet = binSplitDataSet(testData, tree['spInd'],
                    tree['spVal'])
    if isTree(tree['left']): tree['left'] = prune(tree['left'], lSet)
    if isTree(tree['right']): tree['right'] =  prune(tree['right'], rSet)
    if not isTree(tree['left']) and not isTree(tree['right']):
        lSet, rSet = binSplitDataSet(testData, tree['spInd'],
                    tree['spVal'])
        errorNoMerge = sum(power(lSet[:,-1] - tree['left'],2)) +\
            sum(power(rSet[:,-1] - tree['right'],2))
        treeMean = (tree['left']+tree['right'])/2.0
        errorMerge = sum(power(testData[:,-1] - treeMean,2))
        if errorMerge < errorNoMerge:
            print "merging"
            return treeMean
        else: return tree
    else: return tree
```

Listing 9.3 contains three functions: isTree(), getMean(), and prune(). The function isTree() tests if a variable is a tree. It returns a Boolean type. You can use this to find out when you've found a branch with only leaf nodes.

The function getMean() is a recursive function that descends a tree until it hits only leaf nodes. When it finds two leaf nodes, it takes the average of these two nodes. This function collapses a tree. You'll see where this is needed in prune().

The main function in listing 9.3 is prune(), which takes two inputs: a tree to prune and testData to use for pruning the tree. The first thing you do in prune() is check to see if the test data is empty ❶. The function prune() gets called recursively and splits the data based on the tree. Our tree is generated with a different set of data from our test data, and there will be instances where the test data doesn't contain values in the same range as the original dataset. In this case, what should you do? Is the data overfit, in which case it would get pruned, or is the model correct and no pruning would be done? We'll assume it's overfit and prune the tree.

Next, you test to see if either branch is a tree. If so, you attempt to prune it by calling prune on that branch. After you've attempted to prune the left and right branches, you test to see if they're still trees. If the two branches aren't trees, then they can be merged. You split the data and measure the error. If the error from merging the two branches is less than the error from not merging, you merge the branches. If there's no measurable benefit to merging, you return the original tree.

Let's set this in action. After you've entered the code from listing 9.3 into regTrees.py, save it and enter the following commands in your Python shell:

```
>>> reload(regTrees)
<module 'regTrees' from 'regTrees.pyc'>
```

To create the largest possible tree, type in the following:

```
>>> myTree=regTrees.createTree(myMat2, ops=(0,1))
```

To load the test data, type in the following:

```
>>> myDatTest=regTrees.loadDataSet('ex2test.txt')
>>> myMat2Test=mat(myDatTest)
```

To prune the tree, enter the following:

```
>>> regTrees.prune(myTree, myMat2Test)
merging
merging
merging
            .
            .
            .
merging
{'spInd': 0, 'spVal': matrix([[ 0.499171]]), 'right': {'spInd': 0, 'spVal':
            .
            .
            .
01, 'left': {'spInd': 0, 'spVal': matrix([[ 0.960398]]), 'right': 123.559747,
    'left': 112.386764}}}, 'left': 92.523991499999994}}}}
```

A large number of nodes were pruned off the tree, but it wasn't reduced to two nodes as we had hoped. It turns out that postpruning isn't as effective as prepruning. You can employ both to give the best possible model.

In the next section we'll reuse a lot of the tree-building code to create a new type of tree. This tree will still have binary splits, but the leaf nodes will contain linear models of the data instead of constant values.

9.5 Model trees

An alternative to modeling the data as a simple constant value at each leaf node is to model it as a piecewise linear model at each leaf node. *Piecewise linear* means that you have a model that consists of multiple linear segments. If you aren't clear, you'll see what it means in a second. Consider for a moment the data plotted in figure 9.4. Do you think it would be better to model this dataset as a bunch of constant values or as two straight lines? I say two straight lines. I'd make one line from 0.0 to 0.3 and one line from 0.3 to 1.0; we'd then have two linear models. This is called piecewise linear because a piece of our dataset is modeled by one linear model (0.0 to 0.3) and another piece (0.3 to 1.0) is modeled by a second linear model.

One of the advantages of decision trees over other machine learning algorithms is that humans can understand the results. Two straight lines are easier to interpret than a big tree of constant values. The interpretability of model trees is one reason why you'd choose them over regression trees. The second reason is higher accuracy.

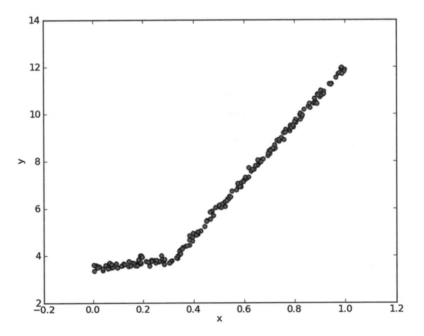

Figure 9.4 Piecewise linear data to test model tree-creation functions

With a simple change, we can use the functions written earlier to generate linear models at the leaf nodes instead of constant values. We'll use the tree-generating algorithm to break up the data into segments that can easily be represented by a linear model. The most important part of the algorithm is the error measurement.

The tree-generating code is already there. But we need to write some code to determine the error of a proposed split. Do you remember when we were writing `createTree()` there were two arguments that we never changed? We made those arguments instead of hard coding them for regression trees so that we could change those arguments for a model tree and reuse the code for model trees.

How do we measure the error and determine the best split? We can't use the same error we used in the regression tree. For a given dataset, we first fit a linear model to the data, and then we measure how much the actual target values differ from values forecasted by our linear model. This error is then squared and summed. Let's write some code to implement this. Open regTrees.py and add in the following code:

> **Listing 9.4 Leaf-generation function for model trees**

```
def linearSolve(dataSet):
    m,n = shape(dataSet)
    X = mat(ones((m,n))); Y = mat(ones((m,1)))          ❶ Format data
    X[:,1:n] = dataSet[:,0:n-1]; Y = dataSet[:,-1]          in X and Y
    xTx = X.T*X
    if linalg.det(xTx) == 0.0:
        raise NameError('This matrix is singular, cannot do inverse,\n\
        try increasing the second value of ops')
    ws = xTx.I * (X.T * Y)
    return ws,X,Y

def modelLeaf(dataSet):
    ws,X,Y = linearSolve(dataSet)
    return ws

def modelErr(dataSet):
    ws,X,Y = linearSolve(dataSet)
    yHat = X * ws
    return sum(power(Y - yHat, 2))
```

The first function in listing 9.4 is called `linearSolve()`, which is used by the other two functions. This formats the dataset into the target variable Y and the independent variable X ❶. X and Y are used to perform a simple linear regression as you did in chapter 8. In this function, you also raise an exception if the inverse of the matrix can't be determined.

The next function, `modelLeaf()`, is used to generate a model for a leaf node once you've determined to no longer split the data. This function is similar to `regLeaf()` from listing 9.2. All this does is call `linearSolve()` on the dataset and return the regression coefficients: ws.

The final function, `modelErr()`, computes the error for a given dataset. This is used in `chooseBestSplit()` to determine which split to take. This will be used in place of the `regErr()` from listing 9.2. This calls `linearSolve()` on the dataset and computes the squared error of yHat and Y.

That's all the code you need to write to create a model tree using the functions from listings 9.1 and 9.2. To see this in action, save regTrees.py and enter the following into your Python shell:

```
>>> reload(regTrees)
<module 'regTrees' from 'regTrees.pyc'>
```

The data from figure 9.4 is stored in a tab-delimited text file called exp2.txt.

```
>>> myMat2 = mat(regTrees.loadDataSet('exp2.txt'))
```

Now to use `createTree()` with our model tree functions, you enter the functions as arguments to `createTree()`:

```
>>> regTrees.createTree(myMat2, regTrees.modelLeaf, regTrees.modelErr,
 (1,10))
{'spInd': 0, 'spVal': matrix([[ 0.285477]]), 'right': matrix([[
 3.46877936], [ 1.18521743]]), 'left': matrix([[  1.69855694e-03],
      [  1.19647739e+01]])}
```

The code created two models, one for the values less than 0.285477 and one for values greater. The data in figure 9.4 was generated with a split value at 0.3. The linear models given by the `createTree()` function are `y=3.468+1.1852x` and `y=0.0016985+11.96477x`. These are close to the actual values I used to generate the data in figure 9.4. The actual models used were `y=3.5+1.0x` and `y=0+12x` with Gaussian noise added. The data from figure 9.4 along with the generated linear models is plotted in figure 9.5.

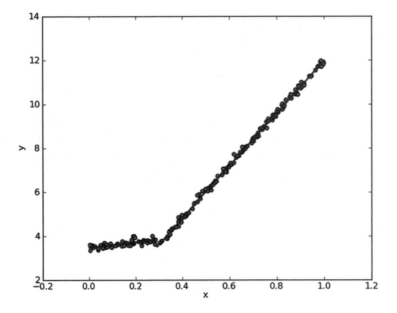

Figure 9.5   Results of model tree algorithm applied to the dataset in figure 9.4

Which is better, model tree, regression tree, or one of the models from chapter 8? By looking at the correlation coefficient, sometimes called the R^2 value, you can get an objective answer. You can calculate the correlation coefficients in NumPy by the command `corrcoef(yHat,y, rowvar=0)`, where `yHat` is the predicted values and `y` is the actual values of the target variable.

You'll now see an example where we compare the results from the previous chapter using standard linear regression to the methods in this chapter using tree-based methods. We'll compare the results using `corrcoef()` to see which one is the best.

9.6   *Example: comparing tree methods to standard regression*

Now that you can create model trees and regression trees and do regular regression, let's test them to see which one is the best. We're going to first write a few quick functions to give us a forecast for any given input once we have a tree. Next, we're going to use this to calculate the test error for three different regression models. We'll test these models on some data relating a person's intelligence with the number of speeds on their bicycle.

The data is nonlinear and can't be easily modeled by a global linear model from chapter 8. Also, the data used in this example is purely fictional.

First, let's write some functions to give us a value, for a given input and a given tree. Open regTrees.py and enter the code from the following listing.

Listing 9.5   Code to create a forecast with tree-based regression

```
def regTreeEval(model, inDat):
    return float(model)

def modelTreeEval(model, inDat):
    n = shape(inDat)[1]
    X = mat(ones((1,n+1)))
    X[:,1:n+1]=inDat
    return float(X*model)

def treeForeCast(tree, inData, modelEval=regTreeEval):
    if not isTree(tree): return modelEval(tree, inData)
    if inData[tree['spInd']] > tree['spVal']:
        if isTree(tree['left']):
                return treeForeCast(tree['left'], inData , modelEval)
        else:
            return modelEval(tree['left'], inData)
    else:
        if isTree(tree['right']):
                return treeForeCast(tree['right'], inData , modelEval)
        else:
            return modelEval(tree['right'], inData)

def createForeCast(tree, testData, modelEval=regTreeEval):
    m=len(testData)
    yHat = mat((m,1))
    for i in range(m):
        yHat[i,0] = treeForeCast(tree, mat(testData[i]), modelEval)
    return yHat
```

The function `treeForeCast()` takes a single data point or row vector and will return a single floating-point value. This gives one forecast for one data point, for a given tree. You have to tell `treeForeCast()` what type of tree you're using so that it can use the proper model at the leaf. The argument `modelEval` is a reference to a function used to evaluate the data at a leaf node. The function `treeForeCast()` follows the tree based on the input data until a leaf node is hit. When a leaf node is hit, it calls `modelEval()` on the input data. The default value for `modelEval()` is `regTreeEval()`.

To evaluate a regression tree leaf node, you call `regTreeEval()`, which returns the value at the leaf node. To evaluate a model tree node, you call `modelTreeEval()`. The function `modelTreeEval()` reformats the input data to account for the 0th order term and then calculates the forecasted value and returns it. `regTreeEval()` has two inputs even though only one is used because it needs to have the same function signature as `modelTreeEval()`.

Finally, the function `createForeCast()` calls `treeForeCast()` multiple times. This function is useful when you want to evaluate a test set, because it returns a vector of forecasted values. You'll see this in action in a moment.

Now consider the dataset in figure 9.6. I plotted data collected for various bicycle riders, relating their IQ to the number of speeds on their bicycle. We're going to build multiple models for this dataset and then test them against a test set. You can find this data in the file bikeSpeedVsIq_train.txt and find a test set in the file bikeSpeedVsIq_test.txt.

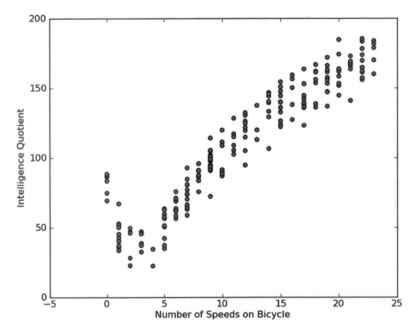

Figure 9.6   Data relating the number of speeds on a person's bicycle to their intelligence quotient; this data will be used to test tree-based regression against standard linear regression.

We're going to build three models for the data in figure 9.6. First, save the code from listing 9.5 in regTrees.py and enter the following in your Python shell:

```
>>>reload(regTrees)
```

Next, you need to build a tree for the data:

```
>>> trainMat=mat(regTrees.loadDataSet('bikeSpeedVsIq_train.txt'))
>>> testMat=mat(regTrees.loadDataSet('bikeSpeedVsIq_test.txt'))
>>> myTree=regTrees.createTree(trainMat, ops=(1,20))
>>> yHat = regTrees.createForeCast(myTree, testMat[:,0])
>>> corrcoef(yHat, testMat[:,1],rowvar=0)[0,1]
0.96408523182221306
```

Now try it with a model tree with the same settings, but you'll make a model tree instead of a regression tree:

```
>>> myTree=regTrees.createTree(trainMat, regTrees.modelLeaf,
    regTrees.modelErr,(1,20))
>>> yHat = regTrees.createForeCast(myTree, testMat[:,0],
    regTrees.modelTreeEval)
>>> corrcoef(yHat, testMat[:,1],rowvar=0)[0,1]
0.9760412191380623
```

Remember, for these R^2 values, the closer to 1.0 the better, so the model tree did better than the regression tree. Now let's see it for a standard linear regression. You don't need to import any code from chapter 8; you have a linear equation solver already written in linearSolve():

```
>>> ws,X,Y=regTrees.linearSolve(trainMat)
>>> ws
matrix([[ 37.58916794],
    [  6.18978355]])
```

To get the yHat values, you can loop over the test data:

```
>>> for i in range(shape(testMat)[0]):
...     yHat[i]=testMat[i,0]*ws[1,0]+ws[0,0]
...
```

Finally, you check the R^2 value:

```
>>> corrcoef(yHat, testMat[:,1],rowvar=0)[0,1]
0.94346842356747584
```

The R^2 value is lower than the other two methods, so we've shown that the trees do a better job at predicting complex data than a simple linear model. I'm sure you're not surprised, but I wanted to show you how to qualitatively compare the different regression models.

We'll now explore a framework for building graphical user interfaces in Python. You can use this GUI to explore different regression tools.

9.7   *Using Tkinter to create a GUI in Python*

Machine learning gives us some powerful tools to extract information from poorly understood data. Being able to present this information to people in an easily understood manner is important. In addition, if you can give people the ability to interact with the data and algorithms, you'll have an easier time explaining things. If all you do is generate static plots and output numbers to the Python shell, you're going to have a harder time communicating your results. If you can write some code that allows people to explore the data, on their own terms, without instruction, you'll have much less explaining to do. One way to help present the data and give people a way to interact with it is to build a GUI, or graphical user interface, as shown in figure 9.7.

Example: building a GUI to tune a regression tree

1. Collect: Text file provided.

2. Prepare: We need to parse the file with Python, and get numeric values.

3. Analyze: We'll build a GUI with Tkinter to display the model and the data.

4. Train: We'll train a regression tree and a model tree and display the models with the data.

5. Test: No testing will be done.

6. Use: The GUI will allow people to play with different settings for prepruning and to choose different types of models to use.

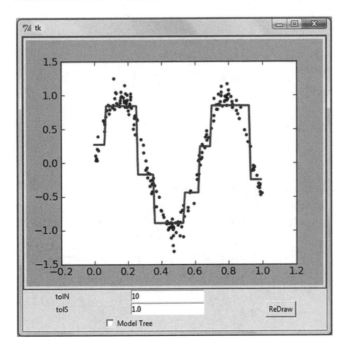

Figure 9.7   Default `treeExplore` GUI, showing a regression tree and the input data with settings `tolN=10` and `tolS=1.0`

In this final section, we're going to look at how to build a GUI in Python. You'll first see how to use an existing module called Tkinter to build a GUI. Next, you'll see how to interface Tkinter with the library we've been using for making plots. We'll create a GUI to give people the ability to explore regression trees and model trees.

9.7.1 Building a GUI in Tkinter

There are a number of GUI frameworks for Python. Tkinter is one framework that's easy to work with and comes with the standard Python build. Tkinter works on Windows, Mac OS, and most Linux builds.

Let's get started with the overly simple Hello World example. In your Python shell, type in the following commands:

```
>>> from Tkinter import *
>>> root = Tk()
```

At this point, a small window will appear, or something is wrong. To fill out this window with our text, enter the following commands:

```
>>> myLabel = Label(root, text="Hello World")
>>> myLabel.grid()
```

Now your text box should display the text you entered. That was pretty easy, wasn't it?

To be complete, you should add the following line:

```
>>> root.mainloop()
```

This kicks off the event loop, which handles mouse clicks, keystrokes, and redrawing, among other things.

A GUI in Tkinter is made up of widgets. Widgets are things like text boxes, buttons, labels, and check buttons. The label we made, `myLabel`, is the only widget in our overly simple Hello World example. When we called the `.grid()` method of `myLabel`, we were telling the geometry manager where to put `myLabel`. There are a few different geometry managers in Tkinter. `grid` puts widgets in a two-dimensional table. You can specify the row and column of each widget. Here we didn't specify any row or columns, and `myLabel` defaulted to row 0, column 0.

Let's put together the widgets for our tree explorer. Create a new Python file called treeExplore.py. Enter the code from the following listing.

> **Listing 9.6 Tkinter widgets used to build tree explorer GUI**

```
from numpy import *

from Tkinter import *
import regTrees

def reDraw(tolS,tolN):
    pass

def drawNewTree():
    pass
```

```
root=Tk()

Label(root, text="Plot Place Holder").grid(row=0, columnspan=3)

Label(root, text="tolN").grid(row=1, column=0)
tolNentry = Entry(root)
tolNentry.grid(row=1, column=1)
tolNentry.insert(0,'10')
Label(root, text="tolS").grid(row=2, column=0)
tolSentry = Entry(root)
tolSentry.grid(row=2, column=1)
tolSentry.insert(0,'1.0')
Button(root, text="ReDraw", command=drawNewTree).grid(row=1, column=2,\
                                                      rowspan=3)
chkBtnVar = IntVar()
chkBtn = Checkbutton(root, text="Model Tree", variable = chkBtnVar)
chkBtn.grid(row=3, column=0, columnspan=2)

reDraw.rawDat = mat(regTrees.loadDataSet('sine.txt'))
reDraw.testDat = arange(min(reDraw.rawDat[:,0]),\
                   max(reDraw.rawDat[:,0]),0.01)
reDraw(1.0, 10)

root.mainloop()
```

The code in listing 9.6 sets up the proper Tkinter modules and arranges them using the grid geometry manager. Two placeholder functions are included also. These will be filled out later. The format of this code is the same as our simple example of how we first created a root widget of type `Tk` and then inserted a label. You can see how we use the `grid()` method, with the row and column settings. You can also specify `columnspan` and `rowspan` to tell the geometry manager to allow a widget to span more than one row or column. There are other settings you can use as well.

New widgets that you haven't seen yet are `Entry`, `Checkbutton`, and `IntVar`. The `Entry` widget is a text box where a single line of text can be entered. `Checkbutton` and `IntVar` are self-explanatory. In order to read the state of `Checkbutton`, you need to create a variable, which is why you have `IntVar`.

At the end, you initialize some global variables associated with `reDraw()`; you'll use these later. I didn't include an exit or quit button. I think if people want to quit, they can close the window. Adding an extra close button is redundant. If you want to add one, you can insert the following code:

```
Button(root, text='Quit',fg="black", command=root.quit).grid(row=1,
column=2)
```

If you save the code in listing 9.6 and execute it, you should see something similar to figure 9.8.

Now that we have the GUI working the way we want it to, let's make it create plots. We're going to plot out a dataset and on the same chart plot out forecasted values from our tree-based regression methods. You'll see how to do this in the next subsection.

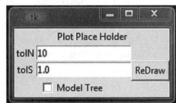

Figure 9.8   Our tree explorer using various TkInter widgets

9.7.2 Interfacing Matplotlib and Tkinter

We've made many plots in this book with Matplotlib. How can we put one of those plots in our GUI? To do this, I'm going to introduce the concept of a backend, and then we'll alter the Matplotlib backend (only in our GUI) to display in the Tkinter GUI.

The creators of Matplotlib have a frontend, which is the user-facing code such as the `plot()` and `scatter()` methods. They've also created a backend, which interfaces the plot with many different applications. You could alter the backend to have your plots displayed in PNG, PDF, SVG, and so on. We're going to set our backend to TkAgg. Agg is a C++ library to make raster images from a figure. TkAgg allows us to use Agg with our selected GUI framework, Tk. TkAgg allows Agg to render on a canvas. We can place a canvas in our Tk GUI and arrange it with `.grid()`.

Let's replace the `Plot Place Holder` label with our canvas. Delete the `Plot Place Holder` label and add in the following code:

```
reDraw.f = Figure(figsize=(5,4), dpi=100)
reDraw.canvas = FigureCanvasTkAgg(reDraw.f, master=root)
reDraw.canvas.show()
reDraw.canvas.get_tk_widget().grid(row=0, columnspan=3)
```

This code creates a Matplotlib figure and assigns it to the global variable `reDraw.f`. It next creates a `canvas` widget, similar to the other widgets.

We can now connect this canvas with our tree-creating functions. To see this in action, open treeExplore.py and add the following code. Remember that we previously made stubs for `reDraw()` and `drawTree()`, so make sure that you don't have two copies of the same function.

Listing 9.7 Code for integrating Matplotlib and Tkinter

```
import matplotlib
matplotlib.use('TkAgg')
from matplotlib.backends.backend_tkagg import FigureCanvasTkAgg
from matplotlib.figure import Figure

def reDraw(tolS,tolN):
    reDraw.f.clf()
    reDraw.a = reDraw.f.add_subplot(111)          ❶ See if check box
    if chkBtnVar.get():                              has been selected
        if tolN < 2: tolN = 2
        myTree=regTrees.createTree(reDraw.rawDat, regTrees.modelLeaf,\
                            regTrees.modelErr, (tolS,tolN))
        yHat = regTrees.createForeCast(myTree, reDraw.testDat, \
                            regTrees.modelTreeEval)
    else:
        myTree=regTrees.createTree(reDraw.rawDat, ops=(tolS,tolN))
        yHat = regTrees.createForeCast(myTree, reDraw.testDat)
    reDraw.a.scatter(reDraw.rawDat[:,0], reDraw.rawDat[:,1], s=5)
    reDraw.a.plot(reDraw.testDat, yHat, linewidth=2.0)
    reDraw.canvas.show()

def getInputs():
```

```
    try: tolN = int(tolNentry.get())
    except:
        tolN = 10
        print "enter Integer for tolN"
        tolNentry.delete(0, END)
        tolNentry.insert(0,'10')
    try: tolS = float(tolSentry.get())
    except:
        tolS = 1.0
        print "enter Float for tolS"
        tolSentry.delete(0, END)
        tolSentry.insert(0,'1.0')
    return tolN,tolS

def drawNewTree():
    tolN,tolS = getInputs()
    reDraw(tolS,tolN)
```

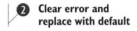

❷ Clear error and replace with default

The first thing you do in listing 9.7 is import Matplotlib and set the backend to TkAgg. There are two more import statements that glue together TkAgg and a Matplotlib figure.

We should first talk about drawNewTree(). If you recall from listing 9.6, this is the function that gets called when someone clicks the button labeled ReDraw. This function does two things: first, it calls getInputs(), which gets values from the entry boxes. Next, it calls reDraw() with the values from the entry boxes, and a beautiful plot is made. We'll discuss each of those functions in turn.

The function getInputs() tries to figure out what the user entered, without crashing the program. We're expecting a float for tolS and an integer for tolN. To get the text a user entered, you call the .get() method on the Entry widget. Form validation can consume a lot of your time when GUI programming, but it's important to have a successful user experience. You use the try:, except: pattern here. If Python can interpret the text as an integer, you use that integer. If it can't recognize it, you print an error, clear the entry box, and restore the default value. ❶ You follow a similar procedure for tolS, and the values are returned.

The function reDraw() is where the tree drawing takes place. This function assumes that the input values are valid. The first thing that's done is to clear the previous figure, so you don't have two plots on top of each other. When the function is cleared, the subplot is deleted, so you need to add a new one. Next, you see whether the check box has been checked. ❷ Depending on the state of the check box, you build a model tree or a regression tree with the tolS and tolN settings. After the tree is built, you create forecasted values from our testDat, which are evenly spaced points in the same range as our data. Finally, the actual data and the forecasted values are plotted. I plotted the actual data with scatter() and the forecasted values with plot(). The scatter() method creates discrete points and the plot() method creates a continuous line.

Let's see how this works. Save treeExplore.py and execute it. If you're writing code in an IDE, you can execute it with a run command. From the command line, you can execute it with python treeExplore.py. You should see something like figure 9.7 at the beginning of this section.

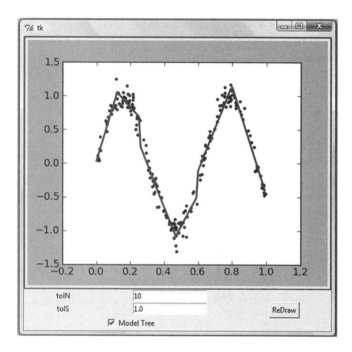

Figure 9.9 The `treeExplore` **GUI building a model tree over the same data and same settings as figure 9.7. The model tree does a better job of forecasting the data than the regression tree.**

The GUI in figure 9.7 has all of the widgets from figure 9.8 with the placeholder label replaced with a Matplotlib plot. The default value shows a regression tree with eight leaf nodes. Let's try out the model tree. Click the Model Tree text box and click the ReDraw button. You should see something similar to figure 9.9.

You should try `treeExplore` with different values. The dataset has 200 points. See what happens when you set `tolN` to 150. To build the biggest tree possible, remember that we set `tolN` to 1 and `tolS` to 0. Try that and see what happens.

9.8   Summary

Oftentimes your data contains complex interactions that lead to nonlinear relationships between the input data and the target variables. One method to model these complex relationships is to use a tree to break up the predicted value into piecewise constant segments or piecewise linear segments. A tree structure modeling the data with piecewise constant segments is known as a regression tree. When the models are linear regression equations, the tree is known as a model tree.

The CART algorithm builds binary trees and can handle discrete as well as continuous split values. Model trees and regression trees can be built with the CART algorithm as long as you use the right error measurements. When building a tree, there's a tendency for the tree-building algorithm to build the tree too closely to the data, resulting in an overfit model. An overfit tree is often more complex that it needs to be. To make the tree less complex, a process of pruning is applied to the tree. Two methods of pruning are prepruning, which prunes the tree as it's being built, and postpruning, which prunes the tree after it's built. Prepruning is more effective but requires user-defined parameters.

Tkinter is a GUI toolkit for Python. It's not the only one, but it's the most commonly used. Tkinter allows you to build widgets and arrange those widgets. You can make a special widget for Tkinter that allows you to display Matplotlib plots. The integration of Matplotlib and Tkinter allows you to build powerful GUIs where people can explore machine learning algorithms in a more natural way.

This is our last chapter on regression. I hope you won't miss it. I may. We'll now leave behind the security of supervised learning and head to the unknown waters of unsupervised learning. In regression and classification (supervised learning), we had a target variable. This isn't the case in unsupervised learning, as you'll see shortly. The next chapter is on k-means clustering.

Part 3

Unsupervised learning

This third part of *Machine Learning in Action* deals with unsupervised learning. This is a break from what was covered in the first two sections. In unsupervised learning we don't have a target variable as we did in classification and regression. Instead of telling the machine "Predict Y for our data X," we're asking "What can you tell me about X?" Things we ask the machine to tell us about X may be "What are the six best groups we can make out of X?" or "What three features occur together most frequently in X?"

We start our study of unsupervised learning by discussing clustering (grouping similar items together) and the k-means clustering algorithm in chapter 10. Next, we look into association analysis or shopping basket analysis with the Apriori algorithm in chapter 11. Association analysis can help us answer the question "What items are mostly commonly bought together?" We finish our study of unsupervised learning in chapter 12 with a more efficient algorithm for association analysis: the FP-growth algorithm.

Grouping unlabeled items using k-means clustering

This chapter covers
- The k-means clustering algorithm
- Cluster postprocessing
- Bisecting k-means
- Clustering geographic points

The 2000 and 2004 presidential elections in the United States were close—very close. The largest percentage of the popular vote that any candidate received was 50.7% and the lowest was 47.9%. If a percentage of the voters were to have switched sides, the outcome of the elections would have been different. There are small groups of voters who, when properly appealed to, will switch sides. These groups may not be huge, but with such close races, they may be big enough to change the outcome of the election.[1] How do you find these groups of people, and how do you appeal to them with a limited budget? The answer is *clustering*.

---

[1] For details on how microtargeting was used successfully in the 2004 U.S. presidential campaign, see Fournier, Sosnik, and Dowd, *Applebee's America* (Simon & Schuster, 2006).

Let me tell you how it's done. First, you collect information on people either with or without their consent: any sort of information that might give some clue about what is important to them and what will influence how they vote. Then you put this information into some sort of clustering algorithm. Next, for each cluster (it would be smart to choose the largest one first) you craft a message that will appeal to these voters. Finally, you deliver the campaign and measure to see if it's working.

Clustering is a type of unsupervised learning that automatically forms clusters of similar things. It's like automatic classification. You can cluster almost anything, and the more similar the items are in the cluster, the better your clusters are. In this chapter, we're going to study one type of clustering algorithm called *k-means*. It's called k-means because it finds k unique clusters, and the center of each cluster is the mean of the values in that cluster. You'll see this in more detail in a little bit.

Before we get into k-means, let's talk about cluster identification. Cluster identification tells an algorithm, "Here's some data. Now group similar things together and tell me about those groups." The key difference from classification is that in classification you know what you're looking for. That's not the case in clustering. Clustering is sometimes called *unsupervised classification* because it produces the same result as classification but without having predefined classes.

With cluster analysis we're trying to put similar things in a cluster and dissimilar things in a different cluster. This notion of similarity depends on a similarity measurement. You've seen different similarity measures in previous chapters, and they'll come up in later chapters as well. The type of similarity measure used depends on the application.

We'll build the k-means algorithm and see it in action. We'll next discuss some drawbacks of the simple k-means algorithm. To improve some of these problems, we can apply postprocessing to produce better clusters. Next, you'll see a more efficient version of k-means called *bisecting k-means*. Finally, you'll see an example where we'll use bisecting k-means to find optimal parking locations while visiting multiple nightlife hotspots.

10.1 *The k-means clustering algorithm*

k-means clustering

Pros: Easy to implement

Cons: Can converge at local minima; slow on very large datasets

Works with: Numeric values

k-means is an algorithm that will find k clusters for a given dataset. The number of clusters k is user defined. Each cluster is described by a single point known as the *centroid*. Centroid means it's at the center of all the points in the cluster.

The k-means algorithm works like this. First, the `k` centroids are randomly assigned to a point. Next, each point in the dataset is assigned to a cluster. The assignment is done by finding the closest centroid and assigning the point to that cluster. After this step, the centroids are all updated by taking the mean value of all the points in that cluster.

Here's how the pseudo-code would look:

Create k points for starting centroids (often randomly)
While any point has changed cluster assignment
　for every point in our dataset:
　　for every centroid
　　　calculate the distance between the centroid and point
　　assign the point to the cluster with the lowest distance
　for every cluster calculate the mean of the points in that cluster
　　assign the centroid to the mean

General approach to k-means clustering

1. Collect: Any method.

2. Prepare: Numeric values are needed for a distance calculation, and nominal values can be mapped into binary values for distance calculations.

3. Analyze: Any method.

4. Train: Doesn't apply to unsupervised learning.

5. Test: Apply the clustering algorithm and inspect the results. Quantitative error measurements such as sum of squared error (introduced later) can be used.

6. Use: Anything you wish. Often, the clusters centers can be treated as representative data of the whole cluster to make decisions.

I mentioned "closest" centroid. This implies some sort of distance measure. You can use any distance measure you please. The performance of k-means on a dataset will be determined by the distance measure you use. Let's get started coding this. First, create a file called kMeans.py and enter the code from the following listing.

Listing 10.1　k-means support functions

```python
from numpy import *

def loadDataSet(fileName):
    dataMat = []
    fr = open(fileName)
    for line in fr.readlines():
        curLine = line.strip().split('\t')
        fltLine = map(float,curLine)
        dataMat.append(fltLine)
    return dataMat

def distEclud(vecA, vecB):
```

```
        return sqrt(sum(power(vecA - vecB, 2)))

def randCent(dataSet, k):
    n = shape(dataSet)[1]
    centroids = mat(zeros((k,n)))                    Create cluster
    for j in range(n):                          ◁──┘ centroids
        minJ = min(dataSet[:,j])
        rangeJ = float(max(dataSet[:,j]) - minJ)
        centroids[:,j] = minJ + rangeJ * random.rand(k,1)
    return centroids
```

The code in listing 10.1 contains a few helper functions you'll need for the k-means algorithm. The first function, `loadDataSet()`, is the same as in previous chapters. It loads a text file containing lines of tab-delimited floats into a list. Each of these lists is appended to a list called `dataMat`, which is returned. The return value is a list containing many other lists. This format allows you to easily pack values into a matrix.

The next function, `distEclud()`, calculates the Euclidean distance between two vectors. This is our initial distance function, which you can replace with other distance metrics.

Finally, the last function in listing 10.1 is `randCent()`, which creates a set of k random centroids for a given dataset. The random centroids need to be within the bounds of the dataset. This is accomplished by finding the minimum and maximum values of each dimension in the dataset. Random values from 0 to 1.0 are then chosen and scaled by the range and minimum value to ensure that the random points are within the bounds of the data. OK, let's see these three functions in action. Save kMeans.py and enter the following code in your Python shell:

```
>>> import kMeans
>>> from numpy import *
```

To create a data matrix from a text file, enter the following (testSet.txt is included with the source code for chapter 10):

```
>>> datMat=mat(kMeans.loadDataSet('testSet.txt'))
```

You can explore this two-dimensional matrix. We'll use it later to test the full k-means algorithm. Let's see if `randCent()` works now. First, let's see what the minimum and maximum values are in our matrix:

```
>>> min(datMat[:,0])
matrix([[-5.379713]])
>>> min(datMat[:,1])
matrix([[-4.232586]])
>>> max(datMat[:,1])
matrix([[ 5.1904]])
>>> max(datMat[:,0])
matrix([[ 4.838138]])
```

Now let's see if `randCent()` produces a value between `min` and `max`.

```
>>> kMeans.randCent(datMat, 2)
matrix([[-3.24278889, -0.04213842],
        [-0.92437171,  3.19524231]])
```

It does, so these functions work as promised. Last, let's test the distance metric.

```
>>> kMeans.distEclud(datMat[0], datMat[1])
5.184632816681332
```

Now that we have the support functions working, we're ready to implement the full k-means algorithm. The algorithm will create k centroids, then assign each point to the closest centroid, and then recalculate the centroids. This process will repeat until the points stop changing clusters. Open kMeans.py and enter the code from the following listing.

Listing 10.2   The k-means clustering algorithm

```
def kMeans(dataSet, k, distMeas=distEclud, createCent=randCent):
    m = shape(dataSet)[0]
    clusterAssment = mat(zeros((m,2)))
    centroids = createCent(dataSet, k)
    clusterChanged = True
    while clusterChanged:
        clusterChanged = False
        for i in range(m):
            minDist = inf; minIndex = -1
            for j in range(k):                                        ❶ Find the
                distJI = distMeas(centroids[j,:],dataSet[i,:])            closest
                if distJI < minDist:                                     centroid
                    minDist = distJI; minIndex = j
            if clusterAssment[i,0] != minIndex: clusterChanged = True
            clusterAssment[i,:] = minIndex,minDist**2
        print centroids                         Update centroid ❷
        for cent in range(k):                        location
            ptsInClust = dataSet[nonzero(clusterAssment[:,0].A==cent)[0]]
            centroids[cent,:] = mean(ptsInClust, axis=0)
    return centroids, clusterAssment
```

The k-means algorithm appears in listing 10.2. The function kMeans() accepts four input parameters. The dataset and the number of clusters to generate are the only required parameters. A function to use as the distance metric is optional, and a function to create the initial centroids is also optional. The function starts out by finding the number of items in the dataset and then creates a matrix to store cluster assignments. The cluster assignment matrix, called clusterAssment, has two columns; one column is for the index of the cluster and the second column is to store the error. This error is the distance from the cluster centroid to the current point. We'll use this error later on to measure how good our clusters are.

You iterate until none of the data points changes its cluster. You create a flag called clusterChanged, and if this is True you continue iterating. The iteration is handled by a while loop. You next loop over all the data points to find the closest centroid. This is done by looping over all the centroids and measuring the distance to each one. ❶ The distance is measured by whatever function you pass to distMeas. The default is distEclud(), which we wrote in listing 10.1. If any of these clusters changes, you update the clusterChanged flag.

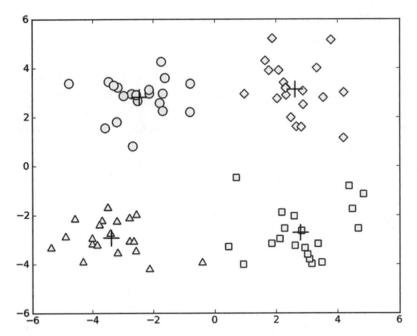

Figure 10.1 Clusters resulting from k-means clustering. After three iterations, the algorithm converged on these results. Data points with similar shapes are in similar clusters. The cluster centers are marked with a cross.

Finally, you loop over all the centroids and update their values. ❷ This is done by first doing some array filtering to get all the points in a given cluster. Next, you take the mean values of all these points. The option `axis=0` in the mean calculation does the mean calculation down the columns. Finally, the centroids and cluster assignments are returned. See figure 10.1.

Let's see the code from listing 10.2 in action. After saving kMeans.py, enter the following in your Python shell:

```
>>> reload(kMeans)
<module 'kMeans' from 'kMeans.pyc'>
```

If you don't have a copy of `datMat` from the previous example, you can enter the following command (remember to import NumPy):

```
>>> datMat=mat(kMeans.loadDataSet('testSet.txt'))
```

Now you can cluster the data points in `datMat`. I have a hunch there should be four clusters, because the image looks like there could be four clusters, so enter the following:

```
>>> myCentroids, clustAssing = kMeans.kMeans(datMat,4)
[[-4.06724228  0.21993975]
 [ 0.73633558 -1.41299247]
 [-2.59754537  3.15378974]
 [ 4.49190084  3.46005807]]
[[-3.62111442 -2.36505947]
```

```
[ 2.21588922 -2.88365904]
[-2.38799628  2.96837672]
[ 2.6265299   3.10868015]]
[[-3.53973889 -2.89384326]
 [ 2.65077367 -2.79019029]
 [-2.46154315  2.78737555]
      [ 2.6265299   3.10868015]]
```

The four centroids are displayed. You can see after three iterations that k-means converges. A plot of these four centroids, along with the original data, is given in figure 10.1.

Everything went smoothly with this clustering, but things don't always go that way. We'll next talk about some possible problems with k-means clustering and how to fix those problems.

10.2 *Improving cluster performance with postprocessing*

We talked about putting data points in k clusters where k is a user-defined parameter. How does the user know that k is the right number? How do you know that the clusters are good clusters? In the matrix with the cluster assignments is a value representing the error of each point. This value is the squared error. It's the squared distance of the point to the cluster center. We'll discuss ways you can use this error to find out the quality of your clusters.

Consider for a moment the plot in figure 10.2. This is the result of running k-means on a dataset with three clusters. k-means has converged, but the cluster assignment isn't that great. The reason that k-means converged but we had poor clustering was that k-means converges on a local minimum, not a global minimum. (A local minimum means that the result is good but not necessarily the best possible. A global minimum is the best possible.)

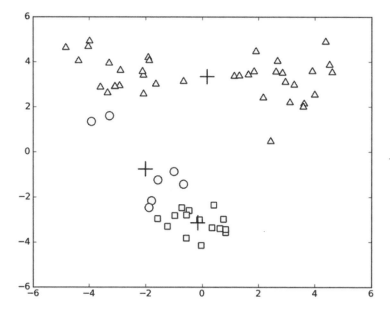

Figure 10.2 Cluster centroids incorrectly assigned because of poor initialization with random initialization in k-means. Additional postprocessing is required to clean up the clusters.

One metric for the quality of your cluster assignments you can use is the SSE, or sum of squared error. This is the sum of the values in column 1 of `clusterAssment` in listing 10.2. A lower SSE means that points are closer to their centroids, and you've done a better job of clustering. Because the error is squared, this places more emphasis on points far from the centroid. One sure way to reduce the SSE is to increase the number of clusters. This defeats the purpose of clustering, so assume that you have to increase the quality of your clusters while keeping the number of clusters constant.

How can you fix the situation in figure 10.2? You can postprocess the clusters. One thing you can do is take the cluster with the highest SSE and split it into two clusters. You can accomplish this by filtering out the points from the largest cluster and then running k-means on just those points with a k value set to 2.

To get your cluster count back to the original value, you could merge two clusters. From looking at figure 10.2, it seems obvious to merge the incorrectly placed centroids at the bottom of the figure. That was easy to visualize in two dimensions, but how could you do that in 40 dimensions?

Two quantifiable ideas are merging the closest centroids or merging the two centroids that increase the total SSE the least. You could calculate distances between all centroids and merge the closest two. The second method would require merging two clusters and then calculating the total SSE. You'd have to repeat this for all pairs of clusters to find the best pair to merge. We'll next discuss an algorithm that uses these cluster-splitting techniques to form better clusters.

10.3 *Bisecting k-means*

To overcome the problem of poor clusters because of k-means getting caught in a local minimum, another algorithm has been developed. This algorithm, known as *bisecting k-means*, starts out with one cluster and then splits the cluster in two. It then chooses a cluster to split. The cluster to split is decided by minimizing the SSE. This splitting based on the SSE is repeated until the user-defined number of clusters is attained.

Pseudocode for bisecting k-means will look like this:

Start with all the points in one cluster
While the number of clusters is less than k
  for every cluster
    measure total error
    perform k-means clustering with k=2 on the given cluster
    measure total error after k-means has split the cluster in two
  choose the cluster split that gives the lowest error and commit this split

Another way of thinking about this is to choose the cluster with the largest SSE and split it and then repeat until you get to the user-defined number of clusters. This doesn't sound too difficult to code, does it? To see this in action, open kMeans.py and enter the code from the following listing.

Listing 10.3 The bisecting k-means clustering algorithm

```
def biKmeans(dataSet, k, distMeas=distEclud):
    m = shape(dataSet)[0]
    clusterAssment = mat(zeros((m,2)))
    centroid0 = mean(dataSet, axis=0).tolist()[0]
    centList =[centroid0]
    for j in range(m):
        clusterAssment[j,1] = distMeas(mat(centroid0), dataSet[j,:])**2
    while (len(centList) < k):
        lowestSSE = inf
        for i in range(len(centList)):
            ptsInCurrCluster =\
                dataSet[nonzero(clusterAssment[:,0].A==i)[0],:]
            centroidMat, splitClustAss = \
                kMeans(ptsInCurrCluster, 2 , distMeas)
            sseSplit = sum(splitClustAss[:,1])
            sseNotSplit = \
              sum(clusterAssment[nonzero(clusterAssment[:,0].A!=i)[0],1])
            print "sseSplit, and notSplit: ",sseSplit,sseNotSplit
            if (sseSplit + sseNotSplit) < lowestSSE:
                bestCentToSplit = i
                bestNewCents = centroidMat
                bestClustAss = splitClustAss.copy()
                lowestSSE = sseSplit + sseNotSplit
        bestClustAss[nonzero(bestClustAss[:,0].A == 1)[0],0] =\
                        len(centList)
        bestClustAss[nonzero(bestClustAss[:,0].A == 0)[0],0] =\
                        bestCentToSplit
        print 'the bestCentToSplit is: ',bestCentToSplit
        print 'the len of bestClustAss is: ', len(bestClustAss)
        centList[bestCentToSplit] = bestNewCents[0,:]
        centList.append(bestNewCents[1,:])
        clusterAssment[nonzero(clusterAssment[:,0].A == \
                        bestCentToSplit)[0],:]= bestClustAss
    return mat(centList), clusterAssment
```

❶ Initially create one cluster

❷ Try splitting every cluster

❸ Update the cluster assignments

The code in listing 10.3 has the same arguments as kMeans() in listing 10.2. You give it a dataset, the number of clusters you want, and a distance measure, and it gives you the clusters. Similar to kMeans() in listing 10.2, you can change the distance metric used.

The function starts out by creating a matrix to store the cluster assignment and squared error for each point in the dataset. Next, one centroid is calculated for the entire dataset, and a list is created to hold all the centroids. ❶ Now that you have a centroid, you can go over all the points in the dataset and calculate the error between that point and the centroid. Later, you'll need the error.

Next, you enter the while loop, which splits clusters until you have the desired number of clusters. You can measure the number of clusters you have by measuring the number of items in the cluster list. You're going to iterate over all the clusters and find the best cluster to split. To do this, you need to compare the SSE after each split. You first initialize the lowest SSE to infinity; then you start looping over each cluster in the centList cluster list. For each of these clusters, you create a dataset of only the points from that cluster. This dataset is called `ptsInCurrCluster` and is fed into `kMeans()`. The k-means algorithm gives you two new centroids as well as the squared error for each of those centroids. ❷ These errors are added up along with the error for the rest of the dataset. If this split produces the lowest SSE, then it's saved. After you've decided which cluster to split, it's time to apply this split. Applying the split is as easy as overwriting the existing cluster assignments for the cluster you've decided to split. When you applied `kMeans()` with two clusters, you had two clusters returned labeled 0 and 1. You need to change these cluster numbers to the cluster number you're splitting and the next cluster to be added. This is done with two array filters. ❸ Finally, these new cluster assignments are updated and the new centroid is appended to `centList`.

When the `while` loop ends, the centroid list and the cluster assignments are returned, the same way that they're done in `kMeans()`.

Let's see this in action. After you've entered the code from listing 10.3, save kMeans.py and enter the following in your Python shell:

```
>>> reload(kMeans)
<module 'kMeans' from 'kMeans.py'>
```

You can run it on our original dataset or you can load the "difficult" dataset in figure 10.2 by entering the following:

```
>>> datMat3=mat(kMeans.loadDataSet('testSet2.txt'))
```

To run `biKmeans()`, enter the following command:

```
>>> centList,myNewAssments=kMeans.biKmeans(datMat3,3)
sseSplit, and notSplit:   491.233299302 0.0
the bestCentToSplit is:   0
the len of bestClustAss is:   60
sseSplit, and notSplit:   75.5010709203 35.9286648164
sseSplit, and notSplit:   21.40716341 455.304634485
the bestCentToSplit is:   0
the len of bestClustAss is:   40
```

Now, let's inspect the centroids:

```
>>> centList
[matrix([[-3.05126255,  3.2361123 ]]), matrix([[-0.28226155, -2.4449763 ]]),
    matrix([[ 3.1084241,  3.0396009]])]
```

You can run this multiple times and the clustering will converge to the global minimum, whereas the original `kMeans()` would occasionally get stuck in the local minimum. A plot of the data points and centroids after running `biKmeans()` is shown in figure 10.3.

Now that you have the bisecting k-means algorithm working, you're ready to put it to use on some real data. In the next section, we'll take some geographic coordinates on a map and create clusters from that.

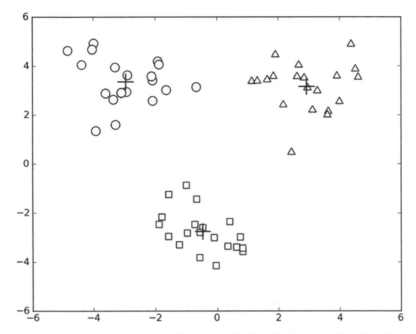

Figure 10.3 Cluster assignment after running the bisecting k-means algorithm. The cluster assignment always results in good clusters.

10.4 Example: clustering points on a map

Here's the situation: your friend Drew wants you to take him out on the town for his birthday. A number of other friends are going to come also, so you need to provide a plan that everyone can follow. Drew has given you a list of places he wants to go. This list is long; it has 70 establishments in it. I included the list in a file called portland-Clubs.txt, which is packaged with the code. The list contains similar establishments in the greater Portland, Oregon, area.

Seventy places in one night! You decide the best strategy is to cluster these places together. You can arrange transportation to the cluster centers and then hit the places on foot. Drew's list includes addresses, but addresses don't give you a lot of information about how close two places are. What you need are the latitude and longitude. Then, you can cluster these places together and plan your trip.

> **Example: using bisecting k-means on geographic data**
>
> 1. Collect: Use the Yahoo! PlaceFinder API to collect data.
> 2. Prepare: Remove all data except latitude and longitude.
> 3. Analyze: Use Matplotlib to make 2D plots of our data, with clusters and map.
> 4. Train: Doesn't apply to unsupervised learning.
> 5. Test: Use `biKmeans()`, developed in section 10.4.
> 6. Use: The final product will be your map with the clusters and cluster centers.

You need a service that will convert an address to latitude and longitude. Luckily, Yahoo! provides such a service. We're going to explore how to use the Yahoo! PlaceFinder API. Then, we'll cluster our coordinates and plot the coordinates along with cluster centers to see how good our clustering job was.

10.4.1 *The Yahoo! PlaceFinder API*

The wonderful people at Yahoo! have provided a free API that will return a latitude and longitude for a given address. You can read more about it at the following URL: http://developer.yahoo.com/geo/placefinder/guide/.

In order to use it, you need to sign up for an API key. To do that, you have to sign up for the Yahoo! Developer Network: http://developer.yahoo.com/. Create a desktop app and you'll get an appid. You're going to need the appid to use the geocoder. A geocoder takes an address and returns the latitude and longitude of that address. The code listing will wrap all this together. Open kMeans.py and add the code from the following listing.

Listing 10.4 Yahoo! PlaceFinder API

```
import urllib
import json
def geoGrab(stAddress, city):
    apiStem = 'http://where.yahooapis.com/geocode?'
    params = {}
    params['flags'] = 'J'
    params['appid'] = 'ppp68N8t'
    params['location'] = '%s %s' % (stAddress, city)
    url_params = urllib.urlencode(params)
    yahooApi = apiStem + url_params
    print yahooApi
    c=urllib.urlopen(yahooApi)
    return json.loads(c.read())

from time import sleep
def massPlaceFind(fileName):
    fw = open('places.txt', 'w')
    for line in open(fileName).readlines():
        line = line.strip()
        lineArr = line.split('\t')
        retDict = geoGrab(lineArr[1], lineArr[2])
        if retDict['ResultSet']['Error'] == 0:
            lat = float(retDict['ResultSet']['Results'][0]['latitude'])
            lng = float(retDict['ResultSet']['Results'][0]['longitude'])
            print "%s\t%f\t%f" % (lineArr[0], lat, lng)
            fw.write('%s\t%f\t%f\n' % (line, lat, lng))
        else: print "error fetching"
        sleep(1)
    fw.close()
```

❶ Set JSON as return type

❷ Print outgoing URL

The code in listing 10.4 contains two functions: geoGrab() and massPlaceFind(). The function geoGrab() gets a dictionary of values from Yahoo, while massPlaceFind() automates this and saves the relevant information to a file.

In geoGrab(), you first set the apiStem for Yahoo APIs; then you create a dictionary. You'll set various values of this dictionary, including flags=J, so that the output will be returned in the JSON format. ❶ (If you're not familiar with JSON, don't worry. It's a format for serializing arrays and dictionaries, but we won't look at any JSON. JSON stands for JavaScript Object Notation. You can find more information at www.json.org.) You next use the urlencode() function from urllib to pack up your dictionary in a format you can pass on in a URL. Finally, open the URL and read the return value. The return value is in JSON format, so you use the JSON Python module to decode it into a dictionary. The decoded dictionary is returned, and you've finished geocoding one address.

The second function in listing 10.4 is massPlaceFind(). This opens a tab-delimited text file and gets the second and third fields. These are fed to geoGrab(). The output dictionary from geoGrab() is then checked to see if there are any errors. If not, then the latitude and longitude are read out of the dictionary. These values are appended to the original line and written to a new file. If there's an error, you don't attempt to extract the latitude and longitude. Last, the sleep function is called to delay massPlaceFind() for one second. This is done to ensure that you don't make too many API calls too quickly. If you do, you may get blocked, so it's a good idea to put in this delay.

After you've saved kMeans.py, enter the following in your Python shell:

```
>>> reload(kMeans)
<module 'kMeans' from 'kMeans.py'>
```

To try out geoGrab, enter a street address and a city string such as

```
>>> geoResults=kMeans.geoGrab('1 VA Center', 'Augusta, ME')
http://where.yahooapis.com/
    geocode?flags=J&location=1+VA+Center+Augusta%2C+ME&appid=ppp68N6k
```

The actual URL used is printed so you can see exactly what's going on. If you get sick of seeing the URL, feel free to comment out that print statement in listing 10.4. ❷ Now let's see what was returned. It should be a big dictionary.

```
>>> geoResults
{u'ResultSet': {u'Locale': u'us_US', u'ErrorMessage': u'No error',
u'Results': [{u'neighborhood': u'', u'house': u'1', u'county': u'Kennebec
County', u'street': u'Center St', u'radius': 500, u'quality': 85, u'unit':
u'', u'city': u'Augusta', u'countrycode': u'US', u'woeid': 12759521,
u'xstreet': u'', u'line4': u'United States', u'line3': u'', u'line2':
u'Augusta, ME  04330-6410', u'line1': u'1 Center St', u'state': u'Maine',
u'latitude': u'44.307661', u'hash': u'B8BE9F5EE764C449', u'unittype': u'',
u'offsetlat': u'44.307656', u'statecode': u'ME', u'postal': u'04330-6410',
u'name': u'', u'uzip': u'04330', u'country': u'United States',
u'longitude': u'-69.776608', u'countycode': u'', u'offsetlon': u'-
69.776528',u'woetype': 11}], u'version': u'1.0', u'Error': 0, u'Found': 1,
u'Quality': 87}}
```

This is a dictionary with one key, ResultSet, which contains another dictionary with the following keys: Locale, ErrorMessage, Results, version, Error, Found, and Quality.

You can explore all these things, but the two we're interested in are `Error` and `Results`.

The `Error` key tells us the error code. 0 means that there were no errors. Anything else means that we didn't get the address we were looking for. You can get this error by typing

```
>>> geoResults['ResultSet']['Error']
0
```

Now let's see the latitude and longitude. You can get these by entering the following:

```
>>> geoResults['ResultSet']['Results'][0]['longitude']
u'-69.776608'
>>> geoResults['ResultSet']['Results'][0]['latitude']
u'44.307661'
```

These are strings, and you'll have to get them as floats using `float()` to use them as numbers. Now, to see this in action on multiple lines, execute the second function in listing 10.4:

```
>>> kMeans.massPlaceFind('portlandClubs.txt')
Dolphin II       45.486502        -122.788346
                       .
                       .

Magic Garden     45.524692        -122.674466
Mary's Club      45.535101        -122.667390
Montego's        45.504448        -122.500034
```

This generates a text file called places.txt in your working directory. We'll now use the points for clustering. We'll plot the clubs along with their cluster centers on a map of the city.

10.4.2 *Clustering geographic coordinates*

Now that we have a list properly formatted with geographic coordinates, we can cluster the clubs together. We used the Yahoo! PlaceFinder API to get the latitude and longitude of each point. Now we need to use that to calculate a distance between points and for cluster centers.

The clubs we're trying to cluster in this example are given to us in latitude and longitude, but this isn't enough to tell us a distance. Near the North Pole, you can walk a few meters, and your longitude will vary by tens of degrees. Walk the same distance at the equator, and your longitude varies a fraction of a degree. You can use something called the spherical law of cosines to compute the distance between two sets of latitude and longitude. To see this implemented in code along with a function for plotting the clustered clubs, open kMeans.py and add the code from the following listing.

Listing 10.5   Spherical distance measure and cluster-plotting functions

```
def distSLC(vecA, vecB):
    a = sin(vecA[0,1]*pi/180) * sin(vecB[0,1]*pi/180)
    b = cos(vecA[0,1]*pi/180) * cos(vecB[0,1]*pi/180) * \
                    cos(pi * (vecB[0,0]-vecA[0,0]) /180)
```

```
    return arccos(a + b)*6371.0
import matplotlib
import matplotlib.pyplot as plt
def clusterClubs(numClust=5):
    datList = []
    for line in open('places.txt').readlines():
        lineArr = line.split('\t')
        datList.append([float(lineArr[4]), float(lineArr[3])])
    datMat = mat(datList)
    myCentroids, clustAssing = biKmeans(datMat, numClust, \
                                        distMeas=distSLC)
    fig = plt.figure()
    rect=[0.1,0.1,0.8,0.8]
    scatterMarkers=['s', 'o', '^', '8', 'p', \
                    'd', 'v', 'h', '>', '<']
    axprops = dict(xticks=[], yticks=[])
    ax0=fig.add_axes(rect, label='ax0', **axprops)
    imgP = plt.imread('Portland.png')
    ax0.imshow(imgP)
    ax1=fig.add_axes(rect, label='ax1', frameon=False)
    for i in range(numClust):
        ptsInCurrCluster = datMat[nonzero(clustAssing[:,0].A==i)[0],:]
        markerStyle = scatterMarkers[i % len(scatterMarkers)]
        ax1.scatter(ptsInCurrCluster[:,0].flatten().A[0],\
                    ptsInCurrCluster[:,1].flatten().A[0],\
                marker=markerStyle, s=90)
    ax1.scatter(myCentroids[:,0].flatten().A[0],\
                myCentroids[:,1].flatten().A[0], marker='+', s=300)
    plt.show()
```

① Create matrix from image

The code in listing 10.5 contains two functions. The first one, distSLC(), is the a distance metric for two points on the earth's surface. The second one, clusterClubs(), clusters the clubs from a text file and plots them.

The function distSLC() returns the distance in miles for two points on the earth's surface. Two points are given in latitude and longitude, and you use the spherical law of cosines to calculate the distance between these two points. Our latitudes and longitudes are given in degrees, but sin() and cos() take radians as inputs. You convert from degrees to radians by dividing by 180 and multiplying by pi. Pi was imported when you imported everything from NumPy.

The second function, clusterClubs(), takes one input that's the number of clusters you'd like to create. This function wraps up parsing a text file, clustering, and plotting. You first create an empty list and then open places.txt and get the fourth and fifth fields, which contain the latitude and longitude. A matrix is then created from the list of latitude/longitude pairs. You next run biKmeans() on these data points and use the distSLC() distance measure for your clustering. You then plot the clusters and cluster centers.

In order to plot the clusters, you first create a figure and a rectangle. You're going to use this rectangle to determine the amount of the figure to dedicate to plotting. Next, you create a list of all the available marker types for scatter plotting. You'll use this later to give a unique marker to each cluster. You next use imread() to create a matrix from an image. ❶ You can plot this matrix using `imshow()`. Next, you create a new plot on the same figure as the image you just plotted. This allows you to use two coordinate systems without any scaling or shifting. Next, you loop over every cluster and plot these out. A marker type is chosen from `scatterMarkers`, which you created earlier. You use the index `i % len(scatterMarkers)` so that you can loop over the list if you have more clusters than available marker types. Finally, the clusters are plotted as crosses, and you show the plot.

To see this in action, enter the following in your Python shell after you've saved kMeans.py:

```
>>> reload(kMeans)
<module 'kMeans' from 'kMeans.py'>
>>> kMeans.clusterClubs(5)
sseSplit, and notSplit:  3073.83037149 0.0
the bestCentToSplit is:  0
                  .
                  .
                  .
sseSplit, and notSplit:  307.687209245 1118.08909015
the bestCentToSplit is:  3
the len of bestClustAss is:  25
```

A figure similar to figure 10.4 should appear after you've executed this command.

Try this out with different cluster numbers. What do you think is a good number of clusters?

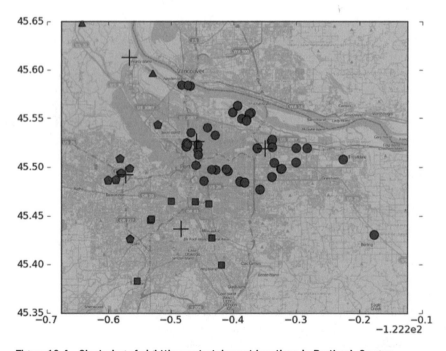

Figure 10.4   Clustering of nighttime entertainment locations in Portland, Oregon

10.5 *Summary*

Clustering is a technique used in unsupervised learning. With unsupervised learning you don't know what you're looking for, that is, there are no target variables. Clustering groups data points together, with similar data points in one cluster and dissimilar points in a different group. A number of different measurements can be used to measure similarity.

One widely used clustering algorithm is k-means, where k is a user-specified number of clusters to create. The k-means clustering algorithm starts with k-random cluster centers known as centroids. Next, the algorithm computes the distance from every point to the cluster centers. Each point is assigned to the closest cluster center. The cluster centers are then recalculated based on the new points in the cluster. This process is repeated until the cluster centers no longer move. This simple algorithm is quite effective but is sensitive to the initial cluster placement. To provide better clustering, a second algorithm called bisecting k-means can be used. Bisecting k-means starts with all the points in one cluster and then splits the clusters using k-means with a k of 2. In the next iteration, the cluster with the largest error is chosen to be split. This process is repeated until k clusters have been created. Bisecting k-means creates better clusters than k-means.

k-means and its derivatives aren't the only clustering algorithms. Another type of clustering, known as hierarchical clustering, is also a widely used clustering algorithm. In the next chapter, we'll examine the Apriori algorithm for finding association rules in a dataset.

Association analysis with the Apriori algorithm

11

A trip to the grocery store provides many examples of machine learning in action today and future uses of it. The way items are displayed, the coupons offered to you after you purchase something, and loyalty programs all are driven by massive amounts of data crunching. The store wants to get as much money as possible from you, and they certainly will use technology for this purpose.

Loyalty programs, which give the customer a discount by using a loyalty card, can give the store a glimpse at what one consumer is purchasing. If you don't use a loyalty card, the store can also look at the credit card you used to make the purchases. If you don't use a loyalty card and pay with cash, a store can look at the items purchased together. (For more ideas on possible uses of technology in the grocery store, see *The Numerati* by Stephen Baker.)

Looking at items commonly purchased together can give stores an idea of customers' purchasing behavior. This knowledge, extracted from the sea of data, can be used for pricing, marketing promotions, inventory management, and so on. Looking for hidden relationships in large datasets is known as *association analysis* or *association rule learning*. The problem is, finding different combinations of items can be a time-consuming task and prohibitively expensive in terms of computing power. Brute-force solutions aren't capable of solving this problem, so a more intelligent approach is required to find frequent itemsets in a reasonable amount of time. In this chapter we'll focus on the Apriori algorithm to solve this problem.

We'll first discuss association analysis in detail, and then we'll discuss the Apriori principle, which leads to the Apriori algorithm. We'll next create functions to efficiently find frequent items sets, and then we'll extract association rules from the frequent items sets. We'll finish up with an example of extracting association rules from congressional voting records and an example of finding common features in poisonous mushrooms.

11.1 Association analysis

Apriori

Pros: Easy to code up

Cons: May be slow on large datasets

Works with: Numeric values, nominal values

Association analysis is the task of finding interesting relationships in large datasets. These interesting relationships can take two forms: frequent item sets or association rules. *Frequent item sets* are a collection of items that frequently occur together. The second way to view interesting relationships is *association rules*. Association rules suggest that a strong relationship exists between two items. I'll illustrate these two concepts with an example. A list of transactions from a grocery store is shown in figure 11.1.

Frequent items sets are lists of items that commonly appear together. One example from figure 11.1 is {wine, diapers, soy milk}. (Recall that sets are denoted by a pair of brackets {}). From the dataset we can also find an association rule such as diapers → wine. This means that if someone buys diapers, there's a good chance they'll buy wine. With the frequent item sets and association rules, retailers have a much better understanding of their customers. Although common examples of association analysis are

Transaction number	Items
0	soy milk, lettuce
1	lettuce, diapers, wine, chard
2	soy milk, diapers, wine, orange juice
3	lettuce, soy milk, diapers, wine
4	lettuce, soy milk, diapers, orange juice

Figure 11.1 A simple list of transactions from a natural foods grocery store called Hole Foods

from the retail industry, it can be applied to a number of other industries, such as website traffic analysis and medicine.

---

diapers → beer

The most famous example of association analysis is diapers → beer. It has been reported that a grocery store chain in the Midwest of the United States noticed that men bought diapers and beer on Thursdays. The store could have profited from this by placing diapers and beer close together and making sure they were full price on Thursdays, but they did not.[†]

[†] DSS News, "Ask Dan! What is the true story about data mining, beer and diapers?" http://www.dssresources.com/newsletters/66.php, retrieved March 28, 2011.

How do we define these so-called interesting relationships? Who defines what's interesting? When we're looking for frequent item sets, what's the definition of *frequent*? There are a number of concepts we can use to select these things, but the two most important are support and confidence.

The *support* of an itemset is defined as the percentage of the dataset that contains this itemset. From figure 11.1, the support of {soy milk} is 4/5. The support of {soy milk, diapers} is 3/5 because of the five transactions, three contained both soy milk and diapers. Support applies to an itemset, so we can define a minimum support and get only the itemsets that meet that minimum support.

The *confidence* is defined for an association rule like {diapers} → {wine}. The confidence for this rule is defined as support({diapers, wine})/support({diapers}). From figure 11.1, the support of {diapers, wine} is 3/5. The support for diapers is 4/5, so the confidence for diapers → wine is 3/4 = 0.75. That means that in 75% of the items in our dataset containing diapers, our rule is correct.

The support and confidence are ways we can quantify the success of our association analysis. Let's assume we wanted to find all sets of items with a support greater than 0.8. How would we do that? We could generate a list of every combination of items and then count how frequently that occurs. It turns out that doing this can be very slow when we have thousands of items for sale. In the next section we'll address this in detail, and we'll look at something called the Apriori principle, which will allow us to reduce the number of calculations we need to do to learn association rules.

11.2 *The Apriori principle*

Let's assume that we're running a grocery store with a very limited selection. We're interested in finding out which items were purchased together. We have only four items: item0, item1, item2, and item3. What are all the possible combinations in which can be purchased? We can have one item, say item0, alone, or two items, or three items, or all of the items together. If someone purchased two of item0 and four of item2, we don't care. We're concerned only that they purchased one or more of an item.

General approach to the Apriori algorithm

1. Collect: Any method.

2. Prepare: Any data type will work as we're storing sets.

3. Analyze: Any method.

4. Train: Use the Apriori algorithm to find frequent itemsets.

5. Test: Doesn't apply.

6. Use: This will be used to find frequent itemsets and association rules between items.

A diagram showing all possible combinations of the items is shown in figure 11.2. To make the diagram easier to read, we use the item number such as 0 instead of item0. Also, the first set is a big Ø, which means the null set or a set containing no items. Lines connecting item sets indicate that two or more sets can be combined to form a larger set.

Remember that our goal is to find sets of items that are purchased together frequently. If you recall from section 11.1, we measured frequency by the support of a set. The support of a set counted the percentage of transactions that contained that set. How do we calculate this

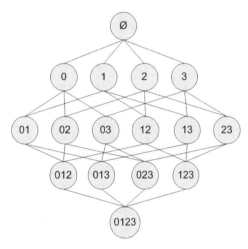

Figure 11.2 **All possible itemsets from the available set {0, 1, 2, 3}**

support for a given set, say {0,3}? Well, we go through every transaction and ask, "Did this transaction contain 0 and 3?" If the transaction did contain both those items, we increment the total. After scanning all of our data, we divide the total by the number of transactions, and we have our support. This result is for only one set: {0,3}. We'll have to do this many times to get the support for every possible set. We can count the sets in figure 11.2 and see that for four items, we have to go over the data 15 times. This number gets large quickly. A data set that contains N possible items can generate 2^N-1 possible itemsets. Stores selling 10,000 or more items aren't uncommon. Even a store selling 100 items can generate $1.26*10^{30}$ possible itemsets. This would take a very long time to compute on a modern computer.

To reduce the time needed to compute this value, researchers identified something called the Apriori principle. The Apriori principle helps us reduce the number of possible interesting itemsets. The Apriori principle says that if an itemset is frequent, then all of its subsets are frequent. In figure 11.2 this means that if {0,1} is frequent, then {0} and {1} have to be frequent. This rule as it is doesn't help us, but if we turn it inside out, it will help us. The rule turned around says that if an itemset is infrequent, then its supersets are also infrequent, as shown in figure 11.3.

> **Apriori**
>
> *A priori* means "from before" in Latin. When defining a problem, it's common to state prior knowledge, or assumptions. This is written as "a priori." In Bayesian statistics, it's common to make inferences conditional upon this a priori knowledge. A priori knowledge can come from domain knowledge, previous measurements, and so on.

In figure 11.3, the shaded itemset {2,3} is known to be infrequent. From this knowledge, we know that itemsets {0,2,3}, {1,2,3}, and {0,1,2,3} are also infrequent. This tells us that once we've computed the support of {2,3}, we don't have to compute the support of {0,2,3}, {1,2,3}, and {0,1,2,3} because we know they won't meet our requirements. Using this principle, we can halt the exponential growth of itemsets and in a reasonable amount of time compute a list of frequent item sets.

In the next section, you'll see the Apriori algorithm based on this Apriori principle. We'll code it in Python and put it to use on a simple data set from our fictional grocery store, Hole Foods.

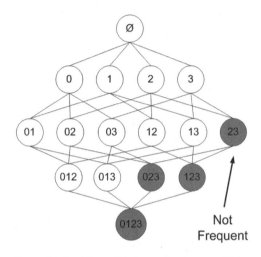

Figure 11.3 **All possible itemsets shown, with infrequent itemsets shaded in gray. With the knowledge that the set {2,3} is infrequent, we can deduce that {0,2,3}, {1,2,3}, and {0,1,2,3} are also infrequent, and we don't need to compute their support.**

11.3 Finding frequent itemsets with the Apriori algorithm

We discussed in section 11.1 that in association analysis we're after two things: frequent item sets and association rules. We first need to find the frequent itemsets, and then we can find association rules. In this section, we'll focus only on finding the frequent itemsets.

The way to find frequent itemsets is the Apriori algorithm. The Apriori algorithm needs a minimum support level as an input and a data set. The algorithm will generate a list of all candidate itemsets with one item. The transaction data set will then be scanned to see which sets meet the minimum support level. Sets that don't meet the minimum support level will get tossed out. The remaining sets will then be combined to make itemsets with two elements. Again, the transaction dataset will be scanned and itemsets not meeting the minimum support level will get tossed. This procedure will be repeated until all sets are tossed out.

11.3.1 Generating candidate itemsets

Before we code the whole algorithm in Python, we'll need to create a few helper functions. We'll create a function to create an initial set, and we'll create a function to scan the dataset looking for items that are subsets of transactions. Pseudocode for scanning the dataset would look like this:

For each transaction in tran the dataset:
For each candidate itemset, can:
>   *Check to see if can is a subset of tran*
>   *If so increment the count of can*
For each candidate itemset:
If the support meets the minimum, keep this item
Return list of frequent itemsets

To see this in action, create a file called apriori.py and add the following code.

Listing 11.1   Apriori algorithm helper functions

```
def loadDataSet():
    return [[1, 3, 4], [2, 3, 5], [1, 2, 3, 5], [2, 5]]

def createC1(dataSet):
    C1 = []
    for transaction in dataSet:
        for item in transaction:
            if not [item] in C1:
                C1.append([item])
    C1.sort()
    return map(frozenset, C1)

def scanD(D, Ck, minSupport):
    ssCnt = {}
    for tid in D:
        for can in Ck:
            if can.issubset(tid):
                if not ssCnt.has_key(can): ssCnt[can]=1
                else: ssCnt[can] += 1
    numItems = float(len(D))
    retList = []
    supportData = {}
    for key in ssCnt:
        support = ssCnt[key]/numItems
        if support >= minSupport:
            retList.insert(0,key)
        supportData[key] = support
    return retList, supportData
```

❶ Create a frozenset of each item in C1

❷ Calculate support for every itemset

Listing 11.1 contains three functions: loadDataSet(), which creates a simple dataset for testing, createC1(), and scanD().

The function createC1() creates—you guessed it—C1. C1 is a candidate itemset of size one. In the Apriori algorithm, we create C1, and then we'll scan the dataset to see if these one itemsets meet our minimum support requirements. The itemsets that do meet our minimum requirements become L1. L1 then gets combined to become C2 and C2 will get filtered to become L2. I think you get the idea.

So here you need a function, createC1(), that creates our first list of candidate itemsets, C1. You need a special function for the first list of candidate itemsets because initially you're reading from input, whereas later lists will be properly stored formatted. The format you're using is frozensets. Frozensets are sets that are frozen, which means they're immutable; you can't change them. You need to use the type frozenset instead of set because you'll later use these sets as the key in a dictionary; you can do that with frozensets but not with sets.

You first create an empty list, C1. This will be used to store all our unique values. Next, you iterate over all the transactions in our dataset. For each transaction, you iterate over all the items in that transaction. If an item isn't in C1, you add it to C1. You don't simply add the item; you add a list containing just one item. You do this to create a set of each item, because later in the Apriori algorithm you'll be doing set operations. You can't create a set of just one integer in Python. It needs to be a list (try it out). That's why you create a list of single-item lists. Finally, you sort the list and then map every item in the list to frozenset() and return this list of frozensets. ❶

The second function in listing 11.1 is scanD(). This function takes three arguments: a dataset, Ck, a list of candidate sets, and minSupport, which is the minimum support you're interested in. This is the function you'll use to generate L1 from C1. Additionally, this function returns a dictionary with support values for use later. This function creates an empty dictionary, ssCnt, and then goes over all the transactions in the dataset and all the candidate sets in C1. If the sets of C1 are part of the dataset, then you'll increment the count in the dictionary. The set is the key in the dictionary. After you've scanned over all the items in the dataset and all the candidate sets, you need to calculate the support. Sets that don't meet your minimum support levels won't be output. First, you create an empty list that will hold the sets that do meet the minimum support. The next loop goes over every element in the dictionary and measures the support. ❷ If the support meets your minimum support requirements, then you add it to retList. You insert any new sets at the beginning of the list with retList.insert(0,key). It isn't necessary to insert at the beginning; it just makes the list look organized. You also return supportData, which holds the support values for your frequent itemsets. This will be useful in the next section.

Let's see this in action! After you've saved apriori.py, enter the following in your Python shell:

```
>>> import apriori
```

Now let's import the dataset:

```
>>> dataSet=apriori.loadDataSet()
>>> dataSet
[[1, 3, 4], [2, 3, 5], [1, 2, 3, 5], [2, 5]]
```

Now create our first candidate itemset, C1:

```
>>> C1=apriori.createC1(dataSet)
>>> C1
[frozenset([1]), frozenset([2]), frozenset([3]), frozenset([4]),
    frozenset([5])]
```

C1 contains a list of all the items in frozenset. Now let's create D, which is a dataSet in the set form:

```
>>> D=map(set,dataSet)
>>> D
[set([1, 3, 4]), set([2, 3, 5]), set([1, 2, 3, 5]), set([2, 5])]
```

Now that you have everything in set form, you can remove items that don't meet our minimum support. For this example use 0.5 as our minimum support level:

```
>>> L1,suppData0=apriori.scanD(D, C1, 0.5)
>>> L1
[frozenset([1]), frozenset([3]), frozenset([2]), frozenset([5])]
```

These four items make up our L1 list, that is, the list of one-item sets that occur in at least 50% of all transactions. Item 4 didn't make the minimum support level, so it's not a part of L1. That's OK. By removing it, you've removed more work from when you find the list of two-item sets.

11.3.2 Putting together the full Apriori algorithm

Pseudo-code for the whole Apriori algorithm would look like this:

While the number of items in the set is greater than 0:
  Create a list of candidate itemsets of length k
  Scan the dataset to see if each itemset is frequent
  Keep frequent itemsets to create itemsets of length k+1

Now that you can filter out sets, it's time to build the full Apriori algorithm. Open apriori.py and add the code from the following listing.

Listing 11.2 The Apriori algorithm

```
def aprioriGen(Lk, k): #creates Ck
    retList = []
    lenLk = len(Lk)
    for i in range(lenLk):
        for j in range(i+1, lenLk):
            L1 = list(Lk[i])[:k-2]; L2 = list(Lk[j])[:k-2]     ❶ Join sets if
            L1.sort(); L2.sort()                                  first k-2 items
            if L1==L2:                                            are equal
                retList.append(Lk[i] | Lk[j])
    return retList

def apriori(dataSet, minSupport = 0.5):
    C1 = createC1(dataSet)
    D = map(set, dataSet)
    L1, supportData = scanD(D, C1, minSupport)
    L = [L1]
```

```
    k = 2
    while (len(L[k-2]) > 0):
        Ck = aprioriGen(L[k-2], k)
        Lk, supK = scanD(D, Ck, minSupport)
        supportData.update(supK)
        L.append(Lk)
        k += 1
    return L, supportData
```

2 Scan data set to get Lk from Ck

The code in listing 11.2 contains two functions: `aprioriGen()` and `apriori()`. The main function is `apriori()`; it will call `aprioriGen()` to create candidate itemsets: `Ck`.

The function `aprioriGen()` will take a list of frequent itemsets, `Lk`, and the size of the itemsets, `k`, to produce `Ck`. For example, it will take the itemsets {0}, {1}, {2} and so on and produce {0,1} {0,2}, and {1,2}. This is accomplished by first creating an empty list and then measuring how many elements are in `Lk`. Next, compare each item in `Lk` with all of the other items in `Lk`. The two `for` loops accomplish that. Next, take two sets in our list and compare them. If the first `k-2` items are equal, then you combine the two sets to make a set of size `k`. **1** The sets are combined using the set union, which is the | symbol in Python.

The `k-2` thing may be a little confusing. Let's look at that a little further. When you were creating {0,1} {0,2}, {1,2} from {0}, {1}, {2}, you just combined items. Now, what if you want to use {0,1} {0,2}, {1,2} to create a three-item set? If you did the union of every set, you'd get {0, 1, 2}, {0, 1, 2}, {0, 1, 2}. That's right. It's the same set three times. Now you have to scan through the list of three-item sets to get only unique values. You're trying to keep the number of times you go through the lists to a minimum. Now, if you compared the first element {0,1} {0,2}, {1,2} and only took the union of those that had the same first item, what would you have? {0, 1, 2} just one time. Now you don't have to go through the list looking for unique values.

Everything gets wrapped up in the `apriori()` function. You give this a dataset and a support number, and it will generate a list of candidate itemsets. This works by first creating `C1` and then taking the dataset and turning that into `D`, which is a list of sets. You use the `map` function to map `set()` to every item in the `dataSet` list. Next, you use `scanD()` from listing 11.1 to create `L1` and place this inside a list, `L`. `L` will contain `L1`, `L2`, `L3`, ... Now that you have `L1`, you want to find `L2`, `L3`, ... This is done with a `while` loop, which creates larger lists of larger itemsets until the next-largest itemset is empty. If this sounds confusing, hold on a second, and you'll see how it works. You use `aprioriGen()` to create `Ck`. Then you use `scanD()` to create `Lk` from `Ck`. `Ck` is a list of candidate itemsets, and then `scanD()` goes through `Ck` and throws out itemsets that don't meet the minimum support levels. **2** This `Lk` list gets appended to `L`, and then you increment `k` and repeat. Finally, when `Lk` is empty, you return `L` and exit.

To see this in action, enter the following after you've saved apriori.py:

```
>>> reload(apriori)
<module 'apriori' from 'apriori.pyc'>
```

This created six unique two-item sets. Now let's check out `apriori`:

```
>>> L,suppData=apriori.apriori(dataSet)
>>> L
[[frozenset([1]), frozenset([3]), frozenset([2]), frozenset([5])],
[frozenset([1, 3]), frozenset([2, 5]), frozenset([2, 3]), frozenset([3, 5])],
[frozenset([2, 3, 5])], []]
```

L contains some lists of frequent itemsets that met a minimum support of 0.5. Let's look at those:

```
>>> L[0]
[frozenset([1]), frozenset([3]), frozenset([2]), frozenset([5])]
>>> L[1]
[frozenset([1, 3]), frozenset([2, 5]), frozenset([2, 3]),
frozenset([3, 5])]
>>> L[2]
[frozenset([2, 3, 5])]
>>> L[3]
[]
```

Each of these itemsets was generated in `apriori()` with `aprioriGen()`. Let's see how `aprioriGen()` works:

```
>>> apriori.aprioriGen(L[0], 2)
[frozenset([1, 3]), frozenset([1, 2]), frozenset([1, 5]),
frozenset([2, 3]), frozenset([3, 5]), frozenset([2, 5])]
```

The six items here are the candidate itemset `Ck`. Four of these items are in `L[1]`, and the other two items get filtered out by `scanD()`.

Let's try it with a support of 70%:

```
>>> L,suppData=apriori.apriori(dataSet,minSupport=0.7)
>>> L
[[frozenset([3]), frozenset([2]), frozenset([5])], [frozenset([2, 5])], []]
```

The variable `suppData` is a dictionary with the support values of our itemsets. We don't care about those values right now, but we'll use them in the next section.

You now know which items occur in 70% of all transactions, and you can begin to draw conclusions from this. You can take this data and begin to draw conclusions, which many applications do, or you can take it and generate association rules to try to get an if-then understanding of the data. We'll do that in the next section.

11.4 *Mining association rules from frequent item sets*

Back in section 11.2, I mentioned that you can look for many interesting things with association analysis. Two common things that people look for are frequent itemsets and association rules. You just saw how you can find frequent itemsets with the Apriori algorithm. Now we need to figure out how to find association rules.

To find association rules, we first start with a frequent itemset. We know this set of items is unique, but we want to see if there is anything else we can get out of these items. One item or one set of items can imply another item. From the grocery store example, if we have a frequent itemset, {soy milk, lettuce}, one example of an association rule is soy milk → lettuce. This means if someone purchases soy milk, then there's a statistically significant chance that they'll purchase lettuce. The converse doesn't always hold. That is, just because soy milk → lettuce is statistically significant, it doesn't mean that lettuce → soy milk is statistically significant. (In the study of logic, the set on the left side of the arrow is called the *antecedent*, and the set on the right side of the arrow is the *consequent*.)

In section 11.3, we quantified an itemset as frequent if it met our minimum support level. We have a similar measurement for association rules. This measurement is called the confidence. The *confidence* for a rule P → H is defined as support(P | H) / support(P). Remember, in Python, the | symbol is the set union; the mathematical symbol is U. P | H means all the items in set P or in set H. We calculated the support for all the frequent itemsets in the previous section. Now, when we want to calculate the confidence, all we have to do is call up those support values and do one divide.

From one frequent itemset, how many association rules can we have? Figure 11.4 shows a lattice with all the different possible association rules from the itemset {0,1,2,3}. To find interesting rules, we generate a list of possible rules and then test the confidence of each rule. If the confidence doesn't meet our minimum requirement, then we throw out the rule.

Similar to frequent itemset generation in the last section, we can generate many association rules for each frequent itemset. It would be good if we could reduce the number of rules to keep the problem tractable. We can observe that if a rule doesn't meet the minimum confidence requirement, then subsets of that rule also won't meet the minimum. Please refer to figure 11.4. Assume that the rule 0,1,2 → 3 doesn't meet the minimum confidence. We know that any rule where the left-hand side is a subset of {0,1,2} will also not meet the minimum confidence. I shaded all of those rules in figure 11.4.

We can use this property of association rules to reduce the number of rules we need to test. Similar to the Apriori algorithm in listing 11.2, we can start with a frequent itemset. We'll then create a list of sets with one item on the right-hand side and test all of those. Next, we'll merge the remaining rules to create a list of rules with two items on the right-hand side. This sort of approach is known as level-wise. To see this in action, open apriori.py and add the following code.

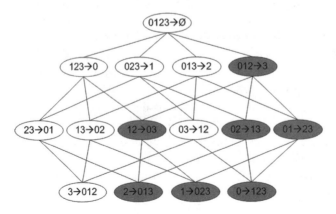

Figure 11.4 Association rule lattice for the frequent itemset {0,1,2,3}. The gray area shows rules with a low confidence. If we find that 0,1,2 → 3 is a low confidence rule, then all other rules with 3 in the consequent (shaded) will also have a low confidence.

Listing 11.3 Association rule-generation functions

```
def generateRules(L, supportData, minConf=0.7):
    bigRuleList = []
    for i in range(1, len(L)):                          ❶ Get only sets with
        for freqSet in L[i]:                              two or more items
            H1 = [frozenset([item]) for item in freqSet]
            if (i > 1):
                rulesFromConseq(freqSet, H1, supportData, bigRuleList,\
                                minConf)
            else:
                calcConf(freqSet, H1, supportData, bigRuleList, minConf)
    return bigRuleList

def calcConf(freqSet, H, supportData, brl, minConf=0.7):
    prunedH = []
    for conseq in H:
        conf = supportData[freqSet]/supportData[freqSet-conseq]
        if conf >= minConf:
            print freqSet-conseq,'-->',conseq,'conf:',conf
            brl.append((freqSet-conseq, conseq, conf))
            prunedH.append(conseq)
    return prunedH

def rulesFromConseq(freqSet, H, supportData, brl, minConf=0.7):
    m = len(H[0])                                       ❷ Try further
    if (len(freqSet) > (m + 1)):                          merging
        Hmp1 = aprioriGen(H, m + 1)
        Hmp1 = calcConf(freqSet, Hmp1, supportData, brl, minConf)
        if (len(Hmp1) > 1):
            rulesFromConseq(freqSet, Hmp1, supportData, brl, minConf)
```

Create Hm+l
new candidates ❸

The code in listing 11.3 contains three functions. The first one, generateRules(), is the main command, which calls the other two. The other two functions, rulesFromConseq() and calcConf(), generate a set of candidate rules and evaluate those rules, respectively.

The generateRules() function takes three inputs: a list of frequent itemsets, a dictionary of support data for those itemsets, and a minimum confidence threshold. It's going to generate a list of rules with confidence values that we can sort through later. These rules are stored in bigRuleList. If no minimum confidence threshold is given, it's set to 0.7. The other two inputs are the exact outputs from the apriori() function in listing 11.2. This function loops over every frequent itemset in L and creates a list of single-item sets: H1 for each frequent itemset. You start with the frequent itemsets that have two or more items because it's impossible to create a rule from a single item. ❶ If you started with the {0,1,2} set, H1 would be [{0},{1},{2}]. If the frequent itemset has more than two items in it, then it could be considered for further merging. The merging is done with rulesFromConseq(), which we'll discuss last. If the itemset only has two items in it, then you calculate the confidence with calcConf().

You're interested in calculating the confidence of a rule and then finding out which rules meet the minimum confidence. All of this is done in calcConf(), and the rest of listing 11.3 prepares rules for this. You'll return a list of rules that meet the minimum confidence; to hold this you create an empty list, prunedH. Next, you iterate over all the itemsets in H and calculate the confidence. The confidence is calculated with support values in supportData. By importing these support values, you save a lot of computing time. If a rule does meet the minimum confidence, then you print the rule to the screen. The passing rule is also returned and will be used in the next function, rulesFromConseq(). You also fill in the list brl, which is the bigRuleList passed in earlier.

To generate more association rules from our initial itemset, you use the rulesFromConseq() function. This takes a frequent itemset and H, which is a list of items that could be on the right-hand side of a rule. The code then measures m, which is the size of the itemsets in H. ❷ You next see if the frequent itemset is large enough to have subsets of size m removed; if so, you proceed. You use the aprioriGen() function from listing 11.2 to generate combinations of the items in H without repeating. ❸ This is stored in Hmp1, which will be the H list in the next iteration. Hmp1 contains all the possible rules. You want to see if any of these make sense by testing their confidence in calcConf(). If more than one rule remains, then you recursively call rulesFromConseq() with Hmp1 to see if you could combine those rules further.

To see this in action, save apriori.py and enter the following in your Python shell:

```
>>> reload(apriori)
<module 'apriori' from 'apriori.py'>
Now let's generate a set of frequent itemsets with a support of 0.5:
>>> L,suppData=apriori.apriori(dataSet,minSupport=0.5)
>>> rules=apriori.generateRules(L,suppData, minConf=0.7)
>>> rules
 [(frozenset([1]), frozenset([3]), 1.0), (frozenset([5]), frozenset([2]),
1.0), (frozenset([2]), frozenset([5]), 1.0)]
frozenset([1]) --> frozenset([3]) conf: 1.0
frozenset([5]) --> frozenset([2]) conf: 1.0
frozenset([2]) --> frozenset([5]) conf: 1.0
```

This gives you three rules: {1} → {3},{5} → {2},and {2} → {5}. It's interesting to see that the rule with 2 and 5 can be flipped around but not the rule with 1 and 3. Let's lower the confidence threshold and see what we get:

```
>>> rules=apriori.generateRules(L,suppData, minConf=0.5)
>>> rules
 [(frozenset([3]), frozenset([1]), 0.6666666666666666), (frozenset([1]),
frozenset([3]), 1.0), (frozenset([5]), frozenset([2]), 1.0),
(frozenset([2]), frozenset([5]), 1.0), (frozenset([3]), frozenset([2]),
0.6666666666666666), (frozenset([2]), frozenset([3]), 0.6666666666666666),
(frozenset([5]), frozenset([3]), 0.6666666666666666), (frozenset([3]),
frozenset([5]), 0.6666666666666666), (frozenset([5]), frozenset([2, 3]),
0.6666666666666666), (frozenset([3]), frozenset([2, 5]),
0.6666666666666666), (frozenset([2]), frozenset([3, 5]),
0.6666666666666666)]
frozenset([3]) --> frozenset([1]) conf: 0.666666666667
frozenset([1]) --> frozenset([3]) conf: 1.0
frozenset([5]) --> frozenset([2]) conf: 1.0
```

```
frozenset([2]) --> frozenset([5]) conf: 1.0
frozenset([3]) --> frozenset([2]) conf: 0.666666666667
frozenset([2]) --> frozenset([3]) conf: 0.666666666667
frozenset([5]) --> frozenset([3]) conf: 0.666666666667
frozenset([3]) --> frozenset([5]) conf: 0.666666666667
frozenset([5]) --> frozenset([2, 3]) conf: 0.666666666667
frozenset([3]) --> frozenset([2, 5]) conf: 0.666666666667
frozenset([2]) --> frozenset([3, 5]) conf: 0.666666666667
```

We got a lot more rules (11) once we lowered the confidence. Now that you see this works on a trivial dataset, let's put it to work on a bigger, real-life dataset. In the next section we'll examine the voting records of the U.S. congress.

11.5 Example: uncovering patterns in congressional voting

Now that we can find frequent itemsets and association rules, it's time to put these tools to use on a real-life dataset. What can we use? Shopping is a good example, but it's played out. Another example is search terms from a search engine. That sounds interesting, but a more interesting example I saw was voting by members of the U.S. congress.

There's a data set of congressional voting records from 1984 in the University of California at Irvine machine learning dataset repository: http://archive.ics.uci.edu/ml/datasets/Congressional+Voting+Records. This is a little old, and the issues don't mean much to me. Let's try to get some more recent data. There are a number of organizations devoted to making government data public. One organization is Project Vote Smart (http://www.votesmart.org), which has a public API. You'll see how to get the data from Votesmart.org into a format that you can use for generating frequent itemsets and association rules. This data could be used for campaign purposes or to forecast how politicians will vote.

Example: finding association rules in congressional voting records

1. Collect: Use the `votesmart` module to access voting records.

2. Prepare: Write a function to process votes into a series of transaction records.

3. Analyze: We'll look at the prepared data in the Python shell to make sure it's correct.

4. Train: We'll use the `apriori()` and `generateRules()` functions written earlier in this chapter to find the interesting information in the voting records.

5. Test: Doesn't apply.

6. Use: For entertainment purposes, but you could use the results for a political campaign or to forecast how elected officials will vote.

Next, we'll take the voting records and create a transaction database. This will require some creative thinking. Finally, we'll use the code written earlier in this chapter to generate a list of frequent itemsets and association rules.

11.5.1 *Collect: build a transaction data set of congressional voting records*

Project Vote Smart has collected a large amount of government data. They have also provided a public API to access this data at http://api.votesmart.org/docs/terms.html. Sunlight Labs has written a Python module to access this data. The Python module is well documented at https://github.com/sunlightlabs/python-votesmart. We're going to get some recent voting data from the U.S. congress and try to learn some association rules from this.

We eventually want the data to be in the same form as shown in figure 11.1. Each row will be a member of the U.S. congress, and the columns will be different things they've voted on. Let's start by trying to get some things that they voted on recently. If you haven't installed `python-votesmart` and gotten an API key, you'll need to do that now. You can see appendix A for how to install `python-votesmart`.

To get started with the `votesmart` API, you need to import `votesmart`:

```
>>> from votesmart import votesmart
```

Next, you need to enter your API key:[1]

```
>>> votesmart.apikey = '49024thereoncewasamanfromnantucket94040'
```

Now you can start using the `votesmart` API. To get the 100 most recent bills enter

```
>>> bills = votesmart.votes.getBillsByStateRecent()
To see what each bill is, enter the following:
>>> for bill in bills:
...     print bill.title,bill.billId
...
Amending FAA Rulemaking Activities 13020
Prohibiting Federal Funding of National Public Radio 12939
Additional Continuing Appropriations 12888
Removing Troops from Afghanistan 12940
                       .
                       .
                       .
"Whistleblower Protection" for Offshore Oil Workers 11820
```

When you get this book, the most recent 100 bills will be different, so I've saved the top 100 titles and billIds to a file called recent100bills.txt.

You can get further information about each of these bills by using the `getBill()` method. We'll use that last bill, the "Whistleblower Protection" bill, which has a `billId` of 11820. Let's see that in action:

```
>>> bill = votesmart.votes.getBill(11820)
```

This returns a `BillDetail` object with a whole lot of information. You can investigate all the information there, but what we're interested in are the actions taken on the bill. You can see these by entering

```
>>> bill.actions
```

---

[1] This key is just an example. You need to request your own key at http://votesmart.org/share/api/register.

This will give you a number of actions—one when the bill is introduced and another when the bill is voted on. We're interested in the one where the voting took place. You can get this by typing in the following commands:

```
>>> for action in bill.actions:
...     if action.stage=='Passage':
...             print action.actionId
...
31670
```

This isn't the full story. There are multiple stages to a bill. A bill is introduced, voted on by congress, and voted on by the House of Representatives before it goes through the executive office. The Passage stage can be deceptive because it could be in the Passage stage at the executive office, where there is no vote.

To get all the votes from a single bill, use the getBillActionVotes() method:

```
>>> voteList = votesmart.votes.getBillActionVotes(31670)
```

voteList is a list of Vote objects. To see what's inside, enter the following:

```
>>> voteList[22]
Vote({u'action': u'No Vote', u'candidateId': u'430', u'officeParties':
    u'Democratic', u'candidateName': u'Berry, Robert'})
>>> voteList[21]
Vote({u'action': u'Yea', u'candidateId': u'26756', u'officeParties':
    u'Democratic', u'candidateName': u'Berman, Howard'})
```

Now that we've played around with all the relevant APIs, we can put all this together. We're going to write a function to go from the billIds in the text file to an actionId. As I mentioned earlier, not every bill has been voted on, and some bills have been voted on in multiple places. We have to filter out the actionIds to get actionIds that will give us some vote data. I've filtered the 100 bills down into 20 bills that I thought were interesting. It's provided in a file called recent20bills.txt. We'll write one function called getActionIds() to handle filtering out the actionIds. Open apriori.py and enter the code from the following listing.[2]

Listing 11.4   Functions for collecting action IDs for bills in Congress

```
from time import sleep
from votesmart import votesmart
votesmart.apikey = '49024thereoncewasamanfromnantucket94040'
def getActionIds():
    actionIdList = []; billTitleList = []
    fr = open('recent20bills.txt')
    for line in fr.readlines():
        billNum = int(line.split('\t')[0])
        try:
            billDetail = votesmart.votes.getBill(billNum)
            for action in billDetail.actions:
```

---

[2] Don't forget to enter your API key instead of the example key!

```
        if action.level == 'House' and \
        (action.stage == 'Passage' or \
          action.stage == 'Amendment Vote'):                    ❶ Filter out
            actionId = int(action.actionId)                        actions that
            print 'bill: %d has actionId: %d' % (billNum, actionId)  have votes
            actionIdList.append(actionId)
            billTitleList.append(line.strip().split('\t')[1])
    except:
        print "problem getting bill %d" % billNum              ❷ Delay to
    sleep(1)                                                       be polite
return actionIdList, billTitleList
```

The code in listing 11.4 imports `sleep` so that you can delay the API calls, and it imports the `votesmart` module. The `getActionsIds()` function will get `actionIds` for the bills stored in recent20bills.txt. You start by importing API key and then creating two empty lists. The lists will be used to return the `actionsIds` and titles. You first open the file recent20bills.txt and then for each line split it by the tab and enter a `try`, `except` block. It's good practice to use these when dealing with outside APIs because you may get an error, and you don't want an error to waste all the time you spent fetching data. So you first try to get a `billDetail` object using the `getBill()` method. You next iterate over all the actions in this bill looking for something with some voting data. There's voting data on the Passage stage and the Amendment Vote stage, so you look for those. Now there's also a Passage stage at the executive level and that doesn't contain any voting data, so you make sure the level is House ❶. If this is `true`, you print the `actionId` to the screen and append it to `actionIdList`. At this time, you also append the bill title to `billTitleList`. This way, if there is an error with the API call, you don't append `billTitleList`. If there is an error, the except block is called, which prints the error to the screen. Finally, there's a sleep of one second to be polite and not bombard Votes-mart.org with a bunch of rapid API calls ❷. The `actionIdList` and `billTitleList` are returned for further processing.

Let's see this in action. After you enter the code from listing 11.4 into apriori.py, enter the following commands:

```
>>> reload(apriori)
<module 'apriori' from 'apriori.py'>
>>> actionIdList,billTitles = apriori.getActionIds()
bill: 12939 has actionId: 34089
bill: 12940 has actionId: 34091
bill: 12988 has actionId: 34229
            .
            .
            .
```

The `actionId` is displayed, but it's also being added to the output, `actionIdList`, so that you can use it later. If there is an error, then the `try..except` code will catch it. I had one error when I was getting all the `actiondIds`. Now you can move on to getting votes on these `actionIds`.

The candidates can vote Yea or Nay, or they can choose not to vote. We need a way of encoding this into something like an itemset and a transaction database. Remember that a transaction data set has only the absence or presence of an item, not the quantity in it. With our voting data, we can treat the presence of a Yea or Nay as an item.

There are two major political parties in the United States: Republicans and Democrats. We'd like to encode this information in our transaction dataset. Luckily this information comes over in the vote data. This is how we'll construct the transaction dataset: we'll create a dictionary with the politician's name as the key. When the politician is first encountered we'll add him/her to the dictionary along with their political affiliation—Democrat or Republican. We'll use zero for a Democrat, and one for a Republican. Now how do we encode the votes? For each bill we'll make two items: bill+'Yea' and bill+'Nay'. This method will allow us to properly encode if a politician didn't vote at all. The translation from votes to items is shown in figure 11.5.

Now that we have a system for encoding the votes to items, it's time to generate our transaction dataset. Once we have the transaction dataset, we can use the Apriori code written earlier. We're going to write a function to take in a series of `actionIds` and fetch the voting records from Votesmart's API. Then we'll encode the voting for each candidate into an itemset. Each candidate is going to be a row or a transaction in the transaction dataset. To see this in action, open apriori.py and add the code from the following listing.

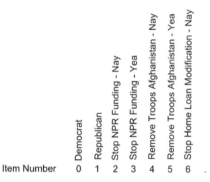

Figure 11.5 Mapping between congressional information and item numbers

---

Listing 11.5 Transaction list population with voting data

```
def getTransList(actionIdList, billTitleList):
    itemMeaning = ['Republican', 'Democratic']
    for billTitle in billTitleList:
        itemMeaning.append('%s -- Nay' % billTitle)
        itemMeaning.append('%s -- Yea' % billTitle)
    transDict = {}
    voteCount = 2
    for actionId in actionIdList:
        sleep(3)
        print 'getting votes for actionId: %d' % actionId
        try:
            voteList = votesmart.votes.getBillActionVotes(actionId)
            for vote in voteList:
                if not transDict.has_key(vote.candidateName):
                    transDict[vote.candidateName] = []
                    if vote.officeParties == 'Democratic':
                        transDict[vote.candidateName].append(1)
                    elif vote.officeParties == 'Republican':
                        transDict[vote.candidateName].append(0)
                if vote.action == 'Nay':
                    transDict[vote.candidateName].append(voteCount)
```

❶ Fill up itemMeaning list

```
              elif vote.action == 'Yea':
                   transDict[vote.candidateName].append(voteCount + 1)
        except:
            print "problem getting actionId: %d" % actionId
        voteCount += 2
    return transDict, itemMeaning
```

The getTransList() function will create the transaction dataset so that you can use the Apriori code written earlier to generate frequent itemsets and association rules. It also creates a title list so that you can easily see what each item means. The first thing you do is create the meaning list, itemMeaning, with the first two elements. When you want to know what something means, all you have to do is enter the item number as the index to itemMeaning. Next, you loop over all the bills you have and add Nay or Yea to the bill title and then add it to the itemMeaning list. ❶ Next you create an empty dictionary to add the items to. You then start going over every actionId you obtained from getActionIds(). The first thing you do is sleep; this is a delay placed in the for loop so that you don't make too many API calls too quickly. Next, you print to screen what you're trying to do so that you can see this is working. You now have the try.except block, which tries to use the Votesmart API to get all the votes on a particular actionId. Then, you loop over all the votes (usually there are more than 400 votes in voteList.) When you loop over all the votes, you fill up transDict by using the politician's name as the dictionary key. If you haven't encountered a politician before, you get his/her party affiliation. Each politician in the dictionary has a list to store the items they voted on or their party affiliation. Then you see if this politician voted Nay or Yea on this bill. If they voted either way, then you add this to the list. If something goes wrong during the API call, the except block is called, and it prints an error message to the screen and the function continues. Finally, the transDict transaction dictionary and the item meaning list, itemMeaning, are returned.

Let's try this out by getting the first two items voted on and see if our code is working:

```
>>> reload(apriori)
<module 'apriori' from 'apriori.py'>
>>>transDict,itemMeaning=apriori.getTransList(actionIdList[:2],
    billTitles[:2])
getting votes for actionId: 34089
getting votes for actionId: 34091
```

Let's see what's inside transDict:

```
>>> for key in transDict.keys():
...     print transDict[key]
[1, 2, 5]
[1, 2, 4]
[0, 3, 4]
[0, 3, 4]
[1, 2, 4]
[0, 3, 4]
[1]
[1, 2, 5]
[1, 2, 4]
[1]
```

```
[1, 2, 4]
[0, 3, 4]
[1, 2, 5]
[1, 2, 4]
[0, 3, 4]
```

Don't be alarmed if many of these lists look similar. Many politicians vote alike. Now, given a list of items, you can quickly decode what it means with the itemMeaning list:

```
>>> transDict.keys()[6]
u' Doyle,  Michael 'Mike''
>>> for item in transDict[' Doyle,  Michael 'Mike'']:
...     print itemMeaning[item]
...
Republican
Prohibiting Federal Funding of National Public Radio -- Yea
Removing Troops from Afghanistan - Nay
```

Your output may be different depending on the results returned from the Votesmart server.

Now, let's try it with the full list:

```
>>> transDict,itemMeaning=apriori.getTransList(actionIdList, billTitles)
getting votes for actionId: 34089
getting votes for actionId: 34091
getting votes for actionId: 34229
                .
                .
                .
```

Now, before you're ready to use the Apriori algorithm we developed earlier, you need to make a list of all the transactions. You can do that with a list comprehension similar to the previous for loop:

```
>>> dataSet = [transDict[key] for key in transDict.keys()]
```

Doing this throws out the keys, which are the politicians' names. That's OK. You aren't interested in that. You're interested in the items and associations among them. We're now going to mine the frequent itemsets and association rules using the Apriori algorithm.

11.5.2 *Test: association rules from congressional voting records*

Now you can apply the Apriori algorithm from section 11.3. If you try the default support setting of 50%, you won't get many frequent itemsets:

```
>>> L,suppData=apriori.apriori(dataSet, minSupport=0.5)
>>> L
[[frozenset([4]), frozenset([13]), frozenset([0]), frozenset([21])],
    [frozenset([13, 21])], []]
```

Using a lower minimum support of 30% gives you many more frequent itemsets:

```
>>> L,suppData=apriori.apriori(dataSet, minSupport=0.3)
>>> len(L)
8
```

With a support of 30%, you have lots of frequent itemsets. You even have six sets with seven items inside:

```
>>> L[6]
[frozenset([0, 3, 7, 9, 23, 25, 26]), frozenset([0, 3, 4, 9, 23, 25, 26]),
    frozenset([0, 3, 4, 7, 9, 23, 26]), frozenset([0, 3, 4, 7, 9, 23, 25]),
    frozenset([0, 4, 7, 9, 23, 25, 26]), frozenset([0, 3, 4, 7, 9, 25, 26])]
```

You now have the frequent itemsets. We could stop here, but let's try to generate association rules using the code we wrote in section 11.4. You can first try the default minimum confidence of 0.7:

```
>>> rules = apriori.generateRules(L,suppData)
```

That generated way too many rules. Let's try increasing the minimum confidence:

```
>>> rules = apriori.generateRules(L,suppData, minConf=0.95)
frozenset([15]) --> frozenset([1]) conf: 0.961538461538
frozenset([22]) --> frozenset([1]) conf: 0.951351351351
                            .
                            .
                            .
frozenset([25, 26, 3, 4]) --> frozenset([0, 9, 7]) conf: 0.97191011236
frozenset([0, 25, 26, 4]) --> frozenset([9, 3, 7]) conf: 0.950549450549
```

Try increasing the confidence even more:

```
>>> rules = apriori.generateRules(L,suppData, minConf=0.99)
frozenset([3]) --> frozenset([9]) conf: 1.0
frozenset([3]) --> frozenset([0]) conf: 0.995614035088
frozenset([3]) --> frozenset([0, 9]) conf: 0.995614035088
frozenset([26, 3]) --> frozenset([0, 9]) conf: 1.0
frozenset([9, 26]) --> frozenset([0, 7]) conf: 0.957547169811
                            .
                            .
                            .
frozenset([23, 26, 3, 4, 7]) --> frozenset([0, 9]) conf: 1.0
frozenset([23, 25, 3, 4, 7]) --> frozenset([0, 9]) conf: 0.994764397906
frozenset([25, 26, 3, 4, 7]) --> frozenset([0, 9]) conf: 1.0
```

These all provide some interesting rules. To find out what each rule means, enter the rule number as the index to itemMeaning:

```
>>> itemMeaning[26]
'Prohibiting the Use of Federal Funds for NASCAR Sponsorships -- Nay'
>>> itemMeaning[3]
'Prohibiting Federal Funding of National Public Radio -- Yea'
>>> itemMeaning[9]
'Repealing the Health Care Bill -- Yea'
```

I've included the following rules in figure 11.6: {3} → {0}, {22} → {1}, and {9,26} → {0,7}.

There are many more interesting and entertaining rules in the data. Do you remember that we initially used the support level of 30%? This means that these rules show up in at least 30% of all the transactions. That is meaningful because what it says is that we're going to see these association rules in at least 30% of the

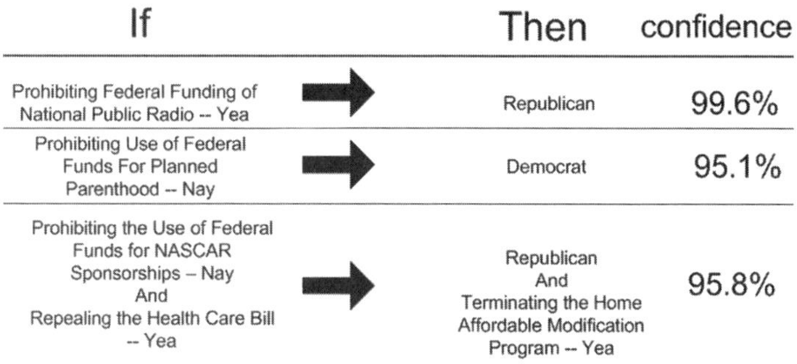

If		Then	confidence
Prohibiting Federal Funding of National Public Radio -- Yea	➡	Republican	**99.6%**
Prohibiting Use of Federal Funds For Planned Parenthood -- Nay	➡	Democrat	**95.1%**
Prohibiting the Use of Federal Funds for NASCAR Sponsorships – Nay And Repealing the Health Care Bill -- Yea	➡	Republican And Terminating the Home Affordable Modification Program -- Yea	**95.8%**

Figure 11.6 Association rules {3} → {0}, {22} → {1}, and {9,26} → {0,7} with their meanings and confidence levels

votes, and in the case of {3} → {0} this rule is right 99.6% of the time. I wish I could bet on this sort of stuff.

11.6 Example: finding similar features in poisonous mushrooms

Sometimes you don't want to look for the frequent itemsets; you may only be interested in itemsets containing a certain item. In the final example, we're going to look for common features in poisonous mushrooms. You can then use these common features to help you avoid eating mushrooms that are poisonous. The UCI Machine Learning Repository has a dataset with 23 features taken from species of gilled mushrooms. Each of the features contains nominal values. We're going to need to transform these nominal values into a set similar to what we did with the votes in the previous example. Luckily, this transformation was already done for us.[3] Roberto Bayardo has parsed the UCI mushrooms dataset into a set of features for each sample of mushroom. Each possible value for each feature is enumerated, and if a sample contains that feature, then its integer value is included in the dataset. Let's take a closer look at the dataset. It's included in the source repository under the name mushroom.dat. Compare this to the original dataset located at http://archive.ics.uci.edu/ml/machine-learning-databases/mushroom/agaricus-lepiota.data.

Take a look at the first few lines of the prepared file mushroom.dat:

```
1 3 9 13 23 25 34 36 38 40 52 54 59 63 67 76 85 86 90 93 98 107 113
2 3 9 14 23 26 34 36 39 40 52 55 59 63 67 76 85 86 90 93 99 108 114
2 4 9 15 23 27 34 36 39 41 52 55 59 63 67 76 85 86 90 93 99 108 115
```

The first feature is poisonous or edible. If a sample is poisonous, you get a 1. If it's edible, you get a 2. The next feature is cap shape, which has six possible values that are represented with the integers 3–8.

To find features in common with poisonous mushrooms, you can run the Apriori algorithm and look for itemsets with feature 2.

```
>>> mushDatSet = [line.split() for line in
open('mushroom.dat').readlines()]
```

---

[3] "Frequent Itemset Mining Dataset Repository" retrieved July 10, 2011; http://fimi.ua.ac.be/data/.

Now let's run the Apriori algorithm on this dataset:

```
>>> L,suppData=apriori.apriori(mushDatSet, minSupport=0.3)
```

Now you can search the frequent itemsets for the poisonous feature 2:

```
>>> for item in L[1]:
...        if item.intersection('2'): print item
...
frozenset(['2', '59'])
frozenset(['39', '2'])
frozenset(['2', '67'])
frozenset(['2', '34'])
frozenset(['2', '23'])
```

You can also repeat this for the larger itemsets:

```
>>> for item in L[3]:
...        if item.intersection('2'): print item
...
frozenset(['63', '59', '2', '93'])
frozenset(['39', '2', '53', '34'])
frozenset(['2', '59', '23', '85'])
frozenset(['2', '59', '90', '85'])
frozenset(['39', '2', '36', '34'])
frozenset(['39', '63', '2', '85'])
frozenset(['39', '2', '90', '85'])
frozenset(['2', '59', '90', '86'])
```

Now you need to look up these features so you know what to look for in wild mushrooms. If you see any of these features, avoid eating the mushroom. One final disclaimer: although these features may be common in poisonous mushrooms, the absence of these features doesn't make a mushroom edible. Eating the wrong mushroom can kill you.

11.7 Summary

Association analysis is a set of tools used to find interesting relationships in a large set of data. There are two ways you can quantify the interesting relationships. The first way is a frequent itemset, which shows items that commonly appear in the data together. The second way of measuring interesting relationships is association rules. Association rules imply an if..then relationship between items.

Finding different combinations of items can be a time-consuming task and prohibitively expensive in terms of computing power. More intelligent approaches are needed to find frequent itemsets in a reasonable amount of time. One such approach is the Apriori algorithm, which uses the Apriori principle to reduce the number of sets that are checked against the database. The Apriori principle states that if an item is infrequent, then supersets containing that item will also be infrequent. The Apriori algorithm starts from single itemsets and creates larger sets by combining sets that meet the minimum support measure. Support is used to measure how often a set appears in the original data.

Once frequent itemsets have been found, you can use the frequent itemsets to generate association rules. The significance of an association rule is measured by confidence. Confidence tells you how many times this rule applies to the frequent itemsets.

Association analysis can be performed on many different items. Some common examples are items in a store and pages visited on a website. Association analysis has also been used to look at the voting history of elected officials and judges.

The Apriori algorithm scans over the dataset each time you increase the length of your frequent itemsets. When the datasets become very large, this can drastically reduce the speed of finding frequent itemsets. The next chapter introduces the FP-growth algorithm.[4] In contrast to Apriori, it only needs to go over the dataset twice, which can lead to a significant increase in speed.

---

[4] H. Li, Y. Wang, D. Zhang, M. Zhang, and E. Chang, "PFP: Parallel FP-Growth for Query Recommendation," RecSys 2008, Proceedings of the 2008 ACM Conference on Recommender Systems; http://portal.acm.org/citation.cfm?id=1454027.

12

Efficiently finding frequent itemsets with FP-growth

This chapter covers

- Finding common patterns in transaction data
- The FP-growth algorithm
- Finding co-occurring words in a Twitter feed

Have you ever gone to a search engine, typed in a word or part of a word, and the search engine automatically completed the search term for you? Perhaps it recommended something you didn't even know existed, and you searched for that instead. That has happened to me, sometimes with comical results when I started a search with "why does...." To come up with those search terms, researchers at the search company used a version of the algorithm we'll discuss in this chapter. They looked at words used on the internet and found pairs of words that frequently occur together.[1] This requires a way to find frequent itemsets efficiently.

[1] J. Han, J. Pei, Y. Yin, R. Mao, "Mining Frequent Patterns without Candidate Generation: A Frequent-Pattern Tree Approach," *Data Mining and Knowledge Discovery 8* (2004), 53–87.

This chapter expands on the topics in the previous chapter. This chapter covers a great algorithm for uncovering frequent itemsets. The algorithm, called FP-growth, is faster than Apriori in the previous chapter. It builds from Apriori but uses some different techniques to accomplish the same task. That task is finding frequent itemsets or pairs, sets of things that commonly occur together, by storing the dataset in a special structure called an FP-tree. This results in faster execution times than Apriori, commonly with performance two orders of magnitude better.

In the last chapter, we discussed ways of looking at interesting things in datasets. Two of the most common ways of looking at things in the dataset are frequent itemsets and association rules. In chapter 11, we did both. In this chapter, we'll focus on frequent itemsets. We'll dive deeper into that task, exploring the FP-growth algorithm, which allows us to mine data more efficiently. This algorithm does a better job of finding frequent itemsets, but it doesn't find association rules.

The FP-growth algorithm is faster than Apriori because it requires only two scans of the database, whereas Apriori will scan the dataset to find if a given pattern is frequent or not—Apriori scans the dataset for every potential frequent item. On small datasets, this isn't a problem, but when you're dealing with larger datasets, this will be a problem. The FP-growth algorithm scans the dataset only twice. The basic approach to finding frequent itemsets using the FP-growth algorithm is as follows:

1 Build the FP-tree.
2 Mine frequent itemsets from the FP-tree.

We'll discuss the FP-tree data structure and then look at how to encode a dataset in this structure. We'll next look at how we can mine frequent itemsets from the FP-tree. Finally, we'll look at an example of mining commonly used words from a stream of Twitter text and an example of mining common patterns in people's web-browsing behavior.

12.1 FP-trees: an efficient way to encode a dataset

FP-growth

Pros: Usually faster than Apriori.

Cons: Difficult to implement; certain datasets degrade the performance.

Works with: Nominal values.

The FP-growth algorithm stores data in a compact data structure called an FP-tree. The FP stands for "frequent pattern." An FP-tree looks like other trees in computer science, but it has links connecting similar items. The linked items can be thought of as a linked list. An example FP-tree is shown in figure 12.1.

Unlike a search tree, an item can appear multiple times in the same tree. The FP-tree is used to store the frequency of occurrence for sets of items. Sets are stored as paths in the tree. Sets with similar items will share part of the tree. Only when they differ will the tree split. A node identifies a single item from the set and the number of times it occurred in this sequence. A path will tell you how many times a sequence occurred. Don't worry if this sounds confusing. Shortly we'll walk through how to create this tree.

The links between similar items, known as *node links*, will be used to rapidly find the location of similar items. Don't worry if this sounds a little confusing right now; we'll work through a simple example. The data used to generate the tree in figure 12.1 is shown in table 12.1.

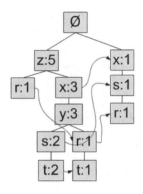

Figure 12.1 An example FP-tree. The FP-tree looks like a generic tree with links connecting similar items.

TID	Items in transaction
001	r, z, h, j, p
002	z, y, x, w, v, u, t, s
003	z
004	r, x, n, o, s
005	y, r, x, z, q, t, p
006	y, z, x, e, q, s, t, m

Table 12.1 Sample transaction dataset, used to generate the FP-tree in figure 12.1

In figure 12.1 the item z appeared five times, and the set {r,z} appeared once. We can conclude that z must have appeared four times with other symbols or on its own. Let's look at the other possibilities for z. The set {t,s,y,x,z} appeared two times, and the set {t,r,y,x,z} appeared once. The item z has a 5 next to it, so it occurred five times, and we have four accounted for, so it must have appeared once on its own. Inspect table 12.1 to verify that this is true. I mentioned that {t,r,y,x,z} appeared once, but in the transaction dataset you can see item 005 was {y,r,x,z,q,t,p}. What happened to q and p?

We used the term *support* in chapter 11, which was a minimum threshold, below which we considered items infrequent. If you set the minimum support to 3 and apply frequent item analysis, you'll get only itemsets that appear three or more times. In generating the tree in figure 12.1, the minimum support was 3, so q and p don't appear in the tree.

The FP-growth algorithm works like this. First, you build the FP-tree, and then you mine it for frequent itemsets. To build the tree, you scan the original dataset twice. The first pass counts the frequency of occurrence of all the items. Remember the Apriori principle from chapter 11. If an item is infrequent, supersets containing that item will also be infrequent, so you don't have to worry about them. You use the first

> ### General approach to FP-growth
> 1. Collect: Any method.
> 2. Prepare: Discrete data is needed because we're storing sets. If you have continuous data, it will need to be quantized into discrete values.
> 3. Analyze: Any method.
> 4. Train: Build an FP-tree and mine the tree.
> 5. Test: Doesn't apply.
> 6. Use: This can be used to identify commonly occurring items that can be used to make decisions, suggest items, make forecasts, and so on.

pass to count the frequency of occurrence and then address only the frequent items in the second pass.

12.2 Build an FP-tree

In the second pass of the dataset, you build the FP-tree. In order to build a tree you need a container to hold the tree.

12.2.1 Creating the FP-tree data structure

The tree in this chapter is more involved than the other trees in this book, so you'll create a class to hold each node of the tree. Create a file called fpGrowth.py and add the code from the following listing.

Listing 12.1 FP-tree class definition

```
class treeNode:
    def __init__(self, nameValue, numOccur, parentNode):
        self.name = nameValue
        self.count = numOccur
        self.nodeLink = None
        self.parent = parentNode
        self.children = {}

    def inc(self, numOccur):
        self.count += numOccur

    def disp(self, ind=1):
        print ' '*ind, self.name, ' ', self.count
        for child in self.children.values():
            child.disp(ind+1)
```

The code in listing 12.1 is a class definition for the nodes of the FP-tree. It has variables to hold the name of the node, a count. The nodeLink variable will be used to link similar items (the dashed lines in figure 12.1). Next, the parent variable is used to refer to the parent of this node in the tree. Often, you don't need this in trees because you're recursively accessing nodes. Later in this chapter, you'll be given a leaf node and you'll need to ascend the tree, which requires a pointer to the parent. Lastly, the node contains an empty dictionary for the children of this node.

There are two methods in listing 12.1; `inc()` increments the `count` variable by a given amount. The last method, `disp()`, is used to display the tree in text. It isn't needed to create the tree, but it's useful for debugging.

Try out this code:

```
>>> import fpGrowth
>>> rootNode = fpGrowth.treeNode('pyramid',9, None)
```

This creates a single tree node. Now, let's add a child node to it:

```
>>> rootNode.children['eye']=fpGrowth.treeNode('eye', 13, None)
```

To display the child node, type

```
>>> rootNode.disp()
   pyramid    9
     eye    13
```

Add another node to see how two child nodes are displayed:

```
>>> rootNode.children['phoenix']=fpGrowth.treeNode('phoenix', 3, None)
>>> rootNode.disp()
   pyramid    9
     eye    13
     phoenix    3
```

Now that you have the tree data structure built, you can construct the FP-tree.

12.2.2 *Constructing the FP-tree*

In addition to the FP-tree shown in figure 12.1, you need a header table to point to the first instance of a given type. The header table will allow you to quickly access all of the elements of a given type in the FP-tree. The header table is shown in figure 12.2.

You'll use a dictionary as your data structure to store the header table. In addition to storing pointers, you can use the header table to keep track of the total count of every type of element in the FP-tree.

The first pass through the dataset will count the frequency of occurrence of each item. Then, you'll eliminate any items that

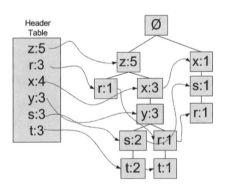

Figure 12.2   FP-tree with header table. The header table serves as a starting point to find similar items.

don't meet the minimum support. In the next step, you'll build the FP-tree. When you build the tree, you'll take each itemset and add it to an existing path if one exists. If it doesn't exist, you'll create a new path. Each transaction is a set, which is an unordered collection. If you have {z,x,y} and {y,z,r}, you need the similar items to overlap. To solve this, you need to sort each set before it's added to the tree. The sort is done using the absolute item frequency. Using the values in the header table in figure 12.2, the filtered and reordered dataset from table 12.1 is shown in table 12.2.

Table 12.2 Transaction dataset with infrequent items removed and items reordered

TID	Items in transaction	Filtered and sorted transactions
001	r, z, h, j, p	z, r
002	z, y, x, w, v, u, t, s	z, x, y, s, t
003	z	z
004	r, x, n, o, s	x, s, r
005	y, r, x, z, q, t, p	z, x, y, r, t
006	y, z, x, e, q, s, t, m	z, x, y, s, t

After you have the transactions filtered and sorted, you can start building the tree. You start with the null set (symbol Ø) and add frequent itemsets to it. The filtered and sorted transactions are successively added to the tree, incrementing existing elements and branching out if no existing element exists. This process is illustrated in figure 12.3 with the first two transactions from table 12.2.

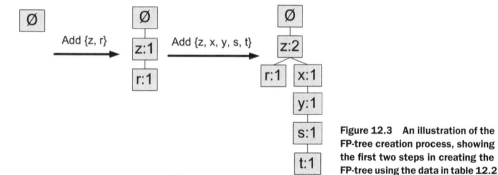

Figure 12.3 An illustration of the FP-tree creation process, showing the first two steps in creating the FP-tree using the data in table 12.2

Now that you have an idea of how to go from a transaction dataset to an FP-tree, let's write some code to create the tree. Open fpGrowth.py and add the code from the following listing.

Listing 12.2 FP-tree creation code

```
def createTree(dataSet, minSup=1):
    headerTable = {}
    for trans in dataSet
        for item in trans:
            headerTable[item] = headerTable.get(item, 0) + dataSet[trans]
```

```
    for k in headerTable.keys():                           ❶ Remove items
        if headerTable[k] < minSup:                          not meeting
            del(headerTable[k])                               min support
    freqItemSet = set(headerTable.keys())
    if len(freqItemSet) == 0: return None, None            ◁─┐ If no items meet
    for k in headerTable:                                  ❷ min support, exit
        headerTable[k] = [headerTable[k], None]
    retTree = treeNode('Null Set', 1, None)
    for tranSet, count in dataSet.items():
        localD = {}
        for item in tranSet:                               ❸ Sort transactions
            if item in freqItemSet:                          by global
                localD[item] = headerTable[item][0]          frequency
        if len(localD) > 0:
            orderedItems = [v[0] for v in sorted(localD.items(),
                                 key=lambda p: p[1], reverse=True)]
            updateTree(orderedItems, retTree, \            ❹ Populate tree with
                       headerTable, count)                    ordered freq itemset
    return retTree, headerTable

def updateTree(items, inTree, headerTable, count):
    if items[0] in inTree.children:
        inTree.children[items[0]].inc(count)
    else:
        inTree.children[items[0]] = treeNode(items[0], count, inTree)
        if headerTable[items[0]][1] == None:
            headerTable[items[0]][1] = inTree.children[items[0]]
        else:
            updateHeader(headerTable[items[0]][1],
                         inTree.children[items[0]])
    if len(items) > 1:
        updateTree(items[1::], inTree.children[items[0]],
                              headerTable, count)           ◁─┐ Recursively call
                                                             updateTree on
def updateHeader(nodeToTest, targetNode):                  ❺ remaining items
    while (nodeToTest.nodeLink != None):
        nodeToTest = nodeToTest.nodeLink
    nodeToTest.nodeLink = targetNode
```

The code in listing 12.2 has three functions. The first one, createTree(), takes the dataset and the minimum support as arguments and builds the FP-tree. This makes two passes through the dataset. The first pass goes through everything in the dataset and counts the frequency of each term. These are stored in the header table. Next, the header table is scanned and items occurring less than minSup are deleted. ❶ If no item is frequent, then you do no further processing. ❷ Next, the header table is slightly expanded so it can hold a count and pointer to the first item of each type. You then create the base node, which contains the null set Ø. Finally, you iterate over the dataset again, this time using only items that are frequent. ❸ These items are sorted, as shown in table 12.2, and the updateTree() method is called. ❹ We'll discuss updateTree() next.

To grow the FP-tree (this is where the *growth* in FP-growth comes from), you call updateTree with an itemset. Figure 12.3 illustrates what happens in updateTree(). It first tests if the first item in the transaction exists as a child node. If so, it updates the count of that item. If the item doesn't exist, it creates a new `treeNode` and adds it as a child. At this time, the header table is also updated to point to this new node. The header table is updated with the `updateHeader()` function, which we'll discuss next. The last thing `updateTree()` does is recursively call itself with the first element in the list removed. **❺**

The last function in listing 12.2 is `updateHeader()`, which makes sure the node links point to every instance of this item in the tree. You start with the first `nodeLink` in the header table and then follow the `nodeLinks` until you find the end. This is a linked list. When working with trees, the natural reaction is to do everything recursively. This can get you in trouble when working with a linked list because if the list is long enough, you'll hit the limits of recursion.

Before you can run this example, you need a dataset. You can get this from the code repo, or you can enter it by hand. The `loadSimpDat()` function will return a list of transactions. These are the same as the transactions in table 12.1. The `createTree()` function will be used later when you're mining the tree so it doesn't take the input data as lists. It expects a dictionary with the itemsets as the dictionary keys and the frequency as the value. A `createInitSet()` function does this conversion for you, so add these to fpGrowth.py, as shown in the following listing.

Listing 12.3   Simple dataset and data wrapper

```
def loadSimpDat():
    simpDat = [['r', 'z', 'h', 'j', 'p'],
               ['z', 'y', 'x', 'w', 'v', 'u', 't', 's'],
               ['z'],
               ['r', 'x', 'n', 'o', 's'],
               ['y', 'r', 'x', 'z', 'q', 't', 'p'],
               ['y', 'z', 'x', 'e', 'q', 's', 't', 'm']]
    return simpDat

def createInitSet(dataSet):
    retDict = {}
    for trans in dataSet:
        retDict[frozenset(trans)] = 1
    return retDict
```

OK, let's see this in action. After you've entered the code from listing 12.3 to fpGrowth.py, enter the following in your Python shell:

```
>>> reload(fpGrowth)
<module 'fpGrowth' from 'fpGrowth.py'>
```

First, let's load the example dataset:

```
>>> simpDat = fpGrowth.loadSimpDat()
>>> simpDat
[['r', 'z', 'h', 'j', 'p'], ['z', 'y', 'x', 'w', 'v', 'u', 't', 's'],
['z'], ['r', 'x', 'n', 'o', 's'], ['y', 'r', 'x', 'z', 'q', 't', 'p'],
['y', 'z', 'x', 'e', 'q', 's', 't', 'm']]
```

Now, you need to format this for `createTree()`:

```
>>> initSet = fpGrowth.createInitSet(simpDat)
>>> initSet
{frozenset(['e', 'm', 'q', 's', 't', 'y', 'x', 'z']): 1, frozenset(['x',
's', 'r', 'o', 'n']): 1, frozenset(['s', 'u', 't', 'w', 'v', 'y', 'x',
'z']): 1, frozenset(['q', 'p', 'r', 't', 'y', 'x', 'z']): 1,
frozenset(['h', 'r', 'z', 'p', 'j']): 1, frozenset(['z']): 1}
```

Now, you can create the FP-tree:

```
>>> myFPtree, myHeaderTab = fpGrowth.createTree(initSet, 3)
```

You can display a text representation of the tree with the `disp()` method:

```
>>> myFPtree.disp()
   Null Set    1
     x    1
       s    1
         r    1
     z    5
       x    3
         y    3
           s    2
             t    2
           r    1
             t    1
       r    1
```

The item and its frequency count are displayed with indentation representing the depth of the tree. Verify that this tree is the same as the one in figure 12.2.

Now that you've created the FP-tree, it's time to mine it for the frequent items.

12.3 *Mining frequent items from an FP-tree*

Most of the hard work is over. We won't be writing as much code as we did in section 12.1. Now that you have the FP-tree, you can extract the frequent itemsets. You'll follow something similar to the Apriori algorithm where you start with the smallest sets containing one item and build larger sets from there. But you'll do this with the FP-tree, and you'll no longer need the original dataset.

There are three basic steps to extract the frequent itemsets from the FP-tree, as follows:

1 Get conditional pattern bases from the FP-tree.
2 From the conditional pattern base, construct a conditional FP-tree.
3 Recursively repeat steps 1 and 2 on until the tree contains a single item.

Now, you'll focus on the first step, which is finding the conditional pattern base. After that you'll create conditional FP-trees from each of the conditional pattern bases. You'll finally write a little code to wrap these two functions together and get the frequent itemsets from the FP-tree.

12.3.1 *Extracting conditional pattern bases*

You'll start with the single items you found to be frequent in the last section. You already have these items in the header table. For each of these items, you'll get the *conditional pattern base*. The conditional pattern base is a collection of paths that end with the item you're looking for. Each of those paths is a *prefix path*. In short, a prefix path is anything on the tree between the item you're looking for and the tree root.

Referring back to figure 12.2, the prefix paths for the symbol r are {x,s}, {z,x,y}, and {z}. Each of these prefix paths also has a count associated with it. The count is the same number as the beginning item. This identifies the number of rs on each path. Table 12.3 lists all of the prefix paths for each frequent item in our example.

Frequent item	Prefix paths
z	{}5
r	{x,s}1, {z,x,y}1, {z}1
x	{z}3, {}1
y	{z,x}3
s	{z,x,y}2, {x}1
t	{z,x,y,s}2, {z,x,y,r}1

Table 12.3   Prefix paths for each frequent item

The prefix paths will be used to create a conditional FP-tree, but don't worry about that for now. To get these prefix paths, you could exhaustively search the tree until you hit your desired frequent item, or you could use a more efficient method. The more efficient method you'll use takes advantage of the header table created earlier. The header table is the starting point for a linked list containing items of the same type. Once you get to each item, you can ascend the tree until you hit the root node.

Code to find the prefix paths is shown in the following listing. Add it to fpGrowth.py.

Listing 12.4   A function to find all paths ending with a given item

```
def ascendTree(leafNode, prefixPath):
    if leafNode.parent != None:
        prefixPath.append(leafNode.name)
        ascendTree(leafNode.parent, prefixPath)

def findPrefixPath(basePat, treeNode):
    condPats = {}
    while treeNode != None:
        prefixPath = []
        ascendTree(treeNode, prefixPath)
        if len(prefixPath) > 1:
            condPats[frozenset(prefixPath[1:])] = treeNode.count
        treeNode = treeNode.nodeLink
    return condPats
```

① **Recursively ascend the tree**

The code in listing 12.4 is used to generate a conditional pattern base given a single item. This is accomplished by visiting every node in the tree that contains the given item. When you were creating the tree, you used the header table to point to the first item of this type and successive item to link together. The findPrefixPath() function iterates through the linked list until it hits the end. For each item it encounters, it calls ascendTree(), which ascends the tree, collecting the names of items it encounters. ❶ This list is returned and added to the conditional pattern base dictionary called condPats.

Let's see this in action with the tree you made earlier:

```
>>> reload(fpGrowth)
<module 'fpGrowth' from 'fpGrowth.py'>
>>> fpGrowth.findPrefixPath('x', myHeaderTab['x'][1])
{frozenset(['z']): 3}
>>> fpGrowth.findPrefixPath('z', myHeaderTab['z'][1])
{}
>>> fpGrowth.findPrefixPath('r', myHeaderTab['r'][1])
{frozenset(['x', 's']): 1, frozenset(['z']): 1,
    frozenset(['y', 'x', 'z']): 1}
```

Check to see if these values match the values in table 12.3. Now that you have the conditional pattern bases, we can move on to creating conditional FP-trees.

12.3.2 *Creating conditional FP-trees*

For each of your frequent items, you'll create a conditional FP-tree. You'll create a conditional tree for z and x and so on. You'll create the conditional pattern bases you just found as the input data to create these trees with the same tree-generating code. Then, you'll recursively find frequent items, find conditional pattern bases, and then find another conditional tree. For example, for the frequent item t, you'll create a conditional FP-tree. Then, you'll repeat this process for {t,y}, {t,x}, ... The creation of the conditional FP-tree for item t is shown in figure 12.4.

In figure 12.4, note that items s and r are part of the conditional pattern bases, but they don't make it to the conditional FP-tree. Why is this? If we're still talking about s

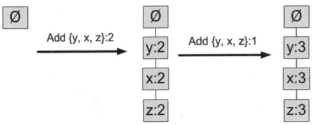

Conditional FP-tree for item: t

Conditional pattern bases: {y, x, s, z}:2 , {y, x, r, z}: 1
Min support = 3
Remove: s & r

Figure 12.4 The creation of the conditional FP-tree for item t. Initially the tree starts out as only the null set as the root. Next, the set {y,x,z} is added from the original set {y,x,s,z}; the character s didn't make it because it didn't meet the minimum support. Similarly, {y,x,z} is added from the original set {y,x,r,z}.

and r, aren't they frequent items? They're frequent items, but they aren't frequent items in t's conditional tree: {t,r} and {t,s} aren't frequent.

Next, you mine the conditional tree for {t,z}, {t,x}, and {t,y}. These will lead to more complex frequent itemsets. This process repeats until you run out of items in the conditional tree. Then you know you can stop. The code to do this is relatively straightforward with a little recursion and the code we wrote earlier. Open fpGrowth.py and add the code from the following listing.

Listing 12.5 The `mineTree` function recursively finds frequent itemsets.

```
def mineTree(inTree, headerTable, minSup, preFix, freqItemList):
    bigL = [v[0] for v in sorted(headerTable.items(),
                            key=lambda p: p[1])]                    ❶ Start from bottom
                                                                       of header table
    for basePat in bigL:
        newFreqSet = preFix.copy()
        newFreqSet.add(basePat)                                    Construct cond. FP-tree from ❷
        freqItemList.append(newFreqSet)                               cond. pattern base
        condPattBases = findPrefixPath(basePat, headerTable[basePat][1])
        myCondTree, myHead = createTree(condPattBases,\
                                minSup)
        if myHead != None:
            mineTree(myCondTree, myHead, minSup, newFreqSet, freqItemList)

                                                                   Mine cond. FP-tree ❸
```

The process of creating conditional trees and prefix paths and conditional bases sounds complex, but the code to do this is relatively simple. The code starts by sorting the items in the header table by their frequency of occurrence. (Remember that the default sort is lowest to highest.) ❶ Then, each frequent item is added to your list of frequent itemsets, `freqItemList`. Next, you recursively call `findPrefixPath()` from listing 12.4, to create a conditional base. This conditional base is treated as a new dataset and fed to `createTree()`. ❷ I added enough flexibility to `createTree()` that it could be reused to create conditional trees. Finally, if the tree has any items in it, you'll recursively call `mineTree()`. ❸

Let's see the code from listing 12.5 in action by putting the whole program together. After you've added the code from listing 12.5 to fpGrowth.py, save the file, and enter the following your Python shell:

```
>>> reload(fpGrowth)
<module 'fpGrowth' from 'fpGrowth.py'>
```

Now create an empty list to store all the frequent itemsets:

```
>>> freqItems = []
```

Now, run `mineTree()` and all the conditional trees will be displayed.

```
>>> fpGrowth.mineTree(myFPtree, myHeaderTab, 3, set([]), freqItems)
conditional tree for: set(['y'])
   Null Set    1
     x    3
```

```
        z    3
conditional tree for:   set(['y', 'z'])
   Null Set   1
      x    3
conditional tree for:   set(['s'])
   Null Set   1
      x    3
conditional tree for:   set(['t'])
   Null Set   1
      y    3
         x    3
            z    3
conditional tree for:   set(['x', 't'])
   Null Set   1
      y    3
conditional tree for:   set(['z', 't'])
   Null Set   1
      y    3
         x    3
conditional tree for:   set(['x', 'z', 't'])
   Null Set   1
      y    3
conditional tree for:   set(['x'])
   Null Set   1
      z    3
```

To get the output like the previous code, I added two lines to `mineTree()`:

```
print 'conditional tree for: ',newFreqSet
myCondTree.disp(1)
```

These were added in the last if statement: `if myHead != None:` before call to the `mineTree`
function.

Now, let's check to see if the itemsets returned matched the condition trees:

```
>>> freqItems
[set(['y']), set(['y', 'z']), set(['y', 'x', 'z']), set(['y', 'x']),
    set(['s']), set(['x', 's']), set(['t']), set(['y', 't']), set(['x',
    't']), set(['y', 'x', 't']), set(['z', 't']), set(['y', 'z', 't']),
    set(['x', 'z', 't']), set(['y', 'x', 'z', 't']), set(['r']), set(['x']),
    set(['x', 'z']), set(['z'])]
```

The itemsets match the conditional FP-trees, which is what you'd expect. Now that you
have the full FP-growth algorithm working, let's try it out on a real-world example.
You'll see if you can get some common words from the microblogging site, Twitter.

12.4   *Example: finding co-occurring words in a Twitter feed*

You'll be using a Python library called `python-twitter`. The source code can be found
at http://code.google.com/p/python-twitter/. As you may have guessed, it allows you
to access the microblogging site, Twitter, with Python. If you aren't familiar with Twit-
ter.com, it's a channel for communicating with others. Posts are limited to 140 characters in length. Each post is called a *tweet*.

The documentation for the Twitter API can be found at http://dev.twitter.com/doc. The keywords aren't exactly the same between the API documentation and the Python module. I recommend looking at the Python file twitter.py to fully understand how to use the library. See appendix A for installation instructions for the module. You'll use only one small portion of the library, but you can do much more with the API, so I encourage you to explore all functionality of the API.

Example: finding co-occurring words in a Twitter feed

1. Collect: Use the `python-twitter` module to access tweets.

2. Prepare: Write a function to remove URLs, remove punctuation, convert to lowercase, and create a set of words from a string.

3. Analyze: We'll look at the prepared data in the Python shell to make sure it's correct.

4. Train: We'll use `createTree()` and `mineTree()`, developed earlier in this chapter, to perform the FP-growth algorithm.

5. Test: Doesn't apply.

6. Use: Not performed in this example. You could do sentiment analysis or provide search query suggestion.

You need two sets of credentials before you can start using the API. The first set is consumer_key and consumer_secret, which you can get from the Twitter Dev site when you register to develop an app (https://dev.twitter.com/apps/new). These keys are specific to the app you're going to be writing. The second set, access_token_key and access_token_secret, are specific to a Twitter user. To get these, you need to check out the get_access_token.py file that comes with the Twitter-Python install (or get them from Twitter Dev site). This is a command-line Python script that uses OAuth to tell Twitter that this application has the right to post on behalf of this user. Once that's done, you can put those values into the previous code and get moving.

You're going to use the FP-growth algorithm to find frequent words in tweets for a given search term. You'll retrieve as many tweets as you can (1,400) and then put the tweets through the FP-growth algorithm. Add the code from the following listing to fpGrowth.py.

Listing 12.6 Code to access the Twitter Python library

```
import twitter
from time import sleep
import re

def getLotsOfTweets(searchStr):
    CONSUMER_KEY = 'get when you create an app'
    CONSUMER_SECRET = 'get when you create an app'
    ACCESS_TOKEN_KEY = 'get from Oauth, specific to a user'
```

```
ACCESS_TOKEN_SECRET = 'get from Oauth, specific to a user'
api = twitter.Api(consumer_key=CONSUMER_KEY,
                  consumer_secret=CONSUMER_SECRET,
                  access_token_key=ACCESS_TOKEN_KEY,
                  access_token_secret=ACCESS_TOKEN_SECRET)
#you can get 1500 results 15 pages * 100 per page
resultsPages = []
for i in range(1,15):
    print "fetching page %d" % i
    searchResults = api.GetSearch(searchStr, per_page=100, page=i)
    resultsPages.append(searchResults)
    sleep(6)
return resultsPages
```

There are three library imports you'll need to add: one for the `twitter` library, one for regular expressions, and the `sleep` function. You'll use the regular expressions to help parse the text later.

The `getLotsOfTweets()` function handles authentication and then creates an empty list. The search API allows you to get 100 tweets at a time. Each of those is considered a page, and you're allowed 14 pages. After you make the search call, there's a six-second sleep to be polite by not making too many requests too quickly. There's also a `print` statement to let you know the program is still running and not dead.

Let's get some tweets. Enter the following in your Python shell:

```
>>> reload(fpGrowth)
<module 'fpGrowth' from 'fpGrowth.py'>
```

I'm going to search for a stock symbol named RIMM:

```
>>> lotsOtweets = fpGrowth.getLotsOfTweets('RIMM')
fetching page 1
fetching page 2
        .
        .
        .
```

The `lotsOtweets` list contains 14 lists with 100 tweets inside. You can explore the tweets by typing

```
>>> lotsOtweets[0][4].text
u"RIM: Open The Network, Says ThinkEquity: In addition, RIMM needs to
reinvent its image, not only demonstrating ... http://bit.ly/lvlV1U"
```

As you can see, some people put URLs in the tweets, and when you parse them, you'll get a mess. You need to remove URLs, so you can get at the words in the tweet. We'll now write some code to parse the tweets into a list of strings, and a function to run the FP-growth algorithm on the dataset. Add the following code to fpGrowth.py:

Listing 12.7 Text parsing and glue code

```
def textParse(bigString):
    urlsRemoved = re.sub('(http[s]?:[/][/]|www.)([a-z]|[A-Z]|[0-9]|[/
    .]|[~])*',
                        '', bigString)
```

```
        listOfTokens = re.split(r'\W*', urlsRemoved)
        return [tok.lower() for tok in listOfTokens if len(tok) > 2]
def mineTweets(tweetArr, minSup=5):
    parsedList = []
    for i in range(14):
        for j in range(100):
            parsedList.append(textParse(tweetArr[i][j].text))
    initSet = createInitSet(parsedList)
    myFPtree, myHeaderTab = createTree(initSet, minSup)
    myFreqList = []
    mineTree(myFPtree, myHeaderTab, minSup, set([]), myFreqList)
    return myFreqList
```

The first function in listing 12.7 is from chapter 4, but I added one line to remove URLs. This calls the regular expression module and removes any URLs. The other function in listing 12.7, `mineTweets()`, calls `textParse` on every tweet. Lastly, `mineTweets()` wraps up some commands we used in section 12.2 to build the FP-tree and mine it. A list of all the frequent itemsets is returned.

Let's try this out:

```
>>> reload(fpGrowth)
<module 'fpGrowth' from 'fpGrowth.py'>
Let's look for sets that occur more than 20 times:
>>> listOfTerms = fpGrowth.mineTweets(lotsOtweets, 20)
How many sets occurred in 20 or more of the documents?
>>> len(listOfTerms)
455
```

The day before I wrote this, a company that trades under the RIMM ticker symbol had a conference call that didn't please investors. The stock opened 22% lower than it had closed the previous day. Let's see if that shows up in the tweets:

```
>>> for t in listOfTerms:
...     print t
set([u'rimm', u'day'])
set([u'rimm', u'earnings'])
set([u'pounding', u'value'])
set([u'pounding', u'overnight'])
set([u'pounding', u'drops'])
set([u'pounding', u'shares'])
set([u'pounding', u'are'])
                        .
                        .
                        .
set([u'overnight'])
set([u'drops', u'overnight'])
set([u'motion', u'drops', u'overnight'])
set([u'motion', u'drops', u'overnight', u'value'])
set([u'drops', u'overnight', u'research'])
set([u'drops', u'overnight', u'value', u'research'])
set([u'motion', u'drops', u'overnight', u'value', u'research'])
set([u'motion', u'drops', u'overnight', u'research'])
set([u'drops', u'overnight', u'value'])
```

It would be interesting to try out some other values for `minSupport` and some other search terms.

Recall that the FP-trees are built by applying one instance at a time. But you assume that all the data is present and you iterate over all the available data. You could rewrite the `createTree()` function to take in one instance at a time and grow the tree with inputs from the Twitter stream. There's a good map-reduce version of FP-growth that can be used to scale this to multiple machines. Google has used it to find frequent co-occurring words, running a large body of text through it, similar to the example we did here.[2]

12.5   *Example: mining a clickstream from a news site*

All right; that last example was cool, but you're probably thinking to yourself, "Dude, this algo is supposed to be fast. That was only 1,400 tweets!" You're right. Let's look at this on a bigger file. In the source repository is a file called kosarak.dat, which contains close to one million records.[3] Each line of this file contains news stories viewed by a user. Some users viewed only a single story, whereas someone viewed 2,498 stories. The users and the stories are anonymized as integers, so there won't be much you can get from viewing the frequent itemsets, but this does a good job of demonstrating the speed of the FP-growth algorithm.

First, load the dataset into a list:

```
>>> parsedDat = [line.split() for line in open('kosarak.dat').readlines()]
```

Next, you need to format the initial set:

```
>>> initSet = fpGrowth.createInitSet(parsedDat)
```

Now, create the FP tree and look for stories or sets of stories that at least 100,000 people viewed:

```
>>> myFPtree, myHeaderTab = fpGrowth.createTree(initSet, 100000)
```

Creating this tree and scanning the one million lines took only a few seconds on my humble laptop. This should demonstrate the power of the FP-growth algorithm. Now you need to create an empty list to hold the frequent itemsets:

```
>>> myFreqList = []
>>> fpGrowth.mineTree(myFPtree, myHeaderTab, 100000, set([]), myFreqList)
```

Let's see how many stories or sets of stories were viewed by 100,000 or more people:

```
>>> len(myFreqList)
9
```

---

2   H. Li, Y. Wang, D. Zhang, M. Zhang, E. Chang, "PFP: Parallel FP-Growth for Query Recommendation," RecSys '08, Proceedings of the 2008 ACM Conference on Recommender Systems; http://infolab.stanford.edu/~echang/recsys08-69.pdf.

3   Hungarian online news portal clickstream retrieved July 11, 2011; from Frequent Itemset Mining Dataset Repository, http://fimi.ua.ac.be/data/, donated by Ferenc Bodon.

Nine. Now let's see which ones:

```
>>> myFreqList
[set(['1']), set(['1', '6']), set(['3']), set(['11', '3']), set(['11', '3',
     '6']), set(['3', '6']), set(['11']), set(['11', '6']), set(['6'])]
```

Try this out with some other settings, perhaps lowering the support level.

12.6 Summary

The FP-growth algorithm is an efficient way of finding frequent patterns in a dataset. The FP-growth algorithm works with the Apriori principle but is much faster. The Apriori algorithm generates candidate itemsets and then scans the dataset to see if they're frequent. FP-growth is faster because it goes over the dataset only twice. The dataset is stored in a structure called an FP-tree. After the FP-tree is built, you can find frequent itemsets by finding conditional bases for an item and building a conditional FP-tree. This process is repeated, conditioning on more items until the conditional FP-tree has only one item.

The FP-growth algorithm can be used to find frequent words in a series of text documents. The microblogging site Twitter provides a number of APIs for developers to use their services. The Python module Python-Twitter allows easy access to Twitter. Applying the FP-growth algorithm to a Twitter feed on a certain topic can give you some summary information for that topic. There are a number of other uses for frequent itemset generation such as shopping transactions, medical diagnosis, and study of the atmosphere.

In the next few chapters we'll be looking at some additional tools. Chapters 13 and 14 will cover some dimensionality-reduction techniques. You can use these techniques to distill your data down to only the important information and remove the noise. Chapter 15 will cover MapReduce, which you'll need when your data exceeds the processing abilities of one machine.

Part 4

Additional tools

This fourth and final part of *Machine Learning in Action* covers some additional tools that are commonly used in practice and can be applied to the material from the first three parts of the book. The tools cover dimensionality-reduction techniques, which you can use to preprocess the inputs before using any of the algorithms from the first three parts of this book. This part also covers map reduce, which is a technique for distributing jobs to thousands of machines.

Dimensionality reduction is the task of reducing the number of inputs you have; this can reduce noise and improve the performance of machine learning algorithms. Chapter 13 is the first chapter on dimensionality reduction; we look at principal component analysis, an algorithm for realigning our data in the direction of the most variance. Chapter 14 is the second chapter on dimensionality reduction; we look at the singular value decomposition, which is a matrix factorization technique that you can use to approximate your original data and thereby reduce its dimensionality.

Chapter 15 is the final chapter in this book, and it discusses machine learning on big data. The term *big data* refers to datasets that are larger than the main memory of the machine you're using. If you can't fit the data in main memory, you'll waste a lot of time moving data between memory and a disk. To avoid this, you can split a job into multiple segments, which can be performed in parallel on multiple machines. One popular method for doing this is map reduce, which breaks jobs into map tasks and reduce tasks. Some common tools for doing map reduce in Python are discussed in chapter 15, along with a discussion of how to break up machine learning algorithms to fit the map reduce paradigm.

13

Using principal component analysis to simplify data

Assume for a moment that you're watching a sports match involving a ball on a flat monitor, not in person. The monitor probably contains a million pixels, and the ball is represented by, say, a thousand pixels. In most sports, we're concerned with the position of the ball at a given time. For your brain to follow what's going on, you need to follow the position of the ball on the playing field. You do this naturally, without even thinking about it. Behind the scene, you're converting the million pixels on the monitor into a three-dimensional image showing the ball's position on the playing field, in real time. You've reduced the data from one million dimensions to three.

In this sports match example, you're presented with millions of pixels, but it's the ball's three-dimensional position that's important. This is known as *dimensionality reduction*. You're reducing data from more than one million values to the three relevant values. It's much easier to work with data in fewer dimensions. In addition, the relevant features may not be explicitly presented in the data. Often, we have to identify the relevant features before we can begin to apply other machine learning algorithms.

This chapter is the first of two that cover dimensionality reduction. In dimensionality reduction we're preprocessing the data. After we've preprocessed the data, we can proceed with other machine learning techniques. This chapter begins with a survey of dimensionality reduction techniques and then moves to one of the more common techniques called principal component analysis. We'll next work through an example showing how principal component analysis can be used to reduce a dataset from 590 features to six.

13.1   *Dimensionality reduction techniques*

Throughout this book one of the problems has been displaying data and results because the book is only two dimensional, but our data frequently isn't. Sometimes, we can show three-dimensional plots or show only the relevant features, but frequently we have more features than we can display. Displaying data isn't the only problem with having a large number of features. A short list of other reasons we want to simplify our data includes the following:

- Making the dataset easier to use
- Reducing computational cost of many algorithms
- Removing noise
- Making the results easier to understand

There are dimensionality reduction techniques that work on labeled and unlabeled data. Here we'll focus on unlabeled data because it's applicable to both types.

The first method for dimensionality reduction is called *principal component analysis (PCA)*. In PCA, the dataset is transformed from its original coordinate system to a new coordinate system. The new coordinate system is chosen by the data itself. The first new axis is chosen in the direction of the most variance in the data. The second axis is orthogonal to the first axis and in the direction of an orthogonal axis with the largest variance. This procedure is repeated for as many features as we had in the original data. We'll find that the majority of the variance is contained in the first few axes. Therefore, we can ignore the rest of the axes, and we reduce the dimensionality of our data. We'll cover this in more depth in section 13.2.

Factor analysis is another method for dimensionality reduction. In factor analysis, we assume that some unobservable *latent variables* are generating the data we observe. The data we observe is assumed to be a linear combination of the latent variables and some noise. The number of latent variables is possibly lower than the amount of observed data, which gives us the dimensionality reduction. Factor analysis is used in social sciences, finance, and other areas.

Another common method for dimensionality reduction is *independent component analysis (ICA)*. ICA assumes that the data is generated by *N* sources, which is similar to factor analysis. The data is assumed to be a mixture of observations of the sources. The sources are assumed to be statically independent, unlike PCA, which assumes the data is uncorrelated. As with factor analysis, if there are fewer sources than the amount of our observed data, we'll get a dimensionality reduction.

Of the three methods of dimensionality reduction, PCA is by far the most commonly used. We'll focus on PCA in this chapter, and we won't cover ICA or factor analysis. In the next section, I'll describe PCA and then you'll write some code to perform PCA in Python.

13.2 *Principal component analysis*

> **Principal component analysis**
>
> Pros: Reduces complexity of data, indentifies most important features
>
> Cons: May not be needed, could throw away useful information
>
> Works with: Numerical values

We'll first discuss some of the theory behind PCA, and then you'll see how to do PCA in Python with NumPy.

13.2.1 *Moving the coordinate axes*

Consider for a moment the mass of data in figure 13.1. If I asked you to draw a line covering the data points, what's the longest possible line you could draw? I've drawn a few choices. Line B is the longest of these three lines. In PCA, we rotate the axes of the data. The rotation is determined by the data itself. The first axis is rotated to cover the largest variation in the data: line B in figure 13.1. The largest variation is the data telling us what's most important.

After choosing the axis covering the most variability, we choose the next axis, which has the second most variability, provided it's perpendicular to the first axis. The real term used is *orthogonal*. On this two-dimensional plot, perpendicular and orthogonal are the same. In figure 13.1, line C would be our second axis. With PCA,

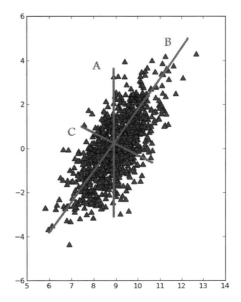

Figure 13.1 Three choices for lines that span the entire dataset. Line B is the longest and accounts for the most variability in the dataset.

we're rotating the axes so that they're lined up with the most important directions from the data's perspective.

Now that you have the axis rotation down, let's talk about dimensionality reduction. Rotating the axes hasn't reduced the number of dimensions. Consider figure 13.2, which has three classes plotted. If we want to separate the classes, we could use a decision tree. Remember that decision trees make a decision based on one feature at a time. We could find some values on the x-axis that do a good job of separating the different classes. We'd have some rule such as if (X<4), then we have class 0. If we used a little more complex classifier, say a support vector machine, we could get better separation of the classes with a hyperplane and a classification rule such as if (w0*x+w1*y+b) > 0, then we have class 0. The support vector machine may give us better margin than the decision tree, but the hyperplane is harder to interpret.

By doing dimensionality reduction with PCA on our dataset, we can have the best of both worlds: we can have a classifier as simple as a decision tree, while having margin as good as the support vector machine. Look at the lower frame of figure 13.2. In this frame, I took the data from the top frame and plotted it after the PCA. The margin on this will be larger than the decision tree margin when using only the original data. Also, because we have only one dimension to worry about, we can have rules to separate the classes that are much simpler than the support vector machine.

In figure 13.2, we have only one axis because the other axis was just noise and didn't contribute to the separation of the classes. This may seem trivial in two dimensions, but it can make a big difference when we have more dimensions.

Now that we've gone over some of what goes on in PCA, let's write some code to do this. Earlier, I mentioned that we take the first principal component to be in the direction of the largest variability of the data. The second principal component will be in the direction of the second largest variability, in a direction orthogonal to the first principal component. We can get these values by taking the covariance matrix of the dataset and doing eigenvalue analysis on the covariance matrix.

Once we have the eigenvectors of the covariance matrix, we can take the top N eigenvectors. The top N eigenvectors will give us the true structure of the N

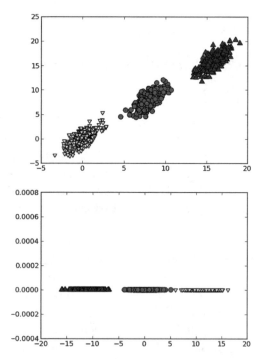

Figure 13.2   Three classes in two dimensions. When the PCA is applied to this dataset, we can throw out one dimension, and the classification problem becomes easier.

Eigenvalue analysis

Eigenvalue analysis is an area of linear algebra that allows us to uncover the underlying "true" structure of the data by putting it in a common format. In eigenvalue analysis, we usually talk about eigenvectors and eigenvalues. In the following equation, $\mathbf{Av} = \lambda\mathbf{v}$, eigenvectors are $\mathbf{v}$ and eigenvalues are λ. Eigenvalues are simply scalar values, so $\mathbf{Av} = \lambda\mathbf{v}$ says when we multiply the eigenvectors by some matrix, $\mathbf{A}$, we get the eigenvectors ($\mathbf{v}$), again multiplied by some scalar values λ. Luckily, NumPy comes with some modules for finding the eigenvectors and eigenvalues. The NumPy `linalg` module has the `eig()` method, which we can use to find the eigenvectors and eigenvalues.

---

most important features. We can then multiply the data by the top N eigenvectors to transform our data into the new space.

13.2.2 *Performing PCA in NumPy*

Pseudocode for transforming out data into the top N principal components would look like this:

Remove the mean
Compute the covariance matrix
Find the eigenvalues and eigenvectors of the covariance matrix
Sort the eigenvalues from largest to smallest
Take the top N eigenvectors
Transform the data into the new space created by the top N eigenvectors

Create a file called pca.py and add the code from the following listing to compute the PCA.

Listing 13.1 The PCA algorithm

```
from numpy import *

def loadDataSet(fileName, delim='\t'):
    fr = open(fileName)
    stringArr = [line.strip().split(delim) for line in fr.readlines()]
    datArr = [map(float,line) for line in stringArr]
    return mat(datArr)

def pca(dataMat, topNfeat=9999999):
    meanVals = mean(dataMat, axis=0)             ❶ Remove
    meanRemoved = dataMat - meanVals                mean
    covMat = cov(meanRemoved, rowvar=0)
    eigVals,eigVects = linalg.eig(mat(covMat))
    eigValInd = argsort(eigVals)                 ❷ Sort top N smallest
    eigValInd = eigValInd[:-(topNfeat+1):-1]        to largest
    redEigVects = eigVects[:,eigValInd]
    lowDDataMat = meanRemoved * redEigVects       ❸ Transform data into
    reconMat = (lowDDataMat * redEigVects.T) + meanVals  new dimensions
    return lowDDataMat, reconMat
```

The code in listing 13.1 contains the usual NumPy import and loadDataSet(). The function loadDataSet() is slightly different from the versions we used in previous chapters because it uses two list comprehensions to create the matrix.

The pca() function takes two arguments: the dataset on which we'll perform PCA and the second optional argument, topNfeat, which is the top N features to use. If you don't provide a value for topNfeat, it will return the top 9,999,999 features, or as many as the original dataset has.

First, you calculate the mean of the original dataset and remove it. ❶ Next, you compute the covariance matrix and calculate the eigenvalues. You use argsort() to get the order of the eigenvalues. You can now use the order of the eigenvalues to sort the eigenvectors in reverse order and get the topNfeat largest eigenvectors. ❷ The top N largest eigenvectors form a matrix that will be used to transform our original data into the new space with N features. ❸ Lastly, you reconstruct the original data and return it for debug along with the reduced dimension dataset.

That wasn't bad, was it? Let's take a look at this in action to make sure you have it right before we get into a big example.

```
>>> import pca
```

I included a dataset with 1000 points in the testSet.txt file. You can load it into memory with

```
>>> dataMat = pca.loadDataSet('testSet.txt')
```

Now, let's do the PCA of this dataset:

```
>>> lowDMat, reconMat = pca.pca(dataMat, 1)
```

lowDMat contains the matrix in our reduced dimensions, which should be one dimension; let's check that out:

```
>>> shape(lowDMat)
(1000, 1)
```

Let's plot it with the original data:

```
>>> import matplotlib
>>>import matplotlib.pyplot as plt
fig = plt.figure()
ax = fig.add_subplot(111)
>>> ax.scatter(dataMat[:,0].flatten().A[0], dataMat[:,1].flatten().A[0],
 marker='^', s=90)
<matplotlib.collections.PathCollection object at 0x029B5C50>
>>> ax.scatter(reconMat[:,0].flatten().A[0], reconMat[:,1].flatten().A[0],
 marker='o', s=50, c='red')
<matplotlib.collections.PathCollection object at 0x0372A210>plt.show()
```

You should see something similar to figure 13.3. Repeat the previous steps, but use

```
>>> lowDMat, reconMat = pca.pca(dataMat, 2)
```

The reconstructed data should overlap the original data because no features are removed. You should see something similar to figure 13.3 but without the straight line.

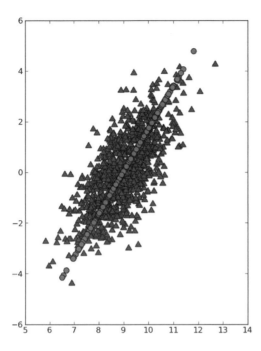

Figure 13.3 The original dataset (triangles) plotted with the first principal component (circles)

Now that we have PCA working on a simple dataset, let's move to a real-world example. We'll reduce the dimensionality of a dataset from a semiconductor factory.

13.3 Example: using PCA to reduce the dimensionality of semiconductor manufacturing data

Semiconductors are made in some of the most high-tech factories on the planet. The factories or fabrications (fabs) cost billions of dollars and take an army to operate. The fab is only modern for a few years, after which it needs to be replaced. The processing time for a single integrated circuit takes more than a month. With a finite lifetime and a huge cost to operate, every second in the fab is extremely valuable. If there's some flaw in the manufacturing process, we need to know as soon as possible, so that precious time isn't spent processing a flawed product.

Some common engineering solutions find failed products, such as test early and test often. But some defects slip through. If machine learning techniques can be used to further reduce errors, it will save the manufacturer a lot of money.

We'll now look at some data for such a task. It's a larger dataset than we've used so far, and it has a lot of features—590 features to be exact.[1] Let's see if we can reduce that. You can find the dataset at http://archive.ics.uci.edu/ml/machine-learning-databases/secom/.

---

[1] SECOM Data Set retrieved from the UCI Machine Learning Repository: http://archive.ics.uci.edu/ml/datasets/SECOM on June 1, 2011.

The data contains a lot of missing values. These values are recorded as NaN, which stands for Not a Number. We can do several things to work with the missing values (see chapter 5). With 590 features, almost every instance has a NaN, so throwing out incomplete instances isn't a realistic approach. We could replace all the NaNs with 0s, but that may be a bad idea because we don't know what these values mean. If they're things like temperature in kelvins, setting the values to zero is a bad idea. Let's try to set the missing values to the mean. We'll calculate the mean from the values that aren't NaN.

Add the code from the following listing to pca.py.

Listing 13.2   Function to replace missing values with mean

```
def replaceNanWithMean():
    datMat = loadDataSet('secom.data', ' ')          Find mean of non-  ①
    numFeat = shape(datMat)[1]                              NaN values
    for i in range(numFeat):
        meanVal = mean(datMat[nonzero(~isnan(datMat[:,i].A))[0],i])

        datMat[nonzero(isnan(datMat[:,i].A))[0],i] = meanVal
                                                         Set NaN values
    return datMat                                      ②  to mean
```

The code in listing 13.2 opens the dataset and counts the number of features. Next, you iterate over all the features. For each feature, you first find the mean value, where there are values to measure. ① Next, you replace any NaN values with the mean. ②

Now that you have the NaN values removed, you can look at the PCA of this dataset. First, let's find out how many features you need and how many you can drop. PCA will tell you how much information is contained in the data. I'd like to emphasize that there's a major difference between data and information. Data is the raw material that you take in, which may contain noise and irrelevant information. Information is the relevant material. These aren't just abstract quantities; you can measure the amount of information contained in your data and decide how much to keep.

Let's see how to do this. First, replace the NaN values in the dataset with mean values using the code we just wrote:

```
dataMat = pca.replaceNanWithMean()
```

Next, borrow some code from the pca() function because we want to look at the intermediate values, not the output. We're going to remove the mean:

```
meanVals = mean(dataMat, axis=0)
meanRemoved = dataMat - meanVals
```

Now, calculate the covariance matrix:

```
covMat = cov(meanRemoved, rowvar=0)
```

Finally, do Eigenvalue analysis on the covariance matrix:

```
eigVals,eigVects = linalg.eig(mat(covMat))
```

Now, let's look at the eigenvalues:

```
>>> eigVals
array([  5.34151979e+07,   2.17466719e+07,   8.24837662e+06,
         2.07388086e+06,   1.31540439e+06,   4.67693557e+05,
         2.90863555e+05,   2.83668601e+05,   2.37155830e+05,
         2.08513836e+05,   1.96098849e+05,   1.86856549e+05,

                                       .
                                       .
                                       .

         0.00000000e+00,   0.00000000e+00,   0.00000000e+00,
         0.00000000e+00,   0.00000000e+00,   0.00000000e+00,
         0.00000000e+00,   0.00000000e+00,   0.00000000e+00,
         0.00000000e+00,   0.00000000e+00,   0.00000000e+00,
         0.00000000e+00,   0.00000000e+00]])
```

You see a lot of values, but what do you notice? Did you notice there are a lot of zeros? Over 20% of the eigenvalues are zero. That means that these features are copies of other features in the dataset, and they don't provide any extra information.

Second, let's look at the magnitude of some of these numbers. The first 15 have magnitudes greater than 105, but after that, the values get really small. This tells you that there are a few important features, but the number of important features drops off quickly.

Last, you may notice a few small negative values. These are caused by numerical errors and should be rounded to zero.

I've plotted the percentage of total variance in figure 13.4. You can see how quickly the variance drops off after the first few principal components.

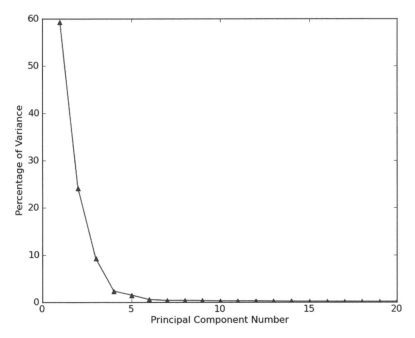

Figure 13.4   Percentage of total variance contained in the first 20 principal components. From this plot, you can see that most of the variance is contained in the first few principal components, and little information would be lost by dropping the higher ones. If we kept only the first six principal components, we'd reduce our dataset from 590 features to 6 features, almost a 100:1 compression.

I also recorded the percentage of variance and the cumulative percentage of variance for these principal components in table 13.1. If you look at the % Cumulative column, you'll notice that after 6 principal components, we've covered 96.8% of the variance. The first 20 principal components cover 99.3% of the variance in the data. This tells us that if we keep the first 6 principal components and drop the other 584, we've achieved a nearly 100:1 compression. Additionally, dropping the higher principal components may make the data cleaner because we're throwing out noisy components.

Table 13.1   % variance for the first 7 principal components of the semiconductor data

Principal component	% Variance	% Cumulative
1	59.2	59.2
2	24.1	83.4
3	9.2	92.5
4	2.3	94.8
5	1.5	96.3
6	0.5	96.8
7	0.3	97.1
20	0.08	99.3

Now that you know how much of the information in our dataset is contained in the first few principal components, you can try some cutoff values and see how they perform. Some people use the number of principal components that will give them 90% of the variance, whereas others use the first 20 principal components. I can't tell you exactly how many principal components to use. You'll have to experiment with different values. The number of effective principal components will depend on your dataset and your application.

The analysis tells you how many principal components you can use. You can then plug this number into the PCA algorithm, and you'll have reduced data for use in a classifier.

13.4   *Summary*

Dimensionality reduction techniques allow us to make data easier to use and often remove noise to make other machine learning tasks more accurate. It's often a preprocessing step that can be done to clean up data before applying it to some other algorithm. A number of techniques can be used to reduce the dimensionality of our data. Among these, independent component analysis, factor analysis, and principal component analysis are popular methods. The most widely used method is principal component analysis.

Principal component analysis allows the data to identify the important features. It does this by rotating the axes to align with the largest variance in the data. Other axes are chosen orthogonal to the first axis in the direction of largest variance. Eigenvalue analysis on the covariance matrix can be used to give us a set of orthogonal axes.

The PCA algorithm in this chapter loads the entire dataset into memory. If this isn't possible, other methods for finding the eigenvalues can be used. A good paper for an online method of finding the PCA is "Incremental Eigenanalysis for Classification."[2] The singular value decomposition, which is the subject of the next chapter, can also be used for eigenvalue analysis.

---

[2] P. Hall, D. Marshall, and R. Martin, "Incremental Eigenanalysis for Classification," Department of Computer Science, Cardiff University, 1998 British Machine Vision Conference, vol. 1, 286–95; http://citeseer.ist.psu.edu/viewdoc/summary?doi=10.1.1.40.4801.

Simplifying data with the singular value decomposition

14

This chapter covers

- The singular value decomposition matrix factorization
- Recommendation engines
- Using the singular value decomposition to improve recommendation engines

Restaurants get rolled into a handful of categories: American, Chinese, Japanese, steak house, vegan, and so on. Have you ever thought that these categories weren't enough? Perhaps you like a hybrid of these categories or a subcategory like Chinese vegetarian. How can we find out how many categories there are? Maybe we could ask some human experts? What if one expert tells us we should divide the restaurants by sauces, and another expert tells us we should divide restaurants by the ingredients? Instead of asking an expert, let's ask the data. We can take data that records people's opinions of restaurants and distill it down into underlying factors.

These may line up with our restaurants categories, a specific ingredient used in cooking, or anything. We can then use these factors to estimate what people will think of a restaurants they haven't yet visited.

The method for distilling this information is known as the *singular value decomposition (SVD)*. It's a powerful tool used to distill information in a number of applications, from bioinformatics to finance.

In this chapter, you're going to learn what the singular value decomposition is and how it can be used to reduce the dimensionality of our data. You'll then see how to do the SVD in Python and how to map our data from the low-dimensional space. Next, you'll learn what recommendation engines are and see them in action. You'll see how you can apply the SVD to recommendation engines to improve their accuracy. We'll use this recommendation engine to help people find a restaurant to visit. We'll conclude by looking at an example of how the SVD could be used for image compression.

14.1 Applications of the SVD

The singular value decomposition (SVD)

Pros: Simplifies data, removes noise, may improve algorithm results.

Cons: Transformed data may be difficult to understand.

Works with: Numeric values.

We can use the SVD to represent our original data set with a much smaller data set. When we do this, we're removing noise and redundant information. Those are noble goals when we're trying to save bits, but we're trying to extract knowledge from data. When viewed from that perspective, we can think of the SVD as extracting the relevant features from a collection of noisy data. If this sounds a little strange, don't worry. I'm going to show a few examples of where and how this is used to explain the power of the SVD.

First, we'll discuss how the SVD is used in search and information retrieval using latent semantic indexing. Next, we'll discuss how the SVD is used in recommendation systems.

14.1.1 Latent semantic indexing

The history of the SVD is over a century old. But it has found more use with the adoption of computers in the last several decades. One of first uses was in the field of information retrieval. The method that uses SVD is called *latent semantic indexing (LSI)* or *latent semantic analysis*.

In LSI, a matrix is constructed of documents and words. When the SVD is done on this matrix, it creates a set of singular values. The singular values represent concepts or topics contained in the documents. This was developed to allow more efficient searching of documents. A simple search that looks only for the existence of words may have problems if the words are misspelled. Another problem with a simple search is that synonyms may be used, and looking for the existence of a word wouldn't tell you if a synonym was used to construct the document. If a concept is derived from thousands of similar documents, both of the synonyms will map to the same concept.

14.1.2 Recommendation systems

Another application of the SVD is in recommendation systems. Simple versions of recommendation systems compute similarity between items or people. More advanced methods use the SVD to create a theme space from the data and then compute similarities in the theme space. Consider for a moment the matrix of restaurant dishes and reviewers' opinions of these dishes in figure 14.1. The reviewers were allowed to rate everything with an integer between 1 and 5. If they didn't try a dish, it was given a 0.

If we did the SVD of this matrix, we'd have noticed two singular values. (Try it out if you don't believe me.) So there appears to be two concepts or themes associated with the dataset. Let's see if we can figure out what these concepts are by looking for the 0s in the figure. Look at the shaded box on the right side. It looks like Ed, Peter, and Tracy rated Tri Tip and Pulled Pork, but it also appears that these three people didn't rate any other dishes. Tri Tip and Pulled Pork are dishes served at American BBQ restaurants. The other dishes listed are found in Japanese restaurants.

We can think of the singular values as a new space. Instead of being five or seven dimensional like the matrix in figure 14.1, our matrix is now two dimensional. What are these two dimensions, and what can they tell us about the data? The two dimensions would correspond to the two groupings in the figure. I shaded one of the groups in the matrix on the right. We could name these two dimensions after the common features of the groups. We'd have an American BBQ dimension and a Japanese food dimension.

	Unagi Don	Chicken Katsu	Chirashi	Tri Tip	Pulled Pork			Unagi Don	Chicken Katsu	Chirashi	Tri Tip	Pulled Pork
Ed	0	0	0	2	2		Ed	0	0	0	2	2
Peter	0	0	0	3	3		Peter	0	0	0	3	3
Tracy	0	0	0	1	1		Tracy	0	0	0	1	1
Fan	1	1	1	0	0		Fan	1	1	1	0	0
Ming	2	2	2	0	0		Ming	2	2	2	0	0
Pachi	5	5	5	0	0		Pachi	5	5	5	0	0
Jocelyn	1	1	1	0	0		Jocelyn	1	1	1	0	0

Figure 14.1   Restaurant dish data and ratings. The SVD of this matrix can condense the data into a few concepts. One concept is shaded in gray on the right side.

How can we get from our original data to this new space? In the next section we'll discuss the SVD in more detail and see how it gives us two matrices called **U** and **VT**. The **VT** matrix maps from users into the BBQ/Japanese food space. Similarly the **U** matrix maps from the restaurant dishes into the BBQ/Japanese food space. Real data usually isn't as dense or as well formatted as the data in figure 14.1. I used this for the sake of illustration.

A recommendation engine can take noisy data, such someone's rating of certain dishes, and distill that into these basic themes. With respect to these themes, the recommendation engine can make better recommendations than using the original data set. In late 2006 the movie company Netflix held a contest that awarded $1M to anyone who would provide 10% better recommendations than the state of the art. The winning team used the SVD in their solution.[1]

In the next section we'll discuss some background material leading up to the SVD, and we'll show how to perform the SVD in Python with NumPy. After that, we'll discuss recommendation engines in further detail. When you have a good understanding of recommendations engines, we'll build a recommendation engine that uses the SVD.

The SVD is a type of matrix factorization, which will break down our data matrix into separate parts. Let's discuss matrix factorization for a moment.

14.2 *Matrix factorization*

Often, a few pieces of data in our dataset can contain most of the information in our dataset. The other information in the matrix is noise or irrelevant. In linear algebra, there are many techniques for decomposing matrices. The decomposition is done to put the original matrix in a new form that's easier to work with. The new form is a product of two or more matrices. This decomposition can be thought of like factoring in algebra. How can we factor 12 into the product of two numbers? (1,12), (2,6), and (3,4) are all valid answers.

The various matrix factorization techniques have different properties that are more suited for one application or another. One of the most common factorizations is the SVD. The SVD takes an original data set matrix called **Data** and decomposes it into three matrices called **U**, Σ, and **V**^{T}. If the original data set **Data** is size mxn, then **U** will be mxm, Σ will be mxn, and **V**^{T} will be nxn. Let's write this out on one line to be clear (the subscript is the matrix dimensions):

$$Data_{mxn} = U_{mxm}\Sigma_{mxn} V_{nxn}^{T}$$

The decomposition creates the Σ, which will have only diagonal elements; all other elements of this matrix are 0. Another convention is that the diagonal elements of Σ are sorted from largest to smallest. These diagonal elements are called *singular values* and they correspond to the singular values of our original data set, **Data**. If you recall from the last chapter, on principal component analysis, we found the eigenvalues of a matrix. These eigenvalues told us what features were most important in our data set.

---

[1] Yehuda Koren, "The BellKor Solution to the Netflix Grand Prize," August 2009; http://www .netflixprize.com/assets/GrandPrize2009_BPC_BellKor.pdf.

The same thing is true about the singular values in Σ. The singular values and eigenvalues are related. Our singular values are the square root of the eigenvalues of `Data*DataT`.

I mentioned earlier that Σ has only diagonal elements sorted from largest to smallest. One common fact that keeps coming up in science and engineering is that after a certain number of singular values (call this `r`) of a data set, the other values will drop to 0. This means that the data set has only `r` important features, and the rest of the features are noise or repeats. You'll see a solid example of this in the next section.

Don't worry about how we're going to break down this matrix. NumPy's linear algebra library has a method for doing the SVD, which you'll see in the next section. If you're interested in how to program the SVD, I'd suggest you check the book *Numerical Linear Algebra*.[2]

14.3 SVD in Python

If the SVD is so great, how can we do it? The linear algebra of doing it is beyond the scope of this book. There are a number of software packages that will do the factorization for us. NumPy has a linear algebra toolbox called linalg. Let's see this in action to do the SVD on the matrix

$$\begin{bmatrix} 1 & 1 \\ 7 & 7 \end{bmatrix}$$

To do this in Python, enter the following commands in your Python shell:

```
>>> from numpy import *
>>> U,Sigma,VT=linalg.svd([[1, 1],[7, 7]])
```

Now you can explore each of these matrices:

```
>>> U
array([[-0.14142136, -0.98994949],
[-0.98994949,  0.14142136]])
>>> Sigma
array([ 10.,    0.])
>>> VT
array([[-0.70710678, -0.70710678],
[-0.70710678,  0.70710678]])
```

Notice that `Sigma` was returned as a row vector, `array([ 10.,    0.])`, not a matrix:

```
array([[ 10.,    0.],
       [ 0.,    0.]]).
```

This is done internally by NumPy because the matrix is all zeros except for the diagonal elements, so it saves space to return just the diagonal elements. Keep that in mind when you see `Sigma` as a vector. OK, let's do some more decomposing, this time on a bigger matrix.

---

[2] L. Trefethen and D. Bau III, *Numerical Linear Algebra* (SIAM: Society for Industrial and Applied Mathematics, 1997).

Create a new file called svdRec.py and enter the following code:

```
def loadExData():
    return[[1, 1, 1, 0, 0],
           [2, 2, 2, 0, 0],
           [1, 1, 1, 0, 0],
           [5, 5, 5, 0, 0],
           [1, 1, 0, 2, 2],
           [0, 0, 0, 3, 3],
           [0, 0, 0, 1, 1]]
```

Now let's do the SVD of this matrix. After you've saved svdRec.py, enter the following at the Python prompt:

```
>>> import svdRec
>>> Data=svdRec.loadExData()
>>> U,Sigma,VT=linalg.svd(Data)
>>> Sigma
array([  9.72140007e+00,   5.29397912e+00,   6.84226362e-01,
         7.16251492e-16,   4.85169600e-32])
```

The first three values are much greater than the others in value. (Don't worry if the last two values are slightly different from the ones listed here; they're so small that running this on different machines will produce slightly different results. The order of magnitude should be similar to those listed here.) We can drop the last two values. Now our original data set is approximated by the following:

$$Data_{mxn} \approx U_{mx3} \Sigma_{3x3} V_{3xn}^{T}$$

A schematic representation of this approximation can be seen in figure 14.2.

Let's try to reconstruct the original matrix. First, we'll build a 3x3 matrix called Sig3:

```
>>> Sig3=mat([[Sigma[0], 0, 0],[0, Sigma[1], 0], [0, 0, Sigma[2]]])
```

Now let's reconstruct an approximation of the original matrix. Because Sig2 is only 2x2, we use only the first two columns of U and the first two rows of V^T. To do this in Python, enter the following:

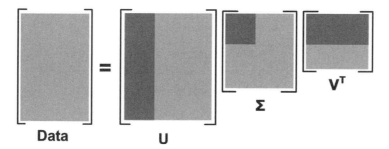

Figure 14.2 Schematic representation of the singular value decomposition. The matrix Data is being decomposed here. The light gray areas show the original data, and the dark gray areas show the only data used in the matrix approximation.

```
>>> U[:,:3]*Sig3*VT[:3,:]
array([[ 1.,   1.,   1.,   0.,   0.],
       [ 2.,   2.,   2.,  -0.,  -0.],
       [ 1.,   1.,   1.,  -0.,  -0.],
       [ 5.,   5.,   5.,   0.,   0.],
       [ 1.,   1.,  -0.,   2.,   2.],
       [ 0.,   0.,  -0.,   3.,   3.],
       [ 0.,   0.,  -0.,   1.,   1.]])
```

How did we know to keep only the first three singular values? There are a number of heuristics for the number of singular values to keep. You typically want to keep 90% of the energy expressed in the matrix. To calculate the total energy, you add up all the squared singular values. You can then add squared singular values until you reach 90% of the total. Another heuristic to use when you have tens of thousands of singular values is to keep the first 2,000 or 3,000. This is a little less elegant than the energy method, but it's easier to implement in practice. It's less elegant because you can't guarantee that 3,000 values contain 90% of the energy in any dataset. Usually you'll know your data well enough that you can make an assumption like this.

We've now approximated the original matrix closely with three matrices. We can represent a big matrix with a much smaller one. There are a number of applications that can be improved with the SVD. I'll discuss one of the more popular uses, recommendation engines, next.

14.4 *Collaborative filtering–based recommendation engines*

Recommendation engines are nothing new to people who've been using the internet in the last decade. Amazon recommends items to customers based on their past purchases. Netflix recommends movies for people to watch. News websites recommend stories for you to read. The list goes on. There are a number of approaches for how to do this, but the approach we're going to use is called *collaborative filtering*. Collaborative filtering works by taking a data set of users' data and comparing it to the data of other users.

The data is conceptually organized in a matrix like the one in figure 14.2. When the data is organized this way, you can compare how similar users are or how similar items are. Both approaches use a notion of similarity, which we'll discuss in more detail in a moment. When you know the similarity between two users or two items, you can use existing data to forecast unknown preferences. For example, say you're trying to predict movies. The recommendation engine will see that there's a movie you haven't viewed yet. It will then compute the similarity between the movies you did see and the movie you didn't see. If there's a high similarity, the algorithm will infer that you'll like this movie.

The only real math going on behind the scenes is the similarity measurement, and that isn't difficult, as you'll see next. We'll first talk about how the similarity between items is measured. Next, we'll discuss the tradeoffs between item-based and user-based similarity measurements. Finally, we'll discuss how to measure the success of a recommendation engine.

14.4.1 *Measuring similarity*

We'd like to have some quantitative measurement of how similar two items are. How would you find that? What if you ran a food-selling website? Maybe you can compare food by ingredients, calorie count, someone's definition of the cuisine type, or something similar. Now let's say you wanted to expand your business into eating utensils. Would you use calorie count to describe a fork? The point is that the attributes you use to describe a food will be different from the attributes you use to describe tableware. What if you took another approach at comparing items? Instead of trying to describe the similarity between items based on some attributes that an expert tells you are important, you compare the similarity by what people think of these items. This is the approach used in collaborative filtering. It doesn't care about the attributes of the items; it compares similarity strictly by the opinions of many users. Figure 14.3 contains a matrix of some users and ratings they gave some of the dishes mentioned earlier in the chapter.

	Unagi Don	Chicken Katsu	Chirashi	Tri Tip	Pulled Pork
Jim	2	0	0	4	4
John	5	5	5	3	3
Sally	2	4	2	1	2

Figure 14.3 Simple matrix for demonstrating similarity measures

Let's calculate the similarity between Pulled Pork and Tri Tip. We can use the Euclidian distance to get started. The Euclidian distance is

$$\sqrt{(4-4)^2 + (3-3)^2 + (2-1)^2} = 1$$

and the Euclidian distance for Pulled Pork and Unagi Don is

$$\sqrt{(4-2)^2 + (3-5)^2 + (2-2)^2} = 2.83$$

From this data, Pulled Pork is more similar to Tri Tip than Unagi Don because the distance between Pulled Pork and Tri Tip is smaller than the distance between Pulled Pork and Unagi Don. We want the similarity, which should vary between 0 and 1 and should be larger for more similar items. We can calculate this by `similarity = 1/(1+distance)`. If the distance is 0, then the similarity is 1.0. If the distance is really big, then the similarity falls to 0.

A second distance measurement is the *Pearson correlation*. This is the correlation that we used in chapter 8 to measure the accuracy of our regression equations. This metric tells us how similar two vectors are. One benefit of this over the Euclidian distance is that it's insensitive to the magnitude of users' ratings. Say one person is manic and rates everything with 5s; another person isn't so happy and rates everything with 1s. The Pearson correlation tells us that these two vectors are equal. The Pearson correlation is built into NumPy as the function `corrcoef()`. We'll use it soon. The values for the Pearson correlation range from -1 to +1. We'll normalize these to the range of 0 to 1.0 by `0.5+0.5*corrcoef()`.

Another commonly used similarity metric is the *cosine similarity*. The cosine similarity measures the cosine of the angle between two vectors. If the angle is 90, then the similarity is 0; if the vectors point in the same direction, then they have a similarity of 1.0. Like the Pearson correlation, this ranges from -1 to +1, so we normalize it to the range of 0 to 1.0. To calculate this, we can take the definition of the cosine of two vectors A and B as

$$cos\theta = \frac{A \cdot B}{\|A\|\|B\|}$$

The two parallel lines around A and B means the L2 norm of the vectors. You can have a norm of any number, but if no number is given, it's assumed to be the L2 norm. The L2 norm of a vector [4, 2, 2] is given by

$$\sqrt{4^2 + 3^2 + 2^2}$$

Once again the linear algebra toolbox in NumPy can compute the norm for you with `linalg.norm()`.

Let's write these similarity measures as functions in Python. Open svdRec.py and insert the code from listing 14.1.

Listing 14.1   Similarity measures

```
from numpy import *
from numpy import linalg as la

def ecludSim(inA,inB):
    return 1.0/(1.0 + la.norm(inA - inB))

def pearsSim(inA,inB):
    if len(inA) < 3 : return 1.0
    return 0.5+0.5*corrcoef(inA, inB, rowvar = 0)[0][1]

def cosSim(inA,inB):
    num = float(inA.T*inB)
    denom = la.norm(inA)*la.norm(inB)
    return 0.5+0.5*(num/denom)
```

The three functions are the three similarity measures we just discussed. The NumPy linalg (Linear Algebra) toolbox is imported as `la` to make the code more readable. The function assumes that `inA` and `inB` are column vectors. The `perasSim()` function checks to see if there are three points or more. If not, it returns 1.0 because the two vectors are perfectly correlated.

Let's give these a try. After you've saved svdRec.py, enter the following in your Python shell:

```
>>> reload(svdRec)
<module 'svdRec' from 'svdRec.pyc'>
>>> myMat=mat(svdRec.loadExData())
>>> svdRec.ecludSim(myMat[:,0],myMat[:,4])
0.12973190755680383
>>> svdRec.ecludSim(myMat[:,0],myMat[:,0])
1.0
```

The Euclidian similarity measure seems to work; now let's try the cosine:

```
>>> svdRec.cosSim(myMat[:,0],myMat[:,4])
0.5
>>> svdRec.cosSim(myMat[:,0],myMat[:,0])
1.0000000000000002
```

Cosine seems to function; let's try the Pearson correlation:

```
>>> svdRec.pearsSim(myMat[:,0],myMat[:,4])
0.20596538173840329>>> svdRec.pearsSim(myMat[:,0],myMat[:,0])
1.0
```

All of these metrics assumed the data was in column vectors. We'll have problems if we try to use row vectors with these functions. (It would be easy to change the functions to compute on row vectors.) Column vectors imply that we're going to use item-based similarity. We'll discuss the reason for that next.

14.4.2 *Item-based or user-based similarity?*

We compared the distance between two restaurant dishes. This is known as *item-based* similarity. A second method that compares users is known as *user-based* similarity. If you refer to figure 14.3, comparing rows (users) is known as user-based similarity; comparing columns is known as item-based similarity. Which one should you use? The choice depends on how many users you may have or how many items you may have. Item-based scales with the number of items, and user-based scales with the number of users you have. If you have something like a store, you'll have a few thousand items at the most. The biggest stores at the time of writing have around 100,000 items. In the Netflix competition, there were 480,000 users and 17,700 movies. If you have a lot of users, then you'll probably want to go with item-based similarity.

For most product-driven recommendation engines, the number of users outnumbers the number of items. There are more people buying items than unique items for sale.

14.4.3 *Evaluating recommendation engines*

How can we evaluate a recommendation engine? We don't have a target value to predict, and we don't have the user here to ask if our prediction is right or wrong. We can do a form of cross-validation that we've done multiple times in other problems. The way we do that is to take some known rating and hold it out of the data and then make a prediction for that value. We can compare our predicted value with the real value from the user.

Usually the metric used to evaluate a recommendation engine is root mean squared error (RMSE). This metric computes the mean of the squared error and then takes the square root of that. If you're rating things on a scale of one to five stars and you have an RMSE of 1.0, it means that your predictions are on average one star off of what people really think.

14.5   Example: a restaurant dish recommendation engine

We're now going to build a recommendation engine. The topic we're going to apply this to is restaurant food. Say you're sitting at home and you decide to go out to eat, but you don't know where you should go or what you should order. This program will tell you both.

We're first going to create the basic recommendation engine, which looks for things you haven't yet tried. The second step is to improve our recommendations by using the SVD to reduce the feature space. We'll then wrap up this program with a human-readable UI so that people can use it. Finally, we'll discuss some problems with building recommendation engines.

14.5.1   Recommending untasted dishes

The recommendation engine will work like this: given a user, it will return the top N best recommendations for that user. To do this we do the following:

1   Look for things the user hasn't yet rated: look for values with 0 in the user-item matrix.
2   Of all the items this user hasn't yet rated, find a projected rating for each item: that is, what score do we think the user will give to this item? (This is where the similarity part comes in.)
3   Sort the list in descending order and return the first N items.

OK, let's do it. Open your svdRec.py and add the code from the following listing.

Listing 14.2   Item-based recommendation engine

```
def standEst(dataMat, user, simMeas, item):
    n = shape(dataMat)[1]
    simTotal = 0.0; ratSimTotal = 0.0
    for j in range(n):
        userRating = dataMat[user,j]
        if userRating == 0: continue
        overLap = nonzero(logical_and(dataMat[:,item].A>0, \       ❶ Find items
                                      dataMat[:,j].A>0))[0]           rated by
        if len(overLap) == 0: similarity = 0                         both users
        else: similarity = simMeas(dataMat[overLap,item], \
                                   dataMat[overLap,j])
        #print 'the %d and %d similarity is: %f' % (item, j, similarity)
        simTotal += similarity
        ratSimTotal += similarity * userRating
    if simTotal == 0: return 0
    else: return ratSimTotal/simTotal

def recommend(dataMat, user, N=3, simMeas=cosSim, estMethod=standEst):
    unratedItems = nonzero(dataMat[user,:].A==0)[1]          ❷ Find unrated
    if len(unratedItems) == 0: return 'you rated everything'    items
    itemScores = []
    for item in unratedItems:
        estimatedScore = estMethod(dataMat, user, simMeas, item)
        itemScores.append((item, estimatedScore))
    return sorted(itemScores, \                               ❸ Return top N
            key=lambda jj: jj[1], reverse=True)[:N]              unrated items
```

Listing 14.2 contains two functions. The first one, called `standEst()`, calculates the estimated rating a user would give an item for a given similarity measure. The second function, called `recommend()`, is the recommendation engine, and it calls `standEst()`. We'll first discuss `standEst()` and then `recommend()`.

The function `standEst()` takes a data matrix, a user number, an item number, and a similarity measure as its arguments. The data matrix is assumed to be organized like figures 14.1 and 14.2 with users as the row and items as the columns. You first get the number of items in the dataset, and then you initialize two variables that will be used to calculate an estimated rating. Next, you loop over every item in the row. If an item is rated 0, it means that this user has not rated it, and you'll skip it. The big picture of this loop is that you're going to loop over every item that the user has rated and compare it with other items. The variable `overLap` captures the elements that have been rated between two items. ❶ If there's no overlap, the similarity is 0 and you exit this loop. But if there are overlapping items, you calculate the similarity based on the overlapping items. This similarity is then accumulated, along with the product of the similarity and this user's rating. Finally, you normalize the similarity rating product by dividing it by the sum of all the ratings. This will give you a number between 0 and 5, which you can use to rank the forecasted values.

The function `recommend()` generates the top `N` recommendations. If you don't enter anything for `N`, it defaults to 3. The other arguments to this function are a similarity measurement and an estimation method. You can use any of the similarity measurements from listing 14.1. Right now you have only one option for the estimation method, but you'll add another one in the next subsection. The first thing you do is create a list of unrated items for a given user. ❷ If there are no unrated items, you exit the function. Otherwise, you loop over all the unrated items. For each unrated item, it calls `stanEst()`, which generates a forecasted score for that item. The item's index and the estimated score are placed in a list of tuples called `itemScores`. Finally, this list is sorted by the estimated score and returned. ❸ The list is sorted in reverse order, which means largest values first.

Let's see this in action. After you've saved svdRec.py, enter the following into your Python shell:

```
>>> reload(svdRec)
<module 'svdRec' from 'svdRec.py'>
```

Now let's load an example matrix. You can use the same matrix from earlier in the chapter with a few modifications. First, load the original matrix:

```
>>> myMat=mat(svdRec.loadExData())
```

This matrix was great for illustrating the SVD, but it's not that interesting, so let's alter a few values:

```
>>> myMat[0,1]=myMat[0,0]=myMat[1,0]=myMat[2,0]=4
>>> myMat[3,3]=2
```

Take a look at the matrix now:

```
>>> myMat
matrix([[4, 4, 0, 2, 2],
        [4, 0, 0, 3, 3],
        [4, 0, 0, 1, 1],
        [1, 1, 1, 2, 0],
        [2, 2, 2, 0, 0],
        [1, 1, 1, 0, 0],
        [5, 5, 5, 0, 0]])
```

OK, now you're ready for some recommendations. Let's try the default recommendation:

```
>>> svdRec.recommend(myMat, 2)
[(2, 2.5000000000000004), (1, 2.0498713655614456)]
```

This says user 2 (the third row down; remember we start with 0) would like item 2 with a project score of 2.5 and item 1 with a project score of 2.05. Now let's try this for other similarity metrics:

```
>>> svdRec.recommend(myMat, 2, simMeas=svdRec.ecludSim)
[(2, 3.0), (1, 2.8266504712098603)]
>>> svdRec.recommend(myMat, 2, simMeas=svdRec.pearsSim)
[(2, 2.5), (1, 2.0)]
```

Try this out with multiple users, and change the data set a little to see how it changes the results.

This example illustrates how the recommendations are done using item-based similarity and a number of similarity measures. You'll now see how you can apply the SVD to your recommendations.

14.5.2 *Improving recommendations with the SVD*

Real data sets are much sparser than the version of myMat we used to demonstrate the recommend() function. A more realistic matrix is shown in figure 14.4.

	Unagi Don	Chicken Katsu	Chirashi	Tri Tip	Salmon Burger	Ruben	Chicken Tandoori	Mapo Tofu	Kung Pao Chicken	Paneer Jalfrazie	Big Dutchman
Brett	2	0	0	4	4	0	0	0	0	0	0
Rob	0	0	0	0	0	0	0	0	0	0	5
Drew	0	0	0	0	0	0	0	1	0	4	0
Scott	3	3	4	0	3	0	0	2	2	0	0
Mary	5	5	5	0	0	0	0	0	0	0	0
Brent	0	0	0	0	0	0	5	0	0	5	0
Kyle	4	0	4	0	0	0	0	0	0	0	5
Sara	0	0	0	0	0	4	0	0	0	0	4
Shaney	0	0	0	0	0	0	5	0	0	5	0
Brendan	0	0	0	3	0	0	0	0	4	5	0
Leanna	1	1	2	1	1	2	1	0	4	5	0

Figure 14.4   Larger matrix of users and dishes. The presence of the many unrated items is more realistic than a completely filled-in matrix.

You can enter this matrix or you can copy the function `loadExData2()` from the code download. Now let's compute the SVD of this matrix to see how many dimensions you need.

```
>>>from numpy import linalg as la
>>> U,Sigma,VT=la.svd(mat(svdRec.loadExData2()))
>>> Sigma
array([ 1.38487021e+01,   1.15944583e+01,   1.10219767e+01,
        5.31737732e+00,   4.55477815e+00,   2.69935136e+00,
        1.53799905e+00,   6.46087828e-01,   4.45444850e-01,
        9.86019201e-02,   9.96558169e-17])
```

Now, let's find the number of singular values that give you 90% of the total energy. First, you square the values in `Sigma`.

```
>>> Sig2=Sigma**2
```

Now, let's see the total energy:

```
>>> sum(Sig2)
541.99999999999932
```

How about 90% of the total energy:

```
>>> sum(Sig2)*0.9
487.79999999999939
```

Let's see how much energy is contained in the first two elements:

```
>>> sum(Sig2[:2])
378.8295595113579
```

That's under 90%. How about the first three:

```
>>> sum(Sig2[:3])
500.50028912757909
```

That should do it. So we can reduce our matrix from an 11-dimensional matrix to a 3-dimensional matrix. Now let's create a function to calculate similarities in our 3-dimensional space. We're going to use the SVD to map our dishes into a lower-dimensional space. In the lower-dimensional space, we'll make recommendations based on the same similarity metrics we used earlier. We'll create a function similar to `standEst()` in listing 14.2. Open svdRec.py and add the code from the following listing.

Listing 14.3 Rating estimation by using the SVD

```
def svdEst(dataMat, user, simMeas, item):
    n = shape(dataMat)[1]
    simTotal = 0.0; ratSimTotal = 0.0
    U,Sigma,VT = la.svd(dataMat)
    Sig4 = mat(eye(4)*Sigma[:4])                    ❶ Create diagonal
    xformedItems = dataMat.T * U[:,:4] * Sig4.I        matrix
    for j in range(n):                              ❷ Create transformed
        userRating = dataMat[user,j]                   items
```

```
        if userRating == 0 or j==item: continue
        similarity = simMeas(xformedItems[item,:].T,\
                            xformedItems[j,:].T)
        print 'the %d and %d similarity is: %f' % (item, j, similarity)
        simTotal += similarity
        ratSimTotal += similarity * userRating
    if simTotal == 0: return 0
    else: return ratSimTotal/simTotal
```

The code in listing 14.3 contains one function, svdEst(). This will be used in place of standEst() when you call recommend(). This function creates an estimated rating for a given item for a given user. If you compare it to standEst() in listing 14.2, you'll see that many of the lines are similar. Something unique to this function is that it does an SVD on the dataset on the third line. After the SVD is done, you use only the singular values that give you 90% of the energy. The singular values are given to you in the form of a NumPy array, so to do matrix math you need to build a diagonal matrix with these singular values on the diagonal. ❶ Next, you use the U matrix to transform our items into the lower-dimensional space. ❷

The for loop iterates over all the elements in a row for a given user. This serves the same purpose as the for loop in standEst() except you're calculating the similarities in a lower dimension. The similarity measure used is passed into this function as an argument. Next, you sum up the similarities and the product of the similarities and the rating that this user gave this item. These are returned to give an estimated rating. I've included one print statement in the for loop so you can see what's going on with the similarity measurements. You can comment it out if the output gets annoying.

Let's see this in action. After you've entered the code from listing 14.3, save svdRec.py and enter the following in your Python shell:

```
>>> reload(svdRec)
<module 'svdRec' from 'svdRec.pyc'>
>>> svdRec.recommend(myMat, 1, estMethod=svdRec.svdEst)
The 0 and 3 similarity is 0.362287.
                    .
                    .
                    .
The 9 and 10 similarity is 0.497753.
[(6, 3.387858021353602), (8, 3.3611246496054976), (7, 3.3587350221130028)]
```

Now let's try it with a different distance metric:

```
>>> svdRec.recommend(myMat, 1, estMethod=svdRec.svdEst,
simMeas=svdRec.pearsSim)
The 0 and 3 similarity is 0.116304.
                    .
                    .
                    .
The 9 and 10 similarity is 0.566796.
[(6, 3.3772856083690845), (9, 3.3701740601550196), (4, 3.3675118739831169)]
```

Try that out with a few different similarity metrics. Compare it to the previous method on this dataset. Which one performs better?

14.5.3 *Challenges with building recommendation engines*

The code in this section works and does an effective job of demonstrating how recommendation engines work and how the SVD distills data into its essential components. I wrote the code to be as easy to understand as possible, not necessarily the most efficient. For one thing, you don't need to do the SVD every time you want a projected value. With our dataset, this didn't make a difference. But on larger datasets, this will slow things down. The SVD could be done once when the program is launched. On large systems, the SVD is done once a day or less often and is done offline.

There are a number of other scaling challenges, such as representing our matrix. The matrix in this example had a lot of 0s, and in a real system it would have many more. Perhaps we could save some memory and computations by storing only the nonzero values? Another potential source of computing waste is the similarity scores. In our program, we calculated the similarity scores for multiple items each time we wanted a recommendation score. The scores are between items, so we reuse them if another user needs them. Another thing commonly done in practice is to compute the similarity scores offline and store them.

Another problem with recommendation engines is how to make good recommendations with no data. This is known as the *cold-start* problem and can be difficult. Another way to phrase this problem is users won't like this unless it works, and it won't work unless users like it. If recommendations are a nice-to-have feature, then this may not be a big problem, but if the success of your application is linked to the success of the recommendations, then this is a serious problem.

One solution to the cold-start problem is to treat recommendations as a search problem. Under the hood these are different solutions, but they can be presented to the user in a transparent manner. To treat these recommendations as a search problem you could use properties of the items you're trying to recommend. In our restaurant dish example we could tag dishes along a number of parameters such as vegetarian, American BBQ, expensive, and so on. You could also treat these properties as data for our similarity calculations. This is known as content-based recommendation. Content-based recommendation may not be as good as the collaborative-filtering methods we discussed earlier, but when it's all you have, it's a good start.

14.6 *Example: image compression with the SVD*

In this last section you'll see a great example of how the SVD can be used for image compression. This example allows you to easily visualize how well the SVD is approximating our data. In the code repository, I included a handwritten digit image. This is one of the images used in chapter 2. The original image is 32 pixels wide and 32 pixels long, with a total of 1024 pixels. Can we represent the same image with fewer numbers? If we're able to compress an image, we can save disk space or bandwidth.

We can use the SVD to reduce the dimensionality of the data and compress an image. Let's see how this works on the handwritten digits. The following listing contains some code for reading the digit and compressing it. To see how good of a job it does, we also reconstruct the compressed image. Open svdRec.py and enter the following code.

```
def printMat(inMat, thresh=0.8):
    for i in range(32):
        for k in range(32):
            if float(inMat[i,k]) > thresh:
                print 1,
            else: print 0,
        print ''

def imgCompress(numSV=3, thresh=0.8):
    myl = []
    for line in open('0_5.txt').readlines():
        newRow = []
        for i in range(32):
            newRow.append(int(line[i]))
        myl.append(newRow)
    myMat = mat(myl)
    print "****original matrix******"
    printMat(myMat, thresh)
    U,Sigma,VT = la.svd(myMat)
    SigRecon = mat(zeros((numSV, numSV)))
    for k in range(numSV):
        SigRecon[k,k] = Sigma[k]
    reconMat = U[:,:numSV]*SigRecon*VT[:numSV,:]
    print "****reconstructed matrix using %d singular values******" % numSV
    printMat(reconMat, thresh)
```

The first function in listing 14.4, printMat(), prints a matrix. The matrix will have floating point values, so you need to define what's light and what's dark. You include a threshold you can tune later. This function iterates over everything in the matrix and prints a 1 if the value in the matrix is over the threshold and a 0 if not.

The next function does the image compression. It allows you to reconstruct an image with any given number of singular values. This creates a list and then opens the text file and loads the characters from the file as numeric values. After the matrix is loaded, you print it to the screen. Next, you take the SVD of the original image and reconstruct the image. This is done by reconstructing Sigma as SigRecon. Sigma is a diagonal matrix, so you create a matrix with all 0s and then fill in the diagonal elements with the first singular values. Finally, SigRecon is used with the truncated **U** and **V**^T matrices to build the reconstructed matrix. This matrix is printed using printMat().

Let's see this function in action:

```
>>> reload(svdRec)
<module 'svdRec' from 'svdRec.py'>
>>> svdRec.imgCompress(2)
****original matrix******
0 0 0 0 0 0 0 0 0 0 0 0 0 0 1 1 0 0 0 0 0 0 0 0 0 0 0 0 0 0 0 0
```

```
0 0 0 0 0 0 0 0 0 0 0 1 1 1 1 1 0 0 0 0 0 0 0 0 0 0 0 0 0 0 0 0
0 0 0 0 0 0 0 0 0 0 0 1 1 1 1 1 1 0 0 0 0 0 0 0 0 0 0 0 0 0 0 0
0 0 0 0 0 0 0 0 0 0 1 1 1 1 1 1 1 1 0 0 0 0 0 0 0 0 0 0 0 0 0 0
0 0 0 0 0 0 0 0 1 1 1 1 1 1 1 1 1 1 0 0 0 0 0 0 0 0 0 0 0 0 0 0
0 0 0 0 0 0 0 1 1 1 1 1 1 1 1 1 1 1 1 0 0 0 0 0 0 0 0 0 0 0 0 0
0 0 0 0 0 0 0 1 1 1 1 1 1 1 1 1 1 1 1 1 0 0 0 0 0 0 0 0 0 0 0 0
0 0 0 0 0 0 0 1 1 1 1 1 1 0 0 0 1 1 1 1 0 0 0 0 0 0 0 0 0 0 0 0
0 0 0 0 0 0 0 1 1 1 1 1 1 0 0 0 0 1 1 1 1 0 0 0 0 0 0 0 0 0 0 0
0 0 0 0 0 0 1 1 1 1 1 1 0 0 0 0 0 0 1 1 1 1 0 0 0 0 0 0 0 0 0 0
0 0 0 0 0 0 1 1 1 1 1 1 0 0 0 0 0 0 1 1 1 1 0 0 0 0 0 0 0 0 0 0
0 0 0 0 0 0 1 1 1 1 1 1 0 0 0 0 0 0 0 1 1 1 1 0 0 0 0 0 0 0 0 0
0 0 0 0 0 0 1 1 1 1 1 1 0 0 0 0 0 0 0 1 1 1 1 0 0 0 0 0 0 0 0 0
0 0 0 0 0 0 0 1 1 1 1 1 1 0 0 0 0 0 0 0 1 1 1 1 0 0 0 0 0 0 0 0
0 0 0 0 0 0 0 1 1 1 1 1 1 0 0 0 0 0 0 0 1 1 1 1 0 0 0 0 0 0 0 0
0 0 0 0 0 0 0 1 1 1 1 1 1 0 0 0 0 0 0 0 1 1 1 1 0 0 0 0 0 0 0 0
0 0 0 0 0 0 0 1 1 1 1 1 1 0 0 0 0 0 0 0 1 1 1 1 0 0 0 0 0 0 0 0
0 0 0 0 0 0 0 1 1 1 1 1 1 0 0 0 0 0 0 0 1 1 1 1 0 0 0 0 0 0 0 0
0 0 0 0 0 0 0 1 1 1 1 1 1 0 0 0 0 0 0 0 1 1 1 1 0 0 0 0 0 0 0 0
0 0 0 0 0 0 0 0 1 1 1 1 1 0 0 0 0 0 0 0 1 1 1 1 1 0 0 0 0 0 0 0
0 0 0 0 0 0 0 0 1 1 1 1 1 0 0 0 0 0 0 0 1 1 1 1 1 0 0 0 0 0 0 0
0 0 0 0 0 0 0 0 1 1 1 1 1 0 0 0 0 0 0 0 1 1 1 1 1 0 0 0 0 0 0 0
0 0 0 0 0 0 0 0 1 1 1 1 1 0 0 0 0 0 0 0 1 1 1 1 1 0 0 0 0 0 0 0
0 0 0 0 0 0 0 0 1 1 1 1 1 0 0 0 0 0 0 1 1 1 1 1 0 0 0 0 0 0 0 0
0 0 0 0 0 0 0 0 1 1 1 1 1 1 0 0 0 0 0 1 1 1 1 1 0 0 0 0 0 0 0 0
0 0 0 0 0 0 0 0 1 1 1 1 1 1 0 0 0 0 1 1 1 1 1 0 0 0 0 0 0 0 0 0
0 0 0 0 0 0 0 0 0 1 1 1 1 1 1 1 1 1 1 1 1 1 1 0 0 0 0 0 0 0 0 0
0 0 0 0 0 0 0 0 0 1 1 1 1 1 1 1 1 1 1 1 1 1 1 0 0 0 0 0 0 0 0 0
0 0 0 0 0 0 0 0 0 1 1 1 1 1 1 1 1 1 1 1 1 1 1 0 0 0 0 0 0 0 0 0
0 0 0 0 0 0 0 0 0 0 1 1 1 1 1 1 1 1 1 1 1 1 0 0 0 0 0 0 0 0 0 0
0 0 0 0 0 0 0 0 0 0 1 1 1 1 1 1 1 1 1 1 1 0 0 0 0 0 0 0 0 0 0 0
0 0 0 0 0 0 0 0 0 0 0 1 1 1 1 1 1 1 1 1 0 0 0 0 0 0 0 0 0 0 0 0
(32, 32)
****reconstructed matrix using 2 singular values******
0 0 0 0 0 0 0 0 0 0 0 0 0 0 0 0 0 0 0 0 0 0 0 0 0 0 0 0 0 0 0 0
0 0 0 0 0 0 0 0 0 0 0 0 0 0 0 0 0 0 0 0 0 0 0 0 0 0 0 0 0 0 0 0
0 0 0 0 0 0 0 0 0 0 0 0 0 1 1 1 1 0 0 0 0 0 0 0 0 0 0 0 0 0 0 0
0 0 0 0 0 0 0 0 0 0 0 0 1 1 1 1 1 1 1 0 0 0 0 0 0 0 0 0 0 0 0 0
0 0 0 0 0 0 0 0 0 0 0 1 1 1 1 1 1 1 1 1 0 0 0 0 0 0 0 0 0 0 0 0
0 0 0 0 0 0 0 0 0 0 1 1 1 1 1 1 1 1 1 1 0 0 0 0 0 0 0 0 0 0 0 0
0 0 0 0 0 0 0 0 0 1 1 1 1 1 1 1 1 1 1 1 0 0 0 0 0 0 0 0 0 0 0 0
0 0 0 0 0 0 0 0 1 1 1 1 0 0 0 0 0 0 1 0 0 0 0 0 0 0 0 0 0 0 0 0
0 0 0 0 0 0 0 0 1 1 1 1 0 0 0 0 0 0 1 1 0 0 0 0 0 0 0 0 0 0 0 0
0 0 0 0 0 0 0 0 1 1 1 1 0 0 0 0 0 0 1 1 1 0 0 0 0 0 0 0 0 0 0 0
0 0 0 0 0 0 0 0 1 1 1 1 0 0 0 0 0 0 1 1 1 0 0 0 0 0 0 0 0 0 0 0
0 0 0 0 0 0 0 0 1 1 1 1 0 0 0 0 0 0 1 1 1 0 0 0 0 0 0 0 0 0 0 0
0 0 0 0 0 0 0 0 1 1 1 1 0 0 0 0 0 0 1 1 1 0 0 0 0 0 0 0 0 0 0 0
0 0 0 0 0 0 0 0 1 1 1 1 0 0 0 0 0 0 1 1 1 0 0 0 0 0 0 0 0 0 0 0
0 0 0 0 0 0 0 0 1 1 1 1 0 0 0 0 0 0 1 1 1 0 0 0 0 0 0 0 0 0 0 0
0 0 0 0 0 0 0 0 1 1 1 1 0 0 0 0 0 0 1 1 1 0 0 0 0 0 0 0 0 0 0 0
0 0 0 0 0 0 0 0 1 1 1 1 0 0 0 0 0 0 1 1 1 0 0 0 0 0 0 0 0 0 0 0
0 0 0 0 0 0 0 0 1 1 1 1 0 0 0 0 0 0 1 1 1 0 0 0 0 0 0 0 0 0 0 0
0 0 0 0 0 0 0 0 1 1 1 1 0 0 0 0 0 0 1 1 1 0 0 0 0 0 0 0 0 0 0 0
0 0 0 0 0 0 0 0 1 1 1 1 0 0 0 0 0 0 1 1 1 0 0 0 0 0 0 0 0 0 0 0
0 0 0 0 0 0 0 0 1 1 1 1 0 0 0 0 0 0 1 1 1 0 0 0 0 0 0 0 0 0 0 0
```

```
0 0 0 0 0 0 0 0 1 1 1 1 0 0 0 0 0 0 0 0 0 0 1 1 1 0 0 0 0 0 0 0
0 0 0 0 0 0 0 0 1 1 1 1 0 0 0 0 0 0 0 0 0 0 1 1 1 0 0 0 0 0 0 0
0 0 0 0 0 0 0 0 1 1 1 1 0 0 0 0 0 0 0 0 0 0 1 1 1 0 0 0 0 0 0 0
0 0 0 0 0 0 0 0 1 1 1 1 0 0 0 0 0 0 0 0 0 0 1 1 0 0 0 0 0 0 0 0
0 0 0 0 0 0 0 0 0 0 1 1 1 1 1 1 1 1 1 1 1 0 0 0 0 0 0 0 0 0 0 0
0 0 0 0 0 0 0 0 0 0 1 1 1 1 1 1 1 1 1 1 1 0 0 0 0 0 0 0 0 0 0 0
0 0 0 0 0 0 0 0 0 0 1 1 1 1 1 1 1 1 1 1 1 0 0 0 0 0 0 0 0 0 0 0
0 0 0 0 0 0 0 0 0 0 0 1 1 1 1 1 1 1 1 1 0 0 0 0 0 0 0 0 0 0 0 0
0 0 0 0 0 0 0 0 0 0 0 1 1 1 1 1 1 1 1 0 0 0 0 0 0 0 0 0 0 0 0 0
0 0 0 0 0 0 0 0 0 0 0 0 0 0 0 0 0 0 0 0 0 0 0 0 0 0 0 0 0 0 0 0
```

With as few as two singular values, the image is reconstructed quite accurately. How many numbers did we use to reconstruct this image? Each of the U and V^T matrices was 32x2, and there were two singular values. That's a total 64+64+2 = 130. Compare this with the original number, which was 1024, and you get an almost 10x compression.

14.7 *Summary*

The singular value decomposition (SVD) is a powerful tool for dimensionality reduction. You can use the SVD to approximate a matrix and get out the important features. By taking only the top 80% or 90% of the energy in the matrix, you get the important features and throw out the noise. The SVD is employed in a number of applications today. One successful application is in recommendation engines.

Recommendations engines recommend an item to a user. Collaborative filtering is one way of creating recommendations based on data of users' preferences or actions. At the heart of collaborative filtering is a similarity metric. A number of similarity metrics can be used to calculate the similarity between items or users. The SVD can be used to improve recommendation engines by calculating similarities in a reduced number of dimensions.

Calculating the SVD and recommendations can be a difficult engineering problem on massive datasets. Taking the SVD and similarity calculations offline is one method of reducing redundant calculations and reducing the time required to produce a recommendation. In the next chapter, we'll discuss some tools for working with massive datasets and doing machine learning on these datasets.

Big data and MapReduce

This chapter covers

- MapReduce
- Using Python with Hadoop Streaming
- Automating MapReduce with mrjob
- Training support vector machines in parallel
  with the Pegasos algorithm

I often hear "Your examples are nice, but my data is *big*, man!" I have no doubt that you work with data sets larger than the examples used in this book. With so many devices connected to the internet and people interested in making data-driven decisions, the amount of data we're collecting has outpaced our ability to process it. Fortunately, a number of open source software projects allow us to process large amounts of data. One project, called *Hadoop*, is a Java framework for distributing data processing to multiple machines.

Imagine for a second that you work for a store that sells items on the internet, and you get many visitors—some purchasing items, some leaving before they purchase items. You'd like to be able to identify the ones who make purchases. How do you do this? You can look at the web server logs and see what pages each person went to. Perhaps some other actions are recorded; if so, you can train a classifier on these actions. The only problem is that this dataset may be huge, and it may take multiple days to train this classifier on a single machine. This chapter will show you some tools you can use to solve a problem like this: Hadoop and some Python tools built on top of Hadoop.

Hadoop is a free, open source implementation of the MapReduce framework. You're going to first learn what MapReduce and the Hadoop project are. You'll next see how you can write MapReduce jobs in Python. You'll test these jobs on a single machine, and then you'll see how you can use Amazon Web Services to run full Hadoop jobs on many machines at one time. Once you're comfortable running MapReduce jobs, we'll discuss common solutions to do machine learning jobs in MapReduce. You'll then see a framework for automating MapReduce jobs in Python called mrjob. Finally, you'll write a distributed SVM with mrjob that could be used to train a classifier on multiple machines.

15.1 *MapReduce: a framework for distributed computing*

MapReduce

Pros: Processes a massive job in a short period of time.

Cons: Algorithms must be rewritten; requires understanding of systems engineering.

Works with: Numeric values, nominal values.

MapReduce is a software framework for spreading a single computing job across multiple computers. It's assumed that these jobs take too long to run on a single computer, so you run them on multiple computers to shorten the time. Some of these jobs are summaries of daily statistics where running them on a single machine would take longer than one day.

A U.S. patent was issued to Google for MapReduce, although others claim to have independently developed similar frameworks. Jeffrey Dean and Sanjay Ghemawat from Google first published the idea in 2004, in a paper titled "MapReduce: Simplified Data Processing on Large Clusters."[1] The name MapReduce comes from the words *map* and *reduce*, which are functions commonly used in functional programming.

MapReduce is done on a cluster, and the cluster is made up of nodes. MapReduce works like this: a single job is broken down into small sections, and the input data is chopped up and distributed to each node. Each node operates on only its data. The code that's run on each node is called the *mapper*, and this is known as the *map* step. The output from the individual mappers is combined in some way, usually sorted. The sorted data is then broken into smaller portions and distributed to the nodes for further processing. This second processing step is known as the *reduce* step, and the code

---

[1] J. Dean, S. Ghemawat, "MapReduce: Simplified Data Processing on Large Clusters," OSDI '04: 6th Symposium on Operating System Design and Implementation, San Francisco, CA, December, 2004.

run is known as the *reducer.* The output of the reducer is the final answer you're look-ing for.

The advantage of MapReduce is that it allows programs to be executed in parallel. If our cluster has 10 nodes and our original job took 10 hours to process, a MapRe-duce version of the job can reach the same result in a little more than 1 hour. For example, say we want to know the maximum temperature in China from the last 100 years. Assume we have valid data from each province for each day over this period. The data looks like <province> <date> <temp>. We could break up the data by the number of nodes we have, and each node could look for the maximum among its data. Each mapper would emit one temperature, <"max"><temp>. All mappers would produce the same key, which is a string "max." We'd then need just one reducer to compare the outputs of the mappers and get our global maximum temperature.

> **NOTE:** At no point do the individual mappers or reducers communicate with each other. Each node minds its own business and computes the data it has been assigned.

Depending on the type of job, we may require different numbers of reducers. If we revisit the Chinese temperature example and say we want the maximum temperature for each year, the mappers would now have to find the maximum temperature for each year and emit that, so the intermediate data would look like <year> <temp>. Now we'd need to make sure all values with the same year go to the same reducer. This is done in the sort between the map and reduce steps. This example illustrates another point: the way data is passed around. Data is passed in key/value pairs. In our second Chinese temperature example, the year was the key and the temperature was the value. We sorted by the year, so we correctly combined similar years; each reducer would receive common key (year) values.

From these examples you may have noticed that the number of reducers isn't fixed. There are a number of flexible options in a MapReduce implementation. The orchestration of this is handled by a master node. The master node handles the orchestration of the whole MapReduce job, including which data is placed on which node, and it handles the timing of the map, sort, and reduce steps, and so on. The master node can also handle fault tolerance. Often, multiple copies of the mapper input data are sent to multiple nodes in the event of a failure. Consider the schematic representation of a MapReduce cluster in figure 15.1.

Each machine in figure 15.1 has two processors and can handle two map or reduce jobs simultaneously. If Machine 0 was destroyed by a robot airplane during the map phase, the master node would recognize this. When the master node sensed a failure, it would remove Machine 0 from the cluster and continue with the job. In some imple-mentations of MapReduce, additional data is stored on each machine. The input data to Machine 0 may also be stored on Machine 1 in case Machine 0 gets destroyed by a robot airplane. In some MapReduce implementations, the nodes need to communi-cate with the master node, indicating that they're alive and functioning. If they aren't

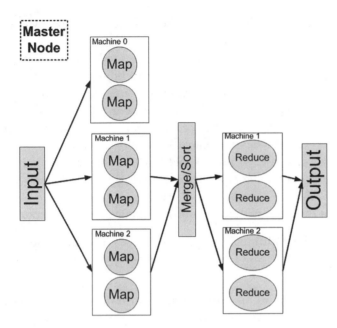

Figure 15.1   A schematic representation of the MapReduce framework. In this example there are three machines with two processors each in the cluster. Machine 0 fails, but the job continues.

alive and properly functioning, the master node may restart them or completely take them out of the pool of available machines.

Some key points about MapReduce from the previous example are these:

- A master node controls the MapReduce job.
- MapReduce jobs are broken into map and reduce tasks.
- Map tasks don't communicate with other map tasks; the same thing is true for reduce tasks.
- Between the map and reduce steps, there's a sort or combine step.
- Redundant copies of the data are stored on separate machines in case of machine failure.
- Data is passed between mappers and reducers in key/value pairs.

One implementation of the MapReduce framework is the Apache Hadoop project. In the next section we'll discuss Hadoop and how you can use it with Python.

15.2   *Hadoop Streaming*

Hadoop is an open source project written in Java. The Hadoop project has a large set of features for running MapReduce jobs. In addition to distributed computing, Hadoop has a distributed filesystem.

This isn't a Java book, nor is it a Hadoop book. You're going to see just enough of Hadoop to run MapReduce jobs in Python. If you're interested in knowing more about Hadoop, I suggest you pick up *Hadoop in Action*[2] or read documentation on

---

[2]   Chuck Lam, *Hadoop in Action* (Manning Publications, 2010).

Hadoop's site (http://hadoop.apache.org/). The book *Mahout in Action*[3] is also a great source of information if you're interested in machine learning with MapReduce.

Hadoop has code that allows you to run distributed programs that are written in languages other than Java. Because this book is written in Python, you'll write some MapReduce jobs in Python and then run them in Hadoop Streaming. Hadoop Streaming (http://hadoop.apache.org/common/docs/current/streaming.html) operates like the pipes in Linux. (If you aren't familiar with pipes, they use the symbol | and take the output from one command and direct it to the input of another command.) If our mapper was called mapper.py and our reducer was called reducer.py, Hadoop Streaming would run something similar to the following Linux command:

```
cat inputFile.txt | python mapper.py | sort | python reducer.py >
outputFile.txt
```

In Hadoop Streaming something like this is done over multiple machines. We can use the Linux command to test our MapReduce scripts written in Python.

15.2.1 *Distributed mean and variance mapper*

We're going to create a MapReduce job that calculates the mean and variance of a bunch of numbers. This is for demonstration purposes, so we'll use a small amount of data. Create a file called mrMeanMapper.py in your favorite editor, and add in the code from the following listing.

> **Listing 15.1 Distributed mean and variance mapper**

```
import sys
from numpy import mat, mean, power

def read_input(file):
    for line in file:
        yield line.rstrip()

input = read_input(sys.stdin)
input = [float(line) for line in input]
numInputs = len(input)
input = mat(input)
sqInput = power(input,2)

print "%d\t%f\t%f" % (numInputs, mean(input), mean(sqInput))
print >> sys.stderr, "report: still alive"
```

This is a straightforward example. You loop over all the input lines and first create a list of floats. Next, you get the length of that list and then create a NumPy matrix from that list. You can then quickly square all of the values. Finally, you send out the mean and the mean of the squared values. These values will be used to calculate the global mean and variance.

> **NOTE** A good practice is to send out a report to standard error. If jobs don't report something to standard error every 10 minutes, then they'll get killed in Hadoop.

---

[3] Sean Owen, Robin Anil, Ted Dunning, and Ellen Friedman, *Mahout in Action* (Manning Publications, 2011).

Let's see the code from listing 15.1 in action. There's an input file with 100 numbers in a file called inputFile.txt in the source code download. You can experiment with the mapper before you even touch Hadoop by typing the following command in a Linux window:

```
cat inputFile.txt | python mrMeanMapper.py
```

You can also do this on Windows by typing the following in a DOS terminal:

```
python mrMeanMapper.py < inputFile.txt
```

You should see something like this:

```
100     0.509570        0.344439
report: still alive
```

The first line is the standard output, which we'll feed into the reducer. The second line, which was written to standard error, will be sent to the master node to report to the master that the node is still alive.

15.2.2 *Distributed mean and variance reducer*

Now that we have the mapper working, let's work on the reducer. The mapper took raw numbers and collected them into intermediate values for our reducer. We'll have many of these mappers doing this in parallel, and we'll need to combine all those outputs into one value. We now need to write the reducer so we can combine the intermediate key value pairs. Open your text editor and create a file called mrMeanReducer.py; then enter the code from the following listing.

Listing 15.2 Distributed mean and variance reducer

```python
import sys
from numpy import mat, mean, power

def read_input(file):
    for line in file:
        yield line.rstrip()

input = read_input(sys.stdin)
mapperOut = [line.split('\t') for line in input]
cumVal=0.0
cumSumSq=0.0
cumN=0.0
for instance in mapperOut:
    nj = float(instance[0])
    cumN += nj
    cumVal += nj*float(instance[1])
    cumSumSq += nj*float(instance[2])
mean = cumVal/cumN
varSum = (cumSumSq - 2*mean*cumVal + cumN*mean*mean)/cumN
print "%d\t%f\t%f" % (cumN, mean, varSum)
print >> sys.stderr, "report: still alive"
```

The code in listing 15.2 is the reducer, and this receives the output of the values from listing 15.1. These values are then combined to form a global mean and variance, which was the goal of this exercise.

You can practice with this on your local machine by typing the following at the command prompt:

```
%cat inputFile.txt | python mrMeanMapper.py | python mrMeanReducer.py
```

In DOS, enter the following command:

```
%python mrMeanMapper.py < inputFile.txt | python mrMeanReducer.py
```

You'll see how to run this on many machines at one time. Perhaps you don't have 10 servers sitting around your house. That's OK. You'll learn where you can rent them by the hour in the next section.

15.3 *Running Hadoop jobs on Amazon Web Services*

If you want to run your MapReduce jobs on 100 machines at the same time, you need to find 100 machines. You could buy them yourself or you could rent them from someone else. Amazon rents out parts of its massive computing infrastructure to developers through Amazon Web Services (AWS) at http://aws.amazon.com/.

AWS powers websites, streaming video, mobile applications, and the like. Storage, bandwidth, and compute power are metered, and you're billed only for your use of each of these, by the hour with no long-term contracts. This is what makes AWS so attractive—you pay only for what you use. Say you have an idea that takes 1,000 computers per day. You can get set up on AWS and experiment for a few days. Then, if you decide it's a bad idea, you can shut it down and you don't have to pay for those 1,000 computers any longer. We'll next talk about a few services currently available on AWS, then we'll walk through getting set up on AWS, and finally we'll run a Hadoop Streaming job on AWS.

15.3.1 *Services available on AWS*

A large number of services are available on AWS. All of them have names that to the informed seem totally logical and to the uninformed seem totally cryptic. AWS is constantly evolving and adding new services. Some basic, stable services that you'll be using are these:

- *S3*—Simple Storage Service is used for storing data on the internet and is used in conjunction with other AWS products. Here you're renting some sort of storage device, so you pay by the amount of data you store and the length of time you store that data.
- *EC2*—Elastic Compute Cloud is a service for using server instances. This is the heart of many common AWS-based systems. You can configure the server to run almost any operating system. A server can be started from a machine image in a matter of minutes. You can create, store, and share machine images. The *elastic*

part of the name comes from the ability to quickly expand the number of servers you're running as your demands require.

- *Elastic MapReduce*—This is the AWS MapReduce implementation. This is built on a slightly older release of Hadoop. (Amazon wanted to have a stable release, and so they made a few modifications, which prevents them from having the bleeding-edge release of Hadoop.) It has a nice GUI and simplifies the setup of Hadoop jobs. You don't have to mess with adding files to Hadoop's filesystem or configuring Hadoop machines. In Elastic MapReduce (EMR) you can run Java jobs or Hadoop Streaming jobs. We'll focus on Hadoop Streaming.

A large number of other services are available for use. We'll focus on EMR, although to use it we need to use S3. EMR takes files from S3 and starts up EC2 instances with Hadoop installed.

15.3.2 *Getting started with Amazon Web Services*

To get started with AWS, you need to create an account on AWS. To use AWS you'll need a credit card; the exercises in the rest of the chapter will cost around $1 USD. Go to http://aws.amazon.com/ and there will be a button in the top right that says "Sign Up Now," similar to figure 15.2. Follow the instructions on the next three pages to get signed up for Amazon Web Services. Make sure you sign up for S3, Elastic MapReduce, and EC2.

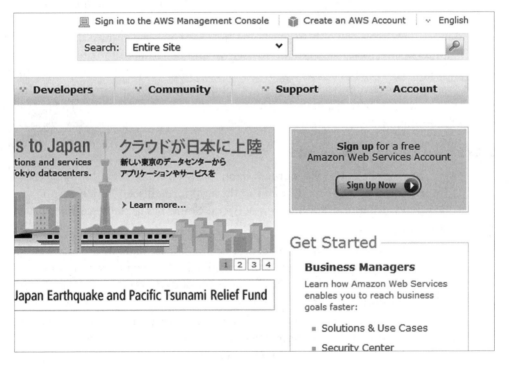

Figure 15.2   The upper-right portion of the landing page at http://aws.amazon.com/, showing where to start the sign-up process for Amazon Web Services

Figure 15.3 AWS Console showing a service I'm not signed up for yet. If you get this window for S3, EC2, or Elastic MapReduce, sign up for those services.

After you've created an account with AWS, log into the AWS console and click the EC2, Elastic MapReduce, and S3 tabs to make sure you signed up to use each of these services. If you aren't signed up for a service, you'll see something similar to figure 15.3.

You're now ready to run a Hadoop job on Amazon's computers. We'll walk through running a Hadoop job on EMR.

15.3.3 *Running a Hadoop job on EMR*

Once you've signed up for all the required Amazon services, log into the AWS console and click the S3 tab. You'll need to upload our files to S3 in order for the AWS version of Hadoop to find our files.

1 First, you'll need to create a new bucket. You can think of a bucket as a drive. Create a new bucket; for example, I created one called rustbucket. Note: bucket names are unique and shared among all users. You should create a unique name for your bucket.

2 Now create two new folders, one called mrMeanCode and one called mrMean-Input. You're going to upload the Python MapReduce files you created earlier to mrMeanCode. The other folder, mrMeanInput, is where you'll store the input to your Hadoop job.

3 Upload the file inputFile.txt to the folder mrMeanInput in your bucket (for example, rustbucket).

4   Upload the files mrMeanMapper.py and mrMeanReducer.py to the folder mrMeanCode in your bucket. Now that you have all the files uploaded, you're ready to launch your first Hadoop job on multiple machines.

5   Click the Elastic MapReduce tab. Next, click the Create New Job Flow button. Name the job flow `mrMean007`. Below that are two check boxes and a drop-down box. Click the Run Your Own Application radio button. On the drop-down menu, select Streaming. Your screen should look like figure 15.4. Click the Continue button.

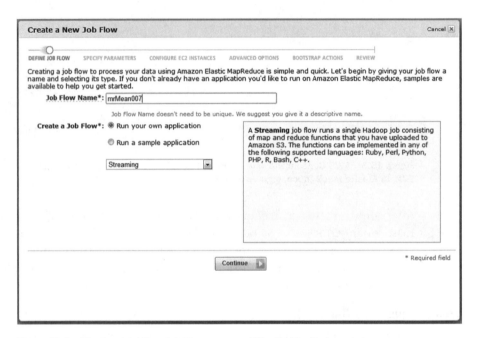

Figure 15.4   The Create a New Job Flow screen of Elastic MapReduce

6   In this step, you give the input arguments to Hadoop. If these settings aren't correct, your job will fail. Enter the values in the following fields on the Specify Parameters screen (be sure to include the quotes):

Input Location*: <your bucket name>/mrMeanInput/inputFile.txt

Output Location*: <your bucket name>/mrMean007Log

Mapper*: "python s3n:// <your bucket name>/mrMeanCode/mrMeanMapper.py"

Reducer*: "python s3n:// <your bucket name>/mrMeanCode/mrMeanReducer.py"

You can leave the Extra Args field blank. This is where you'd specify extra arguments such as restricting the number of reducers. Your screen should look like figure 15.5. Click Continue.

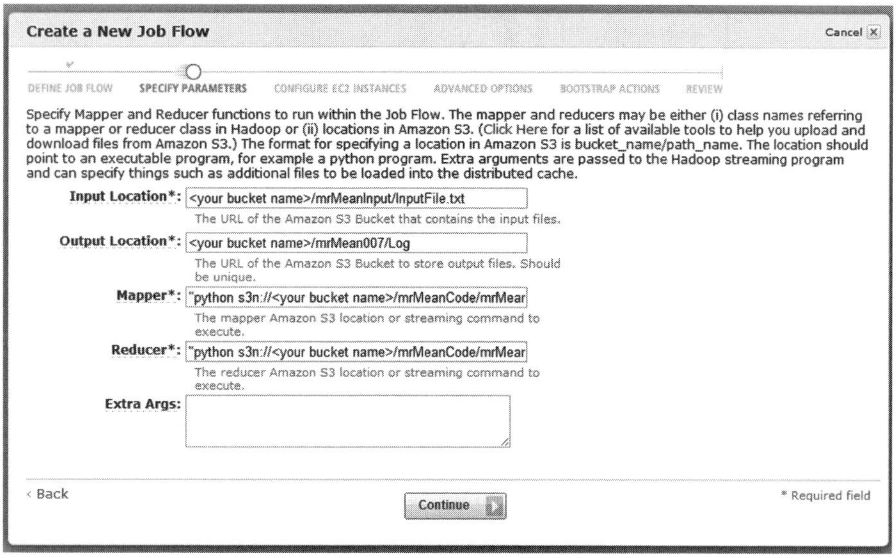

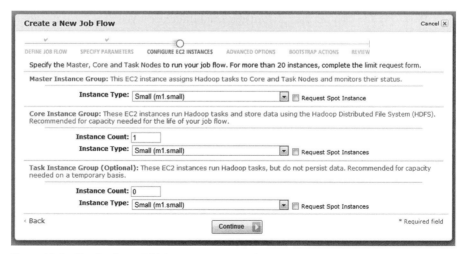

Figure 15.5   The Specify Parameters screen of Elastic MapReduce

7   The next window is the Configure EC2 Instances window, where you specify the number of servers that will crunch your data. The default is 2; you can change it to 1. You can also specify the type of EC2 instance you want to use. You can use a more powerful machine with larger memory, but it will cost more. In practice, big jobs are usually run on Large (or better) instances. Please refer to http://aws.amazon.com/ec2/#instance for more details. For this trivial demonstration, you can use one Small machine. Your screen should look like figure 15.6. Click Continue.

Figure 15.6   The Configure EC2 Instances screen of Elastic MapReduce. Here you set the size of the servers and number of servers you'll use on your MapReduce job.

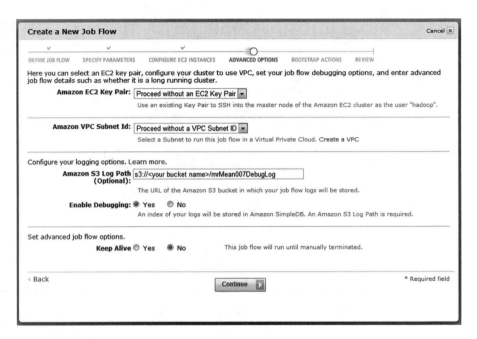

Figure 15.7   The Advanced Options screen of Elastic MapReduce. Here you set the path of where the debug files will be placed. You can also set Keep Alive and a key pair to log into the machine if a job fails. This is a good idea when you want to inspect the exact environment your code will be run on.

8   The next screen is Advanced Options, where you can set options for debugging. Make sure you enable logging. For the Amazon S3 Log Path, enter `s3n://` `<your bucket name>`/mrMean007DebugLog. You won't be able to enable Hadoop debugging unless you've signed up for SimpleDB. SimpleDB is an Amazon tool for easy access to nonrelational databases. We won't use it. We should be able to debug our Hadoop Streaming jobs without it. When a Hadoop job fails, a lot of information is written to this directory. If your job does fail, you can go back and read some of this information to see what went wrong. Your screen should look like figure 15.7. Click Continue.

9   The critical settings are now finished. You can select the defaults on the Bootstrap Actions page and continue to the Review page. Make sure everything looks right; then click the Create Job Flow button at the bottom. Your job has now been created. Click the Close button on the next page, and you'll be brought back to the Elastic MapReduce console. As your job runs, its progress will be displayed in this console. Don't worry if it takes a while to run such a trivial job. A new server instance is being configured. You should see something like figure 15.8. (You probably won't have as many failed jobs as shown here.)

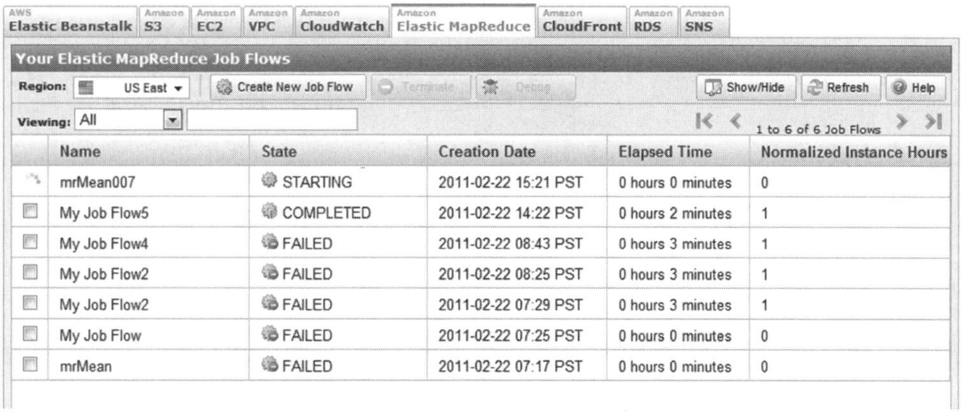

Figure 15.8 The Elastic MapReduce console showing MapReduce jobs. The MapReduce job in this chapter has started in this figure.

A few minutes after your job has started running, it will finish. You can inspect the outputs in S3 by clicking the S3 tab at the top of the console. When the S3 console comes up, click the bucket you created earlier (rustbucket in this example). Inside this bucket, you should see a mrMean007Log folder. Double-click the folder, and the console will open it. Inside, you should see a file called part-00000. Double-click this file to download it to your local machine. This is the output of your reducer. Open it with a text editor. The output should be

```
100     0.509570     0.344439
```

This is the same output that we got when testing the job on our local machine using pipes. Things worked on this job, but if they didn't work, how would you know what went wrong? Back on the Elastic MapReduce tab, if you click a completed job, you'll see a Debug button with the cartoon of a small green insect on it. Clicking this will bring up a debug window, which gives you access to different log files. Click the Controller link, and you'll see the Hadoop command. You can also see the Hadoop version.

Now that you have a taste of what it's like to run a Hadoop Streaming job, we're going to discuss how to execute machine learning algorithms on Hadoop. MapReduce is a system that allows you to run many programs on many computers, but these programs need to be written a little differently for MapReduce.

Skipping AWS

If you don't want to get your credit card out or are afraid that someone on the internet will steal your information, you can run this same task on a local machine. These steps assume you have Hadoop installed (http://hadoop.apache.org/common/docs/stable/#Getting+Started).

1. Copy data to HDFS:

```
>hadoop fs -copyFromLocal inputFile.txt mrmean-i
```

(continued)

2. Start the job:

```
>hadoop   jar    $HADOOP_HOME/contrib/streaming/hadoop-0.20.2-stream-
ing.jar -input mrmean-i -output mrmean-o -mapper "python mrMeanMap-
per.py" -reducer "python mrMeanReducer.py"
```

3. Check the data:

```
>hadoop fs -cat mrmean-o/part-00000
```

4. Get the data:

```
>hadoop fs -copyToLocal mrmean-o/part-00000 .
```

That's it.

15.4 *Machine learning in MapReduce*

Using MapReduce with 10 machines isn't the same as having a computer 10 times big-ger than your current computer. If the MapReduce jobs are written properly, it may feel like this. But you can't take every program and get an instant speedup. The map and reduce tasks need to be properly written.

Many machine learning algorithms don't intuitively fit in a MapReduce frame-work. It doesn't matter. As the old adage goes, "Necessity is the mother of invention." Inventive scientists and engineers have written MapReduce solutions to almost every popular machine learning algorithm.

The following brief list identifies popular machine learning algorithms from this book and their MapReduce implementations:

- Naïve Bayes—This is one of a few algorithms that's naturally implementable in MapReduce. In MapReduce, it's easy to calculate sums. In naïve Bayes, we were calculating the probability of a feature given a class. We can give the results from a given class to an individual mapper. We can then use the reducer to sum up the results.

- k-Nearest Neighbors—Trying to find similar vectors in a small dataset can take a large amount of time. In a massive dataset, it can limit daily business cycles. One approach to speed this up is to build a tree, such as a tree to narrow the search for closest vectors. This works well when the number of features is under 10. A pop-ular method for performing a nearest neighbor search on higher-dimensional items such as text, images, and video is locality-sensitive hashing.

- Support vector machines—The Platt SMO algorithm that we used in chapter 6 may be difficult to implement in a MapReduce framework. There are other implementations of SVMs that use a version of stochastic gradient descent such as the Pegasos algorithm. There's also an approximate version of SVM called proximal SVM, which computes a solution much faster and is easily applied to a MapReduce framework.[4]

---

[4] Glenn Fung, Olvi L. Mangasarian, "PSVM: Proximal Support Vector Machine," http://www.cs.wisc.edu/dmi/svm/psvm/.

- Singular value decomposition—The Lanczos algorithm is an efficient method for approximating eigenvalues. This algorithm can be applied in a series of MapReduce jobs to efficiently find the singular values in a large matrix. The Lanczos algorithm can similarly be used for principal component analysis.

- k-means clustering—One popular version of distributed clustering is known as canopy clustering. You can calculate the k-means clusters by using canopy clustering first and using the canopies as the k initial clusters.

If you're interested in learning how a few more common machine learning tasks are solved in MapReduce, check out the Apache Mahout project (http://mahout.apache.org/) and *Mahout in Action*. The book is especially good at explaining common implementation details for dealing with massive datasets. The Apache Mahout project is written in Java. Another great source for properly writing MapReduce jobs is a book called *Data Intensive Text Processing with Map/Reduce* by Jimmy Lin and Chris Dyer.

Now let's explore a Python tool for running MapReduce jobs.

15.5 *Using mrjob to automate MapReduce in Python*

Of the algorithms listed previously, a number of them are iterative. They can be completed in a few MapReduce jobs but not one. The simple example we looked at in section 15.3 on Amazon's EMR ran in a single job. What if we wanted to run AdaBoost on a very large dataset? What if we wanted to run 10 MapReduce jobs?

There are some frameworks for automating MapReduce job flow, such as Cascading and Oozie, but none of these run on Amazon's EMR. Amazon's EMR supports Pig, which can use Python scripts, but doing this would require learning another scripting language. (Pig is an Apache project which provides a higher-level language for data processing. Pig turns the data processing commands into Hadoop MapReduce jobs.) There are a few tools for running MapReduce jobs from within Python, and one I'm particularly fond of is called mrjob.

Mrjob (http://packages.python.org/mrjob/)[5] was an internal framework at Yelp (a restaurant review website) until they made it open source in late 2010. You can see appendix A for how to install it. We're going to show how to use mrjob next, and then we'll rewrite the global mean and variance calculation we did earlier in mrjob. I think you'll find mrjob both helpful and convenient. (Mrjob is useful as a learning tool, but it's still Python. To get the best performance, you should use Java.)

15.5.1 *Using mrjob for seamless integration with EMR*

Mrjob runs Hadoop Streaming on Elastic MapReduce as we did in section 15.3. The main difference is that you don't have to worry about uploading your data to S3 and then typing in the commands correctly. All of this is handled by mrjob. With mrjob you can also run MapReduce jobs on your own Hadoop cluster or in nondistributed

---

[5] Mrjob documentation: http://packages.python.org/mrjob/index.html; source code can be found here: https://github.com/Yelp/mrjob.

mode for testing. The switch from running a job locally to running it on EMR is easy. For example, to run a job locally, you'd enter something like this:

```
% python mrMean.py < inputFile.txt > myOut.txt
```

Now to run that same job on EMR you'd type

```
% python mrMean.py -r emr < inputFile.txt > myOut.txt
```

All of the uploading and form filling that we did in section 15.3 is done automatically from mrjob. You can add another command to run the job on your local Hadoop cluster if you happen to have one. You can also add numerous command-line arguments to specify the number of servers you want on EMR or the type of server.

In section 15.3 we had two separate files for our mapper and reducer. In mrjob the mapper and reducer can reside in the same script. We'll now look inside a script to see how it works.

15.5.2 *The anatomy of a MapReduce script in mrjob*

You can do a lot of things with mrjob, but to get started we'll go over a typical MapReduce job. The best way to explain this is with an example. We'll solve the same mean/variance problem so that we can focus on the subtleties of the framework. The code in listing 15.3 serves the same purpose as listings 15.1 and 15.2. Open a text editor, create a new file called mrMean.py, and enter the code from the following listing.

Listing 15.3 Mrjob implementation of distributed mean variance calculation

```
from mrjob.job import MRJob

class MRmean(MRJob):
    def __init__(self, *args, **kwargs):
        super(MRmean, self).__init__(*args, **kwargs)
        self.inCount = 0
        self.inSum = 0
        self.inSqSum = 0

    def map(self, key, val):                         ◁ Receives streaming inputs
        if False: yield
        inVal = float(val)
        self.inCount += 1
        self.inSum += inVal
        self.inSqSum += inVal*inVal

    def map_final(self):                             ◁ Processing after all inputs have arrived
        mn = self.inSum/self.inCount
        mnSq = self.inSqSum/self.inCount
        yield (1, [self.inCount, mn, mnSq])

    def reduce(self, key, packedValues):
        cumVal=0.0; cumSumSq=0.0; cumN=0.0
        for valArr in packedValues:
            nj = float(valArr[0])
            cumN += nj
            cumVal += nj*float(valArr[1])
```

```
            cumSumSq += nj*float(valArr[2])
        mean = cumVal/cumN
        var = (cumSumSq - 2*mean*cumVal + cumN*mean*mean)/cumN
        yield (mean, var)

    def steps(self):
        return ([self.mr(mapper=self.map, reducer=self.reduce,\
            mapper_final=self.map_final)])
if __name__ == '__main__':
    MRmean.run()
```

This code calculates a distributed mean and variance. The input text is broken up into multiple mappers and these calculate intermediate values, which are accumulated in the reducer to give a global mean and variance.

You need to create a new class that inherits from the class MRjob. In this example, I've called that class MRmean. Your mapper and reducer are methods of this class. There's another method called steps(), which defines the steps taken. You don't have to do just map-reduce. You could do map-reduce-reduce-reduce, or map-reduce-map-reduce-map-reduce. You'll see an example of this in the next section. In the steps() method you tell mrjob the names of your mapper and reducer. If you don't specify anything, it will look for methods called mapper and reducer.

Let's talk about the behavior of mapper. The mapper acts like the inside of a for loop and will get called for every line of input. If you want to do something after you've received all the lines of the input, you can do that in mapper_final. This may seem strange at first, but it's convenient in practice. You can share state between mapper() and mapper_final(). So in our example we accumulate the input values in mapper(), and when we have all the values we compute the mean and the mean of the squared values and send these out. Values are sent out of the mapper via the yield statement.

Values are represented as key/value pairs. If you want to send out multiple values, a good idea is to pack them up in a list. Values will be sorted after the map step by the key. Hadoop has options for changing how things are sorted, but the default sort should work for most applications. Values with the same key value will be sent to the same reducer. You need to think through what you use for the key so that similar values will be collected together after the sort phase. I used the key 1 for all the mapper outputs because I want one reducer, and I want all of the mapper outputs to wind up at the same reducer.

The reducer in mrjob behaves differently than the mapper. At the reducer, the inputs are presented as iterable objects. To iterate over these, you need to use something like a for loop. You can't share state between the mapper or mapper_final and the reducer. The reason for this is that the Python script isn't kept alive from the map and reduce steps. If you want to communicate anything between the mapper and reducer, it should be done through key/value pairs. At the bottom of the reducer, I added a yield without a key because these values are destined for output. If they were going to another mapper, I'd put in a key value.

Enough talk. Let's see this in action. To run the mapper only, enter the following commands in your Linux/DOS window, not in your Python shell. The file inputFile.txt is in the Ch15 code download.

```
%python mrMean.py --mapper < inputFile.txt
```

You should get an output like this:

```
1     [100, 0.50956970000000001, 0.34443931307935999]
```

To run the full function, remove the `--mapper` option.

```
%python mrMean.py < inputFile.txt
```

You'll get a lot of text describing the intermediate steps, and finally the output will be displayed to the screen:

```
                              .
                              .
                              .
streaming final output from c:\users\peter\appdata\local
\temp\mrMean.Peter.20110228.172656.279000\output\part-00000
0.50956970000000001      0.34443931307935999
removing tmp directory c:\users\peter\appdata\local\
temp\mrMean.Peter.20110228.172656.279000
To stream the valid output into a file, enter the following command:
%python mrMean.py < inputFile.txt > outFile.txt
```

Finally, to run on Amazon's Elastic MapReduce, enter this command. (Make sure you have `AWS_ACCESS_KEY_ID` and `AWS_SECRET_ACCESS_KEY` environment variables set. See appendix A on how to set these.)

```
%python mrMean.py -r emr < inputFile.txt > outFile.txt
```

Now that you know how to use mrjob, let's put this to use on a machine learning problem. In the next section we'll do an iterative algorithm with mrjob, something that we couldn't do with just Elastic MapReduce.

15.6 *Example: the Pegasos algorithm for distributed SVMs*

In chapter 4, we looked at an algorithm for text classification called naïve Bayes. If you remember from chapter 4, we treated our text documents as vectors in a space of our vocabulary. In chapter 6, we looked at support vector machines, or SVMs, for classification. SVMs can work well on text classification; we treat each document as a vector with tens of thousands of features.

Doing text classification on a large number of documents presents a large machine learning challenge. How do we train our classifier over so much data? The MapReduce framework can help if we can break up our algorithm into parallel tasks. If you remember from chapter 6, the SMO algorithm optimized two support vectors at a time. The SMO algorithm also looped through the entire dataset, stopping at values that needed attention. This algorithm doesn't seem to be easy to parallelize.

> **General approach to MapReduce SVM**
>
> 1. Collect: Data provided in text file.
> 2. Prepare: The input data is in a useable format already, so preparation isn't needed. If you need to prepare a massive data set, it probably would be a good idea to write this as a map job so you could parse in parallel.
> 3. Analyze: None.
> 4. Train: With SVMs, we spend most of the time and effort on training. This is no different in MapReduce.
> 5. Test: Visually inspect the hyperplane in two dimensions to see if the algorithm is working.
> 6. Use: This example won't build a full application, but it demonstrates how to train an SVM on a massive dataset. An application of this is text classification, where we have tens of thousands of features and many documents.

One alternative to the SMO algorithm is the Pegasos algorithm. The Pegasos algorithm can easily be written for MapReduce. We'll investigate the Pegasos algorithm next, and then you'll see how to write a distributed version of Pegasos. Finally, we'll run the distributed version in mrjob.

15.6.1 *The Pegasos algorithm*

Pegasos is an acronym for Primal Estimated sub-GrAdient Solver. This algorithm uses a form of stochastic gradient descent to solve the optimization problem defined by support vector machines. It's shown that the number of iterations required is determined by the accuracy you desire, not the size of the dataset. Please see the original paper for more detail.[6] There are two versions, a long and a short version: I recommend the long version of the paper.

Recall from chapter 6 that in a support vector machine we're trying to find a separating hyperplane. In our two-dimensional examples we're trying to find a line that properly separates the two classes of data. The Pegasos algorithm works like this: A set of randomly selected points from our training data is added to a batch. Each of these points is tested to see if it's properly classified. If so, it's ignored. If it's not properly classified, it's added to the update set. At the end of the batch, the weights vector is updated with the improperly classified vectors. The cycle is repeated.

Pseudocode would look like this:

Set w to all zeros
For each batch
　　Choose k data vectors randomly
　　　For each vector

---

[6] S. Shalev-Shwartz, Y. Singer, N. Srebro, "Pegasos: Primal Estimated sub-GrAdient SOlver for SVM," Proceedings of the 24th International Conference on Machine Learning 2007.

> *If the vector is incorrectly classified:*
> *Change the weights vector: w*
> *Accumulate the changes to w*

To show you this algorithm in action, I've include a working Python version of it in the following listing.

Listing 15.4   The Pegasos SVM algorithm

```
def predict(w, x):
    return w*x.T

def batchPegasos(dataSet, labels, lam, T, k):
    m,n = shape(dataSet); w = zeros(n);
    dataIndex = range(m)
    for t in range(1, T+1):
        wDelta = mat(zeros(n))
        eta = 1.0/(lam*t)
        random.shuffle(dataIndex)
        for j in range(k):
            i = dataIndex[j]
            p = predict(w, dataSet[i,:])
            if labels[i]*p < 1:
                wDelta += labels[i]*dataSet[i,:].A          ❶ Accumulate
        w = (1.0 - 1/t)*w + (eta/k)*wDelta                      changes
    return w
```

The code in listing 15.4 is the sequential version of the Pegasos algorithm. The inputs T and k set the number of iterations and the batch size, respectively. In each of the T iterations you recalculate eta, which determines the learning rate or how much the weights can change. In the outer loop you also select a new set of data points to use in the next batch. The inner loop is the batch, where you accumulate ❶ the values of the incorrectly classified values and then update the weights vector.

You can run this example with some of the data from chapter 6 if you wish to try it out. We aren't going to do much with this code except use it for a starting point for a MapReduce version. In the next section we'll build and run a MapReduce version of Pegasos in mrjob.

15.6.2 *Training: MapReduce support vector machines with mrjob*

We'll implement the Pegasos algorithm from listing 15.4 in MapReduce. We'll use the mrjob framework explored in section 15.5 to implement the algorithm. First, we have to decide how to break up the algorithm into map and reduce steps. What can we do in parallel? What can't be done in parallel?

If you looked at all the computations going on when running the code from listing 15.4, you'd see that a lot of the time is spent doing the inner product. We can parallelize these inner products, but we can't parallelize the creation of a new w vector. This gives us a good starting point for writing the MapReduce job. Before we write the mapper and reducer, let's write some supporting code. Open your text editor and create a new file called mrSVM.py; then add the code from the following listing.

Listing 15.5 Distributed Pegasos periphery code in mrjob

```
from mrjob.job import MRJob

import pickle
from numpy import *

class MRsvm(MRJob):
    DEFAULT_INPUT_PROTOCOL = 'json_value'

    def __init__(self, *args, **kwargs):
        super(MRsvm, self).__init__(*args, **kwargs)
        self.data = pickle.load(open(\
                '<path to your Ch15 code directory>\svmDat27'))
        self.w = 0
        self.eta = 0.69
        self.dataList = []
        self.k = self.options.batchsize
        self.numMappers = 1
        self.t = 1

    def configure_options(self):
        super(MRsvm, self).configure_options()
        self.add_passthrough_option(
            '--iterations', dest='iterations', default=2, type='int',
            help='T: number of iterations to run')
        self.add_passthrough_option(
            '--batchsize', dest='batchsize', default=100, type='int',
            help='k: number of data points in a batch')

    def steps(self):
        return ([self.mr(mapper=self.map, mapper_final=self.map_fin,\
                            reducer=self.reduce)]*self.options.iterations)

if __name__ == '__main__':
    MRsvm.run()
```

The code from listing 15.5 sets up everything so you can do the map and reduce steps properly. You have an `include` statement for mrjob, NumPy, and Pickle. Then you create the mrjob class called `MRsvm`. The `__init__()` method initializes some variables you'll use in the map and reduce steps. The Python module Pickle doesn't like to load to files pickled with different versions of Python. I've included data files pickled with Python 2.6 and 2.7 in files called svmDat26 and svmDat27, respectively.

The `configure_options()` method sets up some values you can enter from the command line. These are the number of iterations (`T`) and the batch size (`k`). Both of those arguments are optional, and if they aren't set, they'll default to the values in listing 15.5.

Finally, the `steps()` method tells mrjob what jobs to do and in what order. It creates a Python list with map, map_fin, and reduce steps, and then multiplies this by the number of iterations, which repeats the list for each iteration. In order for this big chain of jobs to work properly, the mapper has to be able to read the data coming out of the reducer. We didn't have this requirement in our single MapReduce job, so we'll have to be more careful with our inputs and outputs.

Let's take a second to define the inputs and outputs:

Mapper

Inputs: <mapperNum, valueList>
Outputs: nothing

Mapper_final

Inputs: nothing
Outputs: <1, valueList >

Reducer

Inputs: <mapperNum, valueList >
Outputs: <mapperNum, valueList >

The values passed in are lists. The first element in the list is a string detailing what type of data is stored in the rest of the list. Two examples of valueList are ['x', 23] and ['w', [1, 5, 6]]. Every mapper_final will emit the same key; this is to make sure that all of the key/value pairs come to one reducer.

With our inputs and outputs defined, let's write the mapper and reducer methods. Open mrSVM.py and add the following methods to the MRsvm class.

Listing 15.6   Distributed Pegasos mapper and reducer code

```
def map(self, mapperId, inVals):
        if False: yield
        if inVals[0]=='w':
            self.w = inVals[1]
        elif inVals[0]=='x':
            self.dataList.append(inVals[1])
        elif inVals[0]=='t': self.t = inVals[1]
    def map_fin(self):
        labels = self.data[:,-1]; X=self.data[:,0:-1]
        if self.w == 0: self.w = [0.001]*shape(X)[1]
        for index in self.dataList:
            p = mat(self.w)*X[index,:].T
            if labels[index]*p < 1.0:
                yield (1, ['u', index])
        yield (1, ['w', self.w])
        yield (1, ['t', self.t])
    def reduce(self, _, packedVals):
        for valArr in packedVals:
            if valArr[0]=='u':  self.dataList.append(valArr[1])
            elif valArr[0]=='w': self.w = valArr[1]
            elif valArr[0]=='t':  self.t = valArr[1]
        labels = self.data[:,-1]; X=self.data[:,0:-1]
        wMat = mat(self.w);    wDelta = mat(zeros(len(self.w)))
        for index in self.dataList:
            wDelta += float(labels[index])*X[index,:]            ◁── ❶ Combines
        eta = 1.0/(2.0*self.t)                                        updates
        wMat = (1.0 - 1.0/self.t)*wMat + (eta/self.k)*wDelta
        for mapperNum in range(1,self.numMappers+1):
            yield (mapperNum, ['w', wMat.tolist()[0] ])
```

```
if self.t < self.options.iterations:
    yield (mapperNum, ['t', self.t+1])
    for j in range(self.k/self.numMappers):
        yield (mapperNum, ['x',\
        random.randint(shape(self.data)[0]) ])
```

The first method in listing 15.6 is the map(); this is the distributed part. This takes in the values and stores them for processing in map_fin(). The inputs could be one of three types: the w vector, the t value, or x. The t value is the iteration number and isn't used in this calculation. You can't save state, so if there are any variables that you want to persist from one iteration to the next, you can either pass them around in key/value pairs or write them to disk. It's easier and faster just to pass this value around.

The map_fin() method is executed when all of the inputs have arrived. At this point you'll have your weights vector w and a list of x values for this batch. Each x value is an integer. It's not the data but an index. The data is stored on disk and loaded into memory when the script is executed. When map_fin() starts, it splits the data into labels and data. Next, it iterates over all of the values in the current batch, which are stored in self.dataList. If any of these values is incorrectly classified, then it's emitted to the reducer. To keep state between the mapper and reducer, the w vector and the t values are sent to the reducer.

Finally, there should be only one reducer. This first iterates over all the key/value pairs and unpacks the values to local variables. Any value in dataList will be used to update the w vector. The updates are accumulated in wDelta. ❶ Then wMat is updated by wDelta and the learning rate eta. After wMat has been updated, it's time to start the whole process over. A new batch of random vectors is chosen and emitted. The key of all these values is the mapper number.

To see this in action, you need to start the job with some data that looks like it came out of the reducer. I've attached a file called kickStart.txt that will do this. To execute the previous code on your local machine, enter the following command:

```
%python mrSVM.py < kickStart.txt
```

```
        .
        .
        .
streaming final output from c:\users\peter\appdata\local\temp
\mrSVM.Peter.20110301.011916.373000\output\part-00000
1       ["w", [0.51349820499999987, -0.084934502500000009]]
removing tmp directory c:\users\peter\appdata\local\temp
\mrSVM.Peter.20110301.011916.373000
```

The output vector is given here. A plot of this vector is shown in figure 15.9 with 2 and 50 iterations.

If you want to run the job on EMR, add the -r emr command. The default number of servers to use for this job is 1. To increase that, add --num-ec2-instances=2 or whatever positive integer you like. Here's an example:

```
%python mrSVM.py -r emr --num-ec2-instances=3 < kickStart.txt > myLog.txt
```

To see all of the options available, enter %python mrSVM.py -h.

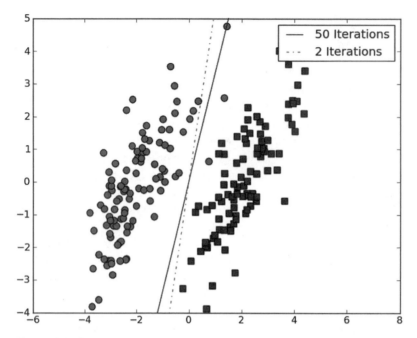

Figure 15.9   Results from the distributed Pegasos algorithm after multiple iterations. The algorithm converges quickly, and further iterations give only a slightly better solution.

Debugging mrjob

Debugging a mrjob script can be much more frustrating that debugging a simple Python script. Here are some suggestions to speed up your debug:

- Make sure you have all the dependencies installed: boto, simplejson, and optionally PyYAML.
- You can set a number of parameters in ~/.mrjob.conf; make sure these are correct.
- Debug as much as you can locally before sending jobs to EMR. There's nothing worse than waiting 10 minutes to find out you made a mistake when you could have found that out in 10 seconds.
- Look in the base_temp_dir; this is set in ~/.mrjob.conf. On my machine it's under /scratch/$USER. You can see the input and output of your jobs there; this is helpful for debugging.
- Run one step at a time.

Now that you know how to write and launch machine learning jobs on many machines, we'll talk about whether doing this is really necessary.

15.7   *Do you really need MapReduce?*

Without knowing who you are, I can say that you probably don't need MapReduce or Hadoop because the vast majority of computing needs can be met with a single computer. These big-data tools were made by the Googles, Yelps, and Facebooks of the world, but how many of those companies are there?

Making the most of your resources can save time and energy. If you find your computing jobs taking too long, ask yourself the following questions: Could you rewrite your code in a more efficient language like C or Java? If you already are using one of those languages, are you writing your code in the most memory-efficient manner? Is your processing constrained by memory or the processor? Perhaps you don't know the answer to these questions. It may be helpful to consult someone who does.

Most people don't realize how much number crunching they can do on a single computer. If you don't have big data problems, you don't need MapReduce and Hadoop. It's great to know they exist and to know what you could do if you had big-data problems.

15.8 *Summary*

When your computing needs have exceeded the capabilities of your computing resources, you may consider buying a better machine. It may happen that your computing needs have exceeded the abilities of reasonably priced machines. One solution to this is to break up your computing into parallel jobs. One paradigm for doing this is MapReduce. In MapReduce you break your jobs into map and reduce steps.

A typical job can use the map step to process data in parallel and then combine the data in the reduce step. This many-to-one model is typical but not the only way of combining jobs. Data is passed between the mapper and reducers with key/value pairs. Typically, data is sorted by the value of the keys after the map step. Hadoop is a popular Java project for running MapReduce jobs. Hadoop has an application for running non-Java jobs called Hadoop Streaming.

Amazon Web Services allows you to rent computing resources by the hour. One tool Amazon Web Services makes available is Elastic MapReduce, which allows people to run Hadoop Streaming jobs. Simple one-step MapReduce jobs can be written and run from the Elastic MapReduce management console. More complex jobs need an additional tool. One relatively new open source tool is called mrjob. With mrjob you can run multiple MapReduce jobs sequentially. With minimal setup, mrjob handles the dirty steps associated with Amazon Web Services.

A number of machine learning algorithms can be easily written as MapReduce jobs. Some machine learning jobs need to be creatively redefined in order to use them in MapReduce. Support vector machines are a powerful tool for text classification, but training a classifier on a large number of documents can involve a large amount of computing resources. One approach to creating a distributed classifier for support vector machines is the Pegasos algorithm. Machine learning algorithms that may require multiple MapReduce jobs such as Pegasos are easily implemented in mrjob.

This concludes the main body of material for this book. Thanks for reading. I hope this book opened many new doors for you. There's much more to be explored in the mathematics of machine learning or the practical implementation in code. I look forward to seeing what interesting applications you create with the tools and techniques from this book.

appendix A:
Getting started with Python

In this appendix we'll go through instructions for installing Python on the three most popular operating systems. In addition, there's a short introduction to Python and instructions for installing the Python modules used in this book. A discussion on NumPy is saved for appendix B, where it more appropriately fits in with a discussion on linear algebra.

A.1 Installing Python

To follow all of the examples in this book, you're going to need Python 2.7, NumPy, and Matplotlib. The examples aren't guaranteed to work with Python 3.X, because Python doesn't provide backward compatibility. The easiest way to get these modules is through package installers. These are available on Mac OS and Linux.

A.1.1 Windows

You can download Python here: http://www.python.org/getit/. Select the appropriate Windows installer (either 64-bit or 32-bit) and follow the instructions.

To get NumPy you can get the binary from http://sourceforge.net/projects/numpy/files/NumPy/. It's much easier than trying to build it yourself.

Once the installer is finished, you can start a Python shell. To do this, first open a command prompt by typing `cmd` in the find window. Then type in the following:

```
>c:\Python27\python.exe
```

This should start a Python shell telling you which version you're using, when it was built, and so on.

If you want to type `c:\Python27\python.exe` every time you start a Python shell, that's fine, but you can also create an alias for the command `python`. I'll leave the details of creating an alias up to you.

You'll also want to get the latest Matplotlib binary. You can find the latest version at the Matplotlib home page: http://matplotlib.sourceforge.net/. Installing this binary is relatively easy; just download the installer and click through the installation steps.

A.1.2 Mac OS X

The best way to get Python, NumPy, and Matplotlib installed on Mac OS X is to use Mac-Ports. MacPorts is a free tool that simplifies compiling and installing software on your Mac. You can read more about MacPorts here: http://www.macports.org/. First, you need to download MacPorts. The best way to do that is to download the appropriate .dmg file. On this site you can select the .dmg file that corresponds to the version of Mac OS X that you have. Once you have the .dmg downloaded, install it. Then when you've installed MacPorts, open a new terminal window and enter the following command:

```
>sudo port install py27-matplotlib
```

This will install Python, NumPy, and Matplotlib. It will take a while depending on how fast your machine and internet connection are. Install times of one hour are not abnormal.

You can install Python, NumPy, and Matplotlib separately if you don't want to install MacPorts. There are now Mac OS X binary installers for all three of these libraries, which make installing super easy.

A.1.3 Linux

The best way to get Python, NumPy, and Matplotlib in Debian/Ubuntu is to use apt-get, or the corresponding package manager in other distributions. If you install Matplotlib, then it will check to see if you have all the dependencies. Since Python and NumPy are dependencies of Matplotlib, installing Matplotlib will ensure that you have the other two.

To install Matplotlib, open a command shell and enter the following command:

```
>sudo apt-get install python-matplotlib
```

This will take some time depending on how fast your machine and internet connection are.

Now that you've installed Python, let's discuss some of the data types used in Python.

A.2 A quick introduction to Python

Now we can go over a few of the features of the language that we use in this book. This is not an exhaustive description of Python; for that I suggest you try "How to Think Like a Computer Scientist" by Elkner, Downey, and Meyers at http://openbookproject.net//thinkCSpy/; the contents are available for free online. We'll go over collection types and control structures, something found in almost every programming language. We'll just review them to see how Python handles them. Finally, in this section we'll review list comprehensions, which I think are the most confusing part of getting started with Python.

A.2.1   *Collection types*

Python has a number of ways of storing a collection of items, and you can add many modules to create more container types. Following is a short list of the commonly used containers in Python:

1 *Lists*—Lists are an ordered collection of objects in Python. You can have anything in a list: numbers, bool, strings, and so on. To create a list you use two brackets. The following code illustrates the creation of a list called `jj` and the addition of an integer and a string:

```
>>> jj=[]
>>> jj.append(1)
>>> jj.append('nice hat')
>>> jj
[1, 'nice hat']
```

Similarly, you can put elements into a list directly. You could create the list `jj` in one pass with the following statement:

```
 >>> jj = [1, 'nice hat']
```

Python also has an array data type, which, similar to other programming languages, can contain only one type of data. This array type is faster than lists when you're looping. We won't use this structure in this book because it could be confused with the array type in NumPy.

2 *Dictionaries*—A dictionary is an unordered key/value type of storage container. You can use strings and numbers for the key. In other languages, a dictionary may be called an associative array or map. In the following code we create a dictionary and adds two items to it:

```
>>> jj={}
>>> jj['dog']='dalmatian'
>>> jj[1]=42
>>> jj
{1: 42, 'dog': 'dalmatian'}
```

You can also create this dictionary in one line with the following command:

```
>>> jj = {1: 42, 'dog': 'dalmatian'}
```

3 *Sets*—A set is just like a set in mathematics. If you aren't familiar with that, it means a unique collection of items. You can create a set from a list by entering the following:

```
>>> a=[1, 2, 2, 2, 4, 5, 5]
>>> sA=set(a)
>>> sA
set([1, 2, 4, 5])
```

Sets can then do math operations on sets, such as the union, intersection, and difference. The union is done by the pipe symbol, |, and the intersection is done by the ampersand symbol, &.

```
>>> sB=set([4, 5, 6, 7])
>>> sB
set([4, 5, 6, 7])
>>> sA-sB
set([1, 2])
>>> sA | sB
set([1, 2, 4, 5, 6, 7])
>>> sA & sB
set([4, 5])
```

A.2.2   Control structures

In Python, indentation matters. Some people actually complain about this, but it forces you to write clean, readable code. In for loops, while loops, or if statements, you use indentation to tell the machine which lines of code belong inside these loops. The indentation can be done with spaces or tabs. In some other languages, you use braces, { }, or keywords. By using indentation instead of braces, Python saves a lot of space. Let's see how to write some common control statements:

1   If—The if statement is quite straightforward. You can use it on one line like so:

```
>>> if jj < 3:  print "it's less than three man"
```

Or, for multiple lines, you can use an indent to tell the interpreter you have more than one line. You can use this indent with just one line of code if you prefer.

```
>>> if jj < 3:
...     print "it's less than three man"
...     jj = jj + 1
```

Multiple conditionals, like else if, are written as elif, and the keyword else is used for a default condition.

```
>>> if jj < 3: jj+=1
... elif jj==3: jj+=0
... else: jj = 0
```

2   For—A for loop in Python is like the enhanced for loop in Java or C++0x. If you're not familiar with those, it simply means that the for loop goes over every item in a collection. Let me give you some examples from lists, sets, and dictionaries:

```
>>> sB=set([4, 5, 6, 7])
>>> for item in sB:
...     print item
...
4
5
6
7
```

Now let's see how to loop over a dictionary:

```
>>> jj={'dog': 'dalmatian', 1: 45}
>>> for item in jj:
...     print item, jj[item]
...
1 45
dog dalmatian
```

The items iterated over are actually the dictionary keys.

A.2.3   List comprehensions

I think the most confusing thing for people new to Python is list comprehensions. List comprehensions are an elegant way of generating a list without writing a lot of code. But the way they work is a little bit backwards. Let's see one in action. Then we'll discuss it.

```
>>> a=[1, 2, 2, 2, 4, 5, 5]
>>> myList = [item*4 for item in a]
>>> myList
[4, 8, 8, 8, 16, 20, 20]
```

List comprehensions are always enclosed in brackets. This one is equivalent to the following code:

```
>>> myList=[]
>>> for item in a:
...     myList.append(item*4)
...
>>> myList
[4, 8, 8, 8, 16, 20, 20]
```

The resulting myList is the same, but we used less code with the list comprehension. The confusing part is that the item that gets appended to the list is in front of the for loop. This is contrary to the way the English text is read, from left to right.

Let's see a more advanced list comprehension. We're now going to use only values greater than 2.

```
>>> [item*4 for item in a if item>2]
[16, 20, 20]
```

You can get really creative with list comprehensions, and if at some point they become difficult to read, you'll be better off writing out the code. That way, other people can read your code. Now that we've reviewed some basics, the next section discusses how to install Python modules used in this book.

For most pure Python modules (modules that don't have bindings to other languages), you can change the directory to where you've unzipped the code and type > python setup.py install. This is the default, and if you're ever unsure how to install something, try this command. Python will install the modules to a directory inside the main Python directory called Libs/site-packages/, so you don't have to worry about where the module was installed or deleting it when you clean out your downloads folder.

A.3   *A quick introduction to NumPy*

Having installed the NumPy library, you may be wondering, "What good is this?" Officially, NumPy is a matrix type for Python, and a large number of functions to operate on these matrices. Unofficially, it's a library that makes doing calculations easy and faster to execute, because the calculations are done in C rather than Python.

Despite the claim that it's a matrix library, there are actually two fundamental data types in NumPy: the array and the matrix. The operations on arrays and matrices are slightly different. If you're familiar with MATLAB™, then the matrix will be most familiar to you. Both types allow you to remove looping operators you'd have to have using only Python. Here's an example of things you can do with arrays:

```
>>> from numpy import array
>>> mm=array((1, 1, 1))
>>> pp=array((1, 2, 3))
>>> pp+mm
array([2, 3, 4])
```

That would have required a `for` loop in regular Python.

Here are some more operations that would require a loop in regular Python: Multiply every number by a constant 2:

```
>>> pp*2
array([2, 4, 6])
```

Square every number:

```
>>> pp**2
array([1, 4, 9])
```

You can now access the elements in the array like it was a list:

```
>>> pp[1]
2
```

You can also have multidimensional arrays:

```
>>> jj = array([[1, 2, 3], [1, 1, 1]])
```

These can also be accessed like lists:

```
>>> jj[0]
array([1, 2, 3])
>>> jj[0][1]
2
```

You can also access the elements like a matrix:

```
>>> jj[0,1]
2
```

When you multiply two arrays together, you multiply the elements in the first array by the elements in the second array:

```
>>> a1=array([1, 2,3])
>>> a2=array([0.3, 0.2, 0.3])
>>> a1*a2
array([ 0.3,   0.4,   0.9])
```

Now let's talk about matrices:

Similar to arrays, you need to import `matrix` or `mat` from NumPy:

```
>>> from numpy import mat, matrix
```

The NumPy keyword `mat` is a shortcut for *matrix*.

```
>>> ss = mat([1, 2, 3])
>>> ss
matrix([[1, 2, 3]])
>>> mm = matrix([1, 2, 3])
>>> mm
matrix([[1, 2, 3]])
```

You can access the individual elements of a matrix like this:

```
>>> mm[0, 1]
2
```

You can convert Python lists into NumPy matrices:

```
>>> pyList = [5, 11, 1605]
>>> mat(pyList)
matrix([[   5,   11, 1605]])
```

Now let's try to multiply two matrices together:

```
>>> mm*ss
Traceback (most recent call last):
  File "<stdin>", line 1, in <module>
  File "c:\Python27\lib\site-packages\numpy\matrixlib\defmatrix.py",
line 330, i
n __mul__
    return N.dot(self, asmatrix(other))
ValueError: objects are not aligned
```

That causes an error and won't be done. The matrix datatype enforces the mathematics of matrix operations. You can't multiply a 1x3 matrix by a 1x3 matrix; the inner numbers must match. One of the matrices will need to be transposed so you can multiply a 3x1 and a 1x3 matrix or a 1x3 and a 3x1 matrix. The NumPy matrix data type has a transpose method, so you can do this multiplication quite easily:

```
>>> mm*ss.T
matrix([[14]])
```

We took the transpose of `ss` with the `.T` method.

Knowing the dimensions is helpful when debugging alignment errors. If you want to know the dimensions of an array or matrix, you can use the `shape` function in NumPy:

```
>>> from numpy import shape
>>> shape(mm)
(1, 3)
```

What if you wanted to multiply every element in matrix mm by every element in ss? This is known as element-wise multiplication and can be done with the NumPy multiply function:

```
>>> from numpy import multiply
>>> multiply(mm, ss)
matrix([[1, 4, 9]])
```

The matrix and array data types have a large number of other useful methods available such as sorting:

```
>>> mm.sort()
>>> mm
matrix([[1, 2, 3]])
```

Be careful; this method does sort in place, so if you want to keep the original order of your data, you must make a copy first. You can also use the argsort() method to give you the indices of the matrix if a sort were to happen:

```
>>> dd=mat([4, 5, 1])
>>> dd.argsort()
matrix([[2, 0, 1]])
```

You can also calculate the mean of the numbers in a matrix:

```
>>> dd.mean()
3.3333333333333335
```

Let's look at multidimensional arrays for a second:

```
>>> jj = mat([[1, 2, 3,], [8, 8, 8]])
>>> shape(jj)
(2, 3)
```

This is a matrix of shape 2x3; to get all the elements in one row, you can use the colon (:) operator with the row number. For example, to get all the elements in row 1, you'd enter

```
>>> jj[1,:]
matrix([[8, 8, 8]])
```

You can also specify a range of elements. To get all the elements in row 1, columns 0–1, you'd use the following statement:

```
>>> jj[1,0:2]
matrix([[8, 8]])
```

This method of indexing can simplify programming with NumPy.

Beyond the array and matrix data types, a large number of other functions in NumPy are very useful. I encourage you to see the full documentation at http://docs.scipy.org/doc/.

A.4 *Beautiful Soup*

We use Beautiful Soup to search and parse HTML. To install Beautiful Soup just download the module: http://www.crummy.com/software/BeautifulSoup/#Download.

Next, unzip it and `cd` into the directory where you've unzipped it. Then enter the following command:

```
>python setup.py install
```

If you're on Linux and it tells you that you don't have permission to install it, type in the following:

```
>sudo python setup.py install
```

With most Python modules this is how you'll install them. Be sure to read the README.txt included with each module you download.

A.5 *Mrjob*

Mrjob is used to launch map reduce jobs on Amazon Web Services. Installing mrjob is as easy as installing other modules in Python. Download the code here: https://github.com/Yelp/mrjob. There's a button on the left side that says ZIP. Click that and download the latest version. Unzip and untar the file, and then `cd` into the directory that you just unzipped. Enter the standard Python install command:

```
>python setup.py install
```

The GitHub listing has a lot of code samples, and there's a good page with official Python documentation here: http://packages.python.org/mrjob/.

Before you actually use it on Amazon Web Services, you need to set two environment variables: `$AWS_ACCESS_KEY_ID` and `$AWS_SECRET_ACCESS_KEY`. These are values unique to your account (I'm assuming you have an account), and you get them when you log into AWS under Account > Security Credentials.

To set these in Windows, open a command prompt and enter the following:

```
>set AWS_ACCESS_KEY_ID=1269696969696969
```

To verify that it worked, type in

```
>echo %AWS_ACCESS_KEY_ID%
```

Make sure you set `AWS_SECRET_ACCESS_KEY` also.

To set these on Mac OS X (newer versions of OS X use the bash shell), open a terminal window and enter the following:

```
>AWS_ACCESS_KEY_ID=1269696969696969
>export AWS_ACCESS_KEY_ID
```

Similarly, you can set `AWS_SECRET_ACCESS_KEY`. Strings don't need quotes.

Ubuntu Linux also uses the bash shell by default, so the Mac OS X instructions should work. If you're using another shell, you'll have to research how to set the environment variables yourself, but it isn't difficult.

A.6   *Vote Smart*

Project Vote Smart is a data source for political data from the United States of America; see http://www.votesmart.org/. They provide a REST API to retrieve their data. Sunlight Labs has written a well-documented Python interface for this API. If you want to use the API, you first need to get an API key, which you can obtain from here: http://votesmart.org/services_api.php.

You can download the Python interface here: https://github.com/sunlightlabs/python-votesmart. On the left side is a download button labeled ZIP. Click that and download the most recent version. Once you've downloaded that file, change your directory to the downloaded and unzipped file folder. Then enter the following command:

```
>python setup.py install
```

Be patient because the API key takes some time to become active. My API key wasn't active until 30 minutes after I applied for it. You'll get an email saying your API key has been approved. Then you're ready to start finding out what those greasy politicians are up to!

A.7   *Python-Twitter*

Python-Twitter is a module to interface with data from Twitter. The code is hosted on Google Code here: http://code.google.com/p/python-twitter/. You can download the code here: http://code.google.com/p/python-twitter/downloads/list. To install this module untar the tarball, and then change to untarred directory and enter

```
>python setup.py install
```

That should be it; you'll need to get a Twitter API key, and then you'll be able to start getting and posting data to Twitter from your Python code.

appendix B:
Linear algebra

To understand advanced machine learning topics, you need to know some linear algebra. If you want to take an algorithm from an academic paper and implement it in code or investigate algorithms outside of this book, you'll probably need a basic understanding of linear algebra. This appendix should serve as a light refresher or introduction if you've had this material before but it's been a while and you need a reminder. If you've never had this material before, I recommend that you take a course at a university, work through a self-study book, or watch a video. Free tutorial videos are available on the internet[1] as well as full recordings of semester-long courses.[2] Have you ever heard "Math is not a spectator sport"? It's true. Working through examples on your own is necessary to reinforce what you've watched others do in a book or video.

We'll first discuss the basic building block of linear algebra, the matrix. Then we'll discuss some basic operations on matrices, including taking the matrix inverse. We'll address the vector norm, which often appears in machine learning, and we'll conclude by discussing how we can apply calculus to linear algebra.

B.1 Matrices

The most basic data type in linear algebra is the matrix. A matrix is made up of rows and columns.

A simple example of this is shown in figure B.1. This matrix contains three rows and three columns. The row numbering usually begins at the top, and column

---

[1] Gilbert Strang has some lectures that are free to view at http://www.youtube.com/watch?v=ZK3O402wf1c. You can also get the course materials at http://ocw.mit.edu/courses/mathematics/18-06-linear-algebra-spring-2010/. His lectures aren't difficult to follow and communicate the key points of linear algebra. In addition, his graduate-level course on computational science is very good: http://www.youtube.com/watch?v=CgfkEUOFAj0.

[2] I've heard many great things about the linear algebra videos on Kahn Academy's website: http://www.khanacademy.org/#linear-algebra.

numbering begins on the left. The first row contains the numbers 9, 9, and 77. Similarly, the third column contains the numbers 77, 18, and 10. In NumPy you can find the number of columns and rows of a given matrix, myMat, by typing numpy.shape(myMat). This returns the results as (columns, rows).

In every chapter in this book we've used vectors, which are special cases of matrices containing only a single column or row. Often, a vector will be mentioned without specifying row or column. If this is the case, assume it's a column vector. Figure B.2 shows a column vector on the left side. The column vector has shape 3x1. On the right side of figure B.2 is a row vector, which has shape 1x3. Keeping track of the shape will be important when we're doing matrix operations such as multiplication.

One of the most basic matrix operations is the transpose. The transpose is flipping the matrix along its diagonal. The rows become columns and the columns become rows. Figure B.3 illustrates this process for a matrix B. The transpose is written with a capital T in superscript. The transpose is often used to manipulate matrices to make calculations easier.

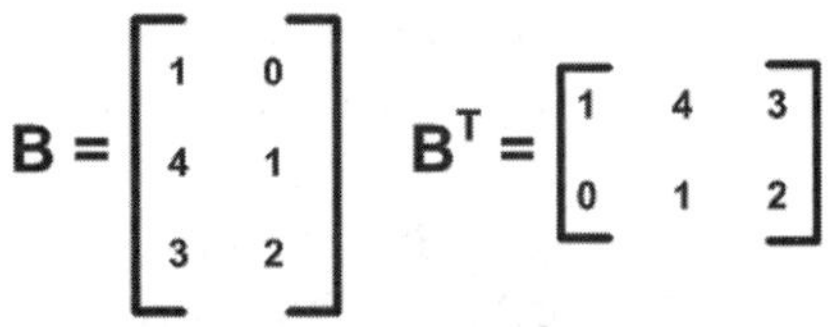

You can add a number to a matrix or multiply a matrix by a number; these operations are applied to each element separately/independently. These are called *scalar operations* because the relative values of the elements in the matrix don't change; only the scale changes. If you want to scale your data by a constant or add a constant offset, you'll need scalar multiplication and addition. Figure B.4 shows scalar multiplication and addition.

Now let's look at some matrix operations. How would you add two matrices together? First of all, the matrices must be the same size. If the matrices are the same size, you can add them together. To do this you add the elements in the same position. An example of this is shown in figure B.5. Matrix subtraction is similar, but you subtract the elements rather than add them.

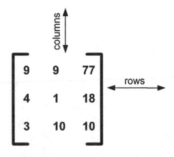

Figure B.1 A simple 3x3 matrix showing the directions of rows and columns

$$\begin{bmatrix} 9 \\ 4 \\ 3 \end{bmatrix} \qquad \begin{bmatrix} 9 & 9 & 77 \end{bmatrix}$$

Figure B.2 A column vector on the left side and a row vector on the right side

$$B = \begin{bmatrix} 1 & 0 \\ 4 & 1 \\ 3 & 2 \end{bmatrix} \qquad B^T = \begin{bmatrix} 1 & 4 & 3 \\ 0 & 1 & 2 \end{bmatrix}$$

Figure B.3 The transpose rotates a matrix, and the rows become columns.

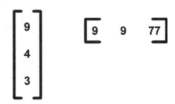

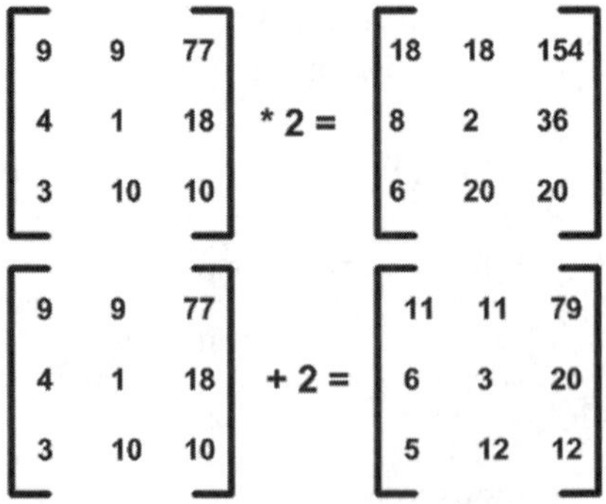

Figure B.4 Scalar operations on our matrix result in every element being multiplied or added by a scalar value.

$$\begin{bmatrix} 9 & 8 \\ 2 & 1 \\ 3 & 4 \end{bmatrix} + \begin{bmatrix} 0 & 3 \\ 3 & 7 \\ 5 & 2 \end{bmatrix} = \begin{bmatrix} 9 & 11 \\ 5 & 8 \\ 8 & 6 \end{bmatrix}$$

Figure B.5 Matrix addition

More interesting, multiplication is multiplying two matrices. Multiplying two matrices isn't as simple as scalar multiplication. To multiply two matrices, they must have a matching inner dimension. For example, you can multiply a 3x4 matrix and a 4x1 matrix but not a 3x4 matrix and a 1x4 matrix. The size of the resulting matrix from multiplying a 3x4 and 4x1 is 3x1. A quick way to check if you can multiply two matrices and the resulting size is to write the dimensions next to each other like this: (3x4)(4x1). Because the middle terms match, you can do the multiplication. By dropping the middle terms, you can see the size of the resulting matrix: 3x1. Figure B.6 illustrates an example of matrix multiplication.

$$\begin{bmatrix} 1 & 0 \\ 4 & 1 \\ 3 & 2 \end{bmatrix} * \begin{bmatrix} 7 \\ 8 \end{bmatrix} = \begin{bmatrix} 1*7 + 0*8 \\ 4*7 + 1*8 \\ 3*7 + 2*8 \end{bmatrix} = \begin{bmatrix} 7 \\ 36 \\ 37 \end{bmatrix}$$

Figure B.6 An illustration of matrix multiplication, showing a 3x2 matrix multiplied by a 2x1, resulting in a 3x1 matrix

Essentially what we did in figure B.6 was take every row of the 3x2 matrix and rotate it to align with the 2x1 matrix and then multiply these together and take the sum. Another way to think of matrix multiplication is a sum of columns. I've rewritten the multiplication from figure B.6 as a sum of columns in figure B.7.

In this second method of matrix multiplication, the same result was achieved but we reorganized how we were looking at the multiplication. Rethinking matrix multiplication as the sum of columns in figure B.7 will be helpful in certain algorithms, such as map reduce versions of matrix multiplication. In general, the definition of matrix multiplication for a matrix **X** and matrix **Y** is

$$(XY)_{ij} = \sum_{k=1}^{m} X_{ik} Y_{kj}$$

$$\begin{bmatrix} 1 & 0 \\ 4 & 1 \\ 3 & 2 \end{bmatrix} * \begin{bmatrix} 7 \\ 8 \end{bmatrix} = 7 * \begin{bmatrix} 1 \\ 4 \\ 3 \end{bmatrix} + 8 * \begin{bmatrix} 0 \\ 1 \\ 2 \end{bmatrix} = \begin{bmatrix} 7 \\ 36 \\ 37 \end{bmatrix}$$

Figure B.7 Matrix multiplication as a sum of columns

If you doubt that two operations are equal, you can always write them out using this summation form.

A common operation in machine learning is the dot product between two vectors. This was done in chapter 6 with support vector machines. The dot product is an element-wise multiplication, then summing up every element in the resulting vector. This is illustrated in figure B.8.

$$\begin{bmatrix} 1 \\ 4 \\ 3 \end{bmatrix} \bullet \begin{bmatrix} 0 \\ 1 \\ 2 \end{bmatrix} = 1*0 + 4*1 + 3*2 = 10$$

Figure B.8 An illustration of the dot product of two vectors

Often there's a physical meaning associated with a dot product, such as how much one vector moves in the direction of another vector. The dot product can be used to find the cosine between two vectors. In any program that supports matrix multiplication, you can get the dot product of two vectors X and Y by multiplying the transpose of X by Y. If X and Y are both length m, they will have dimensions mx1, so X^T will have dimensions 1xm and X^T*Y will have dimensions 1x1.

B.2   *Matrix inverse*

The matrix inverse comes up a lot when you're manipulating algebraic equations of matrices. The matrix X is the inverse of matrix Y if XY=I where I is the identity matrix. (The identity matrix often written as I is a matrix that's all 0s except for the diagonals, which are 1s. You can multiply other matrices by the identity matrix and get the original matrix.) The practical drawback to the matrix inverse is that it becomes messy for matrices larger than a few elements and is rarely computed by hand. It helps to know when you can't take the inverse of a matrix. Knowing this will help you avoid making errors in your programs. You write the inverse of a matrix B as B^{-1}.

A matrix has to be square to be invertible. By *square*, I mean the number of rows and columns has to be equal. Even if the matrix is square, it may not be invertible. If a matrix is not invertible, we say that it's *singular* or *degenerate*. A matrix can be singular if you can express one column as a linear combination of other columns. If you could do this, you could reduce a column in the matrix to all 0s. An example of such a matrix is shown in figure B.9. This becomes a problem when computing the inverse of the matrix, because you'll try to divide by zero. I'll show you this shortly.

$$\begin{bmatrix} 9 & 4 & 0 \\ 5 & 8 & 0 \\ 8 & 6 & 0 \end{bmatrix}$$

Figure B.9   An example of a singular matrix. This matrix has a column of 0s, which means you won't be able to take the inverse of this matrix.

There are many ways to calculate the inverse of a matrix. One way is to rearrange some terms in the matrix and divide every element by the determinant. The *determinant* is special value associated with a square matrix that can tell you a number of things about the matrix. Figure B.10 shows the hand calculations for taking the inverse of a 2x2 matrix. Note how the determinant written with det() is calculated. You multiply every term by this determinant. If one column of the matrix was all 0s,

$$B = \begin{bmatrix} b11 & b12 \\ b21 & b22 \end{bmatrix} \qquad B^{-1} = \frac{1}{\det(B)} \begin{bmatrix} b22 & -b12 \\ -b21 & b11 \end{bmatrix}$$

Figure B.10 Calculating the inverse of a square matrix B. Since we're multiplying every element by 1/det(B), det(B) can't be zero. If we have a singular matrix, det(B) will be zero and we can't take the inverse.

$$\det(B) = b11b22 - b12b21$$

then your determinant would also be 0. This leads to dividing by 0, which isn't possible, so you can't take the inverse of such a matrix. This is why you must have a matrix that's full rank in order to take the inverse.

You've seen how the inverse of a 2x2 matrix is calculated. Now, let's look at how the inverse of a 3x3 matrix would be calculated; you'll see it gets much more complex. Figure B.11 shows the calculations involved in computing the inverse of a 3x3 matrix.

$$C = \begin{bmatrix} c11 & c12 & c13 \\ c21 & c22 & c23 \\ c31 & c32 & c33 \end{bmatrix}$$

$$C^{-1} = \frac{1}{\det(C)} \begin{bmatrix} c22c33 - c23cc32 & c13c32 - c12c33 & c12c23 - c13c22 \\ c23c31 - c21c33 & c11c33 - c13c31 & c13c21 - c11c23 \\ c21c32 - c22c31 & c31c12 - c11c32 & c11c22 - c12c21 \end{bmatrix}$$

$$\det(B) = c11(c22c33 - c23c32) + c12(c23c31 - c33c21) + c13(c21c32 - c22c31)$$

Figure B.11 The inverse of a 3x3 matrix, C. With larger matrices the inverse becomes more difficult to calculate by hand. The determinant of a matrix with size n contains n! elements.

The take-home lesson is that computing the inverse gets really messy after two or three terms because the determinant has n! elements. You don't deal with such small matrices often, so calculating the inverse is usually done by a computer.

B.3 Norms

The *norm* is something that comes up often in machine learning literature. The norm of a matrix is written with two vertical lines on each side of the matrix like this: $\|A\|$. Let's talk about vector norms first.

The vector norm is an operation that assigns a positive scalar value to any vector. You can think of this as the length of the vector, which is useful in many machine learning algorithms such as k-Nearest Neighbors. If you have a vector $z = [3, 4]$ the length is $\sqrt{3^2 + 4^2} = 5$. This is also known as the L2 norm and is written as $\|z\|$ or $\|z\|^2$.

Using a different norm can give better results in some machine learning algorithms, such as the lasso for regression. The L1 norm is zalso popular, and this is sometimes known as the Manhattan distance. The L1 norm of z is 3+4=7, and it's written as $\|z\|_1$. You can have a norm of any number, and in general they're defined as

$$\|z\|_p = \left(\sum_{i=1}^{n} |z|^p \right)^{1/p}$$

The vector norms are used when determining the magnitude or significance of vectors, as in an input. In addition to the function defined here, you could create a vector norm any way you wanted as long as it converted from a vector to a scalar value.

B.4   *Matrix calculus*

In addition to adding, subtracting, and dividing matrices and vectors, you can do calculus operations, such as the derivative on vectors and matrices. This is needed in algorithms such as gradient descent. These are no harder than the standard calculus operations. It just involves understanding the notation and definitions.

If you have a vector $A = \begin{bmatrix} sin\,x - y \\ sin\,3x - 4y \end{bmatrix}$, you can take the derivative of A with respect to

x as $\dfrac{dA}{dx} = \begin{bmatrix} cos\,x \\ 3\,cos\,x \end{bmatrix}$, which gives you another vector. Now if you want to take the derivative

of A with respect to another vector, you'll have a matrix. Say you have another vector

$B = \begin{bmatrix} x \\ y \\ z \end{bmatrix}$

Now if you want to take the derivative of **A** (a 2x1 vector) with respect to **B** (a 3x1 vector), you'll have a 3x2 matrix:

$$\frac{dA}{dB} = \begin{bmatrix} cos\,x & 3\,cos\,x \\ -1 & -4 \\ 0 & 0 \end{bmatrix}$$

More generally, this is

$$\frac{dA}{dB} = \begin{bmatrix} \dfrac{dA1}{dx1} & \dfrac{dA2}{dx2} \\ \dfrac{dA1}{dx1} & \dfrac{dA2}{dx2} \\ \dfrac{dA1}{dx1} & \dfrac{dA2}{dx2} \end{bmatrix}$$

appendix C:
Probability refresher

In this appendix we'll go through some of the basic concepts of probability. The subject deserves more treatment than this appendix provides, so think of this as a quick refresher if you've had this material in the past but need to be reminded about some of the details. For someone who hasn't had this material before, I recommend studying more than this humble appendix. A number of good tutorials and videos are available from the Khan Academy that can be used for self-study.[1]

C.1   Intro to probability

Probability is defined as how likely something is to occur. You can calculate the probability of an event occurring from observed data by dividing the number of times this event occurred by the total number of events. Let me give some examples of these events:

- A coin is flipped and lands heads up.
- A newborn baby is a female.
- An airplane lands safely.
- The weather is rainy.

Let's look at some of these events and how we can calculate the probability. Say we've collected some weather data from the Great Lakes region of the United States. We've classified the weather into three categories: {clear, rainy, snowing}. This data is shown in table C.1.

From this table we can calculate the probability the weather is snowing. The data in table C.1 is limited to seven measurements, and some days are missing in the sequence. But this is the only data we have. The probability of an event is

---

[1] Khan Academy. http://www.khanacademy.org/?video=basic-probability#probability.

Table C.1   Weather measurements for late winter in the Great Lakes region

Reading number	Day of week	Temperature (°F)	Weather
1	1	20	clear
2	2	23	snowing
3	4	18	snowing
4	5	30	clear
5	1	40	rainy
6	2	42	rainy
7	3	40	clear

written as `P(event)`. Let's calculate the probability the weather is snowing as `P(weather = snowing)`:

$$P(weather = snowing) = \frac{number\ of\ times\ weather = snowing}{total\ number\ of\ readings} = \frac{2}{7}$$

I wrote this as `P(weather = snowing)`. But weather is the only variable that can take the value of snowing, so we can write this as `P(snowing)` to save some writing. With this basic definition of probability we calculate the probabilities of weather = rainy and weather = clear. Double-check that `P(rainy) = 2/7` and `P(clear) = 3/7`. You've seen how to calculate the probability of one variable taking one specific value, but what if we're concerned with more than one variable?

C.2   *Joint probability*

What if we want to see the probability of two events happening at the same time, such as weather = snowing and day of week = 2? You can probably figure out how to calculate this; you count the number of examples where both of these events are true and divide it by the total number of events. Let's calculate this simple example: There's one data point where weather = snowing and day of week = 2, so the probability would be 1/7. Now this is usually written with a comma separating the variables: `P(weather = snowing, day_of_week = 2)` or `P(X,Y)` for some events X and Y.

Often you'll see some symbol like `P(X,Y|Z)`. The vertical bar is used to represent conditional probability, so this statement is asking for the probability of X AND Y conditioned on the event Z. A quick refresher on conditional probability is given in chapter 4 if you want to review it.

You just need a few basic rules to manipulate probabilities. Once you have a firm grasp on these, you can manipulate probabilities like algebraic expressions and infer unknown quantities from known quantities. The next section will introduce these basic rules.

C.3   *Basic rules of probability*

The basic rules (axioms) of probability allow us to do algebra with probabilities. These are as fundamental as the rules of algebra and should not be ignored. I'll discuss each of them in turn and show how it relates to our weather data in table C.1.

The probabilities we calculated were fractions. If on all the days we recorded it was snowing, then `P(snowing)` would be 7/7 or 1. Now if on none of the days it was snowing, `P(snowing)` would be 0/7 or 0. It shouldn't be a huge surprise then that for any event X, `0?P(x)?1.0`.

The compliment operator is written as `~snowing`, `¬snowing`, or `snowing`. This compliment means any event except given (`snowing`). In our weather example from table C.1, the other possible events were rainy and clear. So in our world of three possible weather events, `P(¬snowing)` = `P(rainy)` + `P(clear)` = 5/7. Remember `P(snowing)` was 2/7, so `P(snowing)` + `P(¬snowing)` = 1. Another way of saying this is `snowing + ¬snowing` is always true. It might help to visualize these events in a diagram. One particularly useful type is a Venn diagram, which is useful for visualizing sets of things. Figure C.1 shows the set of all possible weather conditions. Snowing takes up the circled area on the diagram. Not snowing takes up the remainder of the diagram.

The last basic rule of probability concerns multiple variables. Consider the Venn diagram in figure C.2 depicting two events from table C.1. The first event is that `weather = snowing`; the second event is `day of week = 2`. These events aren't mutually exclusive; this just means that they can happen at the same time. There are some days when it's snowing and the `day of week = 2`; there are some other days when it's snowing but the day of week is not 2. There's an area where these two regions overlap, but they don't completely overlap.

The area of overlap in figure C.2 can be thought of as the intersection of the two events. This is written as `(weather = snowing) AND (day of week = 2)`. That is

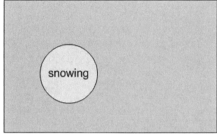

Figure C.1   The top frame shows the event snowing in the circle while all other events are outside the circle. The bottom frame shows not snowing or all other events. The sum of snowing and not snowing makes up all known events.

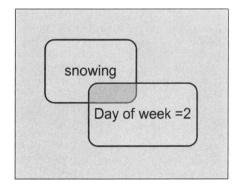

Figure C.2   A Venn diagram showing the intersection of two non–mutually exclusive events.

straightforward. What if we want to calculate `P((weather = snowing) OR (day of week = 2))`? This can be calculated by `P(snowing or day of week = 2) = P(snowing) + P(day of week = 2) - P(snowing AND day of week = 2)`. We have that last subtracted part to avoid double counting the intersection. Let me write this in simpler terms: `P(X OR Y) = P(X) + P(Y) - P(X AND Y)`. This also leads us to an interesting result, a way of algebraically moving between `AND`s and `OR`s of probabilities.

With these basic rules of probability, we can accomplish a lot. With assumptions or prior knowledge, we can calculate the probabilities of events we haven't directly observed.

appendix D:
Resources

Collecting data can be a lot of fun, but if you have a good idea for an algorithm or want to try something out, finding data can be a pain. This appendix contains a collection of links to known datasets. These sets range in size from 20 lines to trillions of lines, so you should have no problem finding a dataset to meet your needs:

- http://archive.ics.uci.edu/ml/—The best-known source of datasets for machine learning is the University of California at Irvine. We used fewer than 10 data sets in this book, but there are more than 200 datasets in this repository. Many of these datasets are used to compare the performance of algorithms so that researchers can have an objective comparison of performance.

- http://aws.amazon.com/publicdatasets/—If you're a big data cowboy, then this is the link for you. Amazon has some really *big* datasets, including the U.S. census data, the annotated human genome data, a 150 GB log of Wikipedia's page traffic, and a 500 GB database of Wikipedia's link data.

- http://www.data.gov—Data.gov is a website launched in 2009 to increase the public's access to government datasets. The site was intended to make all government data public as long as the data was not private or restricted for security reasons. In 2010, the site had over 250,000 datasets. It's uncertain how long the site will remain active. In 2011, the federal government reduced funding for the Electronic Government Fund, which pays for Data.gov. The datasets range from products recalled to a list of failed banks.

- http://www.data.gov/opendatasites—Data.gov has a list of U.S. states, cities, and countries that hold similar open data sites.

- http://www.infochimps.com/—Infochimps is a company that aims to give everyone access to every dataset in the world. Currently, they have more than 14,000 datasets available to download. Unlike other listed sites, some of the datasets on Infochimps are for sale. You can sell your own datasets here as well.

- http://www.datawrangling.com/some-datasets-available-on-the-web—Data Wrangling is a private blog with a large number of links to various data sources on the internet. It's a bit dated, but many of the links are still good.
- http://metaoptimize.com/qa/questions/—This isn't a data source but a question-and-answer site that's machine learning focused. There are many practitioners here willing to help out.

index

Mahout in Action
by Sean Owen, Robin Anil, Ted Dunning,
    and Ellen Friedman

ISBN: 978-1-935182-68-9
416 pages
$44.99
October 2011

Event Processing in Action
by Opher Etzion and Peter Niblett

ISBN: 978-1-935182-21-4
384 pages
$49.99
August 2010

For ordering information go to www.manning.com

Algorithms of the Intelligent Web
by Haralambos Marmanis
    and Dmitry Babenko

ISBN: 978-1-933988-66-5
368 pages
$44.99
May 2009

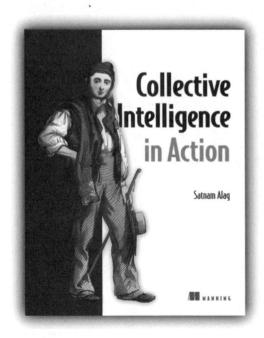

Collective Intelligence in Action
by Satnam Alag

ISBN: 978-1-933988-31-3
424 pages
$44.99
October 2008

For ordering information go to www.manning.com

MongoDB in Action
by Kyle Banker

ISBN: 978-1-935182-87-0
312 pages
$44.99
December 2011

Hadoop in Action
by Chuck Lam

ISBN: 978-1-935182-19-1
336 pages
$44.99
December 2010

For ordering information go to www.manning.com

MORE TITLES FROM MANNING

Lucene in Action, Second Edition
by Michael McCandless, Erik Hatcher,
   and Otis Gospodnetić

  ISBN: 978-1-933988-17-7
  532 pages
  $49.99
  July 2010

The Quick Python Book, Second Edition
by Vernon L. Ceder

  ISBN: 978-1-935182-20-7
  360 pages
  $39.99
  January 2010

For ordering information go to www.manning.com